Christine M. Hassenstab

Body Law and the Body of Law

A Comparative Study of Social Norm Inclusion in Norwegian and American Laws

Christine M. Hassenstab

Body Law and the Body of Law

A Comparative Study of Social Norm Inclusion in Norwegian and American Laws

Managing Editor: Katarzyna Michalak

Associate Editor: Łukasz Połczyński

DE GRUYTER
OPEN

Published by De Gruyter Open Ltd, Warsaw/Berlin
Part of Walter de Gruyter GmbH, Berlin/Munich/Boston

ISBN: 978-3-11-041276-5
e-ISBN: 978-3-11-041277-2

Bibliographic information published by the Deutsche Nationalbibliothek. The Deutsche Nationalbibliothek lists this publication in the Deutsche Nationalbibliografie; detailed bibliographic data are available in the Internet at http://dnb.dnb.de.

Managing Editor: Katarzyna Michalak
Associate Editor: Łukasz Połczyński

www.degruyteropen.com

Cover illustration: © Thinkstock/aodaodaod

This work is dedicated to the memory of my father,
Robert Arthur Hassenstab
29 January 1924 Redwood Falls, Minnesota – 11 March 1973 Redwood Falls, Minnesota
and to the memory of my mother,
Delores Annette (Puchner) Hassenstab
24 January 1924 Springfield, Minnesota – 17 November 1997 St. Louis Park, Minnesota
and to my siblings, Mark Joseph, Annette Marie and Frank Joseph (+).

Contents

Acknowledgements

First, I want to thank my dissertation supervisor, Professor Ann R. Sætnan. Without her generosity, expertise, and kindness, this work would neither have been attempted nor have been finished.

I also want to thank the Kennedy Institute of Ethics (KIE) at Georgetown University in Washington, D.C. for allowing me to be affiliated with them as a Visiting Scholar from 2005 to 2006. I am especially thankful to Prof. Madison Powers, Prof. LeRoy B. Walters and Sally Scofield. I also thank Professor of Linguistics Jeffrey T. Connor-Linton from Georgetown University.

Other inspirational teachers that I want to thank are Professors Jon Bridgeman and Mary O'Neill (University of Washington), Robert Calhoun, Drucilla Stender Ramey and Bernard L. Segal (Golden Gate University School of Law), Willy Parsons (The Evergreen State College), Dinah Shelton (University of Santa Clara) and Loualta Vogel (Centralia Community College).

I am grateful to the staff of the NTNU Library as well as to the staff of the Bioethics Library of the Joseph and Rose Kennedy Institute of Ethics at Georgetown University in Washington, D.C. The librarians at NTNU and the KIE are among the most professional that I have had the privilege to know. I also want to thank Janet Spikes and her colleagues at the Woodrow Wilson Center for Scholars, Washington, D.C.

The friends who have helped and encouraged me in various ways are too numerous to mention. They include Patrice Eihlers, O.P., G. Heimark, Betty Johanna (+), Thomas Lubchenco (+), Jo Maynes (+), Rob Keyes-Beck (+) and members of the Trondheim Writers Circle. Thank you to VyVy, Cheryl, Marik and Gyrid, who are not afraid of the unknown.

Finally, I want to thank the light of my life, Sabrina Petra Ramet who proofread and helped to copy-edit this manuscript, checked footnotes and compiled the Bibliography. I also profited from her counsel on earlier drafts of this dissertation.

Christine Marie Hassenstab
Trondheim, Norway, 2010

Abbreviations

ABCL	American Birth Control League
ACLU	American Civil Liberties Union
Ap	Arbeiderparti (Labor Party)
ATL	Autonomy Thesis of Law
AV	*Adresseavisen* (Newspaper with offices in Trondheim, Sør-Trondelag)
CBCL	Connecticut Birth Control League
CCC	Civilian Conservation Corps
CDA	Critical Discourse Analysis
CHMVS	Committee on Health, Medicine and Vital Statistics
DNJ	Den Norske Jordmorforening (Norwegian Midwives Association)
DNK	Den Norske Kirke (The Norwegian [State] Church)
DNL	Den norske lægforening (Norwegian Doctor's Association)
ERA	Equal Rights Amendment
FASA	Folksaksjon mot selbestemt abort (People's Action Against Abortion)
FrP	Fremskritparti (Progress Party)
GE	General Electric Corporation
H	Høire/Høyre (Conservative Party)
HME	Indremisjon ("Inner", i.e Norwegian Mission)
HVF	Hjemmenes vels landsforbund (Good Home Association, precursor to the NHMF)
HUAC	House Un-American Activities Committee
HF	Hjemmes vel (Good Home)
IKPK	International Kriminalpolizeilichen Kommission (International Criminal Police Commission)
ISM	Institutt for samfunnsmedisin (Institute for Social Medicine)
IVF	*In-vitro* fertilization
KAF	Kristne Arbeideres Forbund (The Christian Workers Association)
KrF	Norske kristifolkeparti (Norwegian Christian People's Party)
LO	Landsorganisasjonnen i Norge (Norwegian Labor Federation)
LPS	Legal Process School
NHMF	Norske husmorforbundet (The Norwegian Housemothers /Housewives Association)
NIS	Norsk Institutt for Sykehusforskning (Norwegian Institute of Hospital Research)
NKN	Norsk nasjonalkvinnersforengingen (Norwegian National Women's Association)
NKNR	Norske Kvinners Nasjonalråd (Norwegian Women's Advisory Association)
NKSF	Norsk Kvinnesaksforening (The Norwegian Feminist Association)
NMF	Norsk medisinske forening (Norwegian Medical Association)
NMBH	Norsk misjon blant hjemløs (Norwegian Mission Among the Homeless

NPV	Norsk Pro Vita (Norwegians for Life)
NRK	Norsk radiokringkasting (Norweigan Radio Broadcasting)
NRKF	Norges Røde Kors landsforening (The National Red Cross Association)
NS	Nasjonal Samling (National Gathering/Association)
NSF	Norsk Sanitetsforeningen (The Norwegian Hygiene Association)
NSA	Norsk Sykepleierforenigen (The Norwegian Nurses Association)
NTF	Norsk Teknisk Forening (Norwegian Technical Association)
NTNU	Norges Tekniske Naturvitenskapelige Universitetet (Norwegian University of Science and Technology)
NYSSV	New York Society for the Suppression of Vice
PPLC	Planned Parenthood League of Connecticut
RikI	Rikshospitalet I Trondheim (National Hosptial in Trondheim)
SP	Senterparti (Center Party). Formerly the Bondepartiet (Farmer's Party)
Sp	Samfundsparti (The Society Party)
SSB	Norwegian Statistik Sentraløbyrå (The Norwegian Central Bureau for Statistics)
SSV	Society for the Supression of Vice
SV	Sosialistisk Venstre (SV)
STL	Separability Thesis of Law
V	Venstre (Liberal Party)
WCTU	Women's Christian Temperance Union
WPA	Works Progress Administration
YMCA	Young Men's Christian Association

Note Regarding Legal Cases and Their Designation

Lawyers in the U.S. and Norway have different ways of citing to a case as precedent. In the United States, for example, in the case of Skinner v. Oklahoma ex rel. Williamson, 316 U.S. 535 (1942), we learn several things just from the citation. First, we know the appellant was a person called Skinner and the respondent was the State of Oklahoma represented by someone called Williamson. We know that the case can be found in the U.S. law periodical, Volume 316 at page 535. We also know the case was decided in 1942. For Supreme Court cases in the U.S., three different citations to the same case can be used, i.e. to the U.S. (United States) set of printed federal decisions, to the S.Ct. (Supreme Court) series and to the L.Ed. (Lawyer's Edition) series. The citation, U.S. v. One Package, 86 F.2d 737, 739 (1936), tells us the case was decided at the federal appellate level and printed in the second series of periodicals from that circuit court. The second number after 737, i.e. 739, gives the specific page in the case where the reference can be found.

American laws can be referred to by the individual state statute number or, on the federal level, by shorthand references such as the American with Disabilities Act or "ADA." Norwegian decisions are referred to in much the same manner as in the American system. Norwegian laws are referred to by the date of passage by the Parliament (Storting).

1 Introduction

1.1 Introduction

Several centuries ago, literary giant Charles Dickens wrote in *Oliver Twist*, that:

> The law is a ass – a idiot. If that's the eye of the law, the law is a bachelor; and the worst I wish the law is, that his eye may be opened by experience – by experience.[1]

William Shakespeare also weighed in on the subject of law and lawyers in his play *Henry VI*, where he had a character announce that all the lawyers should be killed.[2] Opinions about the law are oftentimes a societal hobby. But these opinions aside, I believe – and argue here – that the law is a chameleon. It can and does change "color" depending on its context and function. For some, this might be obvious. Whether obvious or not, however, and time after time, the law becomes a chameleon-like monster.

The chameleon nature of law is connected to the numerous functions of Law; laws might be grounded in the sociological, the political, and even – or especially – concepts of normalized morality and ethics. And as common understandings of morality evolve, law adapt to their new moral environment. Even mathematics and physics might even be implicated if one considers laws about driving safety. But in terms of context, however, the one consistent context that Law cannot avoid is history. Due to procedurally correct laws, being labeled Jewish in Germany had horrific consequences before and during World War II, as did being non-white in South Africa during apartheid. Previously, taking the name of God in vain was an illegal act in colonial America which put some lackadaisical colonists in stocks, on public display. Even earlier, practicing herbal medicine and perhaps living without male "supervision" sent many women to be burned at the stake as witches in Catholic medieval Europe. Law may be a chameleon always changing functions, combining them or prioritizing one over the other but it is permanently bound to history, to a specific time and place and society.

This brings up the question of "good" law. For some legal philosophers, if a law is procedurally correct, enacted in ways constitutionally known and agreed upon, then the content is of no significance. It is a "good" law, no matter what it does or justifies. Whether or not one agrees or disagrees with any particular law is merely set aside as a political quarrel. The assumption is that a certain procedure and logic in law production has taken place and this can be changed by a change in political leaders in a

---

1 Charles Dickens, *Oliver Twist* (New York and Toronto: Vintage Classics, 2012) p. 400.

2 William Shaespeare, *Henry VI*, (New York: Bantam Dell Classic Books, 1988) p. 275. (Part II, Sct IV, Scene II, Dick the Butcher to Jack Cade, line 74.)

subsequent political election. But this focus and this assumption obscure an uncomfortable fact. Some laws can be "bad" or "immoral."

Another remedy, some argue, is that if one dislikes a particular law, one can pursue that matter in the appellate courts. But most courts are bound by what jurisprudential scholars call the Autonomy Thesis of Law (ATL). The ATL is a type of Berlin Wall that means one cannot go behind an enacted law every time it is used in order to question if it is just. If one could, the security and order of society would suffer. Police officers might never know if an arrest was legal or not. Was or wasn't a contract valid under the existing commercial code? One needs some assurances that law is law – and remains law – for a consistent, lengthy period of time.

This leads us to consider the question of how we know what we think we know, often called epistemology. And this is a serious question which is raised here, given the often strange twists and turns of history and political whims. History is no epistemological safe harbor either in this respect if one chooses to believe that the law is a source of security and order. As already implied above, the course of history changes, in part, because societal norms change. Norms can change slowly or rapidly, even within a lifetime. One may not feel on safe ground doing a particular act as a 20 year old but might freely engage in it as a 60 year old person. The main character in the play, *A Man for All Seasons*, is lawyer Thomas More who is King Henry VIII's Chancellor of the Realm. Eventually he is threatened by the King because of his religious beliefs and More tells his son-in-law that:

> I'm *not* God. The currents and eddies of right and wrong, which you find such plain sailing, I can't navigate. I'm no voyager. But in the thickets of the law, oh there I'm a forester. I doubt there's a man alive who could follow me in there, thank God...[3]

Few knew the law better than More, but he was nevertheless eventually executed.

This book is about how law was driven by scientific and social norms during the first and closing decades of the twentieth century. Prior to and at the turn of the century, huge technological breakthroughs had been made, such as steam power, spreading both the advantages and disadvantages of the Industrial Revolution. Although genetic concepts had been discovered at the end of the 19th century, the first three decades of the twentieth were a time of experimentation. But it was "blind" experimentation in a sense, since knowledge of some of the most significant genetic structures and functions such as chromosomes and genes were unknown, much less knowledge of weak hydrogen bonds connecting adenine, guanine, cytosine and thymine in a helical molecule called DNA (deoxyribonucleic acid). This is the historical period in which Case One is situated and the two countries that are compared are the USA (state of Indiana) and Norway.

---

3 Robert Bolt, *A Man for All Seasons* (New York: Vintage International, 1990), p. 65–66.

At the end of the twentieth century, although more scientific information was known, the "betterment" of society through controlled reproduction, which had come to be the ostensible goal at the beginning of the century, took back seat to socio-political factors. At mid-century, laws had been conceived, written and enacted which had given women no or little control over reproduction. In the USA, condoms were illegal. But, as science and technology progressed, better ways of controlling reproduction did emerge. However, as far as the law was concerned, these laws were problematic. This is the period in which Case Two is situated and, in a sense, it is the antithesis of Case One. In Case One, legislators created and passed laws based on what they considered to be cutting-edge science and in the best interests of their societies. In Case Two, the demand for cutting-edge scientific technology (birth control pills) came from below and legislators balked at allowing this. Again, the two countries that are compared are Norway and the USA.

We should also remember that the philosophy of law and the social science of sociology begin with different assumptions, although both claim to use logic. Both claim the scientific process is at work in the discipline. In 1870, Harvard Professor Christopher Columbus Langdell, who will be introduced below, envisioned the law school library as a "laboratory" much like any chemistry or biology laboratory. But words which create precedent and the logic of legal argument seem to have a basic difference from, for example, the certainty of what the outside temperature might be, and at a given pressure, in degrees Celsius or Fahrenheit. These ideas are also examined below.

The scientific method requires that we work from a theory, collect data and make conclusions; it also requires reproducibility. The main theory that I will use here is a theory that comes from STS (Science and Technology Studies) circles often associated with its French originator, Bruno Latour. Harvard Professor Sheila Jasanoff also subscribes to work done in the field of STS and has advanced a theory of how knowledge is co-produced. She writes that four "fields" co-produce knowledge; these are representations, institutions, discourse and identities. These four fields will be explained and used to examine the data presented in the print media at the time the laws were passed.

I use these four "fields" in this book but, since the data set can be large, I also use a theory to supplement the work of Jasanoff and that is the theory of "intersubjectivity." This idea comes from feminist scholarship and argues that we can look at "intersubjective categories" of race/ethnicity, class, gender, citizen status and ability because there are common linkages among the categories due to hierarchical power and oppression.

The theory that I will use to look at creation of law is one used by Brian Tamanaha, called the socio-legal positivist theory of law. Positive law is simply law that is written down "on the books" so to speak. Some thinkers describe their work in terms of positive law but go no further to ask, "is that all there is?" They maintain that if a law is "unjust", it is still positive law and should therefore be obeyed. Still others reach different conclusions along a spectrum culminating, at the opposite end, in the position a tired Rosa Parks found herself one December day in Alabama when she decided to sit in the front of a bus instead of the back – which was illegal – because it was positive law that required Black African Americans to sit in the back of the bus.

This brings me to the concept of "body law" as used in this book. While working on these cases, it struck me that the most basic thing we have which is subject to the law is our bodies. Our minds are free enough so that we can imagine breaking any number of laws every day without consequence. Every law that is enacted by freely elected politicians applies to citizens of a country unless otherwise noted. Sometimes, the "otherwise noted" applies to bodies that are not white and not rich, or without status or influence, as the Baldus (Death Penalty) Study shows below. For example, different penalties under federal law for possession of cocaine, have depended on the type of cocaine used. Use of crack cocaine, mostly used by non-white, poor citizens carried harsher penalties than that found waiting in the restrooms at a corporate Christmas party.

This brings us to consider the people who make law and their epistemic realities. I mention below the theory of "legisprudence" coined by Luc Wintgens and to the work of Kaarlo Tuori. Tuori theorizes that where law and politics might appear connected at a top, superficial level, they are autonomous at lower levels of law formation. At the lowest level of Tuori's three levels is what Michel Foucault calls the "episteme", the prelogical and preconceptual foundations of legal norm creation. And again, we come back to epistemology.

But, more often, the law affects the specific bodies mentioned above, as the historical composition of prisons in the USA – and elsewhere – demonstrates. Critical legal theory suggests that there are often two (or more) sets of laws, and it makes no difference if Lady Justice is blindfolded or not. As children, what we first learn to notice about another person is his or her gender, then race and later, class. As I heard a Black man scream outside court in San Francisco one day, "There ain't no justice, there's only just us!" McCall's theory of intersubjectivity, mentioned above, helps to describe this situation as well as critical legal theory on the ground. It basically says that oppression is an interlocking affair and comes into being because of race, class and gender hierarchies.

Most citizens of a country probably assume that making law is a complicated procedure. But, as this book helps to show, it is an infinitely more complicated matter than we often realize. Different hierarchies are at work, directly or indirectly, different assumptions about what the "polis" wants or doesn't want, different epistemic understandings of what is "best", sometimes impacted by misinformed and misleading propaganda from religion, politics and even science, all informing any given law.

It seems that only the passage of time gives us the luxury of looking backward with some trepidation to see the consequences of these "bad" laws. But I also ask in this book if there might be a way that one could anticipate "bad" law, even before the consequences are known, or a way to lessen "bad" consequences.

1.2 How this Book is Organized

The pseudo-science of Eugenics burst into what was called the Progressive Era in the USA at the end of the 19th century and the beginning of the 20th. Legislators thought it might be some sort of panacea to any number of problems, including crime, poverty and lack of education. Case One examines eugenic laws in the USA state of Indiana and Norway. A law permitting the castration laws of "confirmed criminals" was passed in Indiana in 1907, the first in history. In Norway, a law was passed in 1934 allowing for the castration/sterilization of people considered societal "parasites."

Case Two looks at the antithesis of the laws passed in Case One. What had been legally mandated from above in 1907 and 1934 with regard to reproduction was later abandoned. However, a caveat should be mentioned here. The laws were no longer "on the books" and there was no longer any obvious eugenical castration/sterilization but eugenics practices did continue into the 1970s and beyond. But the laws from 1907 and 1934 had been technically abandoned. Case Two is about the birth control/ abortion debate – begun from below – in both countries throughout the late 1960s and 1970s. Women wanted control over reproductive matters, but they did not fit into the categories of people seen in Case One. This became a problem for politicians.

Both cases involve the body of the individual based on certain classifications of that body by society and assumptions about their worth. They have in common what a person may or may not legally do with her or his body. What a body looks like, the epistemics of sight knowledge, can often determine what that person may and may not do. Black citizens in 1907 Indiana could not do things that white citizens could. European citizens – Roma – cannot do things in Norway today that ordinary Norwegians can do. But the problem with visually "knowing" a body is that it can also be misleading. One could not be sure if a Norwegian citizen was "insane" in 1934 simply by looking at her any more than one could know if a man was a habitual criminal or not in 1907 in Indiana, or that a person is "gay" today. "Out of place" persons were also a major theme in Norway in 1934, possibly due to its small Roma population.[4]

Therefore, some un-readable bodies became the subject of the law in a pro-active manner and law became the instrumentalized force in the search for a pro-active public policy. Here, I look at the social and cultural norms at work in both societies at

4 "Out-of-place" persons continue to be feared. This is exemplified by the arrest of Harvard Professor Henry Gates after trying to get into his own house. Please see Rupert Cornwell, "The arrest that divided America", *The Independent*, 24 July 2009 at http://license.icopyright.net/user/viewFreeUse.act?fuid=NDI0MDU1NA%3D%3D, last accessed 7 July 2009.

the time that these laws were passed. I assume that these norms can be inserted into the formation of laws at a variety of junctures, or "injection points." These include, but are not limited to, 1. the public at large, 2. the electorate, i.e. those that fit the criteria of "citizen", 3. social movement organizations (SMOs) of the time, 4. smaller, specialized interest groups, and 5. the individual legislator or parliamentarian. These injection points are therefore located at all levels of society, the macro-, meso- and micro-levels and these are the three levels that I often use for examples in each case.[5] Another question that is briefly taken up is the timing of the legislation. Besides the eugenics craze, was anything else at work that may have affected societal norms at these times? In this respect, I examine episodic social/moral panics and major structural changes in society are major factors that can trigger legal norm attachment directly to the unreadable body.

This book is divided into seven chapters. Chapter 1 includes an Introduction and short overview of how the book is organized, chapter by chapter.[6]

In Chapter 3, I look directly at societal norms in Indiana and Norway around the time their similar laws were passed. I examine questions of large scale structural changes as well as social/moral panics at the time these laws were legislated.

Chapter 4 examines how people were eventually selected as subjects/objects of the laws passed in Indian and Norway. It is here, that I go beyond what I call the "injection points" available to the individual citizen and look at which SMOs and smaller interest groups were involved, pressing legislators for involuntary sterilization in Indiana and Norway. I also examine some of the individual legislators or parliamentarians involved in each country and the social and political networks/movements in which they were enmeshed.

In Chapter 5, I look at the social and cultural processes that took place *after* the sterilization laws were passed that supported their invalidation or which were engaged in reversing what could be seen as extra-judicial processes. At this point, I also look at later parallel cases, involving laws passed in 1965 in the United States and 1978 in Norway. In those years, normative legal formation again addressed specific persons. I begin by tracing the United State Supreme Court (USSC) case of Griswold v. Connecticut, 381 U.S. 479 (1965), generally understood as bringing into force a "right of privacy." This case allowed married couples the use of contraception as

---

5 SMOs interact with "scientific/intellectual movements" (SIMs). Please see Scott Frickel and Neil Gross, "A General Theory of Scientific/Intellectual Movements" in *American Sociological Review*, 70 (2005), 204–232.

6 Please see George Ritzer, *Sociological Theory*, 7th Ed, (Boston, etc.: McGraw-Hill, 2008) and Kaarlo Tuori, "Legislation Between Politics and Law" in Luc J. Wintgens, (ed.) *Legisprudence: A New Theoretical Approach to Legislatio: Proceedings of the Fourth Benelux-Scandinavian Symposium on Legal Theory* (Oxford and Portland: Hart Publishing Co., 2002) and Kaarlo Tuori, Zenon Bankowski and Jyrki Uusitalo (eds.), *Law and Power: Critical and Socio-Legal Essays* (Liverpool: Deborah Charles Publishing, 1997).

prescribed by a doctor and is generally regarded as the precursor to Roe v. Wade, 410 U.S. 113 (1973), allowing for the right to a legal abortion in the United States.

Chapter 6 looks at how this reversal process was carried out in Norway. The two countries fashioned these normative "body laws" through very dissimilar political and legal processes and I argue that the differences in legal procedural apparati in place were of no significance since it was – in the main – the normative changes that were based at a more fundamental level in society and its culture that allowed for the changes. It is true that law can change norms and that this is often the hope of many policy makers; this strategy has been tried at various times and places. But it is my thesis that the normative ebb and flow between culture and law, during these particular stressful times is from culture to law.

Chapter 7 summarizes the comparisons between the two countries in terms of social and cultural norms and which groups advocated for and against these norms. I also introduce an overview of race/ethnicity, class and ability as it related to the law in the earlier sterilization laws as well as the later contraception/abortion laws. Norway and the United States have different legal and political histories and I consider these in relation to law formation. Finally, I turn to my argument that norms are seen to be embodied in physical bodies and that the law, at opportune times, will create a one-to-one correspondence with intersubjective bodies, based on relative political power, the settled epistemic knowledge of the time, large scale structural changes and the presence or absence of a moral panic.

I also argue that this does not mean the Law is always a relative entity but that laws should be assessed as "just" or "unjust" before enactment, *despite* having met their procedural safeguards; this assessment can be based on the relative social and political position of members of within a country's population. This helps put in place a type of "transparency" that legal scholars Olsen and Toddington argue for with regard to the Autonomy Thesis[7], that Brian Tamanaha searches for in his theory of socio-legal positivist theory of law[8] and that others such as, Duncan Kennedy[9], Liam Murphy[10] and Bonaventura de Sousa Santos[11], directly or indirectly, consider as a necessary antidote to strong positivism.

---

7 Henrik Palmer Olsen and Stuart Toddington, *Law in its Own Right* (Oxford and Portland: Hart Publishing, 1999).
8 Brian Z. Tamanaha, *A General Jurisprudence of Law and Society* (Oxford: Oxford University Press, 2001).
9 Duncan Kennedy, *A Critique of Adjudication (fin de siècle)* (Cambridge, London: Harvard University Press, 1997).
10 Liam Murphy, "The Political Question of the Concept of Law" in Jules Coleman (ed.), *Hart's Postscript: Essays on the Postscript to "The Concept of Law"* (Oxford: Oxford University Press, 2001).
11 Bonaventura de Sousa Santos, *Toward a New Common Sense: Law, Science and Politics in the Paradigmatic Transition* (New York, London: Routledge, 1995).

In conclusion, my work addresses the "how" and the "why" of norm-inclusion in what I term "body law." To do this, I examine both social and legal norms and theories of how they are both created. I then use various sociological theories to untie the various strands of social history as well as legal history and look at two cases of legislation from the United States and Norway. I ask if there is a set of confluences in socio-legal history and/or theory where one might expect to see tendencies in legislatures or Parliaments, to pass "body-law." As part of this analysis, I also include secondary conclusions, about the role of the trans-national social movements, such as Eugenics, as historical forces.

2 Theories Explained and Methodology Used

> Knowledge is a resource with a capacity to flow, but within channels defined by the social structure of any particular period.
>
> Vilhelm Aubert[12]

2.1 Introduction

Works of social science require that we use theory or theories upon which we base our sampling or data collection. And in interdisciplinary research, there are sometimes more theories than normal since two, or more, disciplines are involved.

In this chapter, I begin with asking what is a "norm?" Then I ask what a social norm is and what a legal norm is and if there is any difference between the two? I then describe a theory that the law uses to separate social norms from legal adjudication. This theory is called the ATL or Autonomy Thesis of Law. Following a description of this I offer more elaboration on the ATL by Brian Tamanaha and his socio-legal positivist theory of law formation.

Finally, I set out the main theories used in this book – the Jasanoff theory of the co-production of knowledge which I use since I want to address the idea of how we know what we think we know at any given time and apply that to how legislators and citizens knew what they thought they knew at the various times these laws were passed. Jasanoff's "field" theory is supplemented by the feminist theory of "intersugjectivity" which I also describe, below.

I also describe the Pescosolido model for large-scale structural changes that societies experienced since the passage of time that I deal with here is so great; fairly monumentous changes took place over this 100 plus year period.[13] I also provide some information on moral panics and how they can impact thinking. I also described critical discourse theory which helps in the selection of data from the discourse field and at address the question of which level – th emicro-, meso-, or macro-level – data must be taken. Social movements are also touched upon.

But first, we need to ask, "What are Social and Legal Norms?" Are social norms and legal norms the same? If they are similar, how do they overlap? It might seem over cautious to discuss this question but experimental designs require that we examine

---

12 Vilhelm Aubert, "The Professions in Norwegian Social Structure" in *Transactions of the Fifth World Congress of Sociology,* Vol. III as reprinted by International Sociological Association, 1964, p. 253. (Emphasis mine.)

13 Bernice A. Pescosolido-Rubin and Beth A. Rubin, "The Web of Group Affiliations Revisited: Social Life, Postmodernism, and Sociology" in *American Sociological Review*, 65 (2000), 67.

apples with apples, etc. If there is a difference between social and legal norms, we need to know this.

2.2 What are Social and Legal Norms?

Theories of social action based on norms have been developed ever since the beginnings of Sociology. By the mid-20th century, Jack Gibbs stressed the lack of agreement on the definition of a norm, citing varying definitions from Robert Bierstadt, Leonard Broom and Philip Selznick, George C. Homans, Harry M. Johnson, Richard T. Morris, Theodore M. Newcomb and Robin M. Williams.[14] However, Norwegian academic Ragnar Rommetveit observed that there was some conceptual agreement on the uses of the term. As he wrote in *Social Norms and Roles* there were three uses of the term. They were:

> 1. to indicate uniformities in behavior, 2. to designate a particular 'frame of reference' and, 3. to express the existence of social obli-gation or pressure.[15]

The problem with finding a definition of "norm" is that so many types of behavior are involved and reduction of these heterogeneous behaviors to one generalizable definition is perhaps impossible. But Gibbs made a convincing case that there is a way to define a generic norm. He gives three attributes of the generic constituents of a norm. They are, 1. collective evaluations, i.e. what *ought* to be, 2. collective expectations, i.e. what *will* be, and 3. reactions to behavior, i.e. the application of *sanctions or inducements* to a particular type of behavior.[16]

Sociologists in the present time are more apt to concentrate on the functions and mechanisms of norms. Peter M. Blau (1918–2002) conceived of norms – and values – as mechanisms by which social structures can mediate among themselves in a society. He wrote:

> Commonly agreed upon values and norms serve as media of social life and as mediating links for social transactions. They make indirect social exchange possible, and they govern the process of social integration and differentiation in complex social structures as well as the development of social organization and reorganization of them.[17]

---

14 Jack P. Gibbs, "Norms: The Problem of Definition and Classification" in *The American Journal of Sociology*, 70 (1965), 586–87.

15 *Ibid.*, p. 587. Also see Ragnar Rommetveit, *Social Norms and Roles* (Minneapolis: University of Minnesota Press, 1955), 18–26.

16 *Ibid.*, 589–90.

17 Peter M. Blau, *Exchange and Power in Social Life* (New York: Wiley, 1965), 255.

The reason that I prefer this definition of norms/values is that it gives a method that extends across the social continuum from the micro- to the macro-level.

Work on human norms is also the provenance of research on the individual, such as in the work of George Homans (1910–1989). Homans based some of his fundamental propositions on interacting individuals and psychological principles. As he wrote:

> The great example of a social fact is a social norm, and the norms of the groups in which they belong certainly constrain toward conformity the behavior of many more individuals. The question is not that of the existence of constraint but of its explanation... The norm does not constrain automatically: individuals conform, when they do so, because they perceive it is to their net advantage to conform, and it is psychology that deals with the effect on behavior of perceived advantage.[18]

I accept what Homans says with the possible exception of his claim that a "fact" is a "norm." However, in these two short quotations, we can find most of the fundamental ideas that influence those who research social and legal norms; for example, what is the role of psychology on adjudication by judges or acceptance of "what everyone knows is true" by a citizen, or does law really induce conformity based on rationality and how do structures, schemas (rules) and resources produce change? Homans was the founder of "exchange theory." Richard Emerson has extended Homans' ideas into what is called the "network exchange theory" and both of these theorists assume that actors are not always rational but that social relations can be explained through the use of both micro-and macro-level processes and phenomena.

Although many have contributed to our understanding of social action and the social norm, I am sympathetic to the Blau and Homan definitions, which I believe, cover both actions and norms. That is, a social norm or a social fact is something that is commonly agreed upon and serves as the medium of social life and as a mediating link for social transactions. Norms/values make indirect social exchange possible, and they govern the process of social integration and differentiation in complex social structures as well as the development of social organization and reorganization of these organizations.

An opposing view to this is taken by Stephen Turner, who has tried to address norms in terms of habits and practices and found that practices cannot be both causal and shared and that we can never hope to "get behind the notion of practice, either in a causal or a justificatory way, because practices are not objects...."[19] In this sense, practices are the "vanishing point" of twentieth century philosophy.[20] I prefer the

18 George C. Homans, *The Nature of Social Science* (New York: Harcourt, Brace and World, 1967), 50.
19 Stephen Turner, *The Social Theory of Practices: Tradition, Tacit Knowledge and Presuppositions* (Cambridge: Polity Press, 1994), 123.
20 *Ibid.*, 1.

ideas of Blau and Homans, even though and admittedly, the idea of a "norm" is still uncomfortable – unless one accepts non-linear and intertwined explanations.

But perhaps the liveliest definition of norms/values, for my taste, is that given by Norwegian legal theorist Nils Kristian Sundby, who wrote,

> My fundamental concept of norms is thus so wide that it could cover the fire regulations on board a boat, ...private contracts, rules on what constitutes "offside" in soccer, individual moral judgments, mathematical proof principles, the commands of a general to his subordinates, the claim of scientifically correct observation,... [and] the ritual of high Mass on Sundays,... among other things.[21]

At this juncture, we turn to legal norms. What are they? Do social norms have some, most, or all, of the same generic constituents as legal norms? In other words, do legal norms even exist? Here I should note that legal theorists refer to "legal norms" as the laws themselves and the normative guidelines within those laws and judges also claim a set of ethical and adjudicatory "norms." Beyond that, legal theorists do not think in terms of "norms." By and large, what the layperson considers "legal norms" are, by and large, "social norms" and what legal theorists call "legal norms" evidence the same characteristics as what a law is.

The "father" of Sociology, Max Weber, approached the law by use of three "ideal types" – the moral, the dogmatic and the sociological. The moral attitude envisions the moral as outside the law, as extra-judicial. Exactly how, or even if, norms are incorporated into the law is not investigated. Law is used to render value judgments, from the "outside." Dogmatic jurisprudence is the vantage point of a judge or legal scholar. He or she can use the law for a purpose. The judge can render a decision in a particular case and the scholar can devise arguments that approve or disapprove of a certain law in the scholar has in mind. But Weber does say that this attitude also "end[s] in value judgments, judgments couched in the normative language of approval and disapproval."[22]

The use of these three "ideal types" gave Weber two advantages. First, ideal typology incorporates the idea of "understanding"[23] the acts of groups or individuals by

---

21 Nils Kristian Sundby, *Om Normer* (Olso: Universitetsforlaget, 1974), p. 2. (My translation). Although Knut Bergo in *Tekst og Virkelighet i Rettskilderlæren* calls *Om Normer*, both "bitter" and "unrelenting" (p. 436), Bergo also notes that Sundby's concept of norms is a "relational" concept ("relasjonsbegrep") which is what I am interested in as an antidote to strong positivism. (p. 459) Please note that I do not rule out the existence of some universally held norms, e.g. torture or killing of innocents is wrong. One can also see why norm investigation has such received such bad press in legal academia, being labeled as "vague" by Eric Engle in "Law: Lex vs. Ius" in The *Journal of Jurisprudence*, 1 (2008), 31.

22 Anthony T. Kronman, *Max Weber* (London: Edward Arnold, 1983), 11. This book is part of a series entitled *Jurists: Profiles in Legal Theory*, whose general editor was William Twining.

23 In German, *"Verständnis"* (noun) or *"verstehen"* (verb).

seeing the world from their standpoint and secondly, it incorporates an "interpretive" method that can be used to categorize social activities as well as helping to understand various societal patterns.[24] This allowed him to "accentuate not [only] the generic similarities between cultural phenomen[a], but [also] their differences."[25] But, this ideal-type dialectic of Weber also had, and continues to have, drawbacks. Nevertheless, this "inside-outside" dichotomy continues to be used and also to create problems.

It is when Weber begins to write about the law vis-a-vis the economy that he notes that social norms can be incorporated into the law. He asks what significance, or "normative meaning ought to be attributed in correct logic to a verbal pattern having the form of a legal proposition"?[26] If we look at the sociological point of view, as opposed to the legal point of view of this question, then one asks:

> What actually happens in a group owing to the probability that persons engaged in social action (*Gemeinschaftshandeln*), especially those exert-ing a socially relevant amount of power, subjectively consider certain norms as valid and practically act according to them, in other words, orient their own conduct towards these norms.[27]

But, is this the last word from an upper-class man who supported the cause of small farmers in his own time, i.e. the Junker movement? Obviously, it is not and Weber's response to another legal thinker of this day, Rudolf Stammler, addresses the fact that social and legal norms can be similar.

Stammler wrote that the difference between a social norm (a convention) and a legal norm was that which utilized the free will of the individual. Weber ignored this idea and called it "of no use whatsoever."[28] And here, we should perhaps stop to consider the common understanding of the sources of law. Most would agree that the sources of law exist in such things as customs, traditions, convention, religions, folkways, etc. Weber took this point of view writing that there "is no socially important moral commandment which has not been a legal command at one time or another."[29] Weber considered that law and convention were so "intertwined as cause and effect in the actions of men, with, against, and beside, one another."[30] For Weber, "law, convention, and custom are by no means the only forces" that control the conduct

---

24 The "verstehen" method is also known as the interpretive or hermeneutic approach.
25 Wolfgang J. Mommsen, *The Political and Social Theory of Max Weber* (Cambridge and Oxford: Polity Press, 1989).
26 Guenther Roth and Claus Wittich (eds.), trans. Ephraim Fischoff et. al. *Max Weber, Economy and Society*:An outline of interpretive sociology (Berkeley and Los Angeles: University of California Press, 1978), 311.
27 *Ibid.*
28 *Ibid.*, 325.
29 *Ibid.*
30 *Ibid.*, 327.

of a person. There is also, for a person or a group, self-interest that conduct will continue. Sociology looks to empirical regularities as well as legal guarantees and "*their underlying normative conceptions* as causes or consequences of these regularities."[31]

This entire discussion leads to the point where one could conclude that both social and legal norms can have their formation in the social and that they can be studied empirically. As Scott Hamish writes, Weber's sociological point of view

> reinforces the possibility that at a certain level of analysis there may be no incompatibility between (legal) conceptual analysis and sociology: indeed they may be *entirely compatible*.[32]

Of course, the vital section of this quotation is "at a certain level of analysis" and Hamish takes care to set these out as a combination of tasks. These tasks are:

> an equally weighted but discriminating *combination* of ... 1. an analysis of existing conceptual frameworks for law, and 2. the use of newly constructed frameworks."[33]

As I noted above in my reference to Rommetveit, social norms have as their features, 1. to indicate uniformities in behavior, 2. to designate a particular 'frame of reference' and, 3. to express the existence of social obligation or pressure, I see no need to prolong this discussion of to what extent social and legal norms overlap. They sometimes overlap, partially or entirely to the point of being virtually congruent. This interwining effect makes it difficult to see much, if any, difference between legal and social norms.[34]

2.3 A Theory of Legal Boundaries

> [T]he Leitmotif of legal positivism can be seen as the aspiration to secure for law an independent sphere within the realm of practical reason, which primarily is a matter of attempting to seal off, at the foundational level, 'law' and legal discourse from 'morality' and moral discourse.
>
> Olsen and Toddington[35]

---

31 Hamish Ross, *Law as a Social Institution*, (Oxford: Hart Publishing, 2001), 90.

32 *Ibid.*, 91.

33 *Ibid.*, 94. Ross relies for this on the work of Robert Summers. Please see, Robert Summers, "The New Analytical Jurists" in *New York University Law Review*, 41 (1966), 861. Hamish also makes references to H.L.A. Hart's "nucleic expository theory."

34 Ragnar Rommeveit, *Social Norms and Roles* (Minneapolis: University of Minnesota Press, 1955), 18–26. I should leave room for the case where they do not overlap at all but this is a difficult case to imagine.

35 Henrik Palmer Olsen and Stuart Toddington, *Law in its Own Right* (Oxford and Portland: Hart Publishing, 1999), 31.

The boundaries between laws and norms are always being negotiated and shifting in one way or another. The current boundaries between the law and social norms have already supposedly been constructed – and reinforced – by legal theorists over a long period of time.[36] I want to emphasize that there are very good reasons for this, especially when one reviews the impact that pre-modern European religious forces had on weak civil laws.

But what has happened is that these boundaries act in a way that supports the idea that social norms might only exist and interact with the goal(s) of legislation up until the minute the law is passed in a procedurally appropriate manner. At that point, the law takes on a life of its own and enters a world of abstraction, of legal dogmatics and adjudication.

The ATL is advocated by theorists such as Gerald Postema.[37] To be fair, the reasoning behind the ATL is persuasive, in the abstract. It also says that since human society is so complex and since we can never hope to achieve agreement by all interested parties, then we need to create a barrier for public officials who must use the law in question and also a cultural myth that claims influence by none of the parties. It is a type of "override mechanism."[38]

Postema has three attached corollaries that are both "logically indispensible and logically interrelated." They are the Limited Domain Thesis (LDT), the Pre-emption Thesis (PET) and the Source Thesis (ST). As Olsen and Toddington write, these three sub-theses mean (indeed, demand) that law is:

> a body of "autonomous" norms, operates in a limited domain of practical reason common to officials and citizens alike; that these norms constitute *exclusionary* reasons for action in that they preclude and override conflicting reasons or normative preferences outside the domain, and these, therefore preemptive, norms be *identifiable at source* without recourse to moral argument or political evaluations which might exist and function in various influential ways outside the limited domain.[39]

This is all very convenient and can sometimes leave a significant minority at odds with enacted or adjudicated law or both. However, defining away problems through

---

36 However, one of the strongest modern proponents of this wall is sociologist Arthur Stinchcombe insofar as he supports the procedural formality of the law as a type of "blueprint" for the process of law. See, Arthur L. Stinchcombe, *When Formality Works: Authority and Abstraction in Law and Organizations* (Chicago: The University of Chicago Press, 2001). "My argument is that when law (or mathematics or organization) works, it is the same substance as the rest of social life, but formalized for one purpose or another." p. 3. Rheinstien notes that there are two types of formality, however, and Stinchcombe emphasized procedural formality at the expense of "sense" knowledge as a type of formality.

37 Gerald Postema, "Law's Autonomy and Public Practical Reason" in R.P. George, *The Autonomy of Law: Essays on Legal Positivism* (Oxford: Clarendon Press, 1996), 79–119.

38 Olsen and Toddington, *Law in its Own Right*, 30.

39 *Ibid.*

the use of theory is not the best way of constructing a new theory. It is a bit like believing viruses do not exist as a source of infection because antibiotics kill bacteria. But, it is, nonetheless, very alluring – especially if far more bacteria than viruses exist.

Thus, the Autonomy Thesis of Law exists as supporting the "Berlin Wall" of social norm non-inclusion that I examine in this book. Many theorists have discussed this theory and found it wanting in one way or another – Gustav Radbruch for one – while others defend it at every turn. At the end of the day, the social (and legal) norms of stability and predictability seem to argue for the continuance of the ATL, in some form or another, although there seems to be no end to "conversions" away from it.[40]

Positive law is basically the written law of a country. It can be the result of legislation and adjudication based on challenges to laws and it can be found in printed form or some sort of media, for all citizens to read. It is published to citizens as part of a social contract. As American jurisprudential great H.L.A. Hart would write, it has no necessary connection with morality.

Positive law has several drawbacks as well as advantages. In some cases, it is vague. It is sometimes not well thought out, passed in haste, It can even be purchased through lobbying. In order to have determinate law at any given time, we cannot go behind it and reconsider it every time it is used. This is one of the reasons for the ATL. The problem with walls is that they not only keep something out but they also restrict what is being confined. For example, as I mentioned above, one can find perfectly acceptable reasons, given Western ideas of the separation of Church and State, for keeping the precepts of one religion or another behind this wall and away from being incorporated in positive law of any kind. But should some type of fundamental ethics or the results of social scientific inquiry also be excluded?

With regard to ethics and morality, some theorists assume that it is not, by definition, included – at least in adjudicated law. On the other hand, as Olsen and Toddington write, there is a "less than inspirational" thesis that there is a "*moderate* connection *in some sense* between law and morality."[41] Here is not the place to delve into the variations on this theme. I will note, however, that this issue can make for strange bedfellows.[42]

---

40 At the end of his life, legal theorist Neil MacCormick seemed to be one such convert to the belief that legal positivism was insufficient in itself. Please see Claudio Michelon, Jr.'s oving remembrance of MacCormick in *Dritto & questioni pubbliche*, No. 9 (2009), 53–62.

41 Olsen and Toddington, *Law in its Own Right*, 18.

42 *Ibid.* These two authors cite to the fact that methodological and substantive natural law theorists such as John Finnis agree with methodological and substantive positivists such as Neil MacCormick that there is a *necessary*, i.e. not contingent, connection between law and morality. While there is often a consistent connection – at the practical level – between law and morality, I am of the opinion that there is no *necessary* connection between the two,and in this work am not advocating for the so-called "new" natural law by any means.

An example of how this ATL Berlin Wall restricts use of social science can be found in McCleskey v. Kemp, 481 U.S. 279 (1987). In McCleskey, the United States Supreme Court (USSC) refused to consider empirical data on who received the death penalty and who did not. The data was part of the Baldus Study, which considered the race of victim and perpetrator as a factor in sentencing. Despite the statistical foundations and persuasiveness of this social science data in this study, the USSC refused to consider the study's conclusions as a means to reevaluating the on-going legal validity of the death penalty in McCleskey. Baldus showed a statistically significant correlation between the race of the victim and the perpetrator and the likelihood of the perpetrator to receive the death penalty. If justice was "blind" as those who support the Wall often presume, this could not be proven by the rejection of the Baldus Study or by its content and conclusions.

The theory of positive law continues as a strong theory although there are cracks in the wall which most simply overlook but which others cannot avoid acknowledging.[43] One of the cracks begins with a very old idea, extant at least since Plato and Aristotle. This is that the law, in ways both large and small, does actually "mirror" society. This is the theme that Brian Tamanaha used to begin his study of a general jurisprudence theory that he calls socio-legal positivism.[44] Indeed, one of the Judges we shall meet in this work, Oliver W. Holmes, the author of Buck v. Bell, 274 U.S. 200 (1927), called law a "magic mirror" of the lives of all people; this theory comes down to us as the "mirror thesis."[45] Justice Holmes both espoused the mirror thesis and also upheld the forced sterilization of Carrie Buck in Buck v. Bell, 274 U.S. 200 (1927) leaving us to wonder if the mirror thesis is a cogent argument against the erosion of this Berlin Wall.[46]

43 The ATL itself is the product of the theory of positive law. Positive law, while attacked from various quarters at various time periods, seems to be undergoing a sustained critique at this time. In point of fact, J.D. Goldsworthy has said that legal positivism has now "self-destructed." See, J.D. Goldsworthy, "Self-destruction of Legal Positivism" in *Oxford Journal of Legal Studies*, 4 (1990), 449.

44 Brian Z. Tamanaha, *A General Jurisprudence of Law and Society* (New York and Oxford: Oxford University Press, 2001).

45 *Ibid.*, 2.

46 Buck v. Bell, 274 U.S. 200 (1927), case decided in the U.S. Supreme Court
While I am concerned with the refusal to admit the existence of this Wall by some who write at the border between sociology and law and with the ensuing schizophrenia in American law, I am also concerned with the function of the border. If the law is not "situated" (contextualized) in any sense of that word, then, and in anything other than an abstract manner, to use Thomas Nagel's phrase, is it not a "view from nowhere"? (Please see Thomas Nagel, *The View from Nowhere* (New York and Oxford: Oxford University Press, 1986). It may function to keep law "pure" in some primal, sacral sense but it also functions to give law a largesse that is unassailable, even when unreasonable, as was seen in McCleskey, above. The reasons for this can also be, at least partially, primal. The idea that "any law is better than no law" retains a salience, even though many now admit law is based in conventions and social norms and that law is overrated as a means for social order.

2.4 Tamanaha's Socio-legal Positivist Theory and Boundaries

Anyone who begins to read jurisprudence will note that some ideas and themes may serve as the starting point for many interpretations. One such theme is the idea of social order. In western political thought from Hobbes to Rawls, this is, if not an obvious concern, then at least an underlying fear. As Tamanaha writes:

> The implied threat of disorder works on our primal fears to render law in heroic terms, as a savior or protector; the metaphor of the mirror makes it *our* savior, *our* protector, a power to identify with, not fear.[47]

And here we have the second half of the mirror thesis, which is that law reflects society... so that order can be maintained. This also is a preview of one of my conclusions, namely, that at times of "moral panic" we often turn to the law as a protector against, for example, "race suicide." The emphasis on "law and order" may also be why the phrase "law and justice" has never held the public imagination as has the former.

Other central ideas in the study of jurisprudence are customs, reason and morality. Since I am concerned here, primarily, about the interaction between law and society, I take Tamanaha's model to demonstrate these ideas. He writes that Custom/Consent and Morality/Reason, each from its own vantage point, impacts the making of Positive Law as demonstrated in Figure 2.1, below.

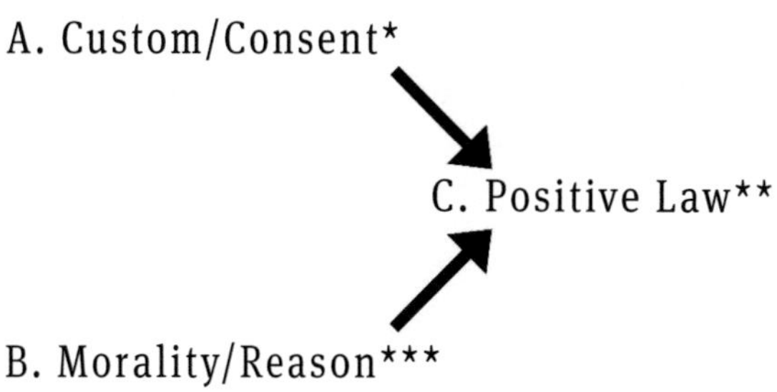

Figure 2.1: The Tamanaha relationship between law and society[48]

47 Tamanaha, *A General Jurisprudence of Law and Society*, 3.

48 *Ibid.*, 4-5. * In this model, Custom/Consent refers to the "customs, usages, habits and practices of society." An example is the common law. ** In this model, Positive Law is law that is written and that can then be enforced through coercion, if necessary, thus implying its attributes of both power and authority. *** Morality/Reason refers to the customs that are perceived as "moral" or to the natural law, but it is not limited to it. In fact, some theorists would deny that positive law need have anything to do with morality (Austin) while others (Dworkin) see them as intertwined.

All this – again – is about the problem of line drawing and the psychological certainty that hard and fast demarcations brings. How and where the lines are drawn among disciplines such as "politics" and "law" or among the various facets of "the social?" And, who draws these lines? And, one question that is sometimes omitted but perhaps the most important is "cui bonum" or "Who benefits by all this line drawing?" Where is the line drawn between, in this case, the Law and the socio-cultural?

It might be worth considering that rather than drawing lines between the worlds of politics and law that we might rather think of them as parallel lines, or layers.[49] Not always unidirectional processes, they are more in the shape of lines indicating the ebb and flow between liquids of different tonic strength, i.e. $\Leftrightarrow$.[50] Or, there might be connections between different layers. The ebb and flow of ions or the connections between multilayered phenomena are metaphors for the fact that history moves forward and backward, at the same time, which brings us to the issue of causation. Tamahana admits that these three areas do not act in a uni-directional fashion and therefore, I would amend his original figure, noted above, to more accurately reflect this so that the symbol $\rightarrow$ becomes the symbol $\Leftrightarrow$.

2.5 Jasanoff and the Idiomatic Co-construction of Knowledge

I use Sheila Jasanoff's social constructivist idiom methodology, although the entire theory of social construction has, and will continue to have, its detractors.[51] Jasanoff, and others, have tried to answer the objections to social constructivism and I agree with her when she writes that the work done by Kuhn and others[52] is captured "imperfectly" by the "dictum that scientific knowledge is socially constructed."[53] The problem with this overly simple formulation is that it "raises two [irresolvable] prob-

49 *Ibid.*, 30. Citation to Pickering.

50 Let us suppose that "politics" might exist as the chemical silver nitrate (Ag2NO3) in a glass beaker. The beaker also holds "the social" or distilled water. In this analogy, when "the law" is added in the form of an acid such as hydrochloric (HCl), various reactions take place in the solution, i.e. there is a precipitate, silver chloride (AgCl). But, by comparison, in an "isotonic" solution, the forward and backward reactions between elements in solution are in equilibrium. But if one has a hypotonic or a hypertonic solution (stress, "moral panic", economic disaster), the direction of fluids can be changed from forward to backward and vice-versa.

51 A recent good discussion of this can be found in John R. Searle's review of Paul A. Boghossian's book *Fear of Knowledge: Against Relativism and Constructivism*, in "Why Should You Believe It?" in The *New York Times Review of Books*, LVI, (2009), 88–91.

52 These others include, for example, Bloor, Collins, Kuhn, Latour and Woolgar.

53 Sheila Jasanoff (ed.), *States of Knowledge: The co-production of science in social order* (London and New York: Routledge), 19.

lems, one theoretical and the other pragmatic."[54] To the first (theoretical) problem, she writes that there is no causal primacy in the "social."

> Constructivism does not imply that social reality is ontologically prior to natural reality, nor that social factors alone determine the workings of nature; yet the rubric "social construction" carries just such connotations.[55]

The second (pragmatic) problem that Jasanoff notes is that, because of the large number of constitutive elements of the "social", there can be no "symmetrical probing" of all the elements at one time.[56] One element has to be made "fundamental, granted agency, and so exempted from further analysis."[57] Thus, she uses the four "fields" of making representation, making institutions, making discourses and making identities – as a method for exploring the factors involved in how knowledge is co-produced; my work will thus be descriptive in nature, looking at factors, perhaps arguing that one or another is "necessary" or "indicative" but not actually arguing causation.

While this may cause some discomfort, she assures us that co-production is neither random nor contingent. As she writes:

> In each of these... areas – the emergence of new phenomena, the resolution of conflicts, the standardization of knowledge or technology, the enculturation of scientific practices – work in the co-productionist idiom stresses the constant intertwining of the cognitive, the material, the scientific and the normative. Co-production is not about ideas alone; it is equally about physical things. It is not only about how people organize or express themselves, but also about how they assume responsibility for their inventions. Equally and to the point, co-production occurs neither at random nor contingently, but along certain well documented pathways.[58]

With this in mind, it should not surprise the reader that some of the information about making representations, institutions, discourse and identities includes such disparate topics as sausage casings, exorcism and women dressed as men.

2.6 Combining Intersubjectivity and the Jasanoff Fields

In addition to Jasanoff's co-productionist idiom with its four fields of co-production, I also use here the theory of intersubjectivity, introduced by Leslie McCall, Patricia

54 *Ibid.*
55 *Ibid.*
56 *Ibid.*, 19–20.
57 *Ibid.*, 20.
58 *Ibid*, 6.

Hill Collins and others.[59] As Collins notes, the construct of intersubjectivity "references two types of relationships: the interconnectedness of ideas and the social structures in which they occur, and the intersecting hierarchies of gender, race, economic class, sexuality and ethnicity."[60] In this theory, the categorical form of complexity takes as its beginning point that "there are relationships of inequality among already constituted social groups."[61] While one must acknowledge that these social groups are "imperfect" and "ever changing", these groups are the centerpieces of the methodology. These groups are the anchor although their use may be provisional.[62] The premise of the categorical complexity approach is that "relationships among social groups are containers of definable and indeed measurable inequalities."[63] The groups that I originally examined were based on ability, class, race/ethnicity, gender, and citizen status. As a sacrifice to space considerations, I will generally use one category as representative of some of the features that the others also show, and that one category is gender.

The ideas which we now know as intersubjectivity are a result of reflexive work done at the end of the twentieth century when traditional feminism was challenged to include a more complete picture of the master-subject relationship through the inclusion of other factors, especially gender, race and class.[64] In the 1990s, these same factors were used to further refine feminist theory. New questions about the nature of repression in any of, or in a mix of, these categories have forced feminists to reconsider a newer "intersubjective" feminist paradigm.

My use of this theory, which includes these containers of identity, is an effort to honor the complexity of the times as well as a way to better outline the full impact that the laws had on these groups.[65] Take, for example, Jasanoff's co-productionist idiom of the identity. In Case 1, one could select various identities through this theoretical lens; these included identities such as handicapped (ability), female (gender), non-white (race), poor (class) and immigrant (citizen status) and look at their role in

---

59 Leslie McCall, "The Complexity of Intersubjectivity" in *Signs: Journal of Women in Culture and Society*, Vol. 30, No. 3 (2005). McCall actually outlines three approaches to intersubjectivity, i.e. anticategorical complexity, intercategorical complexity and intracategorical complexity. Intersubjectivity is also called intersectionality by Feminist theorists.

60 Patricia Hill Collins, "Moving Beyond Gender: Intersectionality and Scientific Knowledge" in Myra Marx Feree, Judith Lorber and Beth B. Hess (eds.) *Revisioning Gender* (Walnut Creek & Lanham: AltaMira Press, a Division of Rowman & Littlefield Publishers, Inc., 2000), 263.

61 *Ibid.*, 1785.

62 *Ibid.*

63 *Ibid.*

64 The "master-subject" reference is to work done by Carole Pateman in her various works such as *The Sexual Contract* (Cambridge: Polity Press, 1988).

65 We see the same groups of non-BMM ("non-benchmark male") people appear in the newspapers in Indiana, 1907 and Oslo, 1934 as well as – again – in Connecticut (1963) and Oslo (1976). As I mentioned earlier, this led me to consider this theory as a way of explaining their re-appearances.

social/moral discourses, i.e. who will feed those who cannot work, what will happen if women can vote, what will happen especially to white women if blacks and whites mix, and what will happen to the country if the poor and "waves" of immigrants reproduce while upper-class white women do not?

The goal of the intersubjective approach is to consider the identity – usually imposed on the individual – of these categories and to compare their relationships, one or two at a time. While this way of managing complexity "at first appears to be a reductionist process", I would argue along with McCall, that it eventually becomes, in the end, "a synthetic and holistic process that brings the various pieces of the analysis together."[66]

In a journal article entitled "The Race to Innocence: Confronting Hierarchical Relations among Women", Marie Louise Fellows and Sherene Razack give an analysis of feminism that includes a discussion of why systems of oppression are so successful. They contend that social strategies and practices must account for the relationships among hierarchical systems.

> Systems of oppression (capitalism, imperialism, and patriarchy) rely on each other in complex ways. This "interlocking" effect means that the systems of oppression come into existence in and through each other so that class exploitation could not be accomplished without gender and racial hierarchies, imperialism could not function without class exploitation, sexism and heterosexism, and so on. Because the systems rely on each other in these complex ways it is ultimately futile to attempt to disrupt one system without simultaneously disrupting others.[67]

I attempt to show how this theory of interlocking systems of oppression, including but not limited to that of women's oppression, can be used to create law for regulation, liberation or further oppression. The fact that oppression is an interlocking process also supports the idea that unjust laws are put into effect when several, or all, of the categories mentioned above are implicated.

Keeping in mind that this thesis is ultimately about how the law impacts the body and its reproductive capacities, in Case One in my discussion of identities I select events that demonstrate the ideograph of wife and mother. An ideograph is a normatively proper concept of woman or wife, i.e. at that time, of who should be deemed a good wife and mother. One of my concerns was to see if the categories stay in a container that remains non-porous even over the short term and in the same

---

66 *Ibid.*, 1787.

67 Mary Louise Fellows and Sherene Razack, "The Race to Innocence: Confronting Hierarchical Relations Among Women" in *Iowa Journal of Race, Gender and Justice*, 1, (1998). In this paper the authors discuss the problem of competing marginalities and the belief that women do not see themselves as being implicated in the subordination of other women – women of color, lesbians, poor women, prostitutes etc. Women often claim that their own marginality is worse than some other sort of marginalism and that they have played no part in the subordination of other women. The authors have named this process "the race to innocence."

place – as well as over the long term. Do the categories become multi-discoursed? If this happens, how do the containers change, do they remain intact or are they semi-porous?

Historical considerations of sociological events are complex. The intersubjective approach posits that complexity derives from the fact that "different contexts reveal different configurations of inequality in [a] particular social formation."[68] The point, as McCall writes, "is not to assume [an] outcome *a priori* but to explore the nature and extent of such differences and inequalities."[69] One can indeed begin with "traditional analytical categories as a starting point" but findings can be more "fruitful" – one of the indices of reliability[70] – and go beyond a single finding to include multiple, interesting and conflicting findings. In her work, for example, she came to question whether the traditional indicators of inequality, such as family income inequality and male earnings could continue to be used as indicators of a "new inequality."[71] Did this mean, in the end, that patterns couldn't be discovered? Some researchers, including N. Katherine Hayles, who have abandoned the predictability aspect of positivism, altogether believe not. They believe that simply because a phenomenon is complex "does not mean that anything goes: reality is complexly patterned but patterned nonetheless."[72]

For example, the category of (degenerate) identity was first linked to the criminal/non-criminal category in the United States and, eventually to the cognitive/physical ability of both males and females, in Norway. The categories "morphed", intersecting with other categories. However, no matter what combination of categories came to exist, if we look at only the sheer number of people sterilized, a dramatically larger number of women than men were sterilized.[73] Why was this so? In the United States in 1942, male criminals were left behind in the protective dust of legal precedent because of the due-process requirements of Skinner v. Oklahoma, while women, especially women of color, disabled and poor women, continued to be sterilized well into the 1970s in both countries.[74] In other words, three-time convicted chicken thieves were

---

68 McCall, *Complexity of Intersubjectivity*, 1791.

69 *Ibid.*

70 Jonathon Potter argues that we can use four considerations to assess our work, 1. deviant case analysis, 2. participants' understandings, 3. coherence and 4. readers' evaluations. Please see, Jonathon Potter, "Discourse analysis and constructionist approaches: theoretical background" in J. Richardson (ed.) *Qualitative Methods for Psychological and the Social Sciences* (Leicester: British Psychological Association, 1996).

71 Please see, Leslie McCall, "Explaining Levels of Within-Group Wage Inequality in U.S. Labor Markets" in *Demography*, 37 (2000), 415–30.

72 McCall, *Complexity of Intersubjectivity*, 1794.

73 Please see as regards the United States, Carey, "Gender and Compulsory Sterilization Programs in America: 1907–1950, Note 208. As regards Norway, please consult Per Haave's work on the sterilization work of Sâmi and "travelers" (Roma) by the Oslo Indremisjonen.

74 *Ibid.*

safer with regard to bodily integrity under the Constitution of the United States than poor, disabled and non-white women were.[75] In Case Two, the same intersubjective categories come to the surface again, also during a time of social turmoil over values and within the same context of how the law regulates human reproduction. In Case Two, the groups that were less powerful in Case One had accumulated more power through various resources, schemas and structures and had changed to a point where an opposite result could be reached.

The problem with this type of argument is that the social script in many countries still normalizes the "benchmark male" (BMM) as a reference point. Benchmark male means "those who are white, able-bodied, heterosexual and middle class, and who constitute the normative standard within the social script."[76] Connell points out that these (male) hegemonic norms of gender can be known "at a given moment in time and cultural space."[77] Connell calls this "hegemonic masculinity" and, when combined with the fact that access to the ballot box for over a century has not produced full participation by women in the liberal democratic process, makes us wonder what exactly has failed in the execution of a modern form of liberal government.

Margaret Thornton notes that "the imagery associated with the body politic has not undergone a sex change."[78] This is so because the liberal project conveniently separated the public and the private sphere. And since "universal language [such as the law] denies embodiment and subjectivity altogether", any type of "particularities are relegated to the private sphere, which encompasses the affective and the corporal, reproduction and nurturing – notions that have all come to be associated with the feminine." But, succinct divisions of the polity as public and the domestic sphere as private are as realistic and possible as putting Humpty Dumpty together again. All BMMs need to do is use the "brain of law" and the view from nowhere, to hide the inconvenient parts of life and to designate them as private" – or "public" – as it suits them.[79] If we look in the space behind the "universal citizen" as defined by the "brain

---

75 As mentioned above, this was the case with Carrie Buck's sister, Doris, who was told she was having an appendectomy and in fact, was sterilized. She later learned this when she and her husband tried to have children.

76 Margaret Thornton, *Sexing the Citizen*, at http://www.law.unimelb.edu.aw/events/citizen/thorton.pdf, last accessed 17 November 2007. Having encountered a number of female partners in large American law firms, I would add to this definition the phrase, "...or women who subscribe to that normative standard as embodied in these males and cannot be distinguished from males based on her actions."

77 Ann Rudinow Sætnan, Nelly Oudshoorn and Marta Kirejczyk (eds.) in *Bodies of Technology* (Columbus: Ohio State University Press, 2000), 6. The reference is to R.W. Connel, *Gender and Power: Society, the Person and Sexual Politics* (Cambridge: Polity Press, 1987).

78 *Ibid.*, 2.

79 *Ibid.*, 4.

of law", an abstract citizen devoid of all characteristics, what we find is a transition from "private to public patriarchy."[80]

Having said the above, I also realize that there can be a problem with this description of patriarchy. As Vanessa Monroe writes, this type of "overly deterministic understanding of the operation of patriarchy" can rest on a problematic understanding of what the interests of women – and men – actually are.[81] While a monolithic vision of patriarchy may indeed not be very helpful, it does give a starting point for evaluating the effects of various historic forms of patriarchy.[82] Because I focus on effects, the "potential paralysis" of women engaged in the "how" of combating a patriarchy need not be analyzed here.[83]

All of the above dovetails nicely with the ideas of sociologist Charles Lemert. The "strong we", and the "weak we", are terms developed by him.[84] The little word "we", he writes is "very potent" and "its value is necessarily derived from the sociology of any situation in which it is used."[85] His example of the language in the American Declaration of Independence is instructive. When that document says "We hold these truths to be self-evident", the "we" refers to a class of powerful white men who "already had the right to use the words 'self-evident'."[86] The relationship between the "strong we" and the "weak we" is that the "weak we" are in the position to ask "Whose We?" as when Jefferson wrote the Declaration of Independence.[87] While not always "self-consciously cruel", it is the "strong we" that:

> throw up barriers of various kinds – fences around refugee camps, gated walls around clusters of fancy homes, and reinforced perimeters on borders with regions where there is an unusual number of the "Weak We" people.[88]

Case One will set out in detail who the "weak we" were who later become part of the "strong we" in Case Two.

---

80 *Ibid.* Thornton cites to Sylvia Walby, "Is Citizenship Gendered?" in *Sociology*, 28 (1994), 379, 392.
81 Vanessa Munroe, *Law and Politics at the Perimeter: Re-Evaluating Key Debates in Feminist Theory* (Oxford and Portland, Oregon: Hart Publishing Company, 2007), 32.
82 *Ibid.*
83 *Ibid.*, 33.
84 Charles Lemert, *Dark Thoughts: Race and the Eclipse of Society* (New York and London: Routledge, 2002), 54–55, 66.
85 *Ibid.*, 52.
86 *Ibid.*, 54.
87 *Ibid.*, 58.
88 *Ibid.*, 59.

2.7 Moral Panic and Large-Scale Structural Change

The idea of moral panic is visible in 1964, when Britain's *Daily Telegraph* reported a "Day of Terror by Scooter Groups" in Clacton, Britain.[89] The *Daily Mirror* went on to report "Wild Ones Invade Seaside" which sociologist Stanley Cohen, who then coined the phrase "moral panic" in his seminal work, *Folk Devils and Moral Panic*.[90]

The idea of a "moral panic" was also used by Mary Douglas, for one, who observed that during "times of social crisis, when natural borders and identities are threatened, there is likely to be a concern with the maintenance of existing bodily boundaries and the purity of bodies."[91] I argue that the framing of some discourses related to race/ethnicity, gender, class, ability and citizenship status occur during socially stressful and times of change and that this matters a great deal in terms of the end legal product of the times, i.e. legislated law.[92]

We know, for example, that individual or communal "distress" is sometimes converted into a medicalized illness that is, at that particular moment, considered "deviance"[93]; in a similar manner a form of societal "moral panic" may accompany

---

89 Please see, http://bbc.co.uk/onthisday/hi/dates/stories/may/18/newsid_2511000/2511245.stm, last accessed 20 June 2009.

90 Stanley Cohen, *Folk Devils and Moral Panics: The Creation of the Mods and the Rockers* (London: MacGibbon & Kee, 1972).

91 Chris Shilling, *The Body and Social Theory* (London, Thousand Oaks, New Dehli: Sage Publications, 2005), p. 64. Please also see Mary Douglas, *Natural Symbols: Explorations in Cosmology* (London: The Cresset Press, 1970).

92 The concept of "framing" originated with Erving Goffman (1922–1982). (Erving Goffman, *Frame Analysis: An Essay on the Organization of Experience* (New York: Harper & Row, 1974). But over the ensuing thirty or more years, the concept can be only "loosely connected" to Goffman's original ideas. (Please see, http://www.lboro.ac.uk/research/mmethods/resources/links/frames_primmer.html, last accessed 3 May 2007.) It even "spans a number of disparate approaches" which are "incompatible with one another." (*Ibid.*) In fact, Robert Benford tells us it has become a bit of a "cliché." (Robert Benford, "An Insider's Critique of the Social Movement Framing Perspective" in *Sociological Inquiry*, 67 (1997), 409–430) But one path away from "cliché", I believe, is to clearly distinguish frames from ideology and ideology from the "master-frame." In addition, in 2000, Benford and Snow asked if the framing literature at that point in time could be said to "congeal or hang together in a fashion suggestive of a coherent perspective" or if "such a perspective [can] be stitched together from various strands of the literature…." (Robert D. Benford and David A. Snow "Framing Processes and Social Movements: An Overview and Asssessment" in *Annual Review of Sociology*, 26 (2000), 611- 639. Their goal was to refine and integrate the relationship between framing and social movements and, through a substantive review of the literature, they found in the affirmative to both questions.

93 Please see the discussion of "Draptomania" above. The idea of social crisis as part and parcel of causation has also impacted the environs of medical anthropology so that, in 1999, Susan M. DiGiacomo could entitle an article "Can There be a 'Cultural Epidemiology'?" In this work, she cites to the realization by Roberto Franzosi, a quantatively trained sociologist, that history was often treated as a "'warehouse of data' to be plundered…" Realizing that his statistical work reflected correlations and

the changing of cultural meanings, values and norms.[94] I do not intend to prove this as a type of rule pertaining to all social and/or cultural upheavals, but only to suggest that it can be a sociological model that can occur, at least in the two cases I present, in the United States and northern Europe.[95]

Furthermore, when societal panic/stress or structural shifts do occur, and when the law becomes involved through either legislative activity or through the appellate interpretation of a set of facts or legal rules applied to those facts, especially in tandem with then "sound" scientific evidence, the panic can flow from this law to bodies that are (often) not male and are (often) not white, with more power and consequence than to the bodies that the law may have originally intended as its subjects and objects (index).

For social constructivists Erich Goode and Nachman Ben-Yehuda, the reality of social problems can be measured or manifested in some of the following ways:

> (i) organized, collective action or campaigns on the part of some of the members of society to do something about, call attention to, protest, or change (or prevent change in) a given condition – in short, "social problems as social movements"...(ii) the introduction of bills in legislatures to criminalize or otherwise deal with the behavior and the individuals supposedly causing the condition...(iii) the ranking of a condition or an issue in the public's hierarchy of the most serious problems facing the country,...and (iv) public discussion of an issue in the media in the form of magazine and newspaper articles..., commentaries,...and dramas...[96]

This grass-roots social model posits that the panic is spontaneous across the society and is propelled by social stresses. The anxiety is displaced onto deviants of one sort or another "who are perceived through cultural symbols, which reflect the real, underlying social stresses."[97] The elite-engineered model uses major institutions –

---

not causal relationships, Franzosi cited to Braudel, bemoaning the fact that "there is hardly ever any real dialogue between sociologist and historian...and no marriage between two disciplines that would seem to be ideally suited mates." Please see, Susan M. DiGiacomo, "Can there be a 'Cultural Epidemiology'?" in *Medical Anthropology Quarterly, New Series,* 13 (1999), pp. 436–457.

94 Margaret Lock, "Cultivating the Body: Anthropology and Epistemologies of Bodily Practice and Knowledge" in the *Annual Review of Anthropology*, 22 (1993), 145.

95 Catastrophic changes can also be a factor in social/moral panics, e.g. changes in weather. A good overview of various types of crises can be found in American Historical Review Forum, "The General Crisis of the Seventeenth Century Revisited" in *The American Historical Review*, 113, No. 4 (2008), 1029–1090. J.B. Shank finds that when used as a "rhetorical term of art rather than as a literal term of scientific and deterministic objectivity, the concept of crisis becomes a powerful tool in Negri's historical analysis of Descartes" and that Rabb's use of the "crisis idea works to open interpretive perspectives, not to shut them down in the name of causal determinism." (p. 1098.)

96 Erich Goode and Nachman Ben-Yehuda, "Culture, Politics, and Social Construction", in *Annual Review of Sociology*, 20 (1994), 152.

97 Jeffrey S. Victor, "Moral Panics and the Social Construction of Deviant Behavior: A Theory and Application to the Case of Ritual Child Abuses" in *Sociological Perspectives*, 41 (1998), 546.

law, medicine, religion – to "generate and sustain moral outrage" against the deviant group."[98] The intention of the elite group, however, is not to solve the "problem." The intention is to "divert attention away from real problems in a society, the solution of which would threaten the economic and political interests of the elite."[99] The interest group model "suggest that moral panics are unintended consequences of moral crusades launched by specific interest groups and their activists..."[100] While the interest groups may be true believers in their cause they are not averse to having the panic function as a boost to their own goals and prestige.

In some form or another, the concept of "moral panic" cannot be denied; it lives on in the literature.[101] R.J. Holton uses the term "sociology of crisis" in his analysis of crises, which has its roots in both Talcott Parsons and Jurgen Habermas.[102] More recently, Ronald N. Jacobs writes about civil society and crisis as reflected in the Rodney King beating.[103] The term also has a function. Thomas Olesen has written about transnational social movements and one of the nine features he identifies with a successful framing of issues is that these frames, such as a moral panic about race suicide, will have a "well-developed elements of diagnosis, prognosis and motivation and establish a coherent internal relation between them." As well, these frames of moral panic will attempt "to provide order and guidance in a complex reality."[104] Moral panic may not be as specific as we would like but it does function in the way that Olesen describes, i.e. it provides a theoretical basis for how to reestablish order again.

Case One and Two take place within the span of nearly 100 years. Can we ignore this as a factor and focus strictly on the Jasanoff fields? We probably could as these fields give evidence of large scale structural change in both the USA and Norway. However, there is a rather succinct model that does the same theoretical work. The Pescosolido model envisions the "modern" or "contemporary" social structure as a circle of intersecting circles all tied by spokes to the individual in the middle of the circle. This emphasis on a new type of network that the individual is engaged in is,

---

98 *Ibid.*, 547.

99 *Ibid.* One of the best descriptions of this from medieval times is found in R.I. Moore, *The Formation of a Persecuting Society: Power and Deviance in Western Europe, 950–1250 A.D.* (Malden and Oxford: Blackwell Publishers, 1987).

100 *Ibid.*, 548.

101 Please see, Erich Goode and Ben-Yehuda Nachman, "No Need to Panic: A Bumper Crop of Books on Moral Panic" in *Sociological Forum*, 15 (2000), 543–52.

102 R.J. Holton, "The Idea of Crises in Modern Society" in *The British Journal of Sociology*, 38 (1987), 502–520.

103 Ronald N. Jacobs, "Civil Society and Crises: Culture, Discourse, and the Rodney King Beating" in *The American Journal of Sociology*, 101 (1996), 1238–1272.

104 Thomas Olesen, "World Politics and Social Movements: "The Janus Face of the Global Democratic Structure" in *Global Society*, 19 (2005), 125.

for these authors, a "bridge" between "postmodernism's concern with the individuals' unique experiences and sociology's focus on social structure."[105] In this new diagram, individuals are not in any of the surrounding interconnected circles but are outside of all of them. The diagram underscores the idea that social life today is "based on serial, ephemeral, short-term, contingent relationships with comparably limited contracts."[106] This contingency is only exacerbated by the fact that the groups themselves can also be temporary. The "family", for example, can be represented by many social circles where the only secure ties between these different social circles are the children.[107]

Along with the advantage of more freedom and flexibility comes the disadvantage of "alienation, isolation and fragmentation."[108] If one focuses on the disadvantages, one could see a

> return to primordial social ties, reflected in hyper-nationalism, ethnic identity, and religious fundamentalism....[where t]hose who profit from the new social forms are likely to be those in power (as in all social forms), those who are resource rich, and those on the cutting edge of societal developments, i.e. technology.[109]

With the individual at the center of the spoke, there is a capacity for "enormous" egoism along with an "underlying numbness"; unique problems are presented for the creation of responsive social policy formation.[110]

2.8 Methodologies for Rhetorical Analyses

Having presented the theories that guide what data I select, I finish this chapter with a discussion of the theories that help those decisions. The first theory is that of critical discourse analysis (CDA) which is a supplement to Jasanoff's "making discourses" field. It is a very common tool with its roots in the "hermeneutical" and "linguistics" turns of the 1980s. Among its chief theoreticians and practitio-

105 *Ibid.*, 62.
106 *Ibid.*, 63.
107 *Ibid.*, 64. Pescosolido-Rubin and Rubin refer to this phenomenon as "stability within change."
108 *Ibid.*
109 *Ibid.*, 65.
110 *Ibid.* Originally, this manuscript was to have a Case Three on ultrasound laws that represented the current period.

ners are Bernstein[111], Norman Fairclough[112], Theo A. von Dijk[113] and Theo von Leeuwen.[114]

There are a number of rhetorical techniques associated with CDA. One is the identification of ideology in a text. Ideology includes ideographs, narratives, myths, characterizations and other discursive units.[115] Ideology works within a society to condition it to accept one or another "warrant or excuse" for action or a set of beliefs.[116] It is also an "essential ingredient in the value structure of a particular community."[117] Ideographs, which are ultimately abstract value terms such as the term "family", serve as "powerful warrants for when members of a collective are willing to take some social action because of their beliefs."[118] People who, as agents, affect social action use ideographs; they are thus intimately connected with social constructions. The practical effect of ideographs is that their use may not need the use of coercion.[119] They are different from "narratives" in that narratives are "stories that are used in the formation of ideologies."[120] While ideographs are more likely single words or phrase, the narrative has a plot and is longer and meant to be retold. Individuals can then choose between competing narratives. Characterizations are "subcomponent elements of narratives" that are made of "agents, acts, scenes and purposes" and taken to fairly accurately represent a class. Myths are larger and are usually stories about "origins and destinies, explanations or pedagogic images of nature and humanity."[121]

---

111 Please see, Basil Bernstein, *The structure of pedagogic discourse: Vol. IV Class, Codes and Control:* (New York and London: Routledge, 1990).

112 Please see, Norman Fairclough, *Analysing Discourse: Textual analysis for social research* (London and New York: Routledge, 2003). This is a fine book with numerous examples ranging from analysis of conversations to cigar wrappers.

113 Please see, T.A. von Dijk (ed.), Discourse, Structure and Process (London and Thousand Oaks: SAGE Publications, Ltd., 1997) and Teun A.Van Dijk, "Chapter 18 Critical Discourse Analysis" in Deborah Schiffrin, Deborah Tannen and Heidi E. Hamilton (eds.) *The Handbook of Discourse Analysis,* (Malden, Oxford and Victoria: Blackwell Publishing Ltd., 2003), 352–72.

114 Theo van Leeuwen, *"The representation of social actors"*, in Carmen Rosa Caldas-Coulthard and Malcolm Coulthard (eds.), Texts and Practices: Readings in Critical Discourse Analysis. Also, Theo van Leeuwen and Ruth Wodak, "Legitimizing immigration control: A discourse – historical analysis" in *Discourse Studies*, Vol. 1. No. 1 (1999), 83–118.

115 Marouf Arif Hasian, Jr., *The Rhetoric of Eugenics in Anglo-American Thought* (Athens and London: The University of Georgia Press: 1996), 159.

116 *Ibid.*, 160.

117 *Ibid.*

118 *Ibid.*, 171. Citing to Celeste M. Condit, "Democracy and Civil Rights: The Universalizing Influence of Public Argumentation" in *Communication Monographs*, 54 (1987), 1–18.

119 This idea subverts the ideology of law that it is needed because it is the only thing that prevents anarchy. Law as the basis of social control is highly overrated but, control aside it is probably needed for decisions in tough cases.

120 *Ibid.*, 160.

121 *Ibid.*, 161. Citing to Lewis, William "Telling America's Story: Narrative Form and the Reagan Pre-

These theories are useful in analyzing the ideological rhetoric in both the Indiana legislature and the Norwegian Parliament. For example, a participant of the Parliamentary committee that debated the Norwegian sterilization law of 1934 analogized the mentally ill and developmental delayed to parasites on the body politic of the nation; they were just like weeds to a farmer and, as such, they cost the nation of Norway millions of kroner very year. The ideological rhetoric in the state of Indiana 1907 was essentially no different.

In this case, the word "parasite" is an example of a rhetorical ideograph.[122] In 1930, well before Hasian's use of the ideograph, Michael McGee proposed the idea of an ideograph as a method of understanding the link between rhetoric and ideology.[123] An ideograph can be defined, as follows:

> An ideograph is an ordinary language term found in political discourse. It is a high-order abstraction representing cohesive commitment to a particular but equivocal and ill-defined normative goal. It warrants the use of power, excuses behavior and belief which might otherwise be perceived as eccentric or antisocial, and guides behavior and belief into channels easily recognized by a community as acceptable and laudable.[124]

McGee's definition of an ideograph and Hasian's enhancement of it help us to analyze newspaper and legislative rhetoric. Other examples of ideographs, especially those associated with intersubjective categories are "family", "healthy people", and "motherhood."

Yet another question presents itself with respect to ideographic narratives or discourses that then intertwine with representations and identities. If societal norms and social action are so intertwined and if they exist on several different layers at the same time, how can these processes possibly be studied? It seems impossible and that one is left with either unmanageable qualitative description or the other extreme of only statistical significant variables.

Various researchers have tried different approaches to this problem. Sociologist Georges Gurvitch (1894–1965) has divided the world along a horizontal, "micro-macro" axis, in much the same way as I do in my discussion of the microtome, below. Gurvitch's horizontal axis, from the micro- to macro-level, includes forms of sociality, groups, social class, social structure and global structures. To this he added, on a vertical level, the most objective social phenomena such as ecological factors and organizations and ending at the "deepest" level subjective social phenomena such

sident" in *The Quarterly Journal of Speech*, 73 (1987), 280 -302.

122 Use of the word "parasite" has lately been recycled in Norwegian politics to refer to those absent from work due to sickness. Please see http://www.db.no/forsiden/politikkSamfunn/article 1816139.ece, last accessed 1 April 2010.

123 Michael Calvin McGee, "The 'Ideograph': A Link Between Rhetoric and Ideology" in *The Quarterly Journal of Speech*, 66 (1930), 1–16.

124 *Ibid.*, 15.

as collective ideas/values and, even, the "collective mind."[125] Gurvitch's vertical level includes, from the objective to the subjective extremes, along a vertical continuum, 1. actors, actions, interactions, bureaucratic structures, law and so forth, 2. mixed types , combining in varying degrees objective and subjective elements, examples include the state, family work world, religion, and 3. social construction of reality, norms values and so forth.

Sociologists George Ritzer and Jeffrey Alexander have since revised the Gurvitch model. The Ritzer model eliminates the multiple levels of Gurvitch. George Ritzer "crosscuts" the two continua (macro-micro and subjective-objective), ending up with only four levels of social research.[126] Ritzer locates "law" in the upper left hand quadrant, i.e. objective and macro-leveled and describes this model as symbolizing a "'snapshot' in time" and yet "embedded in an ongoing historical process."[127] While this is an attractive model, I believe that Ritzer makes the same mistake about the law as most non-sociologists of law generally make, namely as "objective."

Gurvitch, Ritzer and Alexander aside, what I have done here is to use the newspapers from each country as indicative of what existed at all three levels, making sure to examine both what were described at the time as "conservative" newspapers and "liberal" newspapers. I believe this time-honored way of trying to capture the micro-, meso- and macro- levels was a manageable way of proceeding since stories about individuals at the micro-level are often alongside macro-level institutional stories, etc.

125 George Ritzer, *Sociological Theory*, 7th Ed, (Boston, etc.: McGraw-Hill, 2008), 502.

126 *Ibid.*

127 I should note, at this point, that when I conceptualized my own research, I also constructed a diagram that I considered would give me a "snapshot" of a historical process at any given point in time. It was based on my use of the microtome, a device that biologists (used to) use to slice an organ, tissue or group of cells embedded in paraffin. I reasoned that if I could make a very, very thin slice of an organ, then surely I could do the same with an historical phenomenon. I have since been convinced that this is not entirely possible which leads me to my reservations of this model.

3 CASE ONE: A Comparison between Indiana (1907) and Norway (1934)

3.1 Structural Changes and Social Movements in Indiana (1907)

The turn of the century brought the United States of America face to face with contradictory social and political tensions. Side by side with the growing power of monopolies were growing demands from progressive political quarters for state and federal government to intervene in the care of the poor, insane and unhealthy as well as to ensure clean food and water, in short, for the beginnings of a "welfare state." Equality and egalitarianism, twin political themes in the United States since colonial times, were now being voiced as demands for equality for women.

The population of the then 46 states was expected to be approximately 46 million in 1900. That year the country also had 8,000 automobiles but only 10 miles of paved road; this would change drastically within a very short time. Life expectancy was 47.3 for white females, 46.3 for white males and 33.0 for all African-Americans. The average weekly wage for workers, many of whom had just immigrated from Eastern Europe and Ireland, was $12.98 for 59 hours of work[128]; child labor laws and protective legislation for women workers were extremely controversial. But "progressive" forces were at work in the United States and during 1906, the first state and federal Food and Drug Act was passed in the United States as a protective measure against pseudo-medical "quackery."[129]

Geographically, Indiana – the "Hoosier state" – is located directly south of one of the Great Lakes, Lake Michigan.[130] At the western intersection of Indiana with Lake Michigan, Gary Indiana now joins the suburbs of Chicago, Illinois to create a major metropolitan area. On 11 December 1816, Indiana was the 19th state admitted to the federal union. The capitol has been Indianapolis since 1825; Indianapolis is almost in the geographical center of this rectangular state, in Marion County. In 1907 it was the largest city in the state, followed by Fort Wayne in the northeast corner, Evansville in

---

128 Statistics taken from Kingwood College Library Internet website at http://kclibrary.nhmccd.edu/decade00.html#events, accessed on 3 December 2007.

129 The first court trial to be held under the new law began in February 1908. U.S. v. Cuforhedake Brane-Fude. The issue was mislabeling about the contents of this headache remedy.

130 Opinions differ as to the derivation of the word "hoosier." A contractor named Samuel Hoosier, who liked to hire Indianans did exist but the word may also come from the phrases "Who's yer?" or "Who's there?" or "hoozer" a local word for "hill." All general geographical and geo-political data in this section is taken from Volume 10, The World Book Encyclopedia (Chicago, London, Sydney, Toronto: World Book, Inc., 1993), 196–219 and from http://www.1911encyclopedia.org/Indiana, accessed 9 March 2007.

the southwest corner, Gary, in the northwest corner, and South Bend on the middle northern border with Michigan.[131]

In 1900, the state had a population of 2,516,462, which rose by approximately 200,000 to 2,700,876 in 1910, making it the 9th most populous state in the Union. In 1900, 34.3% of the state was "urban" where "urban" was defined as cities of 2,500 or more inhabitants. This meant that 65.7 % of the population lived in rural areas, dropping by 7.4 % in just ten years from 73.1% in 1890.[132] By 1920, 50.6% of the state's population would live in urban areas; in just 30 years 25% of those who had been living in rural areas were relocated with a corresponding increase in the urban population of about 20%. The five cities that qualified as urban centers in 1900 were Indianapolis (169,164), Evansville (59,007), Fort Wayne (45,115), Terre Haute (36,673) and South Bend (35,999). There were 14 cities with a population range from more than 10,000 to less than 21,000. The foreign born population of Indiana in 1900 was 142,121 or 5.6% and the African-American population was 57,505 or 2.3%. In 1906, members of religious congregations were counted. The total numbers of those claiming membership was 938,405 or 37.3% of the entire population. The three largest Church memberships were Methodists (233,443), Roman Catholics (174,849) and Disciples of Christ (108,188).[133]

In 1900, 95.1% of the land area of Indiana was farmland with 28.6% of this farmed by tenant farmers rather than farm-owners. From 1850 to 1900, the size of farms steadily decreased from 136.2 acres in 1850 to 105.3 acres in 1880 and 97.4 acres in 1900. Farmers used a three-crop rotation system for their main crops of corn, wheat and hay. In 1907, the Department of Agriculture estimated that Indiana's agricultural acreage was 7th in the nation for corn (4,690,000 acres), 6th for wheat (2,328,000 acres) and 8th for hay (2,328,000). Although furnishing about 200,000 officers and soldiers for the Union effort, Indiana saw little actual fighting within the state proper during the Civil War. After the War, farmers were plagued by debt and low prices for their products. This, combined with periodic ecological infestations and high freight prices, made the economics of ante-bellum Indiana troublesome.

In 1906, the United States Steel Corporation began building the city of Gary and erected its largest steel plant there. This was after the Standard Oil Company built one of the world's largest oil refineries in Whiting on Lake Michigan. In 1900, the state had 7,128 manufacturing establishments characterized as "factories"; their invested

---

131 Today, there are 92 counties in Indiana with 77 legislative districts. In 1907 there were also 92 counties.

132 Justin E. Walsh, *The Centennial History of the Indiana General Assembly (1816–1978)* (Indianapolis: The Select Committee on the Centennial History of the Indiana General Assembly and The Indiana Historical Bureau, 1987), 287.

133 The remaining Church memberships were Baptist (92,705), Presbyterians (58,633), Lutheran (55,768), United Brethren (52,700) and the German Evangelical Synod (21,624).

capital was $219,321,080. Five years later, that invested capital rose to $312,071,234, which was an increase of 42.3%. In the 1880s the predominant form of transportation was the steam-powered railroad but by 1900, electric railroads were the main means of intrastate transportation.[134] In part, the combination of an increase in railroad connections, the discovery of natural gas and the proximity of coalfields made this surge possible. By 1909, Indiana had 7,286 meters[135] of railway with trunk lines that ensured transportation of products to the burgeoning Midwest industrial centers, such as Chicago. The first Indianapolis 500 automobile race took place in 1911 and demonstrates the surge in car production associated with urbanization and industrialization of life in Indiana's major cities.

The air quality in Indianapolis in 1907 was, if we interpret correctly from a series of cartoons in the *Indianapolis News* – filthy. On 25 April a large square filled with 10 smaller cartoons bearing the headline "A Simple Sum in Arithmetic" appeared. The top figure showed a series of smoke-belching smokestack followed by a plus sign (+) followed by the Indianapolis Smoke Inspector sitting, smoking a cigar, in a seat surrounded by cobwebs. The balloon coming from the Inspector reads, "There is no preventive for smoke" and this was followed by an equal sign (=). Below this were nine smaller cartoons showing The Indianapolis Collar (dirty), the Indianapolis Skirt (dirty hem), Gloves After an Hour's Wear (dirty), the Indianapolis Desk (dirty), the Indianapolis Face (swirling dirt around it), the Indianapolis Affliction Called Cinderitis (tongs taking a huge cinder from a man's eye), the Indianapolis Apology ("Indianapolis would be all right if it weren't for the smoke"), the Visitor's Comment ("New York wouldn't stand for this smoke nuisance for a minute!") and an Indianapolis Building at Six Months Old (filthy).[136]

Indiana State was home to a number of social movements at the turn of the century; in many cases these reflected the same movements at a federal level. These included the women's right to vote movement, the prohibition movement, various movements based on interpretations of Social Darwinism and Eugenics, the right to clean food and drink movement, etc. Many of these can be viewed as existing under the umbrella of the "progressive movement." In part, this is due to the fact that the progressive movement in the United States in 1907 included several rhetorical "masterframes" that legitimated different types of social activity by that movement.

While the rhetorical devices that were mentioned above stand as general rhetorical devices, a special vocabulary has been developed for the study of social movements. Rudolf Heberle uses the idea of "constitutive ideas" to mean ideas that are "most essential to a social movement [and] that form the basis of its solidarity and of

134 Walsh, *Centennial History*, 287.

135 4.3 miles.

136 *Indianapolis News*, 23 April 1907, 3.

concerted action for the pursuit of common goals."[137] Much study of the "framing" of issues also exists and has focused on the meso-level, e.g. rhetorical strategies of civil rights movement organizations.[138] However, such meso-level frames must also resonate with overarching cultural frames, called "masterframes." As Owen Wooley notes "masterframes" are ideas that are "simply collective action frames *writ large* that are adopted by multiple social movements."[139]

The idea of historical masterframes has been seen as a "cultural equivalent to cycles of protest" in the resource mobilization school because they explain the "temporal clustering of movements."[140] Wooley admits the idea has been underutilized because of "theoretical inconsistencies", the main problem being that a clustering of protests is necessary to form a masterframe yet a masterframe is necessary to bring about such a clustering. The answer to this has been to emphasis that masterframes are "cultural codes that movements adopt from external sources" and thereby separating out movements from the larger milieu.[141] The definition of ideology incorporates the idea of "constitutive ideas", i.e. "masterframes" which allows two further activities – solidarity and activity justification.

The idea of "framing" needs to be discussed here for a moment and distinguished from ideology. While the making of frames indicates an active process of meaning making, ideology can be either a resource or a constraint within collective action frames ("CAF"). Oberschall reviews the literature on ideology for us and points out that Herbert McClosky's 1964 definition of ideology is that it is "'a system of belief that is elaborate, integrated, more or less coherent, which justifies the exercise of power, explains and judges historical events, identifies political rights and wrong, and furnishes guides for action.'"[142] Philip Converse's definition from the same year uses the term "belief systems" rather than "ideology" to mean a "'configuration of ideas and attitudes in which elements are bound together by some form of constraint or functional interdependence'."[143]

---

137 W.A. Gamson, *Talking Politics* (Cambridge, New York and Melbourne: Cambridge University Press, 1992), 111.

138 Please see, Aldon D.Morris and Carol McChug Mueller (eds.), *Frontiers in Social Movement Theory* (New Haven and London: Yale University Press, 1992), and Sidney Tarrow, *Power in Movement: Social Movements and Contentious Politics* (2nd Ed.) (Cambridge: Cambridge University Press, 2006).

139 Owen Wooley, "Locating Masterframes in History: An analysis of the Religious Masterframe of the Abolition Movement and its Influence on Movement Trajectory" in *Journal of Historical Sociology*, 17 (2004), 493.

140 *Ibid.* The idea of historical master frames has been seen as a "cultural equivalent to cycles of protest" in the resource mobilization school because they explain the "temporal clustering of movements."

141 *Ibid.*, 494.

142 Anthony Oberschall, *Social Conflict and Social Movements* (Englewood Cliffs, New Jersey: Prentice Hall, Inc., 1973), 178.

143 *Ibid.*

Framing, of course, occurs at all social levels – the macro-, meso-, and micro-levels. In 1907, a number of masterframes supported a feeling of moral panic in society-at-large. What was society to do with poor, uneducated women and children? How could society ensure that these people would have correct morals and maintain the decency expected of them? All of the schemas and resources that were associated with this movement are beyond the scope of this work, but suffice it to say that this movement possessed relatively deep structures that appear to emerge from time to time – for example in the 1960s in the United States.

The progressive movement saw itself as basically reformist in nature and worked in all areas of economic, social and political life. In terms of economic history, we know the United States had experienced an economic depression from 1893 until 1897 and that this depression affected the entire nation. The progressive movement is generally thought to have begun during this period and ended in 1917 with the entry of the nation into World War I. To be sure, some of the goals and methods of the progressive movement produced significant results. But the point to be made here is that its goals and methods often intersected with the eugenics movement itself, and for that matter, the emerging feminist movement.

The discursive work of the progressive movement rested on quite different interpretations of themes and ideas than were in circulation before the financial crises of 2009.[144] At the turn of the 19th century in the 20th century, the words "liberty" and "freedom" had a certain "outmoded" and "unscientific" salience among the movement.[145] Civil society had been able, at the turn of the century, to see through cries for "personal freedom" because of the damage done in its name. Society demanded a more paternalistic attitude in government. At exactly the same time, the eugenics movement was gaining momentum and the two merged under some of the same ambiguous ideographs, i.e. "social control" and "individualism." Martin Barr was an early proponent of the sterilization of the "unfit" and his writings demonstrate the alignment process between of the two movements which allows for frame bridging between movements:

> What in the beginning was a philanthropic purpose pure and simple, having as its object the most needy and therefore naturally directed toward paupers and idiots now assumes the proportions of a socialistic reform as a matter of self-preservation, a necessity to preserve the nation from the encroachments of imbecility, of crime, and of all the fateful heredities of a highly nervous age.[146]

---

144 An extreme capitalism along with an extreme individualism was exported to eastern European countries at the demise of Communism. Some of these countries are beginning to rethink the model. The equation "liberty" = "no rules" is also being rethought, especially by governments vis-à-vis the banking sector.

145 Hasian, *The Rhetoric of Eugenics*, 26.

146 *Ibid.*, 27.

What can be noted in this quotation is a frame bridging between the progressive movement and socialism. But this did not ensure that either survived. While the progressive movement went into remission with Great Depression and its contingencies in the United States, the eugenics movement continued through a process of frame transformation aided by the credibility of scientific framers.[147] This frame transformation continued well into the 1970s, its former moving target – "paupers and idiots" – having mutated into "welfare mothers."

Discourses that were embedded in the eugenics movement contributed to the sense of "moral panic" in Indiana in 1907. In order to see how this happened, we return to social movement theory. Sidney Tarrow writes that "collective challenges, based on common purposes and social solidarities, in sustained interaction with elites, opponents and authorities" can be seen in social movements.[148] I will examine a number of these elites, opponents and authorities below. Tarrow quotes Charles Tilly as saying that:

> Authorities and thoughtless historians commonly describe popular contention as disorderly... But the more closely we look at that same contention, the more we discover order. We discover order created by the rooting of collective action in the routines and organization of **everyday social life**, and by its involvement in a continuous process of signaling, negotiation, and struggle with other parties whose interests the collective action touches."[149]

One of the simplest examples of the "rooting of collective action in the routines and organization of everyday social life" is seen when we examine the eugenics-inspired "Better-Baby" contests held around the United States at this time. One such Better Baby Contest was held in Indiana in 1906. These better baby contests, part of the routine of everyday life in Indiana, are an example of what has been later referred to as "positive" eugenics. Such a harmless daily activity in a society under stress, even at the micro-level, cannot be ignored. Through the mere naming of them as "**Better** Baby Contests", and relegating them to the domestic realm, it was possible to overlook their power.[150] But the rhetorical naming of them as "**Better** Baby Contests" signifies gradation of worth and they worked to advance both progressive and eugenics ideas, even if at a micro-level.[151]

---

147 The diagnostic variety of an "injustice frame" is never fully eliminated, however, and still retains a resonance in the United States, resurfacing again in the 1960s.

148 Sidney Tarrow, *Power in Movement*, 4. Note 333.

149 Charles Tilly, *The Contentious French* (Cambridge, Massachusetts: Harvard University Press, 1986), 4. (Emphasis mine.)

150 Please see Martin S. Pernick, M.D., "Taking Better Baby Contests Seriously" (Editorial), in the *American Journal of Public Health*, 92 (2002), 707–708.

151 I am not questioning the fact that some babies have, for example, redder hair than others, only that the standards by which "better" is judged need to be closely examined.

Alexandra Minna Stern has examined the records of the Committee on Mental Defectives, begun in Indiana in 1915 by then Governor Samuel Ralston as well as other records reaching in to the 1950s and found that in 1920, the eugenics movement in Indiana was "thriving."[152] She found that:

> Gauged in terms of the involvement of state leaders and agencies 1910 to 1930 was the zenith of Hoosier eugenics. However, hereditarian ideas started to reverberate across Indiana in the 1880s and justification for sterilization based on inferior genetic worth did not dissipate until the 1950s.[153]

Although 1910 to 1915 may have been the "zenith" for the eugenics movement in Indiana, the movement continued and Stern reports that between 1929 and 1974, about 2,000 inmates of the Indiana state institutions – for the feebleminded, insane, epileptic, and delinquent – were forcibly sterilized.[154] This substantiates the evidence found by Allison Carey who has researched the continued use of forcible sterilization of women into and beyond the 1950s.[155]

Indiana also had a direct connection inside the Cold Spring Harbor laboratory, which, a this time, was the eugenics "hub" in the United States. In early April, the *News* printed an extensive story on the work being conducted at the Carnegie Institute in Washington, D.C. A "Professor Davenport", most likely Charles B. Davenport, was quoted as saying that the work being done there "points a way – a new way – to the improvement of the human race." Davenport's remarks, if they were remarks and not meant as text, were quoted extensively and addressed the discoveries of Mendel. Davenport discussed the work of the Cold Spring Harbor Station, especially the experiments with poultry.[156] And, one of the scientists working with Davenport at Cold Spring Harbor was Prof. W.J. Moenkhaus of Indiana University.[157]

---

152 Alexandra Minna Stern, "We Cannot Make a Silk Purse out of a Sow's Ear": Eugenics in the Hoosier Heartland, 1900–1960" in *Indiana Magazine of History*, 107 (2007), 20.

153 *Ibid.*, p. 27. I disagree with Stern that the "inferior genetic worth" masterframe dissipated in the 1950s and would suggest it merely "morphed", or lay dormant until another opportunity arose for it to again gain momentum. Please see the works of Troy Duster, "Lessons from History: Why Race and Ethnicity Have Played a Major Role in Biomedical Research" in *Journal of Law, Medicine and Ethics*, 34 (2006), 489.

154 *Ibid.*, 20.

155 Allison C. Carey, "Gender and Compulsory Sterilization, 74–105. Note 208.

156 In 1910, Davenport would become the head of the Eugenics Records Office "ERO" at the Cold Spring Harbor facility. The founding of this office came from the widow of railroad magnate, E.H. Harriman. Mrs. E.H. Harriman, whose daughter Mary had spent the summer of 1905 at the Cold Spring Biological Station as an undergraduate from Barnard College, agreed in 1910 to help finance the ERO. The work of the ERO was also assisted by funding from John D. Rockefeller, Jr. Please see Kevles, *Name of Eugenics*, 54–55.

157 "Evolution Tests At Carnegie's Expense. Interesting Experiments at Cold Spring Harbor. Possibility of New Race?" *Indianapolis News*, April 5, 1907, 8.

3.2 Welfare Institutions and Political Governance in Indiana

State government, pursuant to the 1851 Constitution, included a Governor, for a four-year term plus a bi-cameral General Assembly consisting of 50 Senators, at least 25 years of age with 4-year terms and 100 Representatives, at least 21 years of age with 2-year terms. From 1897 through 1909, the state elected three Republican governors in succession: James A Mount (s. 1897–1901), Winfield T. Durbin (s. 1901–1905) and J. Frank Hanley (s. 1905–1908).[158] After Governor Hanley's administration, during which the world's first coercive sterilization law was passed, two Democrats were then elected in succession, Thomas R. Marshall (s. 1909–1912) and Samuel M. Ralston (s. 1913–1916).

In 1907, Indiana, like others states, had a number of prisons. "Far-reaching" reforms had been made in the prison system in 1897 under the Republican governorship of James Atwell Mount (1843–1901), elected in 1896. The General Assembly had passed an indeterminate sentence and parole law, which had been recommended two years earlier by a legislatively sponsored commission.[159] This penal scheme allowed for the release of male prisoners older than 16 years of age who had been convicted of a felony and had served their minimum sentence. Excluded from release were men convicted of murder or treason; later excluded were those convicted of a third felony or of the rape of child less than 12 years of age. Some saw this law as a "coddling" of the criminal element but, after the Indiana Supreme Court upheld its constitutionality in 1898, this outcry lessened.[160] In 1898, the same penal scheme was applied to women prisoners 18 years of age or older. A Parole Board was set up to decide on releases and for the one-year supervision following release. During Governor Hanley's administration, in 1907, the General Assembly also authorized circuit and criminal court judges to suspend the sentences of persons convicted of some crimes, both felonies and misdemeanors, and to be placed under supervision, a form of probation or parole. From April 1, 1897 to September 30, 1915, approximately 9,338 prisoners were paroled with 5,685 or 61% successfully completing the following year of supervision.[161]

In 1900, the state had five penal institutions. These were the Indiana Boys' School, opened in 1868 and known by various names thereafter such as the Plainfield School. Other penal institutions included the Indiana Girls' School (1873), opened in Indianapolis and then moved to Clermont in 1907, a Women's Prison (1873) – the first in the United States. Other penal institutions included a Reformatory using the "Elmira Plan" opened in 1897, a State Prison South (Jeffersonville), opened in 1860,

158 My notation "s" indicates the dates that the person served in office during the indicated dates.
159 Clifton J. Phillips, vol. IV of *Indiana in Transition: The Emergence of an Industrial Commonwealth, 1880–1920* (Indianapolis: Indiana Historical Bureau and Indiana Historical Society, 1968), 490.
160 *Ibid.*
161 *Ibid.*, 491. The failure rate is given as 26.9% and no explanation is given for the remainder.

and a State Prison North (Michigan City) opened the same year.[162] These individual state institutions were under the control of a separate bi-partisan board of four members.

The entire state system of public charity was also under a similar system, the Indiana State Board of State Charities (1889) (ISBC), in which the Governor appointed all four members. Complementing this system at the county level were unsalaried boards of county charities and correction and county boards of children's guardian, appointed by circuit court judges. A total of 1,016 township trustees in Indiana were overseers of the poor and were the authorities who dispensed official relief. Each county provided for the indoor care of the poor in poor asylums and children's homes as well as for prisoners in county jails. A child could be made a ward of state only by Juvenile Court order; these children were then place into other homes by agents of the above Board of State Charities.

In general, institutional composition as well as their placement and goals were in a state of flux in Indiana, as well as elsewhere around the United States. An example of this was the establishment in Indiana in 1915 of the Indiana State Farm in Putnamville for male misdemeanants, 16 years or older, mentioned above. Legislative thinking was that these persons could serve their time in a "healthful, unprisonlike surroundings" rather than in a county jail, where they might be exposed to older, "hardened" criminals.[163] Indeed, within the first year of the opening of Putnamville, 1,174 prisoners from 73 of Indiana's 90 county jails were transferred there.[164] Convict labor was also present in Indiana and was called one of its "thorniest" problems.[165]

Aside from state institutions that dealt with the criminal, poor and juvenile populations, several state and private charitable institutions were also established by 1906. Indeed, they had largely been established between 1820 and 1840, the "age of the asylum", according to historian David J. Rothman.[166] An Institution for the Education of the Deaf was established in 1844 and an Institution for the blind in 1847, both located in Indianapolis and both being two of the first such institutions in the Union. Additionally a State Hospital for the Insane was opened in 1848 (Indianapolis), all three touted as legislative "showcases." At that time the legislature was "reeling from the collapse of the internal improvements system" and needed to show also that its "representative government could operate in an enlightened, progressive way" since, until the 1840s, Indiana had "lagged behind" many other states in its responsibili-

162 Walsh at p. 251 indicates that the Jeffersonville Prison was opened in 1821 but because of its sanitary conditions, medical problems (typhus and scurvy) and overcrowding, the Michigan City prison was legislatively mandated in 1859.

163 *Ibid.*, 491–92.

164 *Ibid.*

165 *Ibid.*, 493.

166 Walsh, *Centennial History*, 105; and David J. Rothman, *The Discovery of the Asylum: Social Order and Disorder in the New Republic* (Boston: Little, Brown & Co., 1971), XIV.

ties to the disenfranchised.[167] In 1844, then Governor James Whitcomb was fortunate to have Democrats in charge of the General Assembly who voted to establish and to finance these institutions.

A "second wave" of institution building – in the sense of both infrastructure and social institutional structures – began after the Civil War. The Northern Indiana Hospital was established in 1888 (Logansport), the Eastern Indiana Hospital in 1890 (Richmond), the Southern Indiana Hospital in 1890 (Evansville) and the South-Eastern Indiana Hospital in 1905 (Madison). A Soldiers' and Sailors' Orphans' Home was opened in 1868 (Knightstown Springs, Rush County)[168], a State Soldiers' Home in 1896 (Lafayette), a School for the Feeble-Minded Youth in 1879 in Knightstown and then moved to Fort Wayne in 1890[169], a village for epileptics in 1907 (New Castle) and one hospital for the treatment of tuberculosis to be built in Rockville, which was authorized in 1907 and the land for which was purchased in 1908. A series of scandals in the late 1880s at the Knightstown Orphans' Hospital (1885), the State Prison South (1885) and the Insane Hospital in Indianapolis (1887) brought more reforms. At the orphanage "pederasty and child abuse" were alleged, at the prison, "sadism and repeated cruelty" were alleged and at the insane asylum, charges of "nepotism, cruelty, extortion and graft" were said to have created a situation where patients "were fed maggoty butter, and pork from a drove of hogs dying of cholera..."[170]

As can be seen from this brief introduction, Indiana was changing in terms of both its population and its economic profile. In response to this and other macro-phenomena, a social panic developed. One of the ways in which this panic was manifested was in the idea of "race suicide." This idea was everyday fare in many newspapers and asserted an ideograph. This ideograph was a discursive unit that warranted that the population of the "right" type of Americans was decreasing. Rich, white, and educated women were often the focus of this argument since it was they who were not having enough children. Poor, immigrant and uneducated women where, on the other hand, having all too many children. As with panic in general, the targets became more and more plentiful so as to accommodate the rhetorical label of "degenerate."

Ideas about the degeneration of the population were also fueled by some social scientists who, with concepts of Darwinian social evolution, sought to influence public policy. Not only were there "scientific" data that could be used by legislatures to support this social Darwinism but, at the very same time, the legal profession of the United States was also undergoing a significant change in the way in which law

167 *Ibid.*, 105 –106.

168 Walsh at p. 251 gives 1867 as the date for establishment of this institution.

169 Walsh at p. 251 gives 1887 as the date for its removal to Fort Wayne.

170 Walsh, *Centennial History*, 252.

was taught, supposedly patterned after the natural sciences.[171] Law was advocated as a science similar to physics, chemistry or biology. And legislation became one of the sites of social and cultural contestation.

In the end, Indiana was perceived by many national groups as accomplishing a great deal of good in terms of social welfare issues. On June 12–13, 1907, Minneapolis Minnesota hosted the 13th annual meeting of the National Conference of Charities. Indianan Dr. Amos Butler would give the President's address to this meeting with Indiana's Senator Beveridge to follow. This was an indication of how important the "Indiana way" was, and how it had gained momentum throughout the United States as well as within the progressive movement itself.[172] But the "Indiana way" didn't end with charitable works that left the beneficiary's body intact. Indiana's own Dr. H. Sharp's development and use of the vasectomy on prisoners, his own form of the "Indiana Plan", soon became a model for compulsory sterilization as well as creating the legislation and institutional practice in a number of states "for many years to come."[173]

3.3 Scientific Discourses and "Race Suicide" in Indiana

While the presence of societal problems and the disarticulation/rearticulation of large-scale societal ways of living are significant, it is only part of the puzzle of law formation at this time. The other half is norm production, its life cycle and denouement or subaltern hibernation. If we refer back to the two norm theories discussed in Chapter 1, we see that at the "micro-objective" level of Rickert's model, he includes "patterns of behavior, action and interaction" while at his "micro-subjective" level, he includes such things as perceptions and beliefs or "the various facets of the social construction of reality."[174] We should remember that, in this theory, these two areas interact continuously with the macro-objective and the macro-subjective.

Before beginning, we should remind ourselves that Darwin's *The Origin of Species*, published in 1859, was a scientific comet that hit the earth, creating deep, perhaps even permanent, fault lines in some societies and throughout societies' numerous activities, most notably religion. Without that realization, what happened in 1907/1934 would make little sense.

---

171 Please see Schweber who has written extensively on Christopher Columbus Langdell and development of the "case-law" technique at Yale.

172 *Indianapolis News*, April 25, 1907, 8.

173 Angela Gugliotta, "Dr. Sharp and His Little Knife: Therapeutic and Punitive Origins of Eugenic Vasectomy - Indiana, 1892–1921" in *Journal of the History of Medicine, 2nd Allied Sciences*, 53, (1998), 386–87.

174 Please see discussion in Chapter 1.

The first example is that of the power of institutional science intersecting with the intersubjective categories of gender and of race/ethnicity. In 1904, Republican and committed prohibitionist James Frank Hanley (1863–1920) (s. 1905–1919) defeated the Democratic candidate, John Worth Kern, to became Governor of Indiana.[175] On the same day as Hanley's inauguration, on the editorial page of the *Indianapolis Star* was a letter entitled "Race Suicide" by J.A. Houser M.D. He concerned himself with the low birth rate, especially between "highly educated and refined women" that produced only 1 or 2 children.[176] Houser minced no words, saying of these women that, "Their education and surroundings have developed them into psychic, esthetic, sensitive, nervous creatures, who are women only in name."[177] Not to be considered unscientific however, he resorted to quantification, claiming that men could also become like this, but "only one-sixth as frequently as women." Two examples of this phenomenon in men were Charles Sumner (1811–1874) and Wendell Phillips (1811–1884) who, while having "brain-power" and leaving wisdom in the world, apparently left no offspring. The article was a hazy blend of racism, genetics and evolutionary thought based on Houser's concern that "[o]ur race is passing away."[178]

A scant two days later was another letter-to-the-editor echoing Dr. Houser's thoughts of the 12th of January with the title "Vitality of the Races in the Light of Science."[179] Signed only with the name "Flandrau", the letter cites three "authorities" on the subject of race vitality. He began by citing the birth rate statistics, which had been published barely a week earlier as a "confirmation of Frederic L. Hoffman's conclusions regarding of the virility of the two races."[180] In Hoffman's book, *Race Traits of the American Negro*, Hoffman advanced a theory that, prior to emancipation, the "negro presented in many respects an excellent physical type, even superior to the white man" but that after emancipation, they migrated to northern and eastern cities and lived "in the midst of the most unsanitary surroundings and under the most immoral influences" with a higher death rate than for whites.[181] Hoffman's use of the statistical method is cited with approval by "Flandrau" who went on to say that the "Aryans can not absorb the negroes by amalgamation."

175 Please see Indiana Government website http://www.in.gov/gov/history/Hanley.html last accessed 11 August 2009.
176 "Race Suicide."*Indianapolis Star*, January 12, 1907, 8.
177 *Ibid.*
178 *Ibid.*
179 "Vitality of the Races in the Light of Science." *Indianapolis Star*, January 14, 1907, 8.
180 *Ibid.*
181 Frederic L. Hoffman, "Race Traits of the American Negro" in the *Publications of the American Economic Association*, Vol. XI, Nos. 1, 2, 3. (New York: Macmillian and Co., 1896), 8. Hoffman's book was reviewed by Gary N. Calkins of Columbia University in the *Political Science Quarterly*, XI (1896), 754–757.

"Flandrau" also cited James Bryce (1871–1922) as showing there is a "decreasing tendency toward the mixing of the two races, not only in America but also in South Africa." Mulatto children "are physically and morally inferior to the pure blacks...lose in vitality what they gain in symmetry and intelligence and they die, early." Flandrau ended his letter by citing Frederick Starr (1858–1933), Professor of Ethnology at the University of Chicago[182], that:

> Recognition of difference between white men and black men is fundamental. The desire and effort to turn bright black boys into inefficient white men should cease. It is imperative that we demand honesty toward the Negro and decency for him but we must expect the race here to die and disappear. If the race is capable of adjustment to American surroundings time will solve the difficulty kindly. If not, time will solve the difficulty, but not severely.[183]

Here, we have the work of three men that informs the basis of "Flandrau's" opinions and it is an easy matter to see how they fit into Tarrow's definition of a national social movement as they present discursive "collective challenges, based on common purposes and social solidarities, in sustained interaction with elites, opponents and authorities."[184]

Frederick L. Hoffman (1865–1946), whom "Flandrau" also cited in this letter, was a professional statistician who worked for the Prudential Insurance Company in Newark, New Jersey.[185] The American Economic Association published Hoffman's first book, mentioned above, in 1896. Hoffman's thesis was that the "Negro was susceptible to many illnesses and constitutionally unfit for survival and was destined to die out."[186] According to Francis Sypher, writing in the conservative Cosmos Club's journal in 2000, Hoffman – a conservative Republican – eventually reversed his opinions, saying that the Negro health was impacted more by environment than by race.[187]

---

182 Frederick Starr was one of the founding members of The American Breeders Association which itself had a long association with the eugenics movement in the United States.
See also, Starr, "The Degeneracy of the American Negro" in *Dial*, XXII (1897), 17–18.

183 Hoffman, "Race Traits", Footnote 311.

184 Tarrow, *Power in Movement*, 4.

185 Please see: http://www.cosmos-club.org/journals/2000/sypher.html, accessed on December 3, 2007. The Cosmos Club calls itself "a private social club" located at 2121 Massachusetts Ave. N.W. in Washington D.C. Although some may dismiss the "grand narrative" style, it is sometimes useful for our historical memory.

186 Francis J. Sypher, "The Rediscovered Prophet: Frederick L. Hoffman (1865–1946)" in George S. Robinson (ed.), *The Cosmos Journal*, 2000. (No volume or number given.) Sypher notes that Hoffman's treatment of the subject of race saying Hoffman's impulses were "primarily humanitarian" and influenced "by the prevailing racism and Darwinism of the time." The sub-lead to this article reads "Prescient and prolific in his writings, F.L. Hoffman is finding new audiences 50 years after his death." In 1897, Kelly Miller wrote a review of Hoffman's work, criticizing Hoffman's methodology and his use of the 1890 census in *Occasional Papers* of the American Negro Academy in Washington D.C.

187 *Ibid.*, citing to the *New York Times*, February 6, 1926.

However, Beatrix Hoffman has a different conception of Frederick Hoffman from that published in today's *The Cosmos Journal.* She places him as a "formidable opponent of the emerging welfare state during the Progressive Era", someone who was a relentless campaigner against "government-run compulsory health insurance between 1915 and 1920."[188] In short, the representations of what science could achieve often promised a scientific solution to the problem of "race suicide."

The micro-subjective discourse level in Indiana also assumed – in the main – that science was benevolent. Members of Indiana's reading public who read the *Indianapolis Star* had access to various and sundry scientific news in it. In an editorial entitled "Scientific Pleasures", the editor of the *Star* mentioned how some scientific work was done in the seclusion of a laboratory, citing work done by Koch or Pasteur; their motive was clearly the "welfare of mankind." But there were also scientists-as-adventurers such as Professor Agassiz and his party of scientists who were about to travel to the West India Islands to take "deep sea soundings" in connection with a recent earthquake in Jamaica.[189] The editor editorializes that:

> Professor Agassiz and his brethren will enjoy the poetry and romance of science on this tour, and though they will doubtless add to the sum of the world's knowledge they will themselves have gained much more than mere dry scientific data. The best rewards of the best work are not covered by a bank account or measured by public applause.[190]

Whether or not the pursuit of science at this time was so unaffected by financial concerns as this editorial assumes is outside the scope of this discussion. What is not, however, is that it was perceived as such by this man at this time and place and that the "welfare of mankind" was represented as the prime motivation in scientific research.

The second example concerns gender. Gender and race/ethnicity were both affected by discursive narratives, which included the "scientific" idea of "race suicide." The micro-level of society does not get much smaller than the toys our children play with. Yet, even at that level, the idea of "race suicide" intersected with discourses of what a "real female" is or should be. It was an advisor to President Teddy Roosevelt (1901–1909), sociologist Edward A. Ross (1866–1951), who actually coined the phrase "race suicide."[191] Around 1901, the teddy bear became a common chil-

---

188 Beatrix Hoffman, "Scientific Racism, Insurance and Opposition to the Welfare State: Ê. Frederick L. Hoffman's Transatlantic Journey" in *Journal of the Gilded Age and Progressive Era*, 2 (2003), 150–190. The James Bryce to whom Flandrau refers may have been a British liberal, The Viscount Bryce of Bechmont, who in 1902, gave a series of lectures entitled "The Relations of the Advanced and Backward Races of Man" and was, in 1888, the author of "The American Commonwealth." Bryce also became the British Ambassador to the United State in 1907.

189 *Indianapolis Morning Star*, February 8, 1907, 8.

190 *Ibid.* (Emphasis mine.)

191 Erich Goode and Nachman Ben-Yehuda, "Moral Panics: Culture, Politics and Social Construction", in *Annual Review of Sociology*, 20 (1994), 149–171.

dren's toy at the same time in both Germany and the United States. As cuddly as the bears seemed, it was not long before the teddy bear took on sinister connotations and came under attack in the name of "race suicide." Mothers had apparently been giving their daughters teddy bears to play with, rather than dolls. In addition to "a clergyman in one of the western states", the editor of "one of the most widely read women's fashion magazines" urged mothers to bring "your babies back to dollies or you will have weaned the grownups of the future from the babies that will never be."[192] The *Boston Globe* took a somewhat less serious view of the matter when its photographer found a group of girls holding "teddy bear dolls" and called upon the "pessimists to lay aside their gloomy forebodings."[193]

Even the Roman Catholic Church became involved in question of the teddy bears. Rev. Michael Esper of St. Joseph's Catholic Church in St. Joseph, Michigan came to the attention of eastern newspapers when he asserted that teddy bears were "destroying all instincts of motherhood" in girls and would "in the future be realized as one of the most powerful factors in race suicide."[194] Esper was reported verbatim as saying:

> There is something natural in the care of a doll by a little girl. It is the first manifestation of the feeling of motherhood . In the development of the motherly instincts is the hope of all nations. It is a monstrous crime to do anything that will tend to destroy these instincts. That is why it is going to be a factor in race suicide problems if the custom is not suppressed.[195]

Esper's sermon earned him space in the *Boston Daily Globe* from which a reporter was sent to interview women at random on the issue. This *Globe* reporter interviewed many women but his search for supporters of Rev. Esper was reported as "fruitless." This "naturalization" of motherhood as a response to "race suicide" is common throughout the period in which sterilization laws were passed and these examples serve to support this idea. They could also be an example of factors at work in the Midwest "countryside", which included Indiana, that were taken less seriously in more "cosmopolitan" seacoast cities, showing an urban-countryside split.[196]

While science was perceived as beneficial, it could also create instability with the knowledge it generated. In the *Star's* "gossip column" for 18 January, the Editor noted that Dr. Hurty "is busy in the lobby...[talking] germs and microbes and cultures to legislators until they almost take to their beds."[197] Hurty gave a speech about tuberculosis in late January to the House of Representatives. Using a cost-benefit rationale, he

192 *Boston Daily Globe*, 27 October 27, 1907, SM 4.
193 *Ibid.* (Emphasis mine.)
194 *The Washington Post*, July 8, 1907, 1.
195 *Ibid.*
196 *Boston Daily Globe*, July 14, 1907, 15.
197 *Indianapolis Star*, January 18, 1907, 6. We will become more acquainted with Dr. Hurty below since it was he who founded the Indiana Department of Public Health, below.

estimated that the disease cost Indiana five million dollars a year, "more than flood, famine, war and earthquake."[198] Hurty's theories on the spread of tuberculosis were reported as dependent on ventilation. He said that:

> fully 30 per cent of you will go home from this Legislature suffering with coughs, colds and diseases of the respiratory organs – all due to the poor ventilation of the chambers in which you are doing your work. Two former legislators, with whom I was well acquainted, died of consumption after returning to their homes, and one of them maintained to the hour of his death that he contracted the disease in this very chamber."[199]

Hurty's speech was described as "frightening" to the Legislature, since many of them knew the two members to whom he referred. While science may have been thought to be beneficial, it could also create both panic as well as a sense of relief with the knowledge it generated.

Science as an institution was involved in many areas of socio-cultural life in Indiana in 1907. As I have mentioned above, this involvement can be studied using the intersubjective categories of race, ethnicity, gender, citizen status, criminal/non-criminal, ability and political philosophy[200]. I will take a moment here to discuss the macro-level discourse of race as viewed through the prism of science.

We would do well to first review the history of race at the turn of the century. In 1906, according to Tuskegee Institute statistics, three whites and sixty-two blacks were subjected to extra-judicial mob violence and lynched in the United States, although

---

198 "Frightens the Legislature. Dr. Hurty shows Them Pictures and Discourses on Death." *Indianapolis Star*, January 30, 1907, 11.

199 *Ibid.* We do know that in 1917, a Senator William T. Green complained that a "poorly vented Senate chamber and the fact that his desk was near a door" brought on his illness. Green died the next day. Again, in 1929, Senator George W. Sims of Terre Haute complained about the physical conditions of the legislature. He said, "The ventilation's bad, the window blinds are a disgrace and the desks so dirty you can't work ten minutes without being a sight!" It was not until after World War II that major improvements in the ventilation system were made in the legislative building.

200 Anarchism came under particular suspicion. On the national level, President William McKinley (1843–1901) had been assassinated five years earlier on 14 September 1901 in Buffalo, New York by an anarchist. More confirmation of the presence of anarchy was found on January 7, 1907, when self-proclaimed anarchists Alexander Berkman and Emma Goldman were reported as both being arrested in New York. Berkman had just been released form a New York prison after serving 14 years for an assault on Henry C. Frick during the Homestead, Pennsylvania riots of 1892. (*Indianapolis News*, January 7, 1907, 11.) In 1907, Goldman has just started to speak to a crowd of around 600 people when the police arrived. She was charged with making an "incendiary speech", a felony, along with Bergman as an accessory.

On the local level, on 3 January 1907, an "alleged maniac" opened fire on Hanley's daughter and her husband as they left the house of Noah Garman, where they had been vacationing. Hanley's daughter, Ethel Hanley Garman, was married to Professor Harry O. Garman who was a member of the faculty at Purdue University in West Lafayette, Indiana. ("Maniac Shoots at Hanley's Daughter." *Indiana Morning Star*, 3 January 3, 1907, 1.)

the NAACP considers these statistics "conservative." Throughout 1907, lynchings were widely reported and, on 5 January 1907, the Indianapolis *Star* wrote of a black man who had "recently returned from the penitentiary" in Alabama. He had entered the room of the daughter of a "prominent banker at Midway", grasped her hand "before she awoke" and was scared away by her screams. After he was caught, "he made a full confession and the lynching followed."[201] Lynching news was regular fare in this Indiana newspaper and the majority of the lynchings were of African Americans. However, five days later another lynching was reported, this time of a white man. In Charles City, Iowa, James Cullen allegedly murdered his wife and 15-year-old stepson. He was then "taken from the Floyd County Jail by a mob and hanged to the Cedar River Bridge, in the heart of the city."[202] The lynch mob even included "four or five ministers and a large number of women..."[203] Other intersubjective groups became involved in the violence as a method of belonging. As Cynthia Skove Nevel writes, joining in the lynching process was also a way in which immigrants, who were seen as neither white nor black, could prove their "whiteness" and establish their credentials as community members.[204]

Discourses concerning race and "race suicide" also articulated with the issue of marriage between races. Race suicide was allegedly practiced through miscegenation. In January 1907, South Carolina Senator Benjamin R. "Pitchfork" Tillman (1847–1918) attracted a large group to the Senate where he spoke on the "race question" in connection with the "Brownsville Affair."[205] The so-called Brownsville Affair took place on 13 August 1906 in Brownsville, Texas where a white bartender was killed and a white police officer was wounded during a disturbance. The disturbance was blamed on an all-Black U.S. Regiment that was camped in town. Roosevelt dishonorably discharged 167 members of the unit without trial or an opportunity to be heard.[206] Theodore Roosevelt himself acted as prosecutor, aided by Joseph Foracker (1846–1917), in the indictment of the 167 enlisted men of the all-Black U.S. Twenty-fifth Regiment. On the 16th, the *News* editorialized about Tillman and the response to his speech. Beginning by noting that Tillman "never makes a speech that is not a direct incitement to race antagonism", we read that Tillman was also "trimmed" by Wisconsin Senator

201 "Mob Hangs Negro. Attempted to Assault Girl. Body is Swung to Tree at Midway, Ala. And Then Riddled With Bullets."*Indianapolis Star*, January 5, 1907, 2.

202 "White Man Lynched. Sheriff Gives Way to Mob. Slayer of Wife and Stepson at Charles City, Ia. Is Hanged to Bridge."*Indianapolis Star*, January 10, 1907, 1.

203 *Ibid.*

204 Cynthia Skove Nevel, *Lynching to Belong: Claiming Whiteness Through Racial Violence* (College Station: Texas A & M University Press, 2007).

205 "Races Will Not Mix, says Tillman. South Carolina Man Fires some Hot Ones at Roosevelt and Foraker. Senate Galleries Packed. Headliner in the Upper House Takes Brownsville Affair as Basis for His Widely Advertise Speech."*Indianapolis News*, January 12, 1907, 1. Lead Story, flush right column.

206 President Richard Nixon later pardoned all of the soldiers.

John C. Spooner (1843–1919) who quoted Tillman as saying of the African-American population that "We shot 'em; we killed 'em, and we'll do it again."[207]

The category of "ethnicity" is porous and often intermixes with status as a citizen. On January 7th, the lead story in the *Star* concerned itself with the subject of Immigration. Frank Sargent, then the Commissioner of General Immigration in Washington, D.C., had submitted a report to Congress at the end of the fiscal year – June 30, 1906 – giving the number of immigrants who had entered the country; the total number was 1,166,353.[208] According to Sargent's information and his interpretation of the situation, they were mostly from central and Eastern Europe, "inhabited by races nearly akin to our own" and they came to the United States because of the "general unrest existing among laboring classes." The headline used for this story is very interesting from a rhetorical standpoint. We can tease out more meaning from the headline if we change the noun "immigration" it to the noun, "immigrants." The immigrants are deemed a "flood", insinuating a threat or a danger of some sort. This only served to accentuate the word "army" in the phrase "army of 1,166,353." Not only is there some sort of threat or disaster implied but there is an additional threat because the quality of these persons is "below standard." We are not told what the standard of comparison is but one could easily think that it was the "bench-mark male" mentioned in Chapter 2. We are merely treated to conclusions in this article, i.e. "That the physical and mental qualities of the aliens we are now receiving is much below that of those who had come in former years, [Sargent] says, is evident."[209]

A third example of scientific discourse at the micro-level in Indiana is as it was applied to youthful criminals. Science became part of the newly established Juvenile Court system in Indiana, the first of its kind the United States, aside perhaps from Pennsylvania. In the Marion County Courthouse, two rooms previously used by the City Park Department were being vacated to allow the establishment of the first ever – in the United States proper – Juvenile Court. One of the rooms was clearly a waiting room and the other was a "court room" in which "no effort has been spared to make them as cheerful and as little like courtrooms as possible." The desk for the presiding Judge – Judge Stubbs – was not on a raised platform and there was no bar separating the Court from participants. The "prevailing theory" of the Court was to give children the sense that they had "a friend in the court" making it easier for them to converse freely and truthfully so that a "heart-to-heart" could be had with the Judge.

A room was also appropriated by the Juvenile Court for use as a medical clinic, operated by Miss Eleanor Ketcham. She had been using jury rooms on the third

---

207 "Spooner and Tillman."*Indianapolis News*, January 16, 1907, 6.

208 "Immigration Flood Breaks All Records. Army of 1,166,353 Aliens Admitted to the United States in One Year. Quality is Below standard. Steamships Blamed for Foreign Labor Importation." *Indianapolis Star*, January 10, 1907, 1. I define "lead" story as the story in the upper left hand side of the newspaper.

209 *Indianapolis Star*, January 10, 1907, 1.

floor of the Courthouse for her clinic and had to vacate the room, taking her "paraphernalia" into the hall when a jury began to deliberate. These medical examinations were "one of the most important branches of this work" since physical defects accounted for the "troubles" that initially brought the children before the Court "in a great many instances." Correction of these physical troubles "worked wonders on the children."[210] In January, when Judge Harold Salamon, a representative of the government of Sweden, visited the one room Court, he had observed "What a wee bit of a courtroom. How do you manage to transact so much business here?... And the odor; it is not well ventilated." Judge Stubbs was reported as "barely kn[owing] how to answer [the question] intelligibly" at that time.[211]

This clinic was a vital part of the entire process and examinations were carried out as a matter of routine. Head of the physical exams was Dr. Walter Hoskins who determined, among other things, if a child was "mentally defective."[212] When a boy entered the clinic the physical director of the Boys Club, Walter Gudel, first interviewed him about his family. The boy then went to Dr. Walter F. Kelly, who was in charge of physical measurements including weight, lung capacity (expanded and collapsed) and head measurements in different directions. Deafness and eyesight are also tested for. The child then went to Dr. Hoskins who was then a lecturer on children at the Indiana Medical College, affiliated with Purdue. The doctor dilated the boy's nostrils and the throat was inspected. Heart and respiration were also checked. If the doctor had any doubts about the health of the child, further examinations were done at other clinics. The examinations for girls were the same as for the boys.

Science was applied those defined as "criminals" even if juveniles. To underestimate the depth of this discourse would be to misunderstand how science was intertwined with daily social life. The legal concept of "insanity" in the sensationalized Thaw case is an example of this. The defendant, Henry Kendal Thaw, had allegedly murdered architect Stanford White who was the cosmopolitan descendant of two American presidents. As part of Thaw's defense, a new concept of legal insanity was used, as modified by modern psychiatry. As part of the *Star's* "gag photographs", a photograph of Stanford White in profile was printed and the skull area divided into five cells, each with an enclosed cartoon. The five compartments were entitled "incapability", "intemperance", "destructiveness", "lack of will power" and "high living." In addition, "science" was again represented in the picture, albeit half-humorously;

---

210 "New Room is Ready for Juvenile Court. Quarters and Room is Vacated by City Park Department to Be Occupied this Week. First Trials On Wednesday. Equipment Does Away with 'Bar of Justice'."*Indianapolis Star*, 10 February 10, 1907, 10.

211 "Juvenile Courts Ask for Larger Quarters. Petition to Be Presented to county Commissioners. Impressions of Visitors." *Indianapolis News*, January 1, 1907, 7.

212 "Systems of Clinic in Juvenile Court. Boys and Girls Examined by Specialist Each Tuesday and Thursday. Observations are Indexed. New Department Find Many Friends and Advocates." *Indianapolis Star*, August 12, 1906, 7.

a solid bold black line was drawn around White's actual skull curvature showing a "normal head" while a dotted bold black line was drawn on the picture to show "the abnormal head."[213] At this time a basic epistemic uncertainty of what was "sane" and "insane" existed within the legal system and this was true not only in the United States but would be true for Norway in 1934. Who and how the new jurisprudence would affect also depended on one's intersubjective group or groups.

3.4 Linking "Race Suicide", Suffrage and Womanhood in Indiana

One of the main discourses in Indiana newspapers in 1907 – if not *the* main one – was that the role of women in a society. In hindsight, we can see that Indiana was inexorably moving in some other direction than that of the pre-modern Pescosolido structure. The two main questions that emerged regarded the role of women in "race suicide" and their right to vote. As to the former, the discursive narrative questioned whether or not women were responsible for "race suicide", and if so, which women?

On the second day of January, 1907 the editor of the *Indianapolis Star*, in his daily column that was normally full of various comments and witticisms, was reduced to saying that the "safe and sane New Year was lost in the shuffle."[214] On the front page that day, another story announced that there was "No Race Suicide in New York" given the fact that the "birth record [for 1906] is the greatest ever reported."[215] However, the state of Indiana was not to be outdone by New York and on 3 January, one day later, the birth statistics for Indianapolis were printed.[216] In 1906 there had been a total of 2,118 males and 2,022 females born in the city. Of this number, the figures were then divided into "white" and "colored."

Despite the numerous discourses about race suicide, these articles concluded there was no such phenomenon. In retrospect, we can see that the total population of the Untied States had risen by 1.6 million, from 85,436,556 to 87,000,271, between 1906 and 1907.[217] Progressive public health reforms also made an impact. As Michael Haines writes:

> Reliable cause of death information for larger areas of the nation become available in 1900 with the initiation of the Death Registration Area (Preston, Keyfitz, and Schoen, 1972). Calculated from these data, the crude death rate declined by 38% between 1900 and 1940, while mortality

213 *Indianapolis Morning Star*, February 15, 1907, 2.

214 *Indianapolis Star*, January 2, 1907, 8.

215 *Ibid.*, 1.

216 *Indianapolis Star*, January 3, 1907, 4.

217 *Vital Statistics of the United States, 2000* (Hyattsville, Maryland: U.S. Department of Health and Human Services, Centers for Disease Control and Prevention National Center for Health Statistics, 2002), Table 4-1.

> from all infectious and parasitic diseases was reduced by 88%. Infectious and parasitic diseases declined from 43% of all deaths to only 15%.[218]

This would tend to imply that people were either ignoring their own experience of life or that the *Indianapolis Star*, among others, was involved in a type of masterframed "propaganda."

But the rhetoric of "race suicide" was very powerful and it persisted in the media. It often pitted various institutionalized religions against one another.[219] For example, in 1908, the *Post* reported on an article by the Rev. G.L. Cady, a Congregationalist Minister from Dorchester, Massachusetts. Cady wrote an article declaring that the "Puritan stock is committing race suicide."[220] Calling the demise of his Puritan church "involuntary harikari", he noted with chagrin that the "Catholic church has a great army of children coming up each year, native born, and the priest knows just what he can count upon for confirmation each year, and he knows that next year there will be just as large'a [sic] crop to harvest."[221] Cady's use of military and agricultural metaphors is interesting and demonstrates just how powerful the idea of a threatened population can be.

Despite evidence to the contrary, the burden of "race suicide" was directly linked with the role of women in society. One of the most obvious signs of the structural shifts that were taking place was that women demanded universal suffrage. No longer were women confined within the concentric circles of a pre-modern Pescosolido model. Women were active in society at all levels from municipal to international and wanted recognition of that fact. For example, on the final day of January, the House Committee on Rights and Privileges, of which Committee on Medicine Health and Vital Statistics (CMHVS)[222] members Keller, Porter and Izard were members, heard testimony from Mrs. Helen Gouger the "foremost exponent of women's rights in Indiana" and the head of the State Suffrage Association.[223] This was not to be her only engage-

---

218 Michael Haines, "The Urban Mortality Transition in the United States, 1800–1940" in *Annales de démographe historique*, 1 (2001), 33–64.

219 This type of rhetoric can be found in more recent times in the speech given by then President S. Milosevic in 1989 where he made the large Albanian families in Kosovo into a threat against Serbia. Kosovar women were having more children than Serbian women. The phenomenon can also be seen from a religious nationalistic perspective in the rhetoric of the Croatian League of Families, in Israeli-Palestine debates and even in Norway within, most notably, the Fremskrittsparti (Frp).

220 *The Washington Post*, November 14, 1908, 6.

221 *Ibid.*

222 The CMHVS (Committee on Medicine Health and Vital Statistics) was the Indiana state legislature committee that reported the sterilization bill back to the legislature as a whole for passage. The CMHVS and its members are examined below.

223 "Women Should Vote. So Said Mrs. Helen Gougar. Noted Suffragist Addressed House Committee, but Found No One Who Would Volunteer to Champion Bills She Wants Presented." *Indianapolis Star*, January 31, 1907, 4.

ment at the General Assembly during the 1907 session. Approximately one week later, she addressed the entire Assembly in the House chamber and asked that a bill be passed giving women the right to vote in municipal elections.[224] She was invited by Rep. J.M. Cravens who himself had introduced a similar resolution the day before in the House, which after being endorsed by Rep. Edwards, had been unanimously accepted. Her 30-minute speech had some effect since, after it was over, Rep. Beyer said he would "introduce her bill and fight for it."[225]

Gouger's talk on women's rights is classic but what is of more interest is that we see in it an example of the articulation of "the attachment or 'joining' of distinct discourses to one another."[226] In her speech, Gouger said:

> Let us vote, and I promise you that you will not have to build an additional cell in your State Prison in the next 100 years. We will reduce the population your insane asylums and we will empty your poor-houses. Besides all this, we will reduce your taxes.[227]

Exactly how this was to be accomplished is not mentioned but, again, this was only a 30-minute speech. In effect, Gouger implicitly set the blame for the chaos in the state's welfare systems at the feet of male legislators, in a "we can do it better" type of logic. We also read that men in the legislature who supported women were called "Miss Nancy's", clearly an attempt to impugn their masculinity.[228] Gouger herself paid keen attention to the bills that were passed in the Assembly. When, for example, a bill was passed that added a period of disenfranchisement for criminals equal to the years the person was in prison, she wrote a letter to the Editor of the *News* in which she noted that it was an "insult to every woman citizen to be made the peer of criminals" and that women would rather "be in the legal companionship of law-abiding decent men."[229]

Two suffrage bills had been set in motion, but on 16 February they had both been set as an order of business for the very last day of the session, March 11. This was done, so the *Star* reported, while the House was in a "jocular" mood but several members said the action would be reversed in time for the bills to be voted on by the Senate.[230] One week after her first speech, two hundred women attended Gougar's

---

224 This was a tactical move. If women could vote in municipal elections it would be more difficult to argue against their participation in state and national elections.

225 "Woman Addresses General Assembly. Mrs. Helen M. Gougar Pleads for Enfranchisement of he Sex in Local Elections. They Would Overcome Evils. Speaker Said Need for Prisons Would Be Decreased." *Indianapolis Star*, February 7, 1907, 4.

226 William Sewell, Jr., *The Logics of History: Social Theory and Social Transformation* (Chicago: University of Chicago Press, 2005), 339.

227 *Indianapolis Star*, February 7, 1907, 4.

228 *Ibid.*

229 *Indianapolis News*, February 15, 1907, 4.

230 *Indianapolis Morning Star*, February 15, 1907, 2 and 23. One day earlier, in Chicago, the executive

second talk and House members "gallantly" gave their seats to the women but most of them "remained away" for the talk. Miss Lydia Blaich, who was supervising Principal of Public School No. 15, opened the meeting by saying she had belief in the "greatness of the American man." Gougar then spoke, denouncing, "the high [liquor] license bill" pending in the House saying if women composed the House, the bill would be defeated. Giving women power would ensure that "the welfare of each shall be the concern of all."

At the end of her speech, Gougar asked all those who supported suffrage to stand. Every woman stood but only two or three men joined them. At that point, Rep. Horace Hanna "strayed into the chamber" and sat down. As several women "glanced sharply at him" he held his ground "bravely and refused to stand."[231] Gougar then asked all those opposed to suffrage to stand. Only one man, Rep. Baker of Elkhart County, had the "temerity" to stand. "Two hundred pairs of eyes looked at him pityingly at him, but he did not flinch." Gougar then asked how many were "on the fence" and no one stood. She retorted that these "are barbed wire times and no one wants to sit on the fence."[232]

Meanwhile, reactions to the demand for universal suffrage in Europe produced actual results. On 18 April 1907, the editor of the *Star* noted in his columns that the

> little duchy of Finland, where, for the first time in the history of modern civilization, the political franchise and the right to legislate and other political office have been fully conferred on women, and where, moreover, these new rights have been energetically and promptly exercised the new Finnish diet will have among its members nineteen women elected by universal suffrage.[233]

Readers were aware, to a greater or lesser degree, that the universal suffrage issue would not disappear. Shifting structural changes were making the "highly nervous times" only more unstable, and the soon to be passed sterilization law would serve to underscore this.[234]

---

committee of the National American Women's Suffrage Association inaugurated a plan to enact a constitutional amendment that would give women the right to vote in national elections, without reference to any property qualifications. This committee was told that "liquor interests" in the Southwest were fighting against suffrage. Miss Laura Gregg of Guthrie, Oklahoma reported, "great corporations of the Southwest are energetically engaged in a propaganda against women suffrage." Relegated to the home – private – sphere, women experienced the real life effects of alcoholism and tended to support anti-drink laws thereby incurring the anger of these "great corporations."

231 *Indianapolis Star*, February 19, 1907, 4.

232 *Ibid.*

233 *Ibid.*, 8.

234 Two articles in adjacent columns on the front page of the *Star* give us an idea as to how the construct of real or natural "womanhood" was in 1907 was in the process of destabilization. In the middle of the page was a story about Mrs. Ruth Prindle, who gave refuge to a young Negro and protected him in her house for an hour against 200 angry glass workers who were "surging against the doors, hurl-

3.5 Structural Changes and Moral Panic in Norway (1934)

In 1907, the similarities between Indiana and Norway were minimal. By 1934, social structures had begun to change, however. Norway had an extremely homogeneous society, with the exception of ethnic Sâmi people and the Romani. Indiana, and the United States in general, was more populated and the movement from rural living to urban living was just beginning, as was industrialization. In 1907, economics in the United States were beginning to indicate just how large an industrial giant it would become in the 20th century. On the other hand, Norway was a relatively poor country with millions of its citizens having departed for a better life, such as in Minnesota, a scant 30 years earlier. All of this changed in the intervening 30 years as, in the words of Jonathon Moses, Norway played economic "catch-up" to the point where, in 1934, it began to face the same challenges that Indiana had faced in 1907.[235] Norway also played a form of "social" catch-up in addition to its economic "catch-up."

When the Norwegian Parliament, the Storting, passed its sterilization law in 1934 reform movements were also at work.[236] The same conditions that had provided momentum for the Progressive Movement in the United States had developed in Norway. Along with Indiana in 1907, "business monopolies, dishonest politics, crowded city slums, and poor working conditions in factories and mines" in Norway, 1934 provided the impetus and rhetoric for an equivalent [progressive] movement there.[237]

In 1934, Norway was a very young country. In 1884, after having established a parliamentarian form of government, Norway faced a fight for independence from Sweden. A consular issue was the trigger that, in 1905, forced the issue of complete independence for Norway. After a parliamentary vote for independence in Norway, Swedes demanded an additional referendum and, with a vote of 368,392 to 184,

---

ing stones and curses." While women had done this before and some would, no doubt, continue to do this, this is a story of the threat of volatile lawlessness in society coupled with the fact that some women could be fearless. In the very next adjacent column, as if the typesetter were (unconsciously?) debating the role of women, was a story about one Miss Geraldine Smith who entered a bar in a "white silk dress, décolleté" with three "bewhiskered Turks in gaudy robes and a bevy of pretty girls, blondes and brunettes, who lined up at the bar and called for highballs, gin fizzes and the whole menu as they put dainty heels against the brass rod, smoked cigarettes, kicked high in the air and behaved most unseemly for ladies." Clearly this was some sort of public theater, but nonetheless mocked societal restrictions on women. Please see "Woman Saves Negro From an Angry Mob. Locks Him in Her Home While Enraged Factory Men Demand Vengeance. Black Stabs White Worker. Police Get Pursued Man and Arrest Mob Leaders." *Indianapolis Star*, March 30, 1907, 1.

235 Jonathon Moses, *Norwegian Catch-Up: Development and Globalization before World War II* (Aldershot and Burlington: Ashgate, 2005).

236 David P. Thelen, Entry for "Progressive Movement" in *The World Book Encyclopedia*, 15 (Chicago, London, Sydney, Toronto: World Book, Inc., 1993), 817.

237 *Ibid.*

Norway became independent in August 1905. The Norwegian Storting chose Prince Carl of Denmark to become King Håkon VII (1905–1957) of Norway.

Between about 1865 and 1914, the gross domestic product "more than doubled" growing from "28,431 to 79,519 million kroner (in constant 2000 prices)."[238] In 1910, 42% of the population was involved in agriculture and forestry. This was reduced by about 5% ten years later, in 1920. The advances made in industrialization were cut short, however by World War I. The war largely reduced the number of ships in Norway's merchant marine, a war wherein Norway remained neutral. In 1920, Norway joined the League of Nations, the precursor to today's United Nations.[239]

Norway again declared itself a non-belligerent as World War II began in Europe. However, this did not prevent Norway putting the 1,000 ships in its merchant fleet at the disposal of the Allies. But, as most had feared, Nazis forces invaded Norway on the morning of 9 April 1940 in *Operation Weserübung*. Norwegians resisted the invasion but Speaker of the Norwegian Storting (Parliament), Carl Hambro, understood the gravity of the situation. The royal family, the Cabinet and 150 members of the Storting left Oslo on a train that same day. Eventually the King and Cabinet left the northern city of Tromsø on 7 June 1940 on a British vessel to set up a government in exile near Windsor Castle.[240]

Six years earlier, in 1934, the political atmosphere in Oslo was like a heated furnace. Approximately one year previous, on 17 May 1933, the Nasjonal Samling (NS) had been founded. Eventually, under the leadership of Vidkun Quisling this party entered into an accommodation with the Nazis, whose forces marched into Norway in June 1940. But six years earlier, in April 1934, members of many political groups in addition to the NS shared the same streets of Oslo – Communists sympathetic to Stalin's government, Workers Party members focused on the unemployment issue, right-wing Høire[241] conservatives planning to take power in the coming October elections, and members of the Farmer's Party as well as followers of Quisling.

However, in the political cauldron of spring, 1934, some groups refused to share the streets of Oslo with each other, especially at night. On the night of 26 April, NS and Communist youth fought in the slushy streets of Oslo. The NS youth had gathered outside the Gjestetova Café in Tullinløkken and, when the Communist group arrived, fistfights broke out. As the fight progressed, rocks were thrown, and the plate-glass window of the restaurant was broken. Five persons were taken by the police, held for an hour and then released. The police announced that they were eager to investigate

238 Jonathon Moses, *Norwegian Catch-Up*, 48. Note 235.

239 Carl Joachim Hambro (1885–1940), was also the President of the League of Nations, when on 3 September 1939, World War II began.

240 On 7 June 1945, King Håkon VII and the royal family returned to Norway aboard a British vessel to face the damage done by occupation Nazis forces.

241 Today the spelling of Høire is usually Høyre.

the whole affair and were sure that after a thorough investigation, at least a couple of people would be arrested.[242]

The year 1934 – the year in which the Norwegian parliament, the Storting, passed into law its sterilization law (1 June 1934 Lov om adgang til sterilisasjon[243]) – was only the 29th year of the formal existence of the modern nation state of Norway. After the population had reached and exceeded the two million mark in 1890–1891, the population of Norway grew to approximately 2,266,200 million people in 1934.[244] True, Norway's economy had improved since the nation's formal birth in 1905, but in 1934, both conservative and liberal media alike universally characterized the economic and political spheres in Norway as in a state of "crisis." Obviously, this crisis had not simply appeared on New Year's Day, 1934.

Hans Fredrik Dahl's description of the interwar period in Norway is extremely helpful as an overview of how this crisis had developed. Further, his descriptions are useful to us since he discusses the social life of Norwegians at this time. For example, in the 1920s and 1930s, he notes that even if cities had grown in size,

> close to 1/5 of all urban dwellers lived in apartments that statistically could be called "over-populated" in that between 2 and 3 persons lived in one room (where the kitchen then counted as a "room"). Most citizens lived in closely populated apartments (1-2 persons per room.) In 1930, in Oslo's eastern section, 1/3 of the entire population lived in conditions where as many as 5 persons lived in one room and a kitchen; in the western section of Oslo the number of people who lived life this was close to 5–10% of the population.[245]

Unemployed men were either in over-crowded homes or walking the streets of Oslo, Bergen and Trondheim, Norway's three largest cities. Work was scarce. In the 1920s, life in Norway can be viewed through the lens of a lack of money but in the 1930s it can be seen as overshadowed by a lack of work, according to Dahl. Strikes and lockouts were common and led to an average annual loss of a million lost workdays, ten times higher than the average after the war, from 1945–1965.[246] Farming as a way of

242 *Aftenposten* (P.M. Edition), April 27, 1934, 2. I use this example of the type of news one finds in the two major daily newspapers of Oslo in 1934, and even today. Norway is still a very small country, around 4.5 million, and this is reflected in the newspaper media. For example, the murder of a single taxi driver in Oslo is headline news while in Indiana today this would probably not be mentioned on the front page of the major newspaper. A positive feature of this smallness is that details are given which one does not find in US print media.

243 Unlike American legal citations, laws in Norway are cited to by the date of their enactment.

244 Chief source: *Statistical Yearbook of Norway,* Norwegian Central Bureau of Statistics, at http://www.ssb.no/histstat/aarbook/1890.pdf, accessed 5 July 5, 2009. Also see, http://www.uu.nl/Bibliotheek/pages/default.aspx, accessed on 5 July 5, 2009.

245 Hans Fredrik Dahl, *Norge Mellom Krigene/Det Norske Samfunnet Krise og Konflict 1918–1940* (Oslo: Pax Forlag A/S, 1971), 10.

246 *Ibid.*, 15.

life was beginning, ever so slightly, to decline. Marriages that in 1920 had produced 4 children per household were, in the interwar period, producing only 3 children per household.[247]

The economic situation of the working class was difficult during this time in Norway. Unemployment was a serious problem and one year before the United States established the CCC (Civilian Conservation Corps) in 1933, Norway had already established conservation camps for the unemployed. After the relative high employment, especially in the ship building industries during WWI, in the 1920s stock prices fell to half their value and timber sales were also cut in half.[248] Unemployment among trade union workers rose from an already high 17.6 per cent in 1921 to 25.5 percent in 1927.[249] The annual report of the Norwegian Electricians and Power Station Association (Norsk Elektriker og Kraftstasjonforbund) said in 1932 that:

> The economic crisis is increasingly ill-natured and the unemployment is reaching...new all-time heights. **This is a picture of a society at war with itself** and those who govern are not capable, or willing, to point out how to get out of this mess.... We have an administration which by all means seeks to load the burden upon the shoulders of the working man...[A government] that conceives new laws to imprison and silence the labor movement and the working class, but is unwilling to carry out measures to deal with the ever increasing numbers of unemployed.[250]

Various social safety nets did exist and were at work. These included, for example, the Poor Relief System[251] and the Norwegian Vagrant Mission[252] but with one of every four workingmen out of work, the concept of "enough" was not open to much interpretive quibbling among that class of citizens.

Nonetheless, in some quarters there were monetary resources. For example, the Høire ("H") Party had announced on 9 February 1934 that the Høires Hus, a new, seven story, modern building would be built under the Chairmanship of attorney Henrik Bergh (1879–1952).[253] With 822 m^2 of available space, there would be more than enough space for the Høire Party to operate, and have its offices and clubs. The ground breaking would be sometime in October, 1934.[254]

---

247 *Ibid.*, 11.

248 Magnus Jensen, *Fra 1905 til våre dager*, (Oslo: Universitetsforlaget, 1968), 44–45.

249 *Ibid.*, 47.

250 Found at http://www.heis.no/search details.aspx?docid=85, accessed December 9, 2007. (Emphasis mine.)

251 "Fattigvesent." *Aftenposten* (A.M. Edition), January 15, 1934, 2.

252 "Den norske omstreifermisjon." *Aftenposten* (A.M. Edition), April 20, 1934, 3. We will encounter this group when we discuss the various "identities" being formed in society, i.e. "others" such as "taterne" ("the travelers"), homosexuals and other ethnic groups such as the nomadic Samí.

253 Bergh would later defend V. Quisling in his trial for treason.

254 *Aftenposten* (A.M. Edition), February 9, 1934, 2.

Politically, the most important parties in Norway in 1934 were the Conservative Party (Høyre[255]), the Liberal Party[256] ("V") and the Labour Party (Arbeiderpartiet, "Ap"). Other parties were present and these included the Farmers Party (Bondepartiet, "BP")[257] founded in 1920, the Society Party (Samfundspartiet, "Sp") founded in the early 1930s, Quisling's Nationalist Party (Nasjonal Samling, "NS")[258] founded in 1933 as well as the secular liberals (Frisindede Venstre, "FV") founded in 1932.[259] At this time, it was virtually impossible to form a stable coalition government, according to Dahl, and during this period, Norway had 10 governments within 15 years with the "average [survival period] of the governments similar to France's Third Republic."[260]

Understandably, Norwegian society was experiencing a sense of angst about the future of the country just as Indianans had experienced their own "moral panic" in 1907 over "race suicide." Whether or not the word "angst" is a technical sociological term that is usually applied to certain historical times, the above data supports the use of the word in relation to this period. As Dahl notes, the processes of industrialization and urbanization plus inadequate and ineffective political institutions, when combined with more forms of communication[261] made for turbulent times. But the most salient point that Dahl makes is that:

> Social life was not calm. And that which was most of all not calm or in equilibrium was the citizens' understanding of each other: as friends, enemies, members of the same class, fellow countryman, patriots, traitors. These things were changed, *essentially*. The history of the interwar period is about them.[262]

Dahl's evaluation can be interpreted to mean that the sociology of the interwar period in Norge was also about these social relationships, relationships between individuals, groups and institutions and the amount of trust each had in the other.

Nevertheless, despite the political unrest, in strictly political terms, Norway was not as left-leaning as other Scandinavian countries. Between 1914 and 1930 the combined percentage of votes from Social Democrats, Communists and the Arbeiderpar-

---

255 This is today's spelling of the older word "Høire."

256 To American ears, this party might sound left of center. In Norway, it is consider right of center.

257 The Bondepartiet changed names in 1959 to become today's Center Party "CP", (Senterpartiet, "SP").

258 The NS was founded on May 13, 1933 by Vidkun Quisling and existed until 1945.

259 The FV party only existed until 1936. "Frisindede Venstre" literally means "open-minded liberals" and was an offshoot of the Liberal Party, itself a "low church" party. While it might be more comfortable for English-speakers to have the acronyms changed from Norwegian to English, i.e. have the Arbeiderpartiet "Ap" changed to "LP" for "Labour Party", I have kept the party acronyms from the Norwegian words.

260 Dahl, *Norge Mellom Krig*, 16.

261 *Ibid.*, 20. The radio had been introduced into Norwegian society in 1925.

262 *Ibid.*

tiet membership in Denmark rose from 29.4% to 42.2%, a 12.7% increase; in the same era, the percentage in Norway increased only half as much, from 26.3% to 33.1%, or, a 6.8% increase. Sweden experienced a 12.4% increase, Finland and Germany a 5.5% increase while England saw a 31.2% increase and France a 13.6% increase.[263] Although the Arbeiderpartiet had broken with the Soviet Komintern in November 1923, the fear of revolution "was not dead" in large part due to the labor problems in pre-WWII Norway.[264]

3.6 Societal Changes and Moral Panic in Norway

> We will rise up to fight against this hedonism. We will rise up under the banner of St. Olav the Holy and proclaim that life is holy and inviolate.
>
> Fru Eller Anker [265]

Various types of "progressive" movements existed in Norway in 1934. The movement composition and institutional design were somewhat different but many of the goals were the same; these goals included addressing the situation of the poor in Norway including the homeless, mothers and children, the sick and the unemployed. By necessity, it also addressed the issue of criminality. As in Indiana, the progressive movement in Norway was, in the main, in the hands of middle and upper class women. Within that group, approaches differed by political conviction, with right-wing women more likely to join the Norges Husmorforbundet (NH) and idolizing its leader, Fru Marie Michelet.[266] Left-wing, especially Arbeiderpartiet, women were more likely to stand in solidarity with Katti Anker Møller (1865–1945), Norway's equivalent of America's birth control pioneer Margaret Sanger.[267]

As we saw above, the eugenics movement was also alive and well in Norway. The ideas of the eugenics movement were in print in daily newspapers just as in Indiana. Those who espoused eugenics as a science were also particularly busy and we will encounter Dr. Alf Mjøen and his Committee on Race Hygiene below. This group took

263 *Ibid.*, 60.

264 *Ibid.*, 65.

265 *Aftenposten*, (a.m. Edition), October 30, 1934, 3.

266 In 1915, Michelet was the first leader of the HVF's precursor, Hjemmenes Vels Landsforbund. She steered both organizations stressing a combination of conservative religious values and "rational", scientific housekeeping. In the 1970s, among other issues, the organization addressed the fact that women who worked in the home should receive "points" for their work there within the national social security systems.

267 Please see, Ida Blom, *Barnebegrensing – synd eller sunn fornuft* (Bergen: Universitetsforlaget, 1980), which is the seminal academic work on birth control in Norway.

as one of its main goals, to influence national legislation and, when we look at the Storting debate, we will see how influential this lobby group actually was.

One narrative that both the eugenics and progressive movements rested on concepts of what it meant to be "healthy" and "unhealthy." One narrative of this idea can be seen in the 1934 Oslo visit of an exhibit that had originated in Dresden. Not only is it part of a narrative but it is also an example of the Jasanoff idea of a "representation", in this case a representation about the power of science as it related to motherhood and nationhood. "Healthy Mothers – Healthy People" was the subject of an article on 10 March in Oslo's afternoon edition of the *Aftenposten*.[268] The article announced an exhibition that would be held in Oslo the coming autumn.[269] It also mentioned that in 1927, another exhibit entitled "Humanity" had been held in Oslo and that no fewer than 83,000 persons had visited the exhibit.[270] The autumn event was to be sponsored by the Hjemmes velstandsforbund[271] (HVF) and the Norges Røde Kors landsforening (NRLF).[272] The newspaper author was clearly excited about the event, mentioning that where it had been shown in other countries, it had a great number of attendees. The exhibit was described as easily intelligible and had many illustrations. It would give clear information on what would be needed in order to have a healthy child, family and lineage.[273] While not named specifically as a "race hygiene" exhibition, it would not be unreasonable to assume that this material was included in the exhibit.

On 20 October 1934, the Crown Prince, HRH Harold, did indeed open "Healthy Mothers – Healthy People" at Håndverkeren.[274] Along with the Prince was the President of the Red Cross, Lieutenant Meinich, Fru Michelet, the venerable President of the Norwegian Housewives Association (NHF), Prof. Arne Sunde, who we will meet when he debates with S.R. Bonde in a committee meeting pertaining to the sterilization law, Superintendent Bergliot Larsson[275], the medical director for Oslo schools Dr. Lauritz Stoltenberg, and the Mayor of the Asker municipality, Lector Schiøtz.

---

268 "Sunde mødre – sundt folk." *Aftenposten*, (p. m. Edition), March 10, 1934, 7. Much ink has been spilled over the translation of the word "folk" in German. There is no exact translation from the German to English especially at this time in history. It would be speculative to render a connotative meaning for the Norwegian "folk" during this time. However, the word is used as a leit motif of health and motherhood.

269 A picture of the German poster for this exhibit can be seen in Sara J. Bloomfield, *Deadly Medicine: Creating the Master Race* (Washington, D.C.: United States Holocaust Memorial Museum, 2004), 24.

270 *Aftenposten* (p.m. Edition), March 10, 1934, 7.

271 For the Good of the Home Association.

272 "Hjemmenes Velstlandsforbund og Norges Røde Kors landsforening." *Aftenposten* (p.m. Edition), March 10, 1934, 7.

273 *Ibid.*

274 *Aftenposten* (p.m. Edition), September 20, 1934, 7. The title "Sunde mødre – sunt folk" could also be translated "Healthy mothers – healthy citizens."

275 *Ibid.* "forstanderinne"

Both the 1927 "Humanity" exhibit and the 1934 "Healthy Mothers – Healthy People" exhibit were on loan and delivered from the Hygiene Museum in Dresden, which Meinich said, "has now for 25 years been at the center of hygiene information in Europe and which our land also stands in gratitude for."[276] We could suppose that if Fru Michelet broke away from her duties at the NHMF national convention, also happening at the same time, numerous other members of the influential NHMF also visited the exhibition. One week after the hygiene exhibit "Healthy Mothers – Healthy People", Norway's national Medical Director N. Heitmann bemoaned the fact that only 10,000 Norwegians had visited the exhibit and that this was "entirely too few." He urged everyone who could, to attend the exhibit since there was much to learn there for all ages and sexes.[277]

The work of the liberal wing of the progressive movements in Norway focused on providing birth control and securing less restrictive abortion laws, something that was not openly considered in the media in Indiana in 1907. The birth control debate itself had been highlighted in Norwegian society at least since Katti Anker Møller had made the concern of "worn out mothers" her life's work in the first decade of the twentieth century.[278] In 1934, however, the issue that was used to address the role of women was the abortion issue.

The birth control question was less significant in 1934 in Norway than in 1907 in Indiana, although advocates in Norway knew that the idea of women's access to it would continue to be attacked.[279] America's birth control pioneer, Margaret Sanger,

---

276 *Ibid.* One of the exhibits, a glass, see-through replica of the human body is pictured in Bloomfield, *Deadly Medicine*, above footnote 1199.

277 *Aftenposten* (a.m. Edition), 27 September 27, 1934, 6.

278 Øyvind Giæver, "Abortion and Eugenics: The role of eugenic arguments in Norwegian abortion debates and legislation, 1920–1978" in *Scandinavian Journal of History*, 30 (2005), 23. Giæver makes the important point that there is a "danger of over-emphasizing" the role of eugenics in light of other "progressive causes" so as to make this period "more palatable" to the modern reader, (p. 39). Other forces were at work and earlier, on 18 October 18, 1913, Katti Anker Møller's letter entitled "Om fosterfordrivelse" (Concerning fetal abortion) was printed in the *Social-Demokraten*, the daily newspaper read by members of the labor movement. Nine years earlier, she had attended a Women's Conference in Berlin in 1904 where she had met other feminist and progressive personalities such as Susan B. Anthony, Maria Stritt, Lady Aberdeen, Mrs. Sewell, and Perkins and Gilman. (Tove Mohr, *Katti Anker Møller – en banebryter* (Oslo: Tiden Norsk Forlag, 1968), 69.

279 That there should be communication between birth control advocates on one continent and researchers on another continent in 1934 should not be a surprise. David Mitchell and Sharon Snyder have coined the term the "eugenic Atlantic" in relation to the building of an international science of eugenics. (David Mitchell and Sharon Snyder, "The Eugenic Atlantic: race, disability and the making of an international Eugenic Science, 1800–1945" in *Disability and Society*, 18 (2003), 843–64.)
They build on work done by Paul Gilroy on how social constructions cross between and among cultures. Gilroy focused on "trans-Atlantic traffic" concerning race and disability, coining the phrase "Black Atlantic" to mean "beliefs about racial and biological inferiority [that] dovetailed for a period of approximately 150 years in the cultural space...the 'Black Atlantic'." (*Ibid.*, 844. Please also see,

had written to Dr. Otto Mohr (1886–1967) asking him to differentiate the Norwegian Mødre hygienekontorer[280] from the German Sexüalbera Frugestellen. Mohr responded to Sanger on 2 August 1928.[281] He wrote that, in contrast to the Norwegian Mothers' Hygiene Offices, the German offices gave advice on "practically any sex questions." The Norwegian offices were primarily concerned with mothers; the head nurse gave answers to questions and contraceptives were sold within the office itself. Mohr compared these offices with the "English ones" in that the Norwegian offices sold literature on birth control, the care of children "and also practical outfit[s] for babies and for pregnant mothers." Although only two such offices existed at the time, as was the case almost exactly one year earlier, Mohr expected "more are going to be [erected] soon." He credited his mother-in-law, Katti Anker Møller "the pioneer in woman's rights in our country" for the existence of these offices but says that they had "now been taken over and run by the Labour Party."[282]

Sanger asked Mohr for suggestions for Norwegians who might be interested in attending a birth control conference to be held in Paris in March the following year. Mohr answered guardedly, saying "I really must be very careful, that it is not easy to find any[one]" willing to attend. He suggested that Katti Anker Møller was the best person to talk to because she "knows from her long experience what to do and how to do it when it comes to the question of practical work." Mohr saw Møller as commit-

---

P. Gilroy, *The Black Atlantic: modernity and double consciousness* (Cambridge: Harvard University Press, 1995). Mitchell and Snyder argue that whatever "socially stigmatized identity" one considers, the "eugenic Atlantic" categorized that particular "insufficiency" as if it were "biologically coded." (*Ibid.*, 860.) And, whatever the nation-states' individual responses were to this, similar cross-national characteristics are found, especially legal cross-national characteristics. (Michael Mintrom, "Policy Entrepreneurs and the Diffusion of Innovation" in *American Journal of Political Science*, 41 (1997), 742.) Research has also been done on how individuals impact this policy formation, so-called "policy entrepreneurs." They play an "important role in articulating innovative ideas onto government agendas." (Michael Mintrom, "Policy Entrepreneurs and the Diffusion of Innovation" in *American Journal of Political Science*, 41 (1997), 742.) In terms of social movement theory, Doug McAdam has written about how both "diffusion" and "brokerage" in social movement theory as "different pathways to scale-shift." (Michael Mintrom, "Policy Entrepreneurs and the Diffusion of Innovation" in *American Journal of Political Science*, 41 (1997), 742.) In typical "cycles of protest" research, diffusion tends to be seen as creating "waves" or "cycles" and "the spread of actions" takes precedence over the work of individual agents. (Pamela E. Oliver and Daniel J. Myers, "Networks, Diffusion, and Cycles of Collective Action" in Mario Diani and Doug McAdam, *Social Movements and Networks: Relational Approaches to Collective Action* (Oxford: Oxford University Press, 2003), 175.) Here, I focus momentarily on one individual, Maragret Sanger, and the "network effect" she participated in with Norwegian feminists. I discuss the network she had with Norwegian actors and what function it had – if any – since the birth control movement in Norway was already fairly well established by 1934.

280 Mothers' Hygiene Offices/Clinics.

281 Library of Congress (Washington, D.C., U.S.A.), *Papers of Margaret Sanger*, Accession Number 16,700, Vol. 29, Reel 19. Letter dated Oslo, 8/2 1928 (Mohr to Sanger).

282 *Ibid.*, End, 1.

ted to "the empowerment of women, in the broadest sense" and himself "of the same opinion."[283] But with regard to Norway, Mohr said:

> judging from your letter, you want members of [a] more scientific type, 'straight thinking economists and sociologists'. I am afraid we don't have any such at present who are really interested in practical birth control. The movement itself has during the latter years had a rapid progress in our country, but few prominent people have so far openly joined.[284]

This is as good a description as one can find from that time period that describes the birth control social movement and its activities and strength in the country.

In 1934, relaxation of the abortion law also very seriously debated in the Norwegian public sphere, even more than the sterilization law was debated; sterilization after an abortion was also seen as a possible solution for poorer women. Indeed, the debate over sterilization of women within the context of a simultaneous abortion was advocated the very same month as the sterilization law itself was passed. Supervising doctors Dr. Kristen Andersen, Schilling and Dr. Widerøe, Dr. med. Skaja, Judge C.E.C. Bonnevie, Judge Hartmann and attornies J.M. Lund and Nørregård had submitted a proposed bill to the Odelsting[285], a separate unit within the Storting, making sterilization an option at the same time as an abortion in cases where "it is reasonable to assume that the woman should not have more children."[286] Here we have an

---

283 Library of Congress (Washington, D.C., U.S.A.), *Papers of Margaret Sanger*, Accession Number 16,700, Vol. 29, Reel 19. Letter dated Oslo, 8/2 1928. End, 2.

284 Otto Mohr was a scientist above all else. On May 4th, the *Aftenposten* reported on a speech that he gave to the Norwegian Scientific Academy on the subject of what he called "intersexuality." Mohr's lecture that day was on the potentiality of the fertilized egg, which he said, "...contained the possibility to develop into both the male and female sex." (*Aftenposten* (p.m. Edition), May 4, 1934, 3.) He acknowledged that the situation was complex and that further research was needed on sex differentiation of the fetus including the control mechanisms, extra-cellular material, and the impact of male and female sex hormones. (*Ibid.*) American Leslie Clarence Dunn (b. 1893), visited Mohr at the University of Oslo in 1927 and he called Mohr an "outstanding investigator" in letters Dunn wrote back to his colleague, Walter Landauer, at the Storrs Agricultural Experimental Station in Connecticut. (Jenny Marie, The Situation in Genetics: Dunn's 1927 Russian Tour, *Mendel Newsletter*, n.s. 12 February 2004. Online at http://www.amphilsoc.org/library/mendel/2003.htm#cain, last accessed December 10, 2007. Dunn was one of the founding members of the Genetics Society of America and its President in 1932. He replaced T.H. Morgan at Columbia after Morgan went to the California Institute of Technology in 1929.

285 After the Storting (Parliament) is gathered in October, and after the President of the Storting is elected, it divides itself into two units, the Odelsting and the Lagting. Please see, http://www.tinget.no/no/Hovedmeny/Hvordan-jobber-stortinget/Storing-Odelsting-Lagting, accessed September 18, 2009.

286 Doktor Ingeborg Aas, *Kvinnen og barnet i fohold til spørsemalet Abortus provacatus* (Oslo: H. Aschehoug & Co. (W. Nygaard), 1935), 45. "Each of these proposals entertains the through that sterilization should be carried out at the same time as an abortion where it is reasonable to assume that the women should not have any more children." Bonnevie was a described as a sorenskriver, which

example of "practical" reason, which is attempting to inject itself into the legislative process to become a legal norm.

That same month in the Storting, a Penal Code Committee was appointed and in August it also decided to take up the abortion issue.[287] The Committee was composed of permanent members, as well as lawyers assisted by three medical doctors, Ingeborg Aas, Tove Mohr (daughter of Katti Anker Møller) and Kristjar Skajaa. Due to "immediate" criticism of the committee as being "radically" biased, the Ministry added 3 more members in October, Stian Erichsen, lawyer Aage Schou and surgeon Dr. Kristen Andersen, who had already brought up the idea of sterilization in connection with abortion procedures in 1929.[288]

This issue was also discussed at the annual meeting of Norwegian jurists in Oslo two months later, just as it had been the subject of Kristen Andersen's introductory remarks to the Norwegian Surgical Association's Annual Meeting seven years earlier, on 2 November 1929.[289] Discussion about abortion was not new to Norway but what should be noted here is how both the legal and medical institutions had become intimately involved in the debate and that the legitimacy of various narratives hung in the balance.

While the Jasanoff "identity" field in relation to women was in epistemic chaos in Norway in the first few months of 1934, other body-law "identities" were forming. The two health problems that were consistently associated with regard to which bodies should be sterilized were mental illness and mental retardation – now called developmental disability. Another body-law identity was also in the process of being formed and this was within certain criminal populations. True, all these groups had women as part of their populations, although the criminal population was primarily male. But it is within the context of the unavailability of birth control to women who "should" not be having so many children, i.e. poor and uneducated women, rural women, and/or religious women who would not use it, where the two discourses intersect. Discussions about changing the medical indications that would make it easier to have an abortion were numerous and it is here that the role of "women as mothers" attaches to the practice of sterilization. What is fascinating is that at this time, the same groups that defended the role of "women as mothers" also defended the sterilization of these "others", i.e. the bodies of the mentally ill and retarded. Just under the surface, this issue was actually framed to mean that "women as mothers" was "the **right kind**

---

is defined as a "judge (chief magistrate of a rural district; office of such a magistrate." Einar Haugen, *Norwegian English Dictionary* (Oslo Madison: Universitetsforlag University of Wisconsin Press), 386.

287 Øyvind Giæver, "Abortion and Eugenics", 26. Note 483.

288 *Ibid.*

289 Kristen Andersen, "Abortus provacatus med særlig henblikk på dens mulige sociale og humanitære indikasjoner" in *Tiddsskrift for Den norske Lægeforening*, 49 (1929), 1191 -1215. On page 1212, Andersen introduces the idea of sterilization in connection with abortion.

of woman as mother" – not coincidentally, the same narrative found in Indiana a quarter of century earlier.

That abortion and birth control were openly debated in Norway in the late 1920s and into the 1930s did not mean that all members of the progressive movement were united over these two issues. Late in October 1934, a protest turned violent at the Calmeyergatens Mission House where a large meeting heard attacks on the "Journal for Sexual Information" and parish vicar Joh. E/M. Wisløff proclaimed a popular uprising against changes to the Criminal Law § 245 concerning abortion. This was a "call to arms" motivational meeting, a "core task" for framing the anti-abortion movement. The lecture hall was "filled from floor to roof" and after singing two verses of "A mighty fortress is our God", Wisløff denounced abortion as a "stake in the heart" and urged a popular uprising "from Lindesnes to the North Cape."[290] Next to speak was res. Kap. Jon Mannsaaker on the theme "Life is holy"; the most important issue was the "religious and moral side of the case." Advokat Ingolf Sundfør (b. 1893)[291] spoke next on the ramifications of legalized abortion on women and "humble folk", saying that they would both be damaged by the changes.[292] Abortion would make women uncivilized and it would be a triumph for the lazy. Sundfør went on to say that the proposed changes would characterize a fetus as some sort of "womanly abscess." Carrying the theme of "abscess" forward, Sundfør said, "One could also say that the legal proposals can also be understood as types of human abscesses which, in the best case, have undergone the surgeon's knife." At the end of his speech, Sundfør proclaimed, "Down with cold-blooded murder! Life must live!"

Priests and attorneys were not the only speakers at the rally; women spoke as well. Dr. Kristine Munch spoke about the status of fathers under the proposal and

---

290 *Aftenposten*, (a.m. Edition), October 30, 1934, 3. The protest was held on 29 October and reported on 30 October 1934.

291 Sundfør was an attorney admitted to practice before the Supreme Court of Norway. He took it upon himself in the *Aftenposten* on 25 August 1934 to remind Oslo readers that there was a split of opinion between those living in the cities and those in the countryside. Sundfør argues that any changes in the law must be based on a moral experience and sets out 13 points. Sundfør's fourth point of the 13 is that marriage is the most important institution and in the fifth point asks if the father is a participant in the abortion issue and whether or not he has rights. His points become points aimed at the medical profession and he asks if a doctor really has the right to evaluate the social and humanitarian indications for abortion. His twelfth point maintains that it is incomprehensible that we recognize the principle that a beginning life can be sacrificed in order that the parents' life can be economically bettered, or more comfortable or so that they can have more possessions. To permit the murder of a beginning life in order to protect a later life that is ruined is like brushing away a mosquito while swallowing a camel. His thirteenth point is interesting from a semiotic standpont. He complains that the phrase "*abortus provocatus*" has such a civil ring to it. "It sounds like the name of a flower or a medicine." The law originally called abortion "fetus murder" and the new (latin) phrase hides the "mission" or "deed" itself.

292 *Ibid.*

Bispinne[293] Petra Fleischer spoke about "sexual literature, which has engulfed the entire country" and the influence it was having on children. Lars Eskelund, a public high school superintendent, spoke on the fall of Greece and Rome because of "depraved" lifestyles. Ella Anker berated Tove Mohr as well as Dr. Kristen Andersen for their "backsliding."[294] Anker told the assembled, "We will rise up to fight against this hedonism. We will rise up under the banner of St. Olav the Holy to proclaim life is holy and inviolate."[295] Parish vicar Ludvig Schübeier ended saying that these were the facts that should speak – and convince – the Norwegian people.[296]

Mohr and Andersen were not the only women to be berated as the next day Aimée Sommerfelt wrote for the *Aftenpostens kronikk297*, the purpose of which was to review a new book by dr. Olga Knopf entitled the "The Art of Being a Woman."[298] In this book review, Sommerfelt attacked dr. Lisa Jacobsen and Margrethe Bonnevie saying:

> we still have a recent memory of two direct opposites [of this type of woman] like dr. Lisa Jacobsen and fru Margrethe Bonnevie whose contributions we see in the daily press.[299]

Jacobsen and Bonnevie were important role models from an elite class of women who acted as "entrepreneurs" in the on going "role of women" debate. Mohr and Andersen were at least perceived by some Norwegian women – including Sommerfelt and Anker – as antithetical to the "real" role and identity of a woman in Norwegian society.

New Year's Day 1934 fell on a Monday and was a non-working day in the towns and villages of Norway. The first working day of the year, however, Norwegian newspapers began by noting that, in Germany, New Years Day 1934 was more than a traditional holiday. On that day, the "Law for the Prevention of Genetically Diseased Offspring" became operational, after becoming law on 14 July of the preceding year. Helping to draft this legislation were such luminaries of the German scientific world as Alfred Ploetz (1860–1940) and Ernst Rüdin (1874–1952), Director of the prestigious Kaiser Wilhelm Institute for Genealogy in Munich.

This was not news to Norwegian doctors. As a general rule, Norwegian doctors traveled to and from Germany at this time and would have known of this legal development. In fact, many doctors who were around 60 years of age in 1934 had visited Germany; as part of the traditional European "study tour", Norwegian physicians

---

293 The title "Bispinne" refers to the wife of a Bishop.

294 *Aftenposten*, (a.m. Edition), October 30, 1934, 3.

295 *Ibid.*

296 *Ibid.*

297 A *"kronikk"* refers to what we now call an "op-ed" piece in a newspaper.

298 *Aftenposten*, (a.m. Edition), October 31, 1934, 2.

299 Olga Knopf, *The Art of Being a Woman* (New York: Blue Ribbon, 1932). Knopf, a psychologist, is probably now known only for her quote "The art of being a woman can never consist of being a bad imitation of a man."

born between 1870 and 1875 preferred to go to Germany. The contrast between this group and those doctors born between 1840 and 1845, who also included France and Austria as a destination, is "striking."[300] Taking information from biographies in Norwegian Doctors (Norges Læger) and the *Norsk Magazin for Lægevidenskaben (Norwegian Magazine for Medical Science)*, Bent Olav Olsen has calculated the most frequently visited of six countries, with one or more destinations in the study tour, as a percentage of all journeys and found that for those doctors born between 1870 and 1875, the percentage visiting Germany was 42.2%. The percentage for Denmark was 25.2%, for Sweden 11.7%, for France and Austria each 9.1% and for Great Britain 6.7%.[301] Although this need not necessarily mean anything sinister, it does speak to the idea that these doctors, who spoke and read German, would also likely have known of this development before it was reported in the press.

Paul Weindling writes that one of the architects of Germany's new law, Alfred Ploetz, "venerated Scandinavia as the motherland of the German [people]."[302] Weindling also notes that the Scandinavians responded to racial hygiene "with great enthusiasm" which served to "reinforce...the ideal of Nordic racial purity" within Germany itself. Another architect of the new German law, Ernst Rüdin, visited Norway and Sweden in March of 1907 where he "recruited seven members" for the International Society for Racial Hygiene (ISRH); Rüdin returned again two years later on 7 May 1909 and recruited another twenty-seven members.[303]

The ISRH had institutional and individual contacts within Norway from its beginnings. It was a "constituent member" of the International Eugenics Committee (IEC) and, for example, on 3 August 1913 Ploetz met with George Darwin and Norwegian Dr. Alf Mjøen in Paris for a meeting of that group.[304] There, Ploetz worked to have an IEC Congress held in Germany but the idea was defeated. Weindling writes that, after that idea was defeated, Ploetz' diary shows that he "consoled himself by drinking brotherhood with Mjøen who was an ardent Nordicist."[305] We have met Dr. A. Mjøen above and will review more fully his contributions to the eugenics movement in Norway below. Suffice it to say, that the eugenics movement had a history dating back to the late 1800s and had been in existence with several highly visible professional supporters.

---

300 Bent Olav Olsen, "Recreation or Professional Necessity? – The Study Tours of Nineteenth Century Norwegian Doctors" in Øivind Larsen and Bent Olav Olsen (eds.) *The Shaping of a Profession: Physicians in Norway, Past and Present* (Canton, Massachusetts: Science History Publications, 1996), 264.
301 Ibid.
302 Paul Weindling, *Health, Race and German Politics Between National Unification and Nazism, 1870 - 1945* (Cambridge: Cambridge University Press, 1989), 150.
303 *Ibid.*
304 *Ibid.*, 153.
305 *Ibid.*, 151. Weindling continues throughout his book to call Mjøen a "racist."

Eugenic ideas had taken root within various institutions, including welfare and religious institutions. Because there were no "waves" of "impure" foreign immigrant bodies to Norway, the only recourse was to examine the indigenous ethnic bodies. Religious structures as well as governmental structures intersected to consider these groups as objects for sterilization. While not a significant percentage of the population, Norway did have a variety of national minority groups, including "Samís, kvener, skogfinner, Jews, gypsies and not least of all, Romani-folk (taterne or 'the travelers')"[306] Dr. Ingeborg Aas and Supervising Doctor Johan Scharffenberg had already raised the question of sterilization of tatarne as early as 1929. Scharffenberg, who played many roles during the interwar period, was from 1919 until 1940 the doctor at a state penitentiary and from 1922 was a member of the council and Head Doctor at the Oslo Hospital's mental hospital.[307]

The treatment of indigenous ethnic populations in Norway was handled largely through religious meso-level organizations. One group, originally known as the Norwegian Mission among the Homeless (Norsk misjon blant hjemløs, NMBH), was just such a "Christian philanthropic group."[308] This group made several assumptions; its members believed that a "mobile lifestyle" was more or less criminal and the life style itself was at least partially biologically pre-determined. In addition, the background of the group had "an association with the politics of criminality and the racial hygiene viewpoint."[309]

Under the influence of the NMBH and Ingvald B. Carlsen who was the Mission's General Secretary from 1918 to 1935, the Church and Education Department issued a letter in 1904 that described taterne as both those that lived as tarterne - even if they were not ethnically so and originally were residents of a particular place - and members of the ethnic group itself.[310] In contrast to this, Dr. Johann Scharffenberg maintained that the larger group of taterne was a distinct and different ethnic group.[311] Many things could be said about how the Mission dealt with the taterne

306 Bjørn Hvinden, "Fra fordømmelse til respect og vergihet: Det norske samfunnets skiftende forhold til romanifolket" in Bjørn Hvinden (ed.), *Romanifolket og det norske samfunnet: Følgene av hundre års politikk for en nasjonal minoritet* (Bergen: Fagbokforlaget, A.S., 2000), 11.

307 *Ibid.*, 67. He held the second position there until 1941 when, under Nazi occupation, he was removed. In 1934, at about the same time as the sterilization legislation, he was prosecuted under Norwegian law for his unflattering publically printed comments about Hitler. He was eventually acquitted of the charge on legal "technicality", in a lovely sleight of (legal) hand.

308 Per Haave, "NS-Regimets 'taterpolitikk' – en minoritetspolitikk i utakt?" in Per Ole Johansen (ed.), *På Siden av Rettsoppgjøret* (Oslo: Unipub Forlag, 2006), 180. "...plannen oppsto ikke i et tomrom."

309 *Ibid.*

310 *Ibid.*, 182.

311 *Ibid.*, 183. Debates about ethnicity and the taterne continued well into the 20th century. What can be said is that some Norwegian politicians had a problematic relationship with ethnically different groups, although after the turbulence of the 1970s, much of this has changed for the better.

but, for our purposes here, the most interesting is that this group believed itself to be doing philanthropic work for the less fortunate. In 1931, Carlson said in an informal radio lecture that:

> it's the Christian feeling of responsibility (or the human feeling of solidarity) that tells us that these are human beings and we must try to give them a sense of human worth.[312]

But despite this, the goal of the Mission was always twofold, to gain social control over the tarterne as well as providing assistance to them. This rhetoric of care, in this case – Christian care – is not unlike the rhetoric of the progressive movement in Indiana. In many cases, the progressive movement allied itself with American churches, mostly protestant, and had identical concerns as this Mission in Norway, albeit to different minority groups.

Per Haave points out that Norway's treatment of the taterne "did not happen in an empty room."[313] Aside from the factors already mentioned, it should also be remembered that during the nation-building phase of Norway's history – which was not more than a few years in the past – the concept of a "real Norwegian" was clearly connected to

> more or less romantic pictures of the life style of farmers and their culture such that this became constituted and cultivated through folk museums, folk music, folk stories, farmer stories, the traditional clothing of farmers, books on farm construction and the like.[314]

In all of these areas, there was simply little social space – and thus very little opportunity – for the ethnic minorities mentioned above to fit into society – should they have even wanted to do so – especially if they were labeled as "transient" or "vagrant."[315]

---

312 Ibid., 185.

313 Per Haave, "NS-Regimets 'taterpolitikk', 180. Note 510.

314 *Ibid.*, 21.

315 The issue of vagrants includes issues of control and surveillance. On May 22, 1928, a directive was sent from the Justice Department in Oslo to all government officials and civil servants in Norway where there was a directory of births and a Church register of births, to register all the vagrants and also settled families and send this information back to both the Mission and the Central Bureau of Statistics. The goal was to create an inclusive and central registration of all vagrants. As Per Haave notes, "this never saw the light of day" but that was not for lack of effort, especially by Oslo's Police Chief Kristian Welhaven and Chief of Education Reidar Sveen. (Per Haave, "NS-Regimets 'taterpolitikk', 195. Note 510. "Sentralen så aldi dagens lys.") Welhaven was the Vice President and Norwegian Representative on the International Kriminalpolizeilichen Kommission (IKPK), the forerunner to Interpol, which was founded in Vienna in 1923. (*Ibid.*) This group was interested in many things but wanted a coordinated effort to stop the migration of gypsies. In 1934 there were about 5,000 to 6,000 gypsies in Norway and about 1,500 to 1,700 tarterne; Welhaven told the IKPK that the Mission would do the registration of vagrants.

3.7 Norwegian Welfare Institutions and Political Governance

> Why have science and the personal way of handling human troubles been introduced as a "health" program? Why have all the new methods of dealing with criminal vagrants, al- coholics, prostitutes, and other asocial persons so closely linked with the idea that these people are sick?
>
> Vilhelm Aubert[316]

While Norway already had a number of institutions such as insane asylums, prisons, and hospitals, there was a need for more such facilities in 1934. All public institutions seemed to be overcrowded and underfunded, just as in Indiana in 1907. Private medical institutions were established in Norway and some doctors had a following from the middle and upper classes at these places. But even private welfare institutions were in need of funds and fund-raising became the raison d'être of some middle and upper class women's groups.

In addition, one cannot help but note the narrative emphasis on "sanity" and "insanity" in the media especially with regard to crime. Newspapers focused relentlessly on the insane and crime, not unlike Indiana in 1907.[317] The two issues articulated and became what I imprecisely call the "dangerous people on the loose and possibly roaming near the reader."[318] But, in point of fact, this phenomenon was part of the Pescosolido Model, discussed above. If the individual is not safely nested within a set of concentric circles – family, community, region and nation – then how do we know s/he is safe? This continued throughout 1934 in Norwegian newspapers, especially in *Aftenposten.*

The wandering person was basically not in the network of social life that Pescosolido described above as pre-modern. And, in Norway, where the Sámi people's way of life included wandering with their herds of reindeer, this had always been a problem. If Norwegians did not know which "gård"[319] a stranger was from, what did s/he really know about the stranger? And a further – practical – question developed for the citizens of the relatively poor nation, i.e. if a wandering stranger was in need or ill, who was responsible for that person?[320] In Norway, during its premodern-modern transi-

---

316 Vilhelm Aubert, "Legal Justice and Mental Health" in *Psychiatry: Journal for the Study of Interpersonal Processes*, 21 (1958), 112. Perhaps Aubert would not have written exactly these same words in the 21st century. However, he might very well have objected to what is called the "sortering" (sorting according to various attributes) of persons in Norwegian society.

317 In fact, during the well-publicized trial of Henry Kendal Thaw, the term "dementia Americana" was used to describe the insanity of the rich and famous.

318 This discursive model was often rearranged with reference to ethnic groups, i.e. the "travelers."

319 Literally, "farm" but can mean a house or building in an urban setting.

320 In the United States, severe social responses were reserved for "strangers", outsiders with mental illnesses who were not considered the community's responsibility. Prior to the mid-nineteenth cention, as disease came to be perceived as an individual condition, the sterilization law addressed the issue of who was responsible. The soon-to-be-passed sterilization law was drafted so as to deal with the "residence" of the mentally ill or dangerous through the institution of the local police chief.

For example, in April 1934, newspapers carried a story of a dangerous mentally disturbed man who had escaped from the Reitgjerdet Asylum in Trondheim.[321] Karl Isidor Braaten, who was 43 years old, had escaped on Holy Thursday after having been at Reitgjerdet for 10 years. His family, who lived in Hurdalen, said that he was not dangerous although the police disagreed and said he should be characterized as dangerous.[322] In some cases, there were legitimate concerns for public safety. In mid-April, yet another mentally ill man tried to kill his wife, his seven-year-old son, and himself in Drammen.[323] As the Pescosolido model's diagrammatic explanation of societal transition demonstrates, the movement from concentric "nested" social networks to "overlapping [and] intersecting social circles" caused the individual to became the center of the etiology of "insanity" and the home or the community were "contaminated." It was thought that this left few options except to confine the insane in "well-ordered asylums" elsewhere that reflected the "demarcation" of these social circles "by socio-demographic characteristics...differentiated...by race, class and status of education, and private hospitals appeared for the affluent."[324]

Reporting on criminal law problems was a regular feature of Oslo newspapers and the first few days of May illustrate this point. On 3 May on the front page of the afternoon edition, *Aftenposten* asked if there were sexual criminals populating Steenstrups gate saying there had been a suspect arrested there the previous day.[325] On 7 May, crime statistics were printed saying that for every 400 adults in Oslo there was one lawbreaker and women were one-tenth of that number.[326] The population of Oslo in 1934 was 266,344; 118,540 men and 147,990 women. This would have given a criminal population of around 665 men and 66 women whom the newspaper named as "criminals" distributed somehow in the public space. Within the space of 5 days,

tury "[t]he policy of "warning out" allowed towns to return individuals with mental illnesses to the towns where they held legal residence." Please see, Bernice A. Pescosolido-Rubin and Beth A. Rubin, "The Web of Group Affiliations Revisited: Social Life, Postmodernism, and Sociology" in *American Sociological Review*, 65 (2000), 67.

321 *Aftenposten* (p.m. Edition), April 3, 1934, 1.

322 *Ibid.*

323 *Aftenposten* (p.m. Edition), April 14, 1934, 1. Directly adjacent to the Karl Braaten story in this newspaper was yet another story of insanity that had not yet had the time to unfold before the country or the world. The headline read: "Hitler i Norge i Sogn og Hardanger ombord på panserskibet "Deutschland."

324 Pescosolido-Rubin and Rubin, "The Web of Group Affiliations", 67.

325 *Aftenposten* (p.m. Edition), May 3, 1934, 1.

326 *Aftenposten* (p.m. Edition), May 7, 1934, 5.

the reading public in Oslo and throughout Norway for that matter, had been exposed to a story written about the possibility of sexual criminals within a certain area of Oslo and then the scientific verification that at least some persons in that area were criminals.

About a week after the suggestion that sexual criminals inhabited Steenstrup gate, *Aftenposten* carried a feature article by Dr. hr. Hospital Director Henrik A. Th. Dedichen (b. 1895) entitled "The Punishment and the Punished."[327] Dedichen, who had his own private psychiatric clinic in East Aker in 1934, made use of this editorial platform to comment on the use of punishment as a "weapon" that society had to protect itself from criminals.[328] Dedichen commented that punishment was viewed with an increasing "distrust" and that Polish and Italian laws were being looked at with interest in "some circles." As was the customary expository style in 1934, Dedichen went back to the laws of Hammarabi to make his point which was that laws were relative to time and place and it was "simplistic ignorance" to believe that jails "pampered" law breakers. Conditions in jails should only be "as tolerable as possible."

Roughly ten days after Dedichen's editorial, Ranke Samuelsen from Trondheim also wrote a feature article entitled "Our Criminally Insane."[329] In a rather sympathetic article, Samuelsen describes the asylums for the criminally insane in the midt-Trøndelag region. Trondheim and Strinda had the "dubious honor" of housing the entire male criminally insane incarcerated population from throughout Norway in 1934. They were either in the criminal asylum in Kongensgate or a half hour from the city at Reitgjerdet.[330] Both institutions had the same director, supervising doctor and administrative unit.[331] Samuelsen was disturbed by the conditions at both places and the transfer of especially dangerous patients from other institutions in Norway to Trondheim, and most especially those with a "tendency to escape."[332] The housing together of the mentally ill, the developmentally delayed and the dangerous criminally insane was not the best of situations and a very serious problem according to Samuelson.[333]

The old Kongensgate asylum in Trondheim was built to hold 36 inmates and Reitgjerdet was built with 135 beds although some patients were housed in private care

327 *Aftenposten* (a.m. Edition), June 9, 1934, 2.

328 The west side of Oslo was more affluent than the east side of Oslo. Accents differ and the social status conferred by a westerly address remains to this day. One cannot help but notice the similarities to mid-1980s America and its sexual abuse hysteria.

329 *Aftenposten*, (a.m. Edition), June 20, 1934, 2.

330 Reitgjerdet continues to be used as a psychiatric institution to this day and in Case Two we also find an escape incident from the same institution. However, at that point the mentally ill population has changed from a "weak we" to a "stronger we."

331 *Ibid.*

332 *Ibid.*

333 *Ibid.*

in the area. Both institutions were full. Reitgjerdet was especially a problem since – whatever its construction – patients did escape. But this phenomenon, in Samuelsen's opinion was "screamed about so often and foolishly in the press." Samuelsen defended the patients at Reitgjerdet noting that they held jobs and should not be seen as criminals. Both Dedichen and Samuelsen are indicative of the progressive attitudes towards institutionalization that were present in Norway at this time and they are similar to ideas circulating in the progressive movement the case of Indiana in 1907. While Norway's progressive movement was less likely to use the term "progressive", it certainly had a great deal of similarity to that movement in Indiana in 1907.

Not everyone agreed with Dedichen and his views on prison conditions. Appellate attorney Håkon Benneche of Stavanger took Dedichen to task, berating Dedichen for laying a "confusion of ideas" before the public. Benneche said that Dedichen's ideas were "no longer modern and would luckily disappear ...soon...along with the soft, sweet sophomoric mentality which has exhausted Europe since [1800]..."[334] Benneche argued that most criminals were not mentally ill and were, in fact, "normal" individuals. On 18 July, Frants Faye Kaltenborn (b. 1901), an assistant chief of police in Oslo, became involved in the semantic fray and countered Benneche with information Kaltenborn had obtained from the Wieneruniversitets Kriminalistiske Institutt. Kaltenborn cited extensively to work done at this Institute, the Department of Criminal Law and Criminology, in his article.[335] Kaltenborn maintained that other factors, including family genetic traits played a roll in criminality.[336]

Here we see frame bridging between the discourses of those reacting against the progressive movement with those in the eugenics movement. The progressive movement was a convenient meeting point for those inclined to left wing politics – obviously – but it also attracted right wing advocates. As the eugenics movement matured, it is easier to see how individual motivation seemed to matter more than principled thinking or argumentation.

3.8 Norm Production at the Shifting Intersections of the Jasanoff Fields

Just as I did with the Indiana half of this case, I now present two examples of the shifting articulations among the Jasanoff fields of knowledge co-production. They reflect,

334 *Aftenposten* (a.m. Edition), July 12, 1934, 2.

335 Wenzeslaus Gleispach (1876–1944) founded the institute in Vienna.

336 *Aftenposten* (a.m. Edition), July 12, 1934, 2. Kaltenborn was trained as a sorenskriver before becoming a police officer. From 1941–1943, he worked as the secretary of Norsk Hydro and from 1943–1945; he was the "sjef" of the "Rikspolitikorpset" in Sweden.

I propose, the micro-subjective level of the Rickert Model and the "preconceptual/ precognitive" (ISLL) level of legal norm formation from the Tuori Model.

Individual professionals who espoused eugenics in its many formulations were often seen in the pages of Oslo's major newspapers, just as in Indiana. One such doctor, Dr. med. Sofus Widerøe, jumped on what seemed to be a fast-moving legal train in 1934 with a book review of "The Law Relating to the Genetically Ill" authored by Gütt, Rüdin and Rüttke.[337] Rüdin has already been mentioned above in reference to the International Society for Race Hygiene. Widerøe's book review presented no new arguments and began with the "economics" of the mentally ill, developmentally delayed and persons with genetic illnesses. Whether or not the numbers of such people in society were actually rising, his perception was that the numbers were steadily increasing. The unique aspect of Widerøe's review was that, for the first time in 1934 in this venue, he used the language of "productivity." He asked, "Do the productive [members in] society have the ability, out of their possible profits, to afford the sum total of these individuals..."[338] Acknowledging that this is a difficult question that had faced Norway for some time, he said, candidly, "It is so difficult and yet so simple!."[339]

Dr. Widerøe asked a series of questions, more routinely situated in the political and legal setting. What were the rights of the individual in relation to the rights of the state? Does the genetically defective person have the right to transmit his sickness or his defective genes to another? Does the state have the right to interfere in the individual's liberty in order to stop the transmission of defective genes and/or genetic illnesses? He then quoted §1 of the German Reichsgesetzblatt I.S. 529 in which 8 conditions of genetic illness are set out and to which that law applied.[340] For Widerøe, this law introduced "a new time" and it was a sign of "a new epoch"; he quoted *Mein Kampf* concerning those who are not "mentally or physicially sound" and pronounces the logic in Hitler's tract as in "order."[341] Dr. Widerøe opined that the German law and its consequences were logically well founded and built on legal principles of the

---

337 *Aftenposten* (a.m. Edition), June 22, 1934, 2. "Gesetz zur Verhütung erbkranken Nachwunches vom 14 juli 1933" Widerøe's 1910 PhD dissertation at the University of Oslo (Christiania) had been entitled "Die Massenverhältnisse des Herzens unter pathologischen Zustände" ("Conditions of the Heart Under Pathological Conditions"). Rüdin is mentioned numerous times throughout this dissertation in various connections with the eugenics movement. Lehman Publishing Company in Munich, which had a direct connection with Darré and the Nordic Ring, published the book that Widerøe reviewed.

338 *Ibid.* (Emphasis mine.)

339 *Ibid.*

340 *Ibid.* They are "1.) born as an "idiot" (with IQ less than 20), which had a specific scientific meaning at this time, 2) schizophrenic, 3.) manic-depressive illness 4.) hereditary epilespy, 5.) hereditary Huntingdons choria), 6.) born blind, 7.) born deaf, 8. born with considerable bodily malformation and chronic alcoholism. Professors Lexer and Døderlein of Munich wrote a chapter in the book on these conditions.

341 *Ibid.*

state. The law was concise and medically and biologically correct; however, Widerøe conceded there would be difficulties in carrying it out.[342]

At one end of eugenic continuum were some enthusiasts who inevitably considered the issue of euthanasia. Again, it was Widerøe who, in August 1934, continued to promote his ideas in another "thought-piece", drawing his inspiration from a rather diverse group of people including Diogenes, Bacon and Somerset Maughum. He cited the history of euthanasia in modern times, including a 1906 legislative proposal in Ohio to allow it. Widerøe asserted that, "euthanasia has been practiced here for a hundred years by all right-minded and medical practitioners [adhering to his Hippocratic Oath]."[343] Clearly, Dr. Widerøe had a rather complete societal picture and of what social policies should be in place to bring this about.

It was within acceptable schemas for an upper-class woman in 1934 to leave the boundaries of the home – if her work were charitable.[344] This allowed for the building of networks, which, in turn, helped to create SMOs, as well as creating culturally pluralistic framing of issues that affected women. Upper and middle class women in Norway at this time were organized into many service groups within several social and religious arenas and September 1934 saw a number of women's national organizations begin and adjourn, one after the other. Between the 11th and the 21st of September 1934, five major women's groups met in Oslo – Norske Sanitetsforening (Norwegian Hygiene Association, NSF), Norske kvinners nasjonalråd (Norwegian Women's Advisory Association, NKNR), Hjemmenes Vel (Good Homes, HV), Norske kvinnesaksforening (Norwegian Women's Legal Association, NKSF) and Norges Husmorforbund (Norwegian Housewives' Association, NHMF). One of these powerful organizations – the NSF – gathered in Oslo on 11 September for its district meeting

342 *Ibid.*

343 *Afternposten* (a.m. Edition), August 17, 1934, 2. To be fair, states attorney Kjerschow rebutted Widerøe's article later on 22 August. (*Aftenposten* (a.m. Edition), 22 August 1934, p. 2.) (Kjerschow had been a member of the committee that did earlier prepatory work on the 1934 sterilization law for the Storting.) He noted that §235 of the current criminal law, in the section on "Crimes against life, the body and health", included the following paragraph:

> In some cases where one's own death is consensual or the occasion or opportunity of significant bodily harm or damage to health has some measure of compassion in a hopeless life of sickness, the punishment can be reduced to a level under that which is normally applied to a less serious level.

(*Ibid.*) Kjerschow wrote that the criminal law still considered euthanasia as murder but that the Court issuing a punishment has access to milder sentences in some situations and that some doctors treated these situations under "unwritten law." Obviously, Kjerschow did not agree with Widerøe, however, that a new law is needed on the subject.

344 Working class women used the worker's associations of their husbands in much the same way. The *Arbeiderbladet* had a Women's Section every Thursday devoted to the political, educational and charitable activities of women.

which brought no less that around 350 women to that meeting.[345] The NSF was otherwise known as the "Gray Ladies", an auxiliary of the Red Cross, whose members offered nonprofessional help to the sick and helped with hygiene education as well as raising money. Professor Olav Hanssen provided a lecture on "Food which Cures..." for the women.[346]

On the second day of the NSF meeting, Dr. Hanssen gave a lecture entitled "Cooperation Between the Kitchen and Doctors at the Hospital." Women attending the conference also discussed how and when to use the money that they had collected. During discussions, which included various doctors and administrators, several questions were asked and, when taken together with other indications, indicated that social schemas were indeed changing. Lina Sørensen noted that there were no dentists available in tuberculosis asylums. In addition, Lulli Lous asked the district doctor why there were no women on the Board of Directors for the Aker Doctors Hospital. The Chairwoman of the meeting, Fru Grundtvig was then moved by this iquestion to remark "We see this again and again that there is no use for women [in the NSF] other than to collect money."[347]

Two days after the NSF opened its meeting in Oslo, the Norwegian National Women's Association (NKF) opened its national meeting under the direction of foreman Betzy Kjelsberg (1866–1950).[348] One cannot help but speculate that this was not a coincidence as members of one organization may have been active in the other. Lorange, Grundt, Kjelsberg, Høe, Sparre, Haslund, Engebrethsen, Holmbie and Lie debated the pros and cons of the impending European war indicating that these women were prepared to debate matters of national and world importance. The next afternoon, at Hjemmenes Vel (1898–1979), the theme of women's right to work was taken up in an introduction by Kjelsberg. She reported that the danger of women losing their right to work, especially after marriage, had been discussed at the International Women's Organization Congress in Paris during that same summer.[349]

---

345 "Sanitetsforening." *Aftenposten* (p.m. Edition), September 11, 1934, 2. The organization was under the leadership of Anna Dahl and Fru Mathilde Kierulf.

346 *Aftenposten* (p.m. Edition), September 11, 1934, 2.

347 *Aftenposten* (a.m. Edition) September 12, 1934, 5.

348 *Aftenposten* (p. m. Edition), September 13, 1934, 1. Norske kvinners nasjonal råd is abbreviated "NKNR." "Norske kvinnersnasjonaldråd åpner sitt årsmøte." Kjelsberg was already a member from the establishment of the NKN in 1904 and became its leader from 1922–1938, sixteen years. Kjelsberg was no stranger to leadership roles and to organizing. In 1884 she was one of the founders of the Norsk Kvindesagssforening. She founded the Kvinnelig handelsstands Forening and the Drammen Sanitetsforening in 1894, tge Drammen Kvinnesaksforening in 1896 and the Drammen Kvinneråd in 1903. In addition to this impressive list, she was the first the first female manufacturing inspector ("fabrikkinspectør") from 1910–1936. She was the first female member of the Venstre (Liberal) party and was also a Vice-Chairwoman ("viseformann") of the International Council of Women.

349 Det internasjonale kvinnersråd kongress.

The Swedish female manufacturing inspector, Kjerstin Hesselgren, expressed the opinion that civilization itself was in danger if women lost the right of self determination, and,

> also here in Norway, the woman must be wakened and be on guard. And it is necessary to use the right to vote in this manner; that women do not vote for someone other than themselves, for those who believe in the same right to work for women as for men.[350]

These groups were not the only ones that were debating the right of women to work after marriage. The Norsk kvinnersaksforening (Norwegian women's legal association, NKSF) was formed in 1884 and in 1934 celebrated its 50th anniversary.[351] The four persons who had led the group since its inception were Anna Stang, Hagbard Berner, Ragna Neilsen and Anne Bugge. *Aftenposten* reported on 15 September 1934 that this group was of the opinion that:

> Norwegian women now have, in theory, full equality with men in society. In practice, however, this equality is not fully carried out. Until this is accomplished, the Norwegian Feminist Association's job is not finished.[352]

A leader of this group, Anna Stang, was the woman Lektor[353] Harald Amundsen complained of above, in the same breath as modern psychology and birth control.

The NHMF also had a leadership course in Oslo, the same day as the celebration of the 50th anniversary of the NKSF.[354] Relations seemed to have been friendly between the two groups, on the surface at the very least. Flowers had been sent to the NKSF from a number of groups including Kjelsberg's NKR, the NSF's governing board, from Altern's Oslo Kvinneråd, the Oslo Women's Business Group, and from the Feminist Association of Drammen.[355]

An example of the work done by the Oslo branch of the NSF was reported the next day in *Aftenposten.* A sanatorium had been started at Grefsen in 1858 and from 1898 until 1909 it was privately administered as a tuberculosis facility.[356] But in 1909, the NSF had assumed full control of the facility as a People's Sanatorium. Largely through its excellent organization and the force of some personalities, it raised much money for the building and maintenance of hospitals and sanitariums and was an active participant in the issues of the day that affected women and children. For example, on

---

350 *Aftenposten* (a. m. Edition), September 15, 1934, 6.

351 "Norsk kvinnesaksforening 1884–1934." *Aftenposten* (a. m. Edition), September 15, 1934, 7.

352 *Ibid.*

353 There is no equivalent in the American university system but "lecturer" is close.

354 "Husmorsforbundet"*Aftenposten* (p. m. Edition), September 17, 1934, 2 and 4.

355 *Aftenposten* (p.m. Edition), September 17, 1934, 4. Frøken Fredrikke Mørck had assumed the editorship of "Nylæende" after the death of Gina Krog.

356 *Aftenposten* (p.m. Edition), September 18, 1934, 5.

3 May the Oslo NSF noted the beginning of a new facility in the autumn because the hospital that was to serve rheumatic sicknesses had been temporarily postponed.[357]

On the 19th of September, the NHMF began its national meeting with and address by Michelet on the mission of the organization. *Aftenposten* was clearly favorably disposed to this group in the person of Michelet. She was presented as a woman who had "good and wise advice" who understood that her "fight was also for the ethical values in human life."[358] Nothing so glowing had been written about women involved in the fight to change abortion laws in Norway at this time. The picture one receives of Michelet is of a woman who could charm yet could talk forcefully about women's rights. The reporter wrote that Michelet was asked a question about women's rights and answered:

> that she, on the whole, believes women must be considered when we think of the national economy and no longer merely as an appendix in the category titled "women and children", she answered with a smile.[359]

Not only the newspaper but also the royal family seems to have been friendly with Michelet. The next day, HRH crown prince Harald of Norway, made an appearance at the NHMF's meeting. Around 300 members met in Oslo and began with the organization of committees and elections. Elected Vice Chair was Amalie Øvergaards and Betzy Kjelsberg personally gave greetings from the NKR before Michelet gave her opening address. The organization then entered "into lively debate" in which the countryside members were pitted against the city member over an issue of the Board of Governors composition. The following day at the NHMF convention was taken up with discussions of Norwegian wool and foods native to Norway. The new Chair was also chosen; Amalie Øvergaard won with a decisive majority against Wiborg Thune and Schnitzler.[360]

The above networking among women who had both money, time and influence is important since we see the discourses that were important to them at this time and place as well as the work they did within Norwegian society, acknowledged or not. We heard Grundtvig complain that there was no use for women in the NSF "other than to collect money" and we also read the statement issued by the NKSF that although women in Norway had equality, it was a restricted equality that was "not fully carried out" in practice. We can only guess at the private conversations these women had but the discourse of dissatisfaction was alive and well in 1934 among these associations and policy entrepreneurs.

---

357 "Revmatiske sygdommer." *Aftenposten* (a.m. Edition), May 3, 1934, 7.

358 *Aftenposten* (a.m. Edition), September 19, 1934, 7.

359 *Aftenposten* (a.m. Edition), September 19, 1934, 7.

360 *Aftenposten* (a.m. Edition), September 21, 1934, 5 and 7.

4 CASE ONE: Legal Norm Injection Points in Indiana and Norway: the Selection of Particular Bodies

4.1 Composition of the Indiana Legislature (1907)

In this Chapter, I look at the composition of the Indiana legislature and the Norwegian Storting at the time these bodies passed their respective sterilization laws. One of my underlying assumptions in doing this examination is that the life experiences of these legislators and parliamentarians impacted their voting, although there is nothing so obvious as a strict correlation. Some legislators, who were from the upper classes, were involved in progressive movement politics just as some legislators, who were from middle and working classes, were involved in fighting against these reforms.

Of course, in 1907, all members of the state Legislature were men. But what were their values, their normative view of the "correct" way the state should proceed? In part, we can answer this through looking at such things as their occupations, ages, religion and life experiences that intersected with other institutions.

Between 1891 and 1929, the largest number of the 1,786 Indianan legislators was lawyers (533/29.7%) followed by farmers (449/25.3%), merchants/storekeepers (127/7.1%), physicians or dentists (89/5.1%), newspapermen/editor (55/3.0%), bankers/financiers (49/2.7%), businessman (47/2.6%), realtors (43/2.5%), teachers (42/2.4%) and manufacturers (40/2.2%).[361] The occupation of the legislators made a difference as to who stood for election or not since mileage and a *per diem* were the only reimbursement to those elected. Between 1877 and 1925 both were fixed at $6 per day and $5 per week for each 25 miles traveled to and from Indianapolis.[362] This, in turn, also had an effect on the turnover in the legislature. Generally, Senators stayed one year longer than Representatives. Between 1891 and 1929, 61.2% of all representatives gave only one year of service, 28.4% gave two years, 6.5% gave three years and 2.0 % gave four years. In the Senate, 6.9% gave one year of service, 74.7% two years, 1.6% three years, 11.6% four years and 2.6% six years.[363]

The mean age for senators between 1891 and 1929 was 48.2 years and for a representative was 48.8 years of age.[364] About sixty percent had held public office at the

361 Justin E. Walsh, *The Centennial History of the Indiana General Assembly (1816–1978)* (Indianapolis: The Select Committee on the Centennial History of the Indiana General Assembly and The Indiana Historical Bureau, 1987), 708–709, Table 7: Occupations of Legislators. The remainder of legislators who accounted for more than 1.0% but less than 2.0% were occupied as Artisan/Mechanic (18/1.0%), Builder/contractor (21/1.2%), Clergyman (18/1.0%), Insurance (27/1.4%), Railroad worker (23/1.2%), salesman (23/1.2%) and "other" (27/1.4%). Of the 18 clergymen, 156 were from rural areas.

362 *Ibid.*, 381.

363 *Ibid.*, 706. Table 6: Tenure in the Indiana General Assembly.

364 *Ibid.*, 400.

"township, city or county level" prior to their election to the Assembly.[365] Generally, 86% of these who were elected to the House and 81.5 % elected to the Senate had not seen military service although it "remained an asset" for those who did run and had served.[366] Between 1901 and 1909, 58% of the elected House members and 74% of the Senate members had attended college.[367] Between 1891 and 1929, most of those attending an Indianan college had attended Indiana University (12%), Indiana State University (5.0%), Purdue University (3.8%), Vincennes University (0.6%) and Ball State University (0.3%).[368] This appears to be a small percentage; however, only 72.7% of the legislators in this time period were actually born in Indiana, up from 34.1% in 1851–1889. While Indiana was becoming a "settled" state, in 1891–1929, many of the legislators were born in neighboring states such as Illinois (2.7%), Ohio, (2.2%), Kentucky (1.6%) and Michigan (1.2%); others were born in Pennsylvania (2.2%), New York (1.5%) and 2.1% were born in Germany.[369]

The religious affiliation of elected legislators between 1891 and 1929 did not exactly follow the pattern of the religions' corresponding representation in the population in 1906.[370] In the former period, most legislators were Methodists (419/23.4) followed by "Unknown" (349/19.5%), Presbyterians (202/11.3%), Disciples of Christ (193/10.9%), "Not a Church Member" (129/7.2%), Baptist (113/6.4%), Roman Catholic (93/5.2%), Lutheran (57/3.2%), Society of Friends or Quakers (54/3.0%), United Brethren (47/2.6%) and Episcopalian (33/1.9%).[371] The 1906 survey would have indicated that the top three faiths of the representatives, in proportion to the general public, would have been Methodists, Roman Catholics and Church of the Brethren. But this is perhaps not significant since we do not know the parameters of both studies, i.e. which churches were included/excluded and the numbers for the 1891–1929 period of "Not a Church member" and "Unknown" are quite large. Nonetheless, the decline in Roman Catholic representatives in relation to their number in the general population may have been related to the fact that the German population might have been at that time largely an immigrant population and that the "Know nothing" movement, aimed specifically at Roman Catholic immigrants may have had some success.[372]

365 *Ibid.*, 403.

366 *Ibid.*, 401, 711, Table 8: Military Service of Legislators.

367 *Ibid.*, 713, Table 9: College Attendance by Legislators.

368 *Ibid.*, 713, Table 10: Attendance by Legislators at State Supported Institutions of Higher Learning.

369 *Ibid.*, 702, Table 4: Birthplace of Legislators.

370 *Ibid.*, 2.

371 Walsh, *Centennial History*, 721, Table 13: Religious Affiliations of Legislators.

372 During 1925, a bill directed at Roman Catholic nuns who taught in public schools was taken up – and defeated – in the Assembly, i.e. the prohibition on the wearing of religious garb or symbols by teachers in public schools. While the Ku Klux Klan targeted African Americans during the night, they targeted other groups - especially Jews and Roman Catholics - during the day, with help of some of their Freemason members in what the KKK called the "Americanization" of Indiana.

Finally, between 1910 and 1911, 45% of House members and 54% of Senate members were "known to be members" of the Freemasons; 47% of the legislature were also "known to be members."[373] Aside from the multitude of network resources that Freemasonry brought to the individual legislator, this is noteworthy because the Klu Klux Klan organization tried to utilize Freemasonry employing "every device to fasten itself upon the Masonic Craft...."[374] In summary, the "average" member of the General Assembly in 1907 was a lawyer, a Republican, 48.5 years of age, a first time member, and a Methodist. The House of Representatives for the State of Indiana began its regular session – its 65th session – on Thursday, 10 January 1907.

What were the scientific discourses that circulated in this Legislature? This was, in part, answered by the above discussion of the macro-leveled eugenics movement in Indiana. But were those discussions the same at the meso-level? What meaning did the identity of "scientist" have and which members, associated with what institutional resources were involved in those discourses? The profession most associated with science was medicine and the *Indianapolis News* noted that, after the legislators themselves, the "first people to appear about the hotels" before the General Assembly had even finished breakfast "were a band of doctors, and they have been there all day since their arrival."[375]

There were also doctors who were legislators. The Senate alone boasted four physicians, Dr. Richard R. McCain of Kentland, Dr. O.M. Keyes of Dana, Dr. Charles R. Lane of Ft. Wayne and Dr. McDowell of Sullivan and Knox County. The House had at least five doctor-legislators, Dr. A.W. Porter of Martin and Orange, Dr. Horace Read of Tipton and Hamilton, Dr. Scholl of Carroll, Howard and Miami, Dr. J. Frank Simison of Montgomery and Tippecanoe and Dr. John W. Vizard of Adams County. Of the entire legislature, these representatives were perceived as understanding scientific concepts and this perception is seen in the fact that doctors composed the majority of the Committee on Mental Health and Vital Statistics (CMHVS). It would be this committee that would initially evaluate the sterilization law in terms of whether or not it should proceed further through the legislative process. The eventual composition of the CMHVS would include Dr. Porter, Coble, Cox, Keller, Dr. Read, Dr. Scholl, Dr. Simison, Dr. Vizard, and Wade, with Read as the Chair of the Committee.[376] (See Appendix C.)

---

373 *Ibid.*, 722, Table 14: Freemasons in the Indiana General Assembly.

374 *Ibid.*, 317. Quotation itself is from Dwight E. Smith, *Goodly Heritage: One Hundred Years of Craft Freemasonry in Indiana* (Franklin, Indiana, 1968), 224–225.

375 "Sounds Caught from General Legislative Hum." *Indianapolis News*, January 7, 1907, 4.

376 Please see Appendix C for party affiliation and the other committees on which the individual CMHVS representative sat. The CMHVS representatives were from the following Counties: Porter (Martin and Orange), Keller (Marion), Cox (Ripley), Read (Hamilton and Tipton), Simison (Tippecanoe and Montgomery), Scholl (Miami, Carroll and Howard), Wade (Posey), Vizard (Adams), Coble (Dubois and Pike).

Newspapers used different techniques to follow activities in the legislature. While the *Star* followed the Legislature with extensive daily reporting, the *News* also used a technique in which a reporter wrote a bi- or tri-weekly piece entitled "In Among the Legislators" authored by a reporter named Blodgett. His was a gadfly school of journalism where we learn – with some caveats – a bit more about the activities of these doctor-legislators than from the more direct reporting approach. For example, we learn that doctor-legislators stayed in touch with one another when Blodgett interviewed a former legislator and physician, Dr. Loren Gage of Grandview County. Gage had dropped in to "chat with old friends" as they gathered in one of the downtown hotels before the Legislature actually began. Gage had been a member of the House two years previously but did "not attempt to secure a renomination" after that term.[377] This is also an example of where professional institutional affiliation granted access to legislators and facilitated an exchange of information. The concept of "networking" was not new to these men even though the term may be a more modern invention.

From Blodgett we also learn that Frank N. Wade of Posey, eventually one of the members of the CMHVS had arrived in Indianapolis on the 7th of January. Wade said "he had no bills to present, but was interested in 'helping to kill some of the bad legislation that will be offered by other members'."[378] Dr. Scholl eventually became the Chair of the CHMVS. Scholl had also served in the House in 1879 and when interviewed by reporter Blodgett, Scholl noted that there wasn't "much difference between then and now." The rules "were about the same" and the "way of doing business now is not much different" either.[379] There was one major difference, however. In 1879, the Democrats had control of the House by six votes. This was exactly the same number of votes that, in 1907, gave the Republicans power in the same chamber.

Members of the CMHVS were busy from the start of the session and not only with science-related matters. For example, Rep. Dr. Scholl, during the same week as his interview with *News* reporter Blodgett, submitted an anti-trust bill and by 14 January, Rep. Dr. Read had submitted a bill concerning sales of personal property. On 15 January, Rep. Vizard submitted a bill on requiring electric companies to provide free meters to customers and Rep. Simison submitted a proposal to allow colleges to change the manner of electing trustees.[380] Yet another member of the CMHVS, Senator Lincoln A. Cox of Marion County, proposed that police pensions be equalized but in no case should they be set at less than \$10 or more than \$50 per month.[381]

---

377 "Legislators Arrive Ready for Action. Fights for Appointive Positions Tame Compared With Those of Previous Years. Party Caucuses Tomorrow. Selection of Branch for Speakership Now Seems Assured." *Indianapolis Star*, January 8, 1907, 3.

378 *Ibid.*

379 *Ibid.*

380 *Indianapolis News*, January 15, 1907, 3.

381 *Indianapolis Star*, January 16, 1907, 3.

The Editor of the *Star* usually reserved the extreme left-hand column on the editorial page for what he considered humorous comments and gossip. He was also familiar with the doctor-legislators and it was not long before we find a first reference in this column to George T. Porter, a member of the CMHVS. Porter was quoted as reminding the *Star* that it was his father, the late Governor Albert G. Porter (1824–1897), "who first urged the appointment of women to a part in the official management of State institutions."[382] In short, these doctor-legislators were involved in all types of matters, not only those scientific or medical.

The Senate also had members who were doctors and one, Sen. Dr. McCain, gave his first speech on 14 February. According to reporter Blodgett, the speech was not long but it was "effective" since "the Kentland doctor voted just as he talked – and that is more than some of the members of the General Assembly do."[383] Procedurally, we know that all bills had to pass through committees in both the House and the Senate. In the Senate, those bills that the House had approved and that dealt with public health needed to come before its Committee on Public Health; Sen. Dr. McCain, from Jasper, Newton, and White Counties was the chairman of this committee. During the 1907 Legislative session, McCain would spend a great deal of time dealing with the sanitary bottle bill, where he and Board of Health Secretary, Dr. Hurty would clash.[384] There is no mention of McCain and his Committee considering the sterilization law.

The final appointments to various other committees of the CMHVS members are included in Appendix C. From this, we can see that Scholl was on the most committees although some of his committee appointments were presumably not as time consuming as others, e.g. comparing the Soldiers Monument Committee and the Ways and Means (Budget) Committee. At least two CMHVS members – Cox and Wade – were on the committees that dealt with prisons and reformatory and so contact with Dr. Sharp and Supt. Whittaker was possible. Scholl was on the State Library Committee and as such, had contact with the State Librarian, Demarchus C. Brown, who was in the process of translating and distributing literature to the legislature from Germany on prison reform; Brown read German and was interested in progressive topics and how reforms were being made in Germany.[385] In summary, it appears as if Porter, Read and

---

382 *Indianapolis Star*, January 15, 1907, 8.
383 "Right in Among Legislators." *Indianapolis News*, February 15, 1907, 4.
384 *Indianapolis Star*, January 30, 1907, 8. Hurty was against the bill.
385 *Indianapolis Star*, May 26, 1907, 28. Demarchus C. Brown was busy translating Professor Berthold Freudenthal's address before the International Penological Society in Germany on Sept. 6, 1906. (*Ibid.*) Although this might not be a remarkable event, the translation was to be used by the Board of State Charities, and it appears, would be passed around to state officials who might be interested. At the time, Freudenthal was a law professor at Frankfurt University who would become one of the architects of Weimar Germany's penal system. The title of Freudenthal's address was "American Criminology" and a substantial portion of the translation was printed in the *Star*. Professor Freudenthal was not entirely enthusiastic about American prisons and reformatories, but, by the same token, did

Simison were the most powerful in CMHVS, next to Scholl. Also, just as today, various personalities and the interest groups they represented had access to members of the CMHVS.

Set alongside these legislative "big but slow-moving [micro-social] processes" is the fact of institutional processes.[386] Analysts who do not look at these larger processes are "prone to a number of serious mistakes."[387] As Pierson says:

> They are particularly likely to miss the role of many "sociological" variables, like demography, literacy, or technology. Their explanations may focus on triggering or precipitating actors rather than more fundamental structural causes. It can get worse. By truncating an analysis of process unfolding over an extended period of time, analysts can easily end up inverting causal relationships.[388]

An example of how sociological variables can be missed is seen in David Carpenter's *The Forging of Bureaucratic Autonomy* where he criticizes the then current (2001) "agent-principal" theory which is based on a cross-sectional approach, in favor of an approach wherein "ambitious and entrepreneurial bureaucrats were able to enhance their reputations for innovativeness and competence and develop strong networks of support among a range of social actors."[389] At that time, what looked like Congressional dominance on the outside was, in fact, Congress asking "for what the bureaucrats

---

not say that Germany had a better system. Citing statistics, he noted that the "picture of American criminal conditions is not spotless." (*Ibid.*) The crux of the problems in America was "American officialdom" where "the men who belong to the party in power, but in point of fact incompetent men, are frequently given positions in the penal institutions [and c]apable men have been removed from their places." Freudenthal also noted a theoretical debate in American criminology that would continue into the present day. He said:

> In America retributive and reformatory punishment have been in conflict, and even yet there are quite often flashes of lightening in the penological heavens of the Union.

Freudenthal presented for his audience a picture of the various stages of the reformatory that should be "built up like classes in school. The higher the class, the nearer the approach to full freedom." He also noted that religion played a role in the reformatory in America as "a means of education of the highest rank...." (*Ibid.*) The Atlantic Ocean may have been "eugenic" but it was also "progressive."

386 The vocabulary from social movements' theory and the vocabulary from Sewell are not always the same. Social movement theorists talk about "institutions" and Sewell writes about "structures." For my purposes, I conceive of "institutions" as part of "structures" in Sewels triad of "structures, schemas and resources."

387 Paul Pierson, "The Study of Policy Development" in *The Journal of Policy History*, 17 (2005), 42.

388 *Ibid.*

389 *Ibid.* See Daniel P. Carpenter, *The Forging of Bureaucratic Autonomy: Reputations, Networks, and Policy Innovation in Executive Agencies, 1862–1928* (Princeton, New Jersey: Princeton Univeresity Press, 2001).

[already] wanted."[390] A particular moment in time, a moment of choice, should be to be seen as part of a cultural, social and political process.

An example of how these larger institutional processes can be overlooked is found in the work of four Indianans. Nowhere in the short, official legislative history of the first sterilization law in the world can we find these four names – Dr. John N. Hurty, Dr. Henry C. Sharp, Dr. Amos W. Butler or Oscar McCullough. These four men were individuals but are also representations of the structures, schemas and resources available to the "progressive" social movement as well as to the eugenics movement in 1907 in Indiana.[391] As noted above in Chapter 3, these two movements often articulated, forming framing bridges with one another as well as with numerous other structures generated by the progressive movement such as the suffragette movement and various religious faiths. As such, they represent the following bridges; medical-legislative structure (Hurty), the progressive-medical structure (Sharp), the progressive-institutional structure (Butler) and the progressive-religious structure (McCullough).

In 1907, Dr. Hurty was the Vice President of the State Medical Association and secretary of the Indiana State Board of Health (ISBOH). The power generated by medical institutions is matched only by government itself and religion and during this period, the medical institution was actively involved in helping to frame issues in collective action with these institutions. Medicine played a hegemonic role in defining and in the amount of flexibility and rigidity accorded the terms "healthy" and "unhealthy." What the ISBOH and its members said possessed a great deal of resonance in the public. Their words had an experiential commensurability since they coincided with the values that had meaning in the lives of their patients.[392]

Dr. Hurty was the "father" of what would become known as the field of "public health" in Indiana. He was one of the more active figures that the *Star* would report

---

390 *Ibid.*

391 Paul Pierson argues that, to look at precipitating actors, without looking at large structural changes, one can mistakenly attribute causality. (Paul Pierson, "The Study of Policy Development, 42. Note 568.) . As he writes:

> They are particularly likely to miss the role of many "sociological" variables, like demography, literacy, or technology. Their explanations may forcus on triggering or precipitating actors rather than more fundamental structural causes. It can get worse. By truncating an analysis of process unfolding over an extended period of time, analysts can easily end up inverting causal relationships.

(*Ibid.*) My work sidesteps this criticism since I try to evaluate institutional changes in addition to the agents involved in the institutions. I also do not claim to prove causation *per se* but rather, important factors in the development of phenomenon.

392 Please see, Robert D. Benford and David A. Snow, *Framing Processes and Social Movements*, 618–622. Salience and experiential commensurability are the criteria the authors use for exploring how successful framing is is social movements.

on throughout the legislative session.[393] For example, on 9 January 1907, the *Star* reported that, at the annual convention of the Tristate Medical Association, at the "earnest" request of Dr. Hurty, the group had endorsed the proposal for a State hospital to treat consumption (tuberculosis).[394]

One legitimating activity of the ISBOH was the collection of facts and figures. It had compiled figures on the nature and spread of epidemics beginning in 1900. In 1907, they published statistics which showed a "remarkable falling off" of epidemics. In 1900, the number of people affected by typhoid fever was 1,329, diphtheria 687 and scarlet fever, 141. By 1906 those numbers had dipped to 846, 341 and 97 respectively.[395] Other public health measures that now seem obvious in hindsight were proposed during the session. The so-called Pearson Bill gave the State Board of Health the power to revoke a physician's license should he not comply, along with householders and others, to report deaths, births, infectious diseases and other information. Senator Pearson's bill also gave the ISBOH – and Hurty – the ability to discharge any local health officer who refused to make proper reports. Even though the Senate thought the bill "too drastic", since it might discharge some citizen who did not know the difference between "infectious" and "contagious" diseases, it was passed, 26 to 19.[396]

Dr. Henry C. Sharp was employed as a physician at the Indiana Reformatory in Jeffersonville. As "early as 1899" he had "begun experimenting with the sterilization of prisoners" but "on a voluntary basis" and extra-judicial basis.[397] I will examine his role in detail below.

Another institutional force was the Indiana Board of State Charities (IBOSC). It secretary was Amos W. Butler, who, on 1 May, reported that all of the State hospitals for the insane were full or overcrowded as was the School for the Feeble-Minded Youth and School for the Deaf. The Reformatory, the State Prison and the Sailors' Home were overcrowded as well. The Epileptic Village in Newcastle would be ready soon and new buildings at the Reformatory and the Feeble-Minded School would decrease overcrowding. The IBOSC also criticized the Marion County Jail. It normally had a capacity of 35. At their last visit, the Jail had 93 inmates, including 35 in the basement that had space and equipment for only 10.[398] While Butler was concerned about this turn

---

393 "Favor State Hospital. Would Fight White Plague. Northern Tristate Medical Association Favors Dr. Hurty's Plan to Care for Tuberculosis Patients and Fight Spread of the Disease." *Indianapolis Star*, January 9, 1907, 8.

394 *Ibid.*

395 *Indianapolis Sunday Star*, February 3, 1907, 1.

396 *Indianapolis Morning Star*, February 16, 1907, 4.

397 Phillips, *Indiana in Transition*, 492. Cited by Gugliotta, Footnote 416 at p. 376, where we also learn that Dr. A.J. Oschner, chief surgeon at St. Mary's Hospital in Chicago and who was later a professor of clinical surgery at the University of Illinois at Chicago, began performing vasectomies in 1887, two years before Sharp. The records from the reformatory that included Sharp's files were burned in a fire.

398 *Indianapolis News*, May 1, 1907, 4.

of events, his solution was to support the work of Dr. Sharp. At a meeting of township trustees in either December, 1906 or January 1907, Butler said that "in time the State would enact legislation to regulate the birth of children in families of the dependent poor and stated also that method was now in use in the penal institutions of the State by which inmates were deprived of the power of reproduction."[399] Here we can see the institutional force of the IBOSC as represented by Butler already advocating for the sterilization law which would become a reality in a mere three months.

Oscar McCullough was leader of the Plymouth Congregational Church in Indianapolis. He also acted as a liaison with business leaders and, twenty-seven years before the legislation in question was passed, founded the Indianapolis Charity Organization Society (ICOS).[400] McCullough represents the socio-religious bridge where religious leaders advocated for legislation that they believed would advance Christian ideals and these ideals were often subsumed into the idea of progress based on positive eugenic ideas. Although a religious leader, McCullough had written a book entitled *Tribe of Ishmael: A Study in Social Degradation* in 1881.[401] He had used records from a group of families in the Indianapolis area to prove that features of degradation were inherited.[402]

McCullough and his ICOS regularly disseminated "healthy-living information." For example, the *Star* noted a lecture by one Dr. U.G. Weatherly, Professor of Economics and Social Science at Indiana University, entitled "The Physical Basis of Society." The lecture was produced under the auspices of the ICOS as part of a two-month long lecture series on social problems. Weatherly himself took a middle ground on the "correct" size of families saying that he was not in agreement with either side of the issue. He did say that "neither the advocates of excessively large families nor those of families so small as to lead to race suicide…."[403]

The varied resources that were available to McCullough, as well as the other three men, were far-reaching. For example, Linton A. Cox – also a member of the CMHVS – was active on welfare issues in the 1907 legislative session from its beginning. On 17 January he proposed legislation on behalf of the Indianapolis Charity Organization Society making abandonment or neglect of a child a criminal felony.[404] The *Star* report gives an indication of the ICOSI's motivation and lobbying ability saying that it "confronts many pitiable cases in which children have been deserted by parents

399 *Indianapolis Star*, (Indianapolis), January 9, 1907, 8.

400 Ruth Hutchinson Crocker, "Making Charities Modern: Business and the Reform of Charities in Indianapolis, 1879–1930" in *Business and Economic History, Second Series*, Vol. 12, (1983), 161.

401 Oscar McCullough, *Tribe of Ishmael: A Study of Social Degradation* (Indianapolis, 1881).

402 Please see, http://www.hmdb.org/marker.asp?marker=1829, accessed May 15, 2009.

403 "Advocates Small Families. Dr. Weatherly Delivers First of a Series of Lectures." *Indianapolis Star*, January 15, 1907, 10.

404 "To Protect Children Strikes At Salaries. Child Desertion A Felony. Through Senator Cox Indianapolis Charity Organization Introduces Stringent Measures." *Indianapolis Star*, January 17, 1907, 4.

and it will work hard for the passage of the bill."[405] The proposed bill provided for imprisonment in either the State Prison or Reformatory for a term of 1 to 3 years or in the county jail or workhouse for no less than 3 months and nor more than 1 year of either or both parents.[406]

In 1907, these four men, and the institutional structures and power that they represented, demonstrate the intersection of agents from strong organizational structures in Indiana, all with numerous resources. Their schemas, or social rules and procedures, were transposable across a "wide range of circumstances" that were not entirely predictable "outside of the context in which they are initially learned."[407] When their schemas were set in motion, they produced "unpredictable qualities and quantities of resources."[408]

4.2 Legislative Discourses: Legislating against Sin

As I have previously noted, between 1890 and 1930, Indiana shifted from a rural-based society to an industrialized state. This shift, however, was **not** reflected in the Legislature, which remained a "bastion" of rural interests.[409] As Walsh points out, "partisan politics, not population shifts, dictated apportionments with rural ascendancy the one constant whether Democrats and Republicans did the dictating."[410] As a result, "appeals to such old-fashioned virtues as hard work, clean living, and tem-

405 *Ibid.*

406 We are told of at least some of the elements of the crime, i.e. the child in question must be less than 16 and the parent must be able to care for the child – but not doing so. If the convicted parent gave a "satisfactory bond" that the child would be cared for, the sentence could be suspended. As today, the "suspended" sentence was suspended only as long as the terms of the suspension were complied with. Should the convicted parent fail to meet the terms, s/he would then be in the same position as before the suspension, i.e. facing imprisonment, fines, etc.

407 Sewell, *Logics*, 140–41.

408 *Ibid.*

409 Walsh, *Centennial History*, 290.

410 Reapportionment of the state into House and Senate districts was a more or less continuous concern of the legislature between, 1816 and 1921 with only a short break for the Civil War. House and Senate Districts were re-mapped in 1821, 1823, 1826, 1829, 1831, 1834, 1836, 1841, 1846, 1851, 1857, 1867, 1872, 1879, 1885, 1891, 1893, 1897, 1905, 1915, 1921, 1963, 1965,1972 (Appendix B, Walsh). Federal Congressional Districts were redrawn in 1822, 1824, 1833, 1843, 1852, 1867, 1872, 1879, 1885, 1891, 1895, 1901, 1911, 1931, 1941, 1965, 1968 and 1972 (Appendix C, Walsh). Re-mapping was initially done to accommodate the push westward but later to accommodate political goals of whichever party was in power. In 1962, in the United States Supreme Court case of Baker v. Carr, 369 US 186 (1962), 82 SCt 691, 7 LEd2d 663, the Supreme Court required that the "one man, one vote" principle meant that each person's vote had to be equally weighted. This took into account growing urban populations and numerous states underwent legislative reapportionment.

perance dominated legislative deliberations."[411] Many types of leisure activity were open for review by the General Assembly including horse racing, baseball – especially if played on the Sunday – boxing, and theatrical performances. Keeping the Sabbath holy, art free of any "obscenity" and Indiana's sober were some of the major concerns of the legislators. In other words, it became a "matter of habit" to "legislate against sin."[412]

Harold Feighter was a reporter for the *Indianapolis News* and covered every General Assembly about 14 years after the sterilization law was passed – from 1921 to 1933. During that time, he noted that what dominated state government was the "Ku Klux Klan, the Anti-Saloon League, and the Horse Thief Detection Association" and that each had a "divine mission."[413] These missions were to

> purify politics, ...stop drinking by means of force and fear of damnation, and...to safeguard chastity in lovers' lanes. Collectively, these forces of righteousness swallowed the Republican Party and caponized [castrated] the Democrats.[414]

As the Republicans were in a majority in the legislature during this period, they – according to Feighter – could be held responsible for the governmental "excesses" imposed by attempts at social purification.[415] Although Freighter describes a period after the sterilization law was passed, his remarks would also seem to apply to 1907, especially in light of the social history outlined below.

On 15 January 1907, the Editor of the *Indianapolis Star* wrote about "Temperance Legislation", one of Governor Hanley's favorite subjects. Buried in his editorial page we find a reference to "temperance laws that are effective" standing in direct opposition to those that do not work. For effective temperance laws, he turns to Norway. He wrote:

> Norway, for example, has in a few years been changed from a nation of drunkards to a nation of sober people by simple law. Under it a drunken man is imprisoned until sober. He is then cleaned up. If his clothing is torn it is mended or he is furnished with new clothing. He is then required to tell where he got his last drink, and is kept in prison until he does tell. The person who sold that drink is then required to pay all expense of incarceration and rehabilitation together with any damage done by the drunken man.[416]

411 *Ibid.*

412 *Ibid.*, 306.

413 Walsh, *Centennial History*, 309. The "Horse Thief Detective Association" is a reference to a detective agency closely linked to the Klu Klux Klan.

414 *Ibid.*

415 *Ibid.*

416 *Indianapolis Star*, January 15, 1907, 8.

This indicates that Indiana was indeed aware of the wider world and that the Editor was not averse to using the conduct of other nations as an argument for change. It also supports the practice, seen in legislation in general, of referring to laws in other countries that seem to support the specific law being discussed.[417] Whatever else changed in Indiana and Norway between 1907 and 1934, the one constant that remained was that at both times and in both countries, "liquor" was the subject of a social movement that was framed in terms of sin and moral weakness.[418]

In addition to doctors, "well dressed men" who looked familiar and came to Indianapolis every time the Assembly met were also the first to appear in the capital. These men, who "like to drop in and pick up a little perfumery money" were lobbyists, "Hessians of the third House", whom reporter Blodgett described as being "without influence, but with a nerve as strong as corrosive sublimate, and an ability to 'cop the dough' under any and all circumstances."[419] Unethical, these men did not care where the money came from, as long as they were paid, according to Blodgett.

The session began with a roll call after which Rep. Hanna of Hendricks County submitted the name of Rep. Emmett F. Branch, Republican from Morgan County, for nomination as Speaker of the House. Branch's opponent was Rep. Thomas J. Honan of Jackson County, nominated by Rep. Behymer of Madison County. By a vote of 53–47, Rep. Branch was declared the Speaker-elect, thus having a "life and death power over bills."[420] In total, this regular session lasted from 10 January 1907 to 11 March 1907 (61 days) and, in addition, a special session was called, lasting from 18–30 September 1907 (13 days).

At 2:00 P.M., Governor Hanley knocked on the doors of the House and was escorted to the podium by four selected men. Hanley then proceeded to give his state of the State address, which he began by noting, "Monetary conditions are at their best."[421] He continued, saying:

> Labor, agriculture, manufacturing, mining and commerce have touched and passed high tide and the ebb is not yet begun... During the last year there was no failure of any financial institution within the State. Taken all in all, conditions are indeed unusual. They present a problem

---

417 Later in 1934, Norwegian Parliament Representative Bjørnson mentions the laws of Germany as examples of effective and useful legislation.

418 It would not be until the advent of Alcoholics Anonymous that alcoholism would be framed as a health issue and not a moral issue.

419 "Whiffs from the Legislative Spice Box." *Indianapolis News*, January 8, 1907, 4. Corrosive sublimate is a reference to acid.

420 *Ibid.*, 373. This power was not seriously challenged until sometime after 1929. The conflict over Branch's election was intense.

421 *Journal of the House of Representatives of the State of Indiana, Sixty-Fifth Session of the General Assembly, Commencing January 11, 1907, Regular Session,* Vol. I (Indianapolis: Wm. B. Burford, Contractor for State Printing and Binding, 1907), 17.

> unlike that which usually confronts state legislatures... The challenge is not "Can we create?" but "Can we administer?"[422]

When Hanley reached the subject of Indiana's state charitable institutions, he specifically mentioned that, although they were run in an efficient and economical manner, that there was room for improvement. His remarks about the State Prison system began with the fact that the labor contracts of Prison employees were due to expire in 1910. Hanley did not mention anything regarding the medical facilities of the State Prison, or the need for the sterilization of "confirmed criminals, idiots, imbeciles, and rapists."[423]

In 1907, tuberculosis, referred to as the "white plague", was a continuing medical problem in the United States and the state of Indiana. When addressing this issue in his speech, Hanley referred to a resolution passed on March 5, 1905 at the 64th General Session, which authorized a commission of 5 persons, 2 Representatives, 2 Senators and one "a practicing physician of prominence in the State", to investigate the establishment of a TB Hospital in Indiana.[424] While this might be interesting information *per se*, the point of its inclusion here is that there was no such equivalent committee formed with regard to the "medical" issue of sterilization at the state prison. Why was tuberculosis a scientific issue worthy of study and sterilization not? I would suggest that tuberculosis affected the bodies of normal citizens – both male and female – some of whom were unable to care for their medical needs and who needed to be separated from the community at large. The bodies of criminals, on the other hand, were in another category, a "degenerate" category. The two categories of "normal" and "degenerate" did not allow the normal citizen to see that criminality could attach itself to his or her family through any number of a series of events, or, if it had, this was a matter kept secret. Therefore, since criminality was seen as only a socially unacceptable category, and not as a medical issue, there was no interest in an investigation by an expert committee.

At the conclusion of his speech, Hanley used a phrase, which after a century, has now taken on a life of its own. He said:

> Special interests, individual and corporate, are wont to exercise undue influence upon all legislation relating to any matter of concern to them. They fill legislative chambers and the approaches thereto...Their attitude [is expressed] with exactness in the couplet, Whose bread I eat,
> His song I sing.
> Such persons are not safe counselors. They are the enemies of the people's interests. Their very presence is inimical to the public welfare. **Human rights** – the rights of the individual citizen, or the **rights of [the] body of the people** – are not safe where legislation can be procured or def-

422 *Ibid.*

423 Statute, *Chapter 215 of the Laws of Indiana*. Please see below for entire text.

424 *Journal of the House of Representatives*, 65.

> eated or government administered through the corrupt and demoralizing influence of the paid [acting for] organized wealth and greed.[425]

Human rights were obviously important enough to be included as rhetorical ideology in this speech and it is especially ironic that Hanley should make mention of it in the very same sentence as the concept of the body politic. This serves to underscore the change in norms over time as well as the idea that the individual body could be abstracted from the corporate body by virtue of a number of classifications.[426]

An individual body within the "body of people" was a very "porous" category at this time, as evidenced by the fact that the law could be extended across a wide spectrum of bodies in a rather short period of time. The "feeble-minded" had already been a legislated category in 1901 when women, ages 16–45, who were "unsupervised" could be made legal wards of the state in order to prevent them from reproducing.[427] And, on 5 March 1905, Governor Hanley approved a law prohibiting "imbeciles, epileptics and those of unsound minds" from obtaining a marriage license.[428] The law was then further extended to criminals who were degenerate.

The 1907 Indiana sterilization bill was not the first attempt to pass such a law in the state of Indiana or indeed, within the United States proper. Angela Gugliotta writes that two years earlier in 1905 under the Republican administration of Governor Winfield Taylor Durbin (s. 1901–1905), a sterilization bill in Indiana had been introduced but "died in committee."[429] Nonetheless, the 1907 Indiana sterilization bill began life – again – as House Bill No. 364.[430] The sole sponsor of the bill was Rep. Dr.

425 *Journal of the House of Representatives*, 68 (Emphasis mine.)

426 *Indianapolis Star*, January 25, 1907, 3.

427 Laws of Indiana, 1901, 156–59.

428 Laws of Indiana, 1905, 215–16.

429 Gugliotta, Sharp and His Little Knife, p. 386–87. Note 330. This was after Pennsylvania Governor Samuel W. Pennypacker (1903–1907) vetoed Pennsylvania Senate Bill No. 35 "An Act for the prevention of idiocy" and sent it back to the legislature saying, tongue-in-cheek, that:

> If idiocy could be prevented by an act of assembly, we may be quite sure that such an act would have long been passed and approved in this state, and that such laws would have been enacted in all civilized countries.

(Tony Platt, "The Frightening Agenda of the American Eugenics Movement" http://hnn.us/articles/1551.html, last accessed 15 March 2006. Within seven years, from 1907 to 1914, twelve states had passed sterilization laws in one form or another.

430 The procedure in a bi-camarel legislature, such as that of Indiana at this time, was similar to today's practice of creating law. Today, under the Constitution of Indiana, a bill may be introduced in either the House or the Senate of the General Assembly and may become "engrossed" (approved) there. The approval process includes a "first reading" in the chamber where it was introduced whereupon it may be sent to the appropriate committee to review. If it is not sent to a committee, the bill "dies." The committee review process may include public hearings. If the committee schedules no hearings, the bill again dies. A vote is taken after the committee review hearing and, if it receives a

Horace D. Read.[431] Read introduced the bill 17 days after the session began, and it had its first reading on 27 January 1907.[432]

After the first reading, the bill was sent to the House Committee on Medicine, Health and Vital Statistics When finally enacted into law the bill read as follows:

> **AN ACT** to prevent the procreation of confirmed criminals, idiots, imbeciles and rapists: Providing that superintendents or boards of managers of institutions where such persons are confined shall have the authority and are empowered to appoint a committee of experts. Consisting of two physicians, to examine into the mental condition of such inmates. WHEREAS, heredity plays a most important part in the transmission of crime, idiocy, and imbecility:
> **THEREFORE, BE IT ENACTED BY THE GENERAL ASSEMBLY OF THE STATE OF INDIANA,** that on and after the passage of this act it shall be compulsory for each and every institution in the state, entrusted with the care of confirmed criminals, idiots, rapists and imbeciles, to appoint upon its staff, in addition to the regular institutional physician, two (2) skilled surgeons of recognized ability, whose duty it shall be, in conjunction with the chief physician and board of experts and the board of managers. If in the judgment of this committee of experts procreation is inad-

simple majority, it is returned to the chamber where it came from where it receives a "second reading." If it does not receive a second reading, the bill again dies. If it does have a second reading, amendments may be proposed and can be added by a simple majority vote. The full chamber then votes on the bill and with the approval of a simple majority it advances to a "third reading." If it does not receive a third reading, it may again die. After a third reading, a vote is taken on amendments where, unlike after the second reading, a 2/3 majority is required for passage of the amendments. If the amendments are approved at this point, it is sent to the entire chamber where a simple majority will ensure that the vote then is sent to the other chamber. If that chamber fails or refuses to act on the bill, it again dies.

In the second chamber the same process as occurred in the first chamber is repeated, with the same possibilities of failure. If the other chamber approves the bill, it is sent to the chamber of origin where that body reviews the amendments, if any, that the other chamber has made. The chamber of origin may then do nothing, whereupon the bill dies, it may approve the amendment made or it may send the bill to the Governor for her signature. If the chamber of origin does not approve the amendments made in the other chamber, the bill is referred to a "conference committee." This committee is composed of two members from both major political parties and the four attempt to reconcile problems; if this cannot be done, the bill dies. If an agreement is reached, the bill is returned to both chambers where it must be approved before finally being sent to the Governor for signature. The bill does not automatically become law however, as the Governor may veto it, sign it into law or simply not sign it and allow it to become law. If the Governor vetoes the bill it goes back to both chambers and, in order to "over-ride" the Governors veto, a simple majority of at least 26 Senators and 51 House members must vote for the bill. Please see http://www.state.in.us/statehouse/tour/Billtolaw.pdf, accessed 10 March 10, 2007.

431 Read was a Joint Representative from the two counties of Hamilton and Tipton. The other representative from Hamilton County was Henry M. Caylor and there was no other representative from Tipton County. The issue of "Joint Representatives" was addressed by the United States Supreme Court in the reapportionment case of Baker v. Carr, 369 U.S. 186 (1962), mentioned above in fn. 587.

432 *Journal of the House of Representatives*, State of Indiana, during the Sixty-Fifth Session General Assembly, Commencing Thursday, January 11, 1907, Regular Session, Volume II (Wm. B. Burford: Contractor for State Printing and Binding, 1907), 302, 367.

> visable, and there is no probability of improvement of the mental and physical condition of the inmate, it shall be lawful for the surgeons to perform such operation for the prevention of procreation as shall be decided safest and most effective. But this operation shall not be performed except in cases that have been pronounced unimproveable. Provided that in no case the consultation fee be more than three dollars to each expert, to be paid out of the funds appropriated for the maintenance of such institution.[433]

The assumptions in this legislation are numerous and, at this point, I will only mention the scientific assumption, i.e. that "heredity plays a most important part in the transmission of crime, idiocy, and imbecility" and that beneficial science will correct the social situation.[434] Most members of the legislature perceived this as a correct scientific statement given how they voted.

Problems with statutory drafting were and are fairly obvious. Does the adjective "confirmed" relate only to criminals or also to the other 3 categories. Also, how is "confirmed" defined and what is the standard of proof for determining "confirmed"? Appellate arguments regarding construction have been made, and won, with these types of questions.

At the end of any legislative session, some policy measures were lost in rush to end the session. In 1923, the *Indianapolis Star* finally complained that the "good measures are lost in the final scramble and occasionally vicious legislation slips through."[435] And this was also true in 1907. The sterilization law was passed on 6 March, only

433 Document URL: http://www.kobescent.com/eugenics/statute.html accessed 3 December 3, 2007.

434 During the first week of March, the Senate passed the sterilization bill into law. The *Star* reported on the bill in its headline as a "modern operation" that had already been employed at the State Reformatory thus legitimating it as "modern", i.e. a means to "progress" and as a *fait accompli* to a procedure already well in place. (*Indianapolis Star*, 7 March 1907, p. 10. "Surgeons to Deal With Criminals. Bill Passes the Senate Authorizing Modern Operations to be Performed. Tried at the Reformatory. Supt. Whittaker Urged Enactment of Such a Law.") Rep. Read's House bill had passed the Senate on 6 March "with few votes being recorded against it." Read's personal interest in the subject was reported to have originated in materials that were given to him by Superintendent William H. Whittaker of the Indianan Reformatory, whom we have encountered above, and where Dr. H. Sharp was already performing extra-judicial vasectomies; these were reportedly performed only upon request. Both Whittaker and Sharp had been "very active in urging upon the members of the Legislature the importance of passing the bill." Angela Gugliotta writes that Whittaker actually was the author of the language in Read's proposed bill. (Gugliotta, Sharp and His Little Knife, 387. Note 330.)

435 Walsh, *Centennial History*, p. 383–384. Between 1900 and 1930 state spending in Indiana doubled and spending at the local level quadrupled. This meant that property taxes in 1930 were 7 times higher than in 1900. Since property valuations could not keep pace with actual spending, nearly every legislative session voted to raise taxes. Inheritance taxes, vessel tonnage taxes, gasoline taxes and the like were also passed since property taxes were not able to generate an adequate tax base. Budget items were generally the last order of business on the last day of the session and "frequently did not pass before the last minutes on the last day" thus requiring legislators to come back in the Fall for a special session. Walsh at 388–389.

5 days before the legislature ended in its mad dash to *sine die*.[436] Also, in 1907, the "number and title of bills bearing a lawmaker's name" determined the continuation of a political career. Aside from the legislator himself, constituents also demanded certain legislation, "as a matter of courtesy." Thirdly, fraternal or professional organization such as the Freemasons or the state Medical Association lobbied for legislation. Private interests and corporations who hired professional lobbyists joined these groups as did state administrative officers and committees or commissions who were under the authority of the state legislature.[437] In virtually every session a bill was considered that "forbade lobbyists to communicate with members on the floor" but, such resolutions were "never effective, however, as the press was filled with accounts of lobbyists jamming the floors of both houses during every session."[438] All these factors impacted the atmosphere in which this law was passed.

These factors have added significance since all that we have in print of the proceedings of the Legislature is in Volume II of the Indiana *House Journal* where one can read the formal compiled history of Bill 364.[439] After being "Read first time" and then "referred to Committee on Medicine, Health and Vital Statistics", it was next "Withdrawn" but then "Reported back favorably."[440] Somewhat further on in the same Journal we read, "By unanimous consent House bill No. 364 was withdrawn from the files."[441] Finally, we read that Rep. Read submitted the report of Medicine, Health and Vital Statistics as a recommendation that the bill be passed.[442] The bill was then read for the second time in the House and was ordered to be engrossed (approved).[443] It was read a third time in the House and then passed by a majority vote of 59–22. It was then referred to the Senate and passed by a majority vote of 28–16. Later House Bill

436 "Sine die" is a Latin phrase, literally meaning "without a day", i.e. without a day to return to the work of the legislature.

437 Walsh, *Centennial History*, 384.

438 *Ibid.*, 426.

439 Private e-mail correspondence with Indiana state librarians. Unlike today, no transcriptions of legislative sessions or of individual committee meetings were made.

440 *Journal of the House of Representatives, State of Indiana, during the Sixty-Fifth Session General Assembly*, Commencing Thursday, January 11, 1907, Regular Session, Volume II (Wm. B. Burford: Contractor for State Printing and Binding, 1907), 302, 367. The Journal digest of the bill on page 302 reads as follows:
Read first time...367, Referred to Committee on Medicine, Health and Vital Statistics...367, Withdrawn...437, Reported back favorably...613, Read second time...718, Engrossed...729, Read third time...1341, Passed the House...1341, Referred to the Senate...1343, Returned from the Senate...2226, Enrolled...2234, Signed by Speaker...2239, Signed by Governor...2415. I have not been able to determine why it was "Withdrawn" and then inexplicably "Reported back favorably." I do know that there was a shouting match one night during a recess of a meeting of the CMHVS.

441 *Ibid.*, 437.

442 *Ibid.*, 612–613. The Indiana State Library, Legislative Section, confirms by personal communication that there are no extant notes from the meeting/s of the Committee.

443 *Ibid.*, 718, 729.

No. 364 was "enrolled", indicating that the Senate had approved it and sent it back to the House.[444] Hanley's handpicked Speaker of the House, Rep. Branch, then signed the bill. [445] On 9 March 1907, Bill 364 was signed by Governor Hanley and was known as Chapter 215, Indiana State Laws.[446]

4.3 Reactions to the Sterilization Law

> Sharp's friend [Dr. G. Henri] Bogart attributed opposition [to the new law] to the equation of sterilization with castration, and to the lawyer's "worship of precedent."
>
> Angela Gugliotta[447]

The sterilization operation itself was reported as bringing "neither mental nor physical pain." Superintendent Whittaker was of the opinion that men with 10 or 12 years of experience in the "handling of criminals...can see the necessity of something being done along this line." This article from the *Star* also gives one of the longer justifications from Dr. Sharp himself.

> Heredity is but one of the many causes of degeneracy, and while refined parents may beget degenerate children I make the statement without fear of successful contradiction that no confirmed criminal or other degenerate ever begot a normal child; and for this reason I enter the plea for society in general and for the unborn child in particular that this will be enacted into a law.[448]

Sharp makes an appeal to the duty not to be born, the exact opposite of arguments seen later in Case Two for "protection" for the "unborn child."

Sharp's understanding of genetics was, in hindsight, wrong. In addition, his initial motivation for this policy that was introduced at a Boys' Reformatory and not an adult penal institution was to deal with the "unrefined" habit of masturbation.[449] We do know that Sharp's very first vasectomy was performed on a 19-year-old man on 11 October 1899. The man was described as being "of criminal heritage", "very dull", "unable to concentrate" and who had "masturbated since age twelve."[450] The man was said to attribute his mental condition "to excessive masturbation" and vol-

---

444 *Ibid.*, 2234.

445 *Ibid.*, 2239.

446 *Ibid.*, 85. In the Index of the Journal of the 1906 Legislature the law itself is not indexed with reference to Medicine or Health or Sterilization. Instead, it is indexed under Criminal Institutions. The editor of the *Star* made no comment on the passage of the bill in his editorial page on the 7th of March.

447 Gugliotta, *Sharp with His Little Knife*, 389. Note 330.

448 *Indianapolis Star*, March 7, 1907, 10.

449 Gugliotta, *Sharp and His Little Knife*, 380. Note 330.

450 *Ibid.*

untarily came to Sharp to ask for help with his problem. Sixty days after the vasectomy, the man had gained weight but his erections were as "vigorous" as ever and he claimed that Sharp had "deceived" him. One year later, however, the man's "mental condition had greatly improved" and he had ceased to masturbate through force of will even though the desire was "as great as ever."[451]

In January, before the legislature began, the *Star* had printed a letter-to-the-editor signed by a Mr. Edward Miller of Ft. Wayne, Indiana, which the Editor entitled "Masculine Instinct Outraged."[452] Here, we have the **only** mention in a Letter-to-the-Editor format of the sterilization law that would eventually be passed. Horace Read's bill itself had its first reading on 27 January 1907, 18 days after Miller's letter. This would indicate that Miller had been alerted in some fashion to Read's intention to propose the bill and was interested enough to write a letter well in advance of the bill's actual proposal. And in fact, in his letter, Miller tells us how he was informed. He was in attendance "a few weeks ago" at a meeting of township trustees, presumably in Fort Wayne, when Dr. Amos Butler had supported the future legislation.[453]

Miller questioned the entire scheme saying that the "unsexing" of people "because of inability to earn a living, is suggesting something that is barbarous, uncivilized and a violation of the God-given law to 'increase and multiply'." Miller did not spare words in attacking this idea. The idea that because someone is poor, that person should be deprived of the ability to have children was anathema especially "with the rich keeping dogs and fondling them in place of children….." When it came to the idea of prisoners becoming "unsexed", Miller became more analytical and asked:

> I would like to know where in the statutes of the [state of] Indiana can be found the authority to do such a thing and even if such a statute was on the law books in Indiana I fail to see where the justice would come in, because the criminal tendency in some form or another runs through every member of the human family, and the fact that men are in the penitentiary does not argue that worse men are not on the outside who are escaping the punishment.[454]

Miller wrote that while eunuchs were "plentiful" in "oriental lands", when "Mr. Butler and his board" turned prisoners into eunuchs and women into "I don't know what to call them", this would not benefit the State in the least. Miller's last impassioned sentence bears repeating:

> Lastly, no natural right exists for doing such a thing and if I were convicted of a crime and sent to Michigan City and during my stay there found that on some morning on waking up out of a sleep, my procreative powers were gone by official act of the surgeon, there would be something

451 *Ibid.*
452 *Indianapolis Star*, January 9, 1907, 8.
453 *Ibid.*
454 *Ibid.*

> doing when I got out and some funerals would take place in advance of the schedule time set by the Creator.[455]

What is interesting is that Miller was the only voice in the pages of the major Indiana newspapers who questioned the impending law. His concerns are based in both legal authority and in a concept of justice, often seen in jurisprudential works under the theme of "practical reason." But practical reason would not be enough to prohibit the law from being passed.

We can conclude that Butler and the IBOSC had actual knowledge of the work of Dr. Harry Sharp in Jeffersonville and that policy entrepreneurs[456] such as Butler, McCulough, and Hurty plus their institutions endorsed Sharp's work. Indeed, between 1899 and 1907, Harry Sharp had already performed approximately 456 vasectomies at the Indiana Reformatory and information regarding this was freely circulating in both medical and governmental institutions.[457] Sharp had presented his work at the Mississippi Valley Medical Association already in 1901 and this account had been later published in the New York Medical Journal in 1902.[458] In 1907, Dr. Sharp also addressed the National Prison Association concerning his work and was elected President of that group on the day after his speech.[459]

Generally the end of a legislative session was unpredictable. It was hectic and dangerous for pending bills and the amount of disorder varied. *Sine die* in 1907 saw members of the House throwing books and papers in the air.[460] Both Dr. Hurty and Dr. Butler were pleased with the legislature. Hurty announced that "every important measure" that the State Board of Health had supported had passed into law.[461] The sterilization law, however, was obviously of small moment to the editor of the *Star* as he did not include it in a list of Indiana's new laws, although the use of the word "among" in the headline did indicate the list was not exhaustive. He did include information on new laws dealing with such subjects as marriage between first cousins, the prevention of the sale of diseased horses and mules, open season on squirrels, and the wages of Superior and Circuit Court Judges. The Session also passed laws on child abandonment, underage females in wine rooms, police pension funds, brakes on locomotives, increased penalties for banks that accept deposits knowing the bank is insolvent, establishing a Probate Court in Marion County, compelling doctors and

---

455 *Ibid.*

456 Please see, Nancy C. Roberts and Paula J.King, "Policy Entrepreneurs: Their Activity Structure and Function in the Policy Process" in *Journal of Public Administration Research and Theory*, 1 (1991), 147–57.

457 Gugliotta, *Sharp and his Little Knife*, 380. Note 330.

458 *Ibid.*

459 *Ibid.*

460 *Indianapolis Morning Star*, March 12, 1907, 4.

461 *Indianapolis News*, March 12, 1907, 2.

health officers to make reports to the State Board of Health, and the "blind tiger" law.[462] Amos Butler also noted that a full 36 bills that were related to charities passed both houses and he expected the Governor to sign at least "most" of them.[463]

In March 1907, two days after the legislative session ended, the *Star's* Editor found time to address the sterilization law. His arguments in favor of the bill were structured around two ideas. The first was that some people are so "abnormally constituted" that they take to crime like "the duckling takes to water or the skylark cleaves the blue vault of heaven."[464] There was something so "radically wrong" with them that it would have been better if they "had...never been born." The second idea, which can be called the "farmer's practical knowledge" is that, in the animal world, "we know how to deal with this problem."[465] By not paying careful attention to breeding in humans, the editor said:

> we have shirked a duty to the unborn degenerate who is called into the world only to be destroyed, soul and body, by the inherited forces of evil that push him on to crime and ruin.[466]

Criminals were not the only focus of the legislation, however. The law applied to "confirmed criminals, idiots, imbeciles and rape fiends." The Editor wrote that the surgeons who would do the operations at the Indiana Reformatory were said to be "of the highest standing." Granted, it was an "experiment" that the "scientific men and criminologists" around the world would watch with interest, but the effort had to be made. And, if the work were "approved by experience" then it would solve the problem of the "multitudes of men and women, foreordained to almost certain physical, social and moral ruin." This type of reductionist thinking predominated the analyses we find at this specific time.

It is also interesting to read the notion that there is a duty to the "unborn degenerate." This can be contrasted with the "fetus as a person" ideograph one reads in today's press. In 1907 this Editor could write of a right not to be born if the birth was of a "degenerate" person, whereas a century later, one could read of a duty to give birth no matter what the condition of the fetus is, because it was a "person." Human rights that accrue to the "personhood" of the fetus, based on the likely future that child might have, have, within a one hundred year period, been successfully exchanged from the duty not to have a particular type of child[467], to the right of the fetus to be

---

462 "Among Indiana's New Laws." *Indianapolis Morning Star*, March 12, 1907, 8. The "blind tiger" bill is a reference to the regulation of alcohol.

463 *Indianapolis News*, March 12, 1907, 4.

464 "Crime at its Source."*Indianapolis Morning Star*, 1March 13, 1907, 8.

465 As we shall see in the second half of this Case, this same approach was used in the Norwegian debates.

466 Gugliotta, *Sharp and his Little Knife*, 380. Note 330.

467 This is as defined by the culture and society of the time.

born, no matter what its likely circumstances. In other words, within a 100-year span, considerations of what type of future the child might have been semiotic ally subtracted from the "personhood" of the fetus.

Passage of Chapter 215 into law was met over the ensuing years with several challenges from several quarters. Indeed, questions as to the constitutionality of the measure appeared immediately after Sharp had given his talk supporting the measure at the National Prison Association in early 1907. A panel assembled after his talk to discuss Indiana's sterilization law. The panel was composed of Dr. Sharp, Superintendent Whittaker, Cuban military officer and leper colony superintendent General Garcia, Indiana Attorney General James Bingham, Ohio State Reformatory Manager H.F. Coates, Representative Dr. Read and Chicago Judge Henry V. Freeman.[468] Of this group, comments by Bingham and Freeman are the most interesting. Freeman was a justice of the Branch Appellate Court for the first district of Illinois in Chicago and also a lecturer on "legal ethics and medical jurisprudence" at the University of Chicago.[469] Bingham "worried about 'the unsoundness of the principle of emasculating a perfectly sane person unless it is imposed as part of the penalty.'"[470] However, he did not have a problem with the right to do the operation as a measure to "relieve disease."[471]

As Gugliotta notes, the panel itself reflected a rivalry between the medical and legal profession over the issue of sterilization. It also reflected the "broader Progressive Era conflict between the courts and elected officials on the one hand and legislatively established panels of experts on the other."[472] Whittaker weighed in on the debate with the opinion that it was the perspective of the medical doctor and not the government or courts or citizenry which should prevail. Garcia worried that sexual unions of the defective only created more defective children who would then become dependent on the state. Coates related his experience with a potential parolee who could not help himself from committing sodomy. The assembled men were concerned about various aspects of crime control, more effective institutionalization and disease control as well as normative morality. None, even the attorneys, voiced the idea of a basic human right to procreate or to have a sexual preference.

After the Hanley term of office, "strong" opposition developed against the law, primarily because of its lack of due process safeguards. Hanley's successors, Governors Thomas Riley Marshall (Democrat) (1854 –1925) and Samuel Moffett Ralston (Democrat) (1857–1925) stopped enforcement of the law during their terms of office, from 1909 to 1917. Finally, in 1921, fourteen years after the passage of the sterilization

468 Gugliotta, *Sharp and his Little Knife*, 390. Note 330.
469 *Ibid.*, Footnote 86.
470 *Ibid.*, 390.
471 *Ibid.*
472 *Ibid.*, 391–392.

law, Chapter 215 was challenged in the Indiana Supreme Court[473] and was found to be invalid as it violated the procedural due process clause under the Fourteenth Amendment of the federal Constitution. This finding is reported at Williams v. Smith, 190 Ind. 526, 131 N.E. 2 (1921).

The Williams challenge had originated from the Clark Circuit County and Judge James W. Fortune, although Gugliotta writes that the successor to Governor Ralston (1913–1917), James P. Goodrich, had "arranged" the constitutional test case, through use of an injunction.[474] It was an action "by Warren Wallace Smith, [and] by Lincoln E. Lankford, his friend, against Charles F. Williams and others."[475] Smith had won at the local level and the defendants had appealed. Ele Stansbury and Edward M. White argued in the highest court for the institutional appellants Williams, while Wilmer T. Fox had represented the prisoner appellee, Smith.

In the end, Judge J. Townsend of the Supreme Court affirmed the ruling by Circuit Court Judge, James Fortune. Townsend's decision is short, consisting of three basic paragraphs and is a classically written decision, based on precedent. The first paragraph merely outlines the statute itself. The second cites to a District Court case from South Dakota, Davis v. Berry, 216 F. 413 (1914) which itself refers to a similar statute from Iowa. Davis had said that:

> The hearing is by an administrative board or officer. There is no actual hearing. There is no evidence. The proceedings are private. The public does not know what is being done until it is done. Witnesses are not produced, or if produced, they are not cross-examined....The prisoner is not advised of the proceedings until ordered to submit to the operation....Due process of...law means that every person must have his day in court, and this is as old as Magna Charta; that sometime in the proceedings he must be confronted by his accuser and given a public hearing.[476]

The third paragraph merely notes that the prisoner and appellant Smith had not had the opportunity to confront his accusers. He had no chance to have experts of his own choosing to present contrary evidence. Smith had no chance "to controvert the scientific question that he is of a class designated in the statute."[477] The statute violated the 14th Amendment of the federal Constitution since Smith's due process rights had been violated. Although Townsend's short opinion meets every requirement of judicial decisional drafting, his reference to the summary taking of the prisoner to the operation is as chilling as any one could ever read. And, his observation of exactly how the class of "confirmed criminal" could be proven and by what scientific evidence

---

473 In 1900, the Supreme Court of Indiana consisted of 5 members who were elected from districts by the state at large. Their term was 6 years in length. An appellate court had been established in 1891 in addition to the circuit and county court system already in place.

474 Gugliotta, *Sharp and his Little Knife*, 403. Note 330.

475 Williams, et. al. v. Smith, 190 Ind. 526 at 526, 131 N.E. 2 (1921).

476 Williams v. Smith, 190 Ind. 526 at 527, 131 N.E. 2 (1921).

477 Williams v. Smith, 190 Ind. 526 at 528, 131 N.E. 2 (1921).

hints at more problems with the statute. Even if the statute had provided for a type of due process, would the legislature have included the "standard of proof" needed for this proof? That the statute should have been successfully challenged speaks to the standards of a small minority of the legal profession in Indiana, especially since the social climate in the state and in the country had produced decidedly different goals than one reads embodied in the statute. It also substantiates Gugliotti's assertion that there was indeed a "rivalry" between the medical and legal professions for control of this epistemic imbroglio.

But this was not the end of the law in Indiana and it was resurrected in 1927 and amended numerous times between 1931 and the 1950s.[478] Defects in the statute were remedied in 1927 in Indiana Acts, Chapter 241. This law provided for a thirty-day notice to the inmate and/or prisoner or their guardians in which to prepare a defense, appeasing those with a due process concern. The Act was further amended in 1931 in Indiana Acts 1931, Chapter 50. This amendment mandated that the physician who applied for sterilization of an idiot, imbecile or feeble-minded person had to certify whether this condition was due to bad genes or if the person was "cacogenic."[479] In 1935, in Indiana Acts, Chapter 12, the bill was again amended to include insane persons as within the jurisdiction of the law.[480] A check of Westlaw Shepard's indicates that the law is still in force and effect, not having been repealed or overturned; it is similar to many laws that are "on the books" but no longer utilized.[481]

Criminals may have been protected – to an extent – from sterilization after the Williams decision in 1921 and the 1927 and 1931 amendments to Chapter 215. Nonetheless, nativism surged in Indiana after World War I. For example, the United States Army had collected data from soldiers entering its ranks during that war and found that while northern Europeans scored "almost as well as native whites...[soldiers who were] black, ...and soldiers born in Latin and Slavic countries averaged significantly lower."[482] This type of information only served to fuel the energies of eugenicists such as Senator Carl E.O. Holmes from Gary, Indiana. Before running for the legislature,

---

478 *Ibid.*

479 "Cacogenics" is defined as "The study of racial degeneration." in William Morris (ed.), *The American Heritage Dictionary of the English Language* (Boston: Houghton Mifflin Company, 1970), p. 185.

480 Please see source http://www.statelib.lib.in.us/www/isl/indiana/eugenics.html, accessed 12 December 12, 2007.

481 Westlaw Shepard's is a method for determining if a case is still "good law" in the United States. In addition to noting if the law has been "overruled", it also notes if various portions of the law have been "questioned", etc. This is not the first time this type of anomaly has occurred, i.e. where older laws remain "on the books", despite presumptive invalidity. See *Indiana Law Journal*, Notes, Volume 38, 1962–1963, p. 276. "Subsequent to the Williams decision, however, procedurally refined statutes providing for the sterilization of the mentally ill and mentally defective were enacted and remain a part of the present law in Indiana [as of 1962–1963]."

482 Walsh, *Centennial History*, 308.

Holmes, a banker and realtor of Swedish ancestry, had been a member of the state Committee on Mental Defectives. After election, he proposed the 1925 amendment to Chapter 215 that would have required the appointment of a state eugenicist who, after studying the wards of the state, could have recommended sterilization for some if they "might reproduce their kin, i.e. more inmates for the states institutions."[483] The act itself was entitled "an act to prevent the procreation of persons socially inadequate from defective inheritance..."[484]

Rep. William Brown of Porter County tried to add an amendment to Holmes' bill to the effect that no one who became a subject of the law could be used for experimentation, but this measure failed.[485] The *Indianapolis News* was an enthusiastic sup-

---

483 *Ibid.*

484 *Ibid.*

485 Prisoners at Jeffersonville were not the only human subjects used in the pursuit of scientific progress. Since the work at Tuskagee is so well known, we often overlook experimentation done before that time. In 1906, the *News* included a story of national importance with the headline "Plague Germs in Prisoners' Bodies. Mistake at Bilibad Likely to Result in Resignation of Dr. R.P. Strong. Wrong Tubes Were Used. Attendents Thought They Were Inoculating Victims with Cholera Serum – Natives Indignant." (*Indianapolis News*, 3 December 1906, p. 1. The *News* misspells the word Bilibid.) Bilibid Prison was the main prison for the Philippines, located in the capitol, Manila. In 1899 Lt. Richard P. Strong along with contract surgeon Joseph J. Curry, as members of the U.S. Army, began to investigate tropical diseases; later, Strong would become the head of the Philippine Biological Laboratory a division of the Philippine Bureau of Science, a civilian laboratory in Manila whose work was to vaccinate against cholera and the plague. On the 16th of November 1906, Strong inoculated 24 prisoners who were inmates at the Bilibid Prison with a cholera vaccine that happened to be either contaminated with bubonic plague microorganisms or with only the plague organism present. Various explanations for this ensued. One such explanation was that a visiting doctor from Chicago had mixed up the test tubes and Strong had not have locks on test tube racks. After being inoculated, thirteen of the twenty-four prisoners died. Another explanation exists which is not so benign and implies intent beyond simple negligence. This explanation posits that the governor-general granted permission for "investigation among inmates of Bilibid Prisons with reference to diseases which prevail among them." *Iatrogenic Plague Disaster* (1906), www.brown.edu/Courses/Bio_160/Projects2000/Ethics/IATROGENICPLAGUEDISASTER.html, accessed on March 8, 2006.

To be fair, Strong did use vaccines on himself as well as the prisoners. But on 16 November he simply asked the prisoners to stand in a line and inoculated them without their permission and without telling them what he was doing. The governor general had used the word "prevalent" in his permission but neither the plague nor cholera was prevalent in 1906 and this permission "did not imply or extend to the trial of prophylactic experiments." (*Ibid.*) A general committee was appointed by the Governor General to investigate the incident and Strong was eventually not found guilty of negligence. No mainland investigation was undertaken either and six years later, Strong was given access to the prisoners to conduct experiments on beriberi, also with fatalities; survivors were compensated with cigars and cigarettes. (Allen M. Hornblum, "They were cheap and available: prisoners as research subjects in twentieth century America", in *BMJ*, 315 (1997), at http://bmj.bmjjournals.com/archive/7120/7120ed1.htm. Please see, Eli Cherin, "Richard Pearson Strong and the Iatrogenic Plague Disaster in Bilibid Prison, Manila, 1906" in *Review of Infectious Diseases*, 11 (1989), 996–1004 and Campbell, K. A., "Knots in the fabric: Richard Pearson Strong and the Bilibid Prison vaccine

porter of the Holmes measure as were Senators Robert L. Moorhead and Thomas A. Daily who, just before the bill passed the Senate by a vote of 31 to 12, stated that every man should set out his pedigree "just as we do for our pedigreed hogs and cattle."[486] The bill went to the House where it was assigned to the Committee on Agriculture – not the CMHVS as before – and where it was reported out without any recommendations. Charles Mendenhall of Marion County then successfully made a motion and it was "indefinitely postponed", essentially a death decree.[487]

Estimates of the total number of persons sterilized before officials either refused to utilize the law or it was ruled invalid, range from 2,000 to 2,500.[488] Alexandra Minna Stern writes that about 2,000 inmates at various state institutions were sterilized between 1927 and 1974; the "the statutory basis for these operations was the 1927 sterilization act and several subsequent amendments that Indiana legislators carefully crafted to preclude problems that doomed the 1907 law."[489]

4.4 Jasanoff Fields Reflected in the Indiana Media

I begin this section with two examples of the shifting articulations among and between the Jasanoff fields of knowledge co-production. They demonstrate the micro-level discursive work that was done by religion and the law to support the pseudo science of Eugenics.

The first example is one where representations of science and progress were fused with the institution of religion. The Indiana sterilization law was the subject of comment on 18 March 1907 at the Roberts Park M.E. (Methodist Episcopal) Church in Indianapolis where Dr. Albert Huristone took as his text Romans xiv, 12 in his sermon "Heredity and Responsibility." That religious groups should comment on this new law is not surprising. The divisions between Christian sects in their support and non-support for sterilization are of interest, however. Using the same "animal improve-

---

trails, 1905–1906" in *Bulletin of Historical Medicine*, 68 (1994), 600 -38.) Strong was later made a Professor of Tropical Medicine at Harvard University.

486 Walsh, *Centenial History*, 308.

487 *Ibid.*

488 Please see, http://www.hmdb.org/marker.asp?marker=1829, accessed May 15, 2009. See footnote number 7.

489 Stern, Sow's Ear, p. 20. Note 347. While it would be soothing to believe that legally and ethically problematic bills such as the sterilization bill of 1907 were a thing of the past, we would do well to note a bill submitted in 98 years later. In 2005, General Assembly of the state of Indiana entertained a proposed bill by Republican Senator Patricia Miller to ban unmarried women, gay men and lesbian women from using assisted reproductive techniques in order to have children. (Ruth Clifford Engs, "Relieved That Indiana Won't Embarrass Itself Again" (Op-Ed), *Indianapolis Star* (Gannett), 9 October 2005.)

ment" argument, Huristone applauded the Legislature asking if "the same common sense 'which is manifested in the improvement of the stock on the farm'" wasn't being used in the Legislature?[490] Echoing the remarks made by the Editor of the *Star* and Dr. Sharp, above, Huristone said society is responsible "not only to the living but to the unborn." When compared with the 21st century religious political rhetoric of life beginning at the moment of conception, Huristone's statement can be seen in at least two ways: either he did not believe – as a minister – that life began at birth or, if he did, he apparently supposed that the greater responsibility was owed to the living and/or future generations.

For Dr. Huristone, science simply "reinforced the doctrines of the Bible."

According to the accounts reported of his sermon, Huristone then wove this idea, that modern concepts of heredity did not abrogate responsibility, into reflections on the political topics of the day. He addressed the legal issue of insanity, which is the subject of my second example, below. Huristone said that "'fits of temporary insanity'" which he called "brain storms" did not absolve one from responsibility. Heredity "did not destroy personality" and thus, even if we inherited certain tendencies, they were only influences and do not destroy "moral responsibility." Huristone also commented on the new Juvenile Court system saying that if the weaker were lead by "some strong probation officer, some worthy citizen", that they could outrun these tendencies.

In the end, Huristone's strategy was to leave no rhetorical space whatsoever between his concepts of religion and "heredity."

> The Christian church has taught the doctrine of heredity for two thousand years, only people did not like the term original sin. But Mr. Darwin has made us all orthodox and now everybody believes in inheritance! The Jewish church long ago taught that the 'iniquity of the father is visited upon the children to the third and fourth generation.' [A]nd in modern times science comes to the side of the moralist teaching that there is as much heredity in crime as in consumption, cancer or insanity; what the pulpit has called 'parental influences' or 'the iniquity of the father,' biology would call heredity.[491]

This is an interesting rhetorical slight of hand, a prescient attempt to reconcile the seemingly insurmountable, inherent problems between religion and science that would soon become apparent.

But the institution of religion was malleable. Huristone could not only use it preemptively as not being antithetical to science but it could also be used in a prospective manner to support nationalism. We find that the very next day in the *Star*, in a letter

490 *Indianapolis Star*, March 18, 1907, 14.
491 *Ibid.*

to the Editor, a Mr. S.O. M'Clung from Williams, Indiana, used the Christian Bible to underpin the idea of "American exceptionalism" or America as the "new Eden."[492]

My second example of how co-productionist fields intersected is that of representations made by Psychology and the institution of the Law. Scientific "experts" were a regular feature in Hoosier newspapers, and especially in connection with the famous Harry Thaw trial. Thaw had allegedly murdered architect Stanford White who was the cosmopolitan descendant of two American presidents. Henry Adams had dubbed White the "Moses of Manhattan's niveau riche."[493] Jealousy of actress Evelyn Nesbitt's previous involvement with White before her marriage to Thaw had lead Thaw – the "eccentric millionaire playboy" – to shoot White on the roof of the old Madison Square Garden.

In January, 1907 opinions about the defendant, Henry Kendall Thaw, by the "famous criminologist" Cesare Lombroso (1836–1909) were printed on page one of the *News*.[494] In the classic rhetoric of eugenics, Lombroso noted that Thaw was a "hereditary degenerate." Lombroso, who worked vigorously to spread eugenic thought in Italy during the early part of the century, concluded that Thaw was "born a degenerate" and that Thaw's "epileptiform madness" was traceable to Thaw's mad aunt and the exhaustion of Thaw's father by the work that made him a millionaire.[495]

For weeks, the trial of Harry Kendall Thaw, held in New York City, had captured the imagination of Indianapolis readers. It was called "copy catnip" and would be, from 1906–1908, the "trial of the century" taking a place alongside other great and better-known American trials such as the Scopes, Lindbergh/Hauptmann, Sheppard and Simpson trials.[496] The *Star* reported on 11 April that the first Thaw trial, begun on 23 January 1907 and ended that day, was on the brink of being called a mistrial, since, after only 6 hours of deliberation, jurors were unable to reach a unanimous decision.[497]

Later, after debating for 47 hours, the jury deadlocked – seven in favor of conviction on the charge of Murder in the First Degree and five for acquittal.[498] Thaw's wife Evelyn had emerged from this trial as "the chief figure around which the drama revolved." The Editor of the *Star* could not help but comment on the mistrial as a "miscarriage of justice" calling Thaw a "conscious murderer if ever there was one." More important for my purposes here, he also commented on the defense that Thaw's attor-

---

492 "Views of the People."*Indianapolis Star*, March 20, 1907, 8.

493 Ronald Goldfarb, "The 'Trial of the Century'" in *Cosmos Journal*, Walter G. Berl, Editor, 1998. This can be viewed at http://www.cosmos-club.org/web/journals/1998/goldfarb.html, accessed December 6, 2007.

494 *Indianapolis News*, January 21, 1907, 1.

495 *Ibid.*

496 Goldfarb, "The 'Trial of the Century'." Note 678.

497 *Indianapolis Star*, April 11, 1907, 1. Upper Left.

498 *Indianapolis Star*, April 13, 1907, 1. Upper Left.

ney, Mr. Delmas, had used – the so-called *"dementia Americana"* defense, denouncing it as "against public policy" and an "anarchistic doctrine of the unwritten law."[499] In a second trial a year later, Thaw was acquitted by reason of insanity, and Thaw was "hailed by the public as a hero in an American morality play."[500]

What this trial did do was to highlight the ever-increasing intersections between the relatively new sciences of Psychology with the Law, just as the Scopes trial would spotlight the science-versus-religion debate in American culture a few years later. Here, a heightened sense of moral panic is alluded to as "dementia Americana" and is malleable enough to be used as a positive notion by a good criminal defense attorney. In his closing statement to the jury, defense attorney Delmas said:

> ...if you desire a name for this species of insanity let me suggest it – call it **dementia Americana**. That is the species of insanity which makes every American man believe his home to be sacred; that is the species of insanity which makes him believe the honor of his daughter is sacred; that is the species of insanity which makes him believe that whosoever invades his home, that whosoever stains the virtue of this threshold, has violated the highest of human laws and must appeal to the mercy of God, if mercy there be for him anywhere in the universe.[501]

But this is also an example of epistemic networks that transgress disciplinary boundaries. And, it is also this very same juridical issue that I will describe in the second half of this Case.

In Norway in 1934, a court addressed the case of a Norwegian woman, Aagot Hansen, who was sent to an insane asylum for years although she was not clinically insane. This is the antithesis of the Thaw case and will be discussed below. These two cases were not simply a "powerful nexus of concerns with national identity, patriarchy, class and the public sphere..."[502] but also were an account of the embryogenesis of new legal epistemology through the use of a dialogic narrative.[503] The two examples also demonstrate which intersubjective group was in power and which was not.

In the United States, changes in the law of insanity were a major phenomenon within the legal community but were also no small matter in society at large. On 16 April, a mirror-image case of Harry Kendall Thaw opened in Lafayette, Indiana, except

499 *Ibid.*, 8.

500 *Goldfarb, Trial of the Century*. Note 678. The fictionalized account of the trial can be had in E.L. Doctorow's novel *Ragtime*.

501 *Chicago Daily Tribune*, April 10, 1907, 1. (Emphasis mine.)

502 Adrienne L. McLean and David A. Cook, "Headline Hollywood: A Century of Film Scandal" in *Film Quarterly*, 55 (2002), 54.

503 Martha Merril Umphrey, "Dialogics of Legal Meaning: Spectacular Trials, the Unwritten Law, and Narratives of Criminal Responsibility" in *Law and Society Review*, (BNET Research Center, 1992) at http://findarticles.com/p/articles/mi_qa3757/is_199901/ai_n8843631/print, accessed December 12, 2007.

that the defendant was a woman, Alice Cooper Lawsen.[504] Lawsen had killed her husband, Charles A. Lawsen, a saloon-owner, and the issue as reported was whether she had done so "deliberately and with premeditation."[505] The reporter speculated that Lawsen would use the new insanity defense.

One final phenomenon must be mentioned in relation to the state of Indiana – the United States – being the state in the first country in the world to successfully legislate a forcible sterilization law. Of the intersubjective categories that I have discussed in Chapter 2, I have chosen – in the main – to write about women as a category, although race/ethnicity is also often mentioned. The Indiana law began with its object as the male body, the bodies of young male prisoners in a juvenile institution. But the law did not confine itself to this category and it soon expanded to the body of an adult male chicken thief before the law was overturned. Meanwhile, the bodies of women were affected and continued to be affected well after the eugenics movement retreated from discourse.[506]

4.5 Eugenic Discourses in the Norwegian Parliament, 1934–1936

> Here we have 100 idiots which cost society so much money. For the same amount of money we can support 200 healthy children. Of these two groups, a significant number will die of inadequate nourishment etc., if we have nothing to support them because we have to use the money for the maintenance of the idiots. What should we do?
>
> Dr. Jørgen H. Berner[507]

> I fear...the so-called 'objective' scientist when they are dealing with problems that are not strictly scientific.
>
> Dr. Otto L. Mohr[508]

The composition of the 150–member Norwegian Storting from 1934–1936 by political party shows a robust plurality identified as Labour Party (Ap) members (68 members of the 150-member Storting, or 45.3%).[509] Conservative (H) members numbered 30

504 *Indianapolis Star*, April 16, 1907, 5.
505 *Ibid.*
506 Please see Allison Carey, "Gender and Compulsory Sterilization Programs in America", 74–105. Note 208. I will analyze her research below.
507 *Aftenposten* (a.m. Edition), August 29, 1934, 2.
508 Library of Congress (Washington, D.C., U.S.A.), *Papers of Margaret Sanger*, Accession Number 16,700, Vol. 29 Reel 19. Letter dated May 11, 1926. Letter dated Oslo, 8/11, 1927 by Otto Mohr, end page two and begin page three.
509 Please see source http://www.norgeslexi.com/politikk/storting/representatnt/34-36.html, accessed December 9, 2007.

(20%), the Liberal Party (V) had 25 members (16.6%) and the Farmers Party (B) had 23 members (15.3%). Other parties had which had only one member were the Society Party (Samfundsparti), the Kr-R Party, the R-F Party and the F-F Party.[510] Together, the latter 4 parties with one member each composed 2.4% of the Storting.

Born in 1859, the oldest member of the Storting was 75-year old C. Hornsrud; he was a Labour Party member and farmer[511] from Buskerud. The youngest Storting member was also a Labour Party member; this was K. Fonstad, a telegraph operator from Hedmark. In addition, the Storting, unlike the Indianan legislature, had three women members; 59 year old Helga A.A. Ramstad, a Labour Party member and caretaker[512] from Akershus, 52 year old Helga A. Karlsen, a Labour Party member and housewife from Oslo, and finally, 46 year old Signe Swensson, a Conservative Party doctor from the Trøndelag area of Norway.[513]

The occupations of the members can be generalized in that, from the professional class of workers, i.e. attorney, doctor, lector and rector, only 6 (4%) were elected to the Storting – a meager number when compared with the Indiana legislature. Of the class of workers that we now term "white collar" workers, i.e. state administrative workers and other professionals, 20 (13.3%) were elected. Those who were identified as employed in a Bank, or identified as a Merchant or Manager numbered 16 (10.6%). These three groups, when combined with the 20 (20%) other "white collar" workers, gave the largest voting bloc – by class – of 62 members (47.9%). The second largest group – by occupation – was composed of farmers, fishermen and other "blue collar" workers. The farming group was comprised of 46 (30.6%) members, fishermen totaled 4 members (2.5%), and 18 (12%) can be identified as "blue collar"; together these three groups had 68 (44.5%) members. Finally, 10 (6.6%) teachers had been elected to this Storting.

In 1934, a majority of the general population of Norway were members of Den Norske Kirke (DNK) and nothing that I have found indicates that any of the members of the 1934–1936 Storting were non-members of the national church of Norway, DNK.

As part of their ordering function, institutions are "stable repositories of knowledge and power" and are also "inscription devices" for society.[514] Institutions can extend across political and geographical boundaries and in this sense, have been – especially since the formation of academic journals – no stranger to the concept of globalization. The globalization effect, in 1934 essentially meant that, although journals flowed freely across the globe, Norway looked to how other Nordic countries

510 I have been unable to find the full names of the last three parties, mentioned only by their acronyms.

511 "Gårdsbruker."

512 "Vaktmester."

513 Appendix D lists the compositioin of the Storting by part affiliation and occupation.

514 Jasanoff (ed.), *States of Knowledge: the co-production of science and social order (London, Routledge, 2004)* 39–40.

were using scientific principles, including eugenics. As we can read in various pre-1934 Justice Committee minutes where the Norwegian sterilization law was discussed, it was Nordic countries that were mentioned with approval as having taken similar steps. This was in addition to the United States, Germany and Great Britain.

As institutions – or institutional structures – both medicine and law in Norway were well established in 1934. In fact, the institution of law was powerful enough for a Norwegian to lead the Congress of Ministers of Justice on 29 November in Stockholm. Attending the Congress, at the instigation of Justice Minister Schyter of Sweden, were Justice Sunde of Norway[515], Zahle of Denmark and Zeriachius of Finland who joined the other 400 participants in Stockholm.[516]

The medical profession was also a powerful institution in Norway, as in Indiana. One of the indications of this is how the subject of euthanasia was addressed as part of the "zeitgeist" of 1934. In *Aftenposten's kronikk* of 29 August 1934, we read the headline "Should Doctors Have the Right to Take the Life of Patients?"[517] Dr. Jørgen H. Berner, who was the General Secretary of the Norwegian Doctor's Association and Editor of its Journal from 1925 to 1949, wrote the editorial.[518] Berner began his editorial by citing to the English Parliament which that fall was set to consider the suggestion in its session. Berner also cited to German criminal law, which, it was rumored, would allow such action under certain conditions.[519]

Berner grabbed the reader's attention by mentioning unfortunate – and emotionally charged – accidents; these included a child who had swallowed lye in Sweden and the case of a child born with central nervous system problems. He then cited newspaper articles by Dr. A. Brinchmann in the 16 November 1933 edition of *Aftenposten* and Dr. Johann Scharffenberg in the 17 October 1933 edition of *Arbeiderbladet* that had both dealt with the question of developmentally delayed children and their right to live.[520] But Berner was more eager to address those who were chronically unhealthy and sick, "in the first place those children with essentially mental or bodily defects which make them a burden for their caretakers and society."[521] Acknowledg-

---

515 Sunde was also a member of the Storting's Justice Committee that approved the 1934 law; his comments can be reviewed in Appendix E.

516 *Aftenposten* (a.m. Edition), November 29, 1934, 3. Halvard Olsen opened the Congress but four Directors were then chosen to lead the meeting including Oscar Torp, who later became Labor Prime Minister from 1951–1955.

517 *Aftenposten* (a.m. Edition), August 29, 1934, 2. *Aftenpostens kronikk*, "Bør lægene ha rett til å avlive patienter?" Please see fn. 495 for definition of "*kronikk*."

518 *Tidskr. Nor Lægeforen* 2002, 122, 121.

519 *Aftenposten* (a.m. Edition), August 29, 1934, 2. "og for ett år siden forlød det at i Tyskland var fremsatt et forslag til ny straffelov, som bestemte at under visse omstendigheter skulde det være tillatt å ta livet av en patient.." The entire question – of euthanasia – had also taken up in a book entitled "And So Life Continues" by Lalli Løvland.

520 *Ibid.*

521 *Ibid.*

ing that the issue of "social" and "humanitarian" indications for the termination of a pregnancy was a matter of debate, Berner noted that a number of "ethical, esteemed people have suggested reforms along this line", allowing abortion, and agreed with Scharffenberg, who would allow abortion.[522] But Berner thought that Schaffenberg and others were inconsistent in that they opposed taking the life of the developmentally delayed but would agree to permit abortion for social and/or humanitarian reasons.

Berner argued that society allowed the "disposal" of fetuses, which for social or economic reasons were not wanted and the killing of a fetus was allowed if it threatened the life of the mother. But with those children who were "deformed", he was of the opinion that it would be better if they had not been born. His opinion was that not to allow for this was a matter of inconsistent thinking, i.e. to assign a newborn rights while not assigning the unborn any similar rights.[523] He argued that a society is judged by how it cares for the "defective" person who cannot care for him or herself.[524] For Berner, it was a slippery slope that society faced when it allowed abortion based on "social" or "humanitarian" indications. "The veneration of life" was an absolute for Berner and the "humanitarian" indication merely a path to ethical slippery slopes. While Berner seemed to be trying to address inconsistencies in the abortion reform movement, he might have done his argument no obvious good by advocating for euthanasia for those who were chronically sick or unhealthy and by proposing that a medical doctor make that decision.

Aftenposten was sometimes used as if it were an academic journal and included many more scientific discussions than did any newspaper in Indiana in 1907. The *Kronikk* in the *Aftenposten* was also basically used as an editorial forum that frequently allowed one or another scientific professional – usually either scientists or doctors – to promote a "scientific" opinion. And the one issue that involved both of these institutions was the issue of whether or not to reform the then-existing abortion law in Norway, the Criminal Law of 22 May 1902, §245 to allow for women to have abortions within three months of conception.

On 3 January 1934, Professor, Dr. R. Ingebrigtsen (b. 1880) wrote an article that was placed on page one of *Aftenposten*, at the upper left had side of the front page, a place routinely used for the most important news of the day.[525] This lengthy article delved into the relative success of the Danish sterilization law, which by 1934, had already been in effect for four years. Danish state's attorney Goll had given results

522 *Ibid.* "...Scharffenberg som dog fordømmer såvel abortus provacatus og avlivning av idioter, etc."
523 *Ibid.* "... så synes det dog å være ganskje inkonsekvent å tildele det fødte barn alle rettigheter ...det ufødte barn dem."
524 *Ibid.*
525 *Aftenposten* (p.m. Edition), January 3, 1934, 1.

from those four years to a meeting of the Criminal Biology Association that had been held in Hamburg, Germany in June of the previous year.[526]

Ingebrigtsen was a medical doctor and he was a crucial part of the articulations between law and medicine at this time, helping to impact the impending sterilization law though feature articles such as this.[527] In his article, after giving a technical explanation of sterilization in men and women, Ingebrigtsen explained under what conditions or "indications" the operation should proceed. The first was as "medically indicated" where the health or life of the patient was in question. As an aside, he noted that one could not consider it a "medical indication" if the patient were castrated because he masturbated excessively or was an exhibitionist. This was a somewhat more liberal position than in the Indiana law because, as he noted, although these conditions were troublesome, and if inherited could lead to imprisonment or punishment, they did not affect the (medical) health of the patient.[528] But Dr. Ingebrigtsen's opinion was that, as the law was written in 1934, castration for "medically" indicated conditions would be allowed. The new draft law, however, would add other categories; these were 1. humanitarian, 2. social, 3. criminal management, and 4. eugenic or any combination of these such as social-eugenic.[529]

Ingebrigtsen went on to give an example of each of the four categories. The example he gave for the first category, "humanitarian" was if a patient were a homosexual or an exhibitionist. After having been dealt with by the criminal system, the offender could be castrated if there were a chance of recidivism or new violations. Ingebrigtsen thought the life of the offender in that situation would become easier with the possibility of uninterrupted freedom.[530] As to the second category "social",

---

526 *Ibid.*, 6.

527 Ingebrigtsen was a Professor of Surgery at the University of Oslo in 1934. Interestingly, he had also been a Fellow at the Rockefeller Institute for Medical Research in New York with Dr. Alexis Carrel (1873–1944) from 1911 to 1913. (Gram, Harald and Steenstrup, Bjørn (Publishers), *Hvem er Hvem?* (Oslo: H. Aschehoug & Co. (W. Nygaard), 1939). p. 319.) In 1912, Carrel won the Nobel Prize for his work in physiology, and along with Charles Claude Guthrie laid the groundwork for the artifical heart. Carrel was recruited to the Rockefeller Institute for Medical Research in 1906 but was later forced to resign. In 1935, he published a book entitled *Man, The Unknown* where his eugenic ideas were included and, in the 1936 Introduction to the German edition alone, praise for the Nazi Regime. In 1941 he became Regent of the Fondation Française pour l'Etude des Problemes Humans from which the Minister of Health suspended him after the liberation of Paris. In the 1990s, historian Arthur Schlesinger, Jr. implicated Carrel in the racism of Charles Lindbergh saying "I suppose he got it a lot of it from Alexis Carrel, the French Biologist who had a kind of racial mysticism of a sort." See PBS interview at http://www.pbs.org/wgbh/amex/lingbergh/filmmore/reference/interview/schlesinger03.html, accessed July 5, 2009. Also see Gugliotta on Carrel.

528 *Aftenposten* (p.m. Edition), January 3, 1934, 1, continued to 6. An example of possible criminal prosecution would be for exhibitionism.

529 *Ibid.*

530 *Ibid.*

Ingebrigtsen mentioned people who are of "inferior value" such as the developmentally disabled and mentally ill, all of whom could be presumed to be unable to care for his or her progeny.[531] The reasoning behind this social category was, for Ingebrigtsen, purely economic. He wrote that these people could be sterilized "**so that** society can be liberated from the economic and moral responsibility which it would otherwise have when faced with these children."[532] The third category was "eugenic" and in a parenthesis the term race-hygiene was used.[533] Ingebrigtsen defined the eugenics category as individuals who were connected with the social category and could certainly be expected to have progeny "as worthless as their origin."[534] The difference between the two categories is the expectation that deficient genes can be eliminated from the population and that the average health of the entire population can be bettered in the long run.[535] The fourth and final category is the "criminal-political" which is similar to category number one, the "humanitarian." Here, Ingebrigtsen again described the exhibitionist who may not need to be incarcerated for prolonged periods if he can be castrated.

It is important here to reflect on the language used above. The use of the phrase "**so that**" is indicative of an "instrumental value expression" in which some action which is identified or controlled by the author gives certain consequences.[536] Other "means-end" relations can be observed in such phrases as "...in order to...", "...will bring about...."[537] Means-end relations are "not conceived of as logically necessary but as potentially empirically verifiable."[538] They are subtle; they are without logic yet they infer scientific verifiability – at some unknown future point – making their use very powerful albeit indirect. In addition, they give us other information. These means-end rhetorical devices can locate values. As Klaus Krippendorf writes, the "hypothetical construct required to identify values in instrumental expressions further suggests viewing values as nodes in a network of asserted instrumental links."[539] Therefore, with some attention, one is able to trace these value-laden "nodes."

---

531 *Ibid.* I have translated "mindreverdige" as "inferior value", "åndssvake" as "developmentally disabled" and "psykisk abnorme" as "mentally ill." I understand that the word "åndssvake" is no longer used in Norwegian speech but if used, has a negative connotation.

532 *Ibid.* (Emphasis mine.)

533 *Ibid.*

534 *Ibid.*

535 *Ibid.*

536 Klaus Krippendorff, "The Expression of Value in Political Documents" in *Journalism Quarterly*, 47 (1970), 514.

537 *Ibid.*

538 *Ibid.*

539 *Ibid.* 515. Krippendorff actually identifies a number of value assertive statements and an entire typology. Instrumental value expressions can be defined as B(1): under condition K, I leads to J; therefore J=V where B(1) is the instrumental value expression, J and K are two further objects regardless of the author's identification, I is an object (action, behavior, situation, abstract conception or ideal)

Ingebritgsen identified the practical results of sterilization as were seen in other countries that had passed such legislation. In his discussion of similar laws passed in the United States, Ingebritsen mentions both Indiana (1907) and California (1909) but dismisses them as essentially race hygiene, or perceived as race hygiene, because individuals were forcibly sterilized. By contrast:

> The draft of the Norwegian law on sexual operations (sterilization) is not essentially race-hygienic in principle and cannot be characterized as forced through legal means.[540]

In retrospect, Ingebritgsen seems to have engaged in semantic sleight of hand here, since he must have known that the law would be "forced" upon those who fit criteria and were sterilized after legal procedure was followed. This is an example of a deft, almost unseen, breach of the Autonomy Theory of Law (ATL), a legal theory that theoretically insulates the Law from normative intrusion.[541]

While dismissive of the laws passed by individual states in the United States, he did take time to compare and contrast, in great detail, the Danish law passed in 1929 and the draft Norwegian law. The Danish law of 1 June 1929 had three categories or indications, i.e. humanitarian, criminal and political. The goal of that law was two-fold, to

> protect society against named sexual criminals (criminal-political indication) and in so doing save these potential sexual criminals from prolonged incarceration which would be the result of their sexual urges leading to (criminal) acts....[542]

The Danish law, as interpreted by Ingebrigtsen, was compatible with eugenics and also applied to those with mental illnesses. There was also a large degree of "harmonization" between the draft Norwegian and the Danish laws.[543]

Next, Ingebrigtsen compared the Danish and draft Norwegian laws with regard to what is now commonly referred to as "informed consent"; in 1934, this dealt with who asked that the operation take place – the individual or a third party. He admitted that the Norwegian draft law goes somewhat further than the Danish law as regarded eugenic indications but, by the same token, the Norwegian law had more steadfast

---

with which the author identifies, and V is a value (goal, principle, standard, ideal) preferred, approved, presented or not. (*Ibid.*, 517 -518.) Instrumental value expressions and other rhetorical devices have been mentioned throughout this work, as well as the semantic notion of the "ideograph", outlined in Chapter 2. (Please also see, Michael Calvin McGee, "The Ideograph as a Unit of Analysis in Political Argument" in, Jack Rhodes and Sara Newell (eds.), *Proceedings of the Summer Conference on Argumentation* (Annandale, Virginia: Speech Communication Association, 1998), 68–87.)

540 *Aftenposten* (p.m. Edition), January 3, 1934, 2.

541 The ATL, also called the Separability Thesis, will be discussed throughout Chapter 8.

542 *Aftenposten* (p.m. Edition), January 3, 1934, 2.

543 *Ibid.*

limitations.[544] And additionally, in contrast to the Danish law, the Norwegian law had a provision for the operation at the initiative of the Chief of Police. In general however, he argued that the two laws were compatible.

Between 1930 and 1934, Denmark had castrated 41 men and no women. The 41 men could be divided into three groups; 1. those without a criminal record, 2. those who had previously been adjudicated as sexual criminals and 3. those who had been adjudicated and had been sentenced to an indeterminate length of time for sexual crimes.[545] From the first group, only one man had been voluntarily castrated; this was on 1 September 1930 involving a 63-year old homosexual who found that his urges had not subsided over the years and who thought that he might not be able to restrain himself in the future. From the second group, nine men had been castrated. The age range was 26 to 59, the average being 44.5 years of age. Four of the men had been adjudicated for exhibitionism, three for sexual behavior with boys, one for sexual behavior with a girl and one, a doctor, for indecent behavior with a male patient while the patient was under anesthesia. From the third group, individuals sentenced to confinement for an indeterminate time for sexual crimes, 84 people had detained and 31 castrated since 1925 pursuant to the Danish criminal law. The categories can be seen in the following chart.

Table 4.1: Number sterilized pursuant to the Danish sterilization law

	From Psychopathic Institution	Dangerous Criminals	Developmentally Delayed	Insane	Epileptics	Total
Number Detained	55	3	20	0	6	84
Number Castrated	17	0	11	0	3	31

An earlier Danish criminal law from 1925 had pertained to those who were "weak or (had) disturbed mental faculties."[546] Leaders of institutional facilities were the first to take advantage of this imprecise language initiate the procedure. The bulk of the 84 detainees were "veterans" who had been already "dismissed" from society and were in state institutions. After castration, the 31 who were castrated were observed for between 6 months to one year. It was noted that they were "calmer" in their presentation, easier to be with in their work place and that the operation had produced results generally beyond expectations.[547]

544 *Ibid.*
545 *Ibid.*
546 *Ibid.*
547 *Ibid.*

Of the 31 castrated, only one had been a recidivist and had been adjudicated three times for inappropriate behavior with boys, the most recent conviction in 1928. This 41 year-old man had been castrated on 1 February 1930 and was released on 1 June 1931. However, this individual was again interned for the same type of behavior after the castration, giving Ingebrigtsen the opportunity to say that the procedure was not entirely without limitations.

In addition to these 31, other Danish citizens who were institutionalized had undergone sterilization pursuant to paragraph 2 of the 1925 criminal law under the hybrid heading of "social-humanitarian" reasons. All of these individuals, both men and women, were developmentally delayed. Eleven men and 51 women had been sterilized. Danish state attorney Goll remarked that this "has been to the happiness of those operated on and a gift to the concerned public treasury."[548] While finances seemed always to be a concern for Goll as well as Ingebrigtsen, Goll did say that these additional people were sterilized with other considerations in mind, i.e. "**so that** their unrestrained sex-drive might not lead them to be blamed for crimes with lasting consequences."[549] Guilt and the financial burden of unwanted children without fathers who might otherwise support them were the two sides to the rationale for sterilization.

Goll noted that the Danish law would be revised but the race-hygiene section of the law would not be affected. If the draft Norwegian law were to be enacted, it was his opinion that there "would be for non-criminal cases a certain degree of <u>stretching</u> [of the law] with regard to the application for permission for the sterilization."[550] Assuming that both Goll and Ingebrigtsen had an accurate working knowledge of the Norwegian law as it was and as it would become under the new law, this is a telling statement. We shall eventually meet this "stretching" of the law, not in theory but in reality, as it unfolded throughout the course of 1934. These men knew what was permissible and what would become a gray-area of practice under the new law. The implication is that they saw an advantage in the new law.

Aside from medical doctors, academic professionals became involved early on with the draft law just as did some attorneys and politicians had. Two individuals mentioned in the Ingebrigtsen article were Dr. Torp, Professor of Physiology in Oslo and Ragnar Vogt, Professor of Psychiatry in Oslo. As early as 1933, the Justice Department, the Norwegian Medical Director and the Medical Faculty in Oslo had solicited these two, along with Ingebritsen, for their input as to the generally known effects of castration.[551] Many others took various positions on the draft law before and after

548 *Ibid.*

549 *Ibid.* (Emphasis mine.)"...**for at** den ubeherskelige kjønnsdrift..."

550 *Ibid.* (Emphasis mine.)

551 *Aftenposten* (p.m. Edition), January 3, 1934, 6. As of 22 February 1933. In a later article in the same newspaper, April 6, 1934, at 5, editors call the results from the sterilization of the developmentally disabled in Denmark favorable ("gunstige").

its passage[552], but Vogt and a Dr. Alfred Mjøen[553], as well as Ingebritsen, were most vociferous in their support of the measure.

What were the "consent" provisions in the draft law? A third party, someone other than the patient could give consent for the procedure and this was provided for in paragraph 3. Despite the fact that Goll had said that one could be justified in foreseeing that if "the Norwegian proposal becomes law [it] can have a larger reach than the Danish law as regards the mentally retarded, institutionalized individuals with an abnormal sex drive and sexual repeaters....", there would still be safeguards to be sure, rules put in place which doctors had missed in the past.[554] Ingebritsen noted that the pending law could not entirely prevent the birth of defective individuals but it could help in elevating the average "quality of life" and in a difficult social and political time, how could one regret this consequence? Ingebrigtsen's last sentence in this extended article is of interest.

> A genetic approach with regard to these questions is, in the meantime, an entirely correct assessment. Research has gone a long way in giving us insight into the prevailing laws of inheritance, which must be the assumption such that one may – if even only negative results, i.e. exclusion of genes – anticipate a more or less regular result.[555]

Several monumental assumptions are at work in these two short sentences, just as in the Indiana law of 1907. The first assumption was that society had a problem, i.e. "these questions" involving abnormal humans, and the second assumption was that activity based in science, i.e. "laws of inheritance", with the help of the Law could solve the problem.

The "problem" was framed as a heady rhetorical brew including the expenditure of public finances, crime and crime prevention and uncontrollable lust. Public finances, whether lacking or not, were assumed to be lacking and paid for through taxation of the hard-working "normal" citizens of the country, be they Danes or Norwegians or Americans. Those who had direct contact with criminals, i.e. the police, attorneys and courts as well as in the church community, perceived crime as an ever-

552 In 1934, one can read editorials in the same newspaper about the impending law from Dr. Johan Lofthus (2 May 1934 – sterilization law), Dr. Henrik A. Th. Dedichen (2 June 1934 – crime and punishement), Dr. Sofus Widerøe (22 June 1934 – Hitler's sterilization law), Attorney Håkon Benneche (12 July 1934 – crime and punishment), and Police Chief Fr. F. Kaltenborn (18 July 1934 – criminal institute in Vienna). These are only the articles written by experts in the editorial section.

553 Dr. Alfred Mjøen was a major figure in the eugenics movements in Norway and we shall meet him shortly. It would be interesting to know why he was not also asked, along with Torp and Vogt, since he obviously had an opinion on the subject. My impression is that, although Mjøen claimed scientific credentials and did what passed for science at his Vindern laboratory, he was not taken as seriously as those who worked within the academic arena.

554 Aftenposten (a.m. Edition), January 3, 1934, 2.

555 Ibid., 6.

increasing problem. The new, reified science of genetics gave a "correct" approach to this societal problem. Furthermore, research supplied an empirical basis and thus a "rational" or "reasonable" approach.

Current scientific thought allowed these experts to presume that, if society could just exclude negative genes, then the outcome would be predictable, i.e. the quality of life would be improved for all. The importance of genes and chromosomes was the biological cutting-edge discovery of the moment. Dr. Ingebritgsen, for example, was clearly aware of the work of American scientist/geneticist, Thomas Hunt Morgan, since he had been awarded the 1933 Nobel Prize in Medicine for his work on chromosomes. Numerous Norwegian scientific luminaries, including both Professors Ragnar Vogt and Otto Mohr – who had nominated Hunt for the award as early as 1923 – were also aware of Hunt's work.[556]

Two months after Ingebrigtsen's lengthy article, Cabinet Minister Sunde decided to put forward the sterilization law in the Storting.[557] The draft law, built upon the Criminal Law Committee's work, gave several ways sterilization could be permitted. First, the Medical Director, on the advice of an expert, had the power to give permission for sterilization or castration. The person him or herself might also ask for the operation when "the request has a worthy reason."[558] If the person requesting the operation was less than 21 years old or was mentally ill or developmentally delayed, the consent of the person's juridical guardian or a specially named trustee was also required. In "certain cases" only the consent of the guardian would be necessary, i.e. cases concerning the mentally ill or the developmentally delayed. These cases had to meet two requirements. There had to be no hope of health or "essential" or "meaningful" improvement and there was reason to suppose that the person would not be in a position to become employed or to care for any children he or she might have or that an abnormal mental condition or a considerable bodily defect might be passed on to the children or that, due to some abnormal sex drive, s/he would commit a sex crime.[559]

Exactly how one could be sure there might be no hope of improvement or how an "abnormal mental condition" or a "considerable bodily defect" would or could be measured was not addressed.[560] In addition, the Chief of Police was given the power to propose these operations for persons meeting the above criteria. Further, the administrator of any jail, workhouse, institution that cared for these persons or edu-

556 *Aftenposten* (p.m. Edition), March 2, 1934, 2.
557 *Ibid.*
558 *Ibid.*
559 *Ibid.*
560 Leaving the law in terms of general principles is standard practice in Norwegian law. The particular definitions and rules are left to administrative authorities (forskrifter). I am thankful to Prof. Sætnan for this input. What this seems to do – as compared to the common law countries – in effect, is to allow the law to change as norms change without a long and costly mudicial process.

cated them could also make the request if the guardian or trustee was in agreement. The Medical Director could also give consent if the person was less than 21 years old, mentally ill or developmentally delayed. In that case, the Director also needed the consent of a council of five members with the Director as Chairman. From a procedural standpoint, the Chief of Police and the Administrative Director of an institution were given a great deal of latitude. Even though it might seem as if a better situation was used when the Medical Director made a decision and a second form of consent was needed from a 5-member group, that group was still headed by the same Director, which makes for a conflict of interest situation.

The proposal did not make any changes to the existing law that allowed a doctor, on his or her own initiative and with the consent of the patient, to sterilize or castrate the patient as long as there was a medical or "other" reason for the operation that was lawful under the provisions of the new law. Although the new law did not advise forced operations, sexual criminals could voluntarily submit to castration after serving his or her sentence. It was anticipated that through this method, preventive detention would in most case be done away with.[561]

Ingebrigtsen's *Afterposten* assessment of the new sterilization law gives a glimpse into what he and others believed would be the effect that science could have in society. He used a means-end rhetoric that essentially circumvented verification. Nonetheless, we can locate the values in that discourse and those values were to "liberate society from the economic and moral responsibility which it would otherwise have when faced with these children."[562] Ingebrigtsen's style was more nuanced than, for example, that of Dr. Jørgen H. Berner, who bluntly asked what do when "we have 100 idiots [who] cost society so much money [and] for the same amount of money we can support 200 healthy children."[563] As noted above, Krippendorf writes, that by identifying values/norms through looking at instrumental expressions, such as Ingebrigtsen's, we can view these values/norms as nodes in a network of asserted instrumental links. This also supports the idea that articulations that are made – and remade – through use of the Jasanoff fields are important evidence of invisible values/norms and their inclusion in law.

Eventually, the number of women and men who were sterilized pursuant to Norway's 1934 sterilization law reflected the same gender imbalance as Allison Carey saw in the case of the United States. From the period 1 June 1934 until 29 December 1942 and from 9 May 1945 to 31 December 1977, there were 46,596 applications for steriliza-

---

561 *Aftenposten* (p.m. Edition), 2 March 1934, p. 2. Preventative detention (sikring") is a Norwegian concept which can mean that a prisoner continues in confinement after he or she has served a sentence. This would most likely take place with regard to violent psycho-sexual persons; in the United States this type of detention would be a civil legal process and not a criminal one.

562 *Aftenposten* (a.m. Edition), January 3, 1934, 1 continued to 6.

563 *Aftenposten* (a.m. Edition), August 29, 1934, 2.

tion in Norway. During the Nazi occupation itself, from 29 December 1942 until 8 May 1945, there were a total of 570 applications.[564] Between 1934 and 1977, the number of women and men applicants under the 1934 law was 32,411 and 14,055 respectively. More than twice the numbers of applications were made by or on behalf of women than men. That imbalance increased to a three-fold difference under the 1942 Nazi inspired sterilization law. Applications by Norway's Medical Director during this period were 281 for women and one for a man.[565]

The number of sterilizations that were actually carried out pursuant to the application procedure was 86.22% of the total number of applications (women) and 97.20% (men) under the 1934 law, 91.28% (women) and 74.77% (men) under the 1942 law, and 86.83% (women) under the Medical Director's application.[566] It must be said that Norway sterilized fewer people than either Sweden or Finland until 1966–1968 when the number of sterilizations in Norwegian hospitals increased dramatically, primarily as a matter of birth control. This continued until the law was changed in 1978 allowing "self decided" abortion until the third month of pregnancy.

Norway did not have the "flood" of immigrants that came to the United States prior to 1907. Nonetheless, it had its own variety of those perceived, as "other" and this group was the focus of sterilization advocates. These were the "taterne" who were an ethnic group who had adopted various ways of life, both settled and mobile, but almost always on the margins of Norwegian social and cultural life. From the middle of the 1800s the DNK had worked with "the travelers." Norway's Christian groups "showed a special interest for this minority and can be seen as what we might call 'moral entrepreneurs' in this area."[567] During this period, the nation-building phase of Norway's history, the idea of a "real Norwegian" was clearly connected to

> more or less romantic pictures of the farmers' life style and culture, such that it became constituted and cultivated through the building of folk museums, through folk music, folk tales, farmer experiences, traditional farmer clothing, village history books and the like.[568]

In all of these areas, there was simply little place – or very little opportunity – for the ethnic minorities mentioned above to fit into society – should they want to - especially if they were labeled as "transient" or "vagrant."

Religious structures as well as the governmental structures intersected to consider this group as a subject for sterilization. In addition, if we look back at the interwar period in Norway, two well-known medical doctors, Ingeborg Aas and Johann

564 Per Haave, *Sterilisering av tatere, 1934–1977: En historisk undersøkelse av lov og praksis* (Oslo, Noreges Forskingsråd, 2000), 152.
565 *Ibid.*
566 *Ibid.*, 154.
567 *Ibid.*, 20–21.
568 *Ibid.*, 21.

Table 4.2: The number of applications for sterilization, 1934–1977. Men and women of tarter ethnicity (Haave's Table 6.10)

	Women	Men	Total
1934-law	113	20	133
1942-law	17	2	19
Medical Director*	3	-	3
Total	133	22	155

* Application made by Medical Director, 1.1.1943–8.5.1945

Table 4.3: Applications for sterilization, consented and completed applications under the 1 June 1934 law with respect to men and women of tater ethnicity (Haave's Table 6.11)

	Women				Men			
	Applications	Consents	Total	Carried Out Percent of the number of applications	Applications	Consents	Total	Carried Out Percent of the number of applications
§3,1	63	61	50	79.4	9	8	7	77.4
§3,2	20	10	18	90.0	6	6	4	66.7
§4	30	28	26	86.7	5	5	4*	80.0
Sum	113	108	94	83.2	20	19	15	75.0

* Sterilization also took place on five (more) men, but instead of being sterilized, they were castrated.

Scharffenberg, had already raised the question of sterilization of the tarterne in 1929. Scharffenberg, who we have mentioned above, played many roles during the interwar period; he was, from 1919 until 1940 the doctor of a Penitentiary and from 1922 was a Chief Resident at the Oslo mental hospital.[569]

The number of taterne who were sterilized under these laws is a bit more difficult to assess than the general population. As a percentage of the total number of people sterilized, they constituted only about a very small portion. If we compare the number of sterilizations on non-"taterslekt"[570], the total number that were carried out between 1935 and 1950 per 1000 citizens in Norway was 2,061. This is from a total

569 *Ibid.*, 67. Scharffenberg held the second position from 1922 until 1941 when, under Nazi occupation, he was removed.
570 Tarter ethnicity.

population of 3,265,126 people, giving us a number of 2.87 per 1000 citizens. Between 1935 and 1977, 155 applications for sterilization of tarter ethnicity were made.[571]

How many of these applications were carried out? Haave gives us the following information.

From these two tables we can see that the percentage of applications from tarter women that were carried out was consistently greater than that for men. But this still does not give us a comparison between applications carried out for tarter persons and non-tarter persons. Haave does, however, give us information about the number of vagrant women who were sterilized as compared to all women in Norway who were born between the years 1900 and 1959 and sterilized under the 1 June 1934 law.

Table 4.4: The number of women in the population sterilized with reference to the 1 June 1934 law on sterilization and who were born between 1900 and 1959 (Haave's Table 6.10)[572]

	§3 first section		**§3 second section**		**§4**		**Total**	
	Number	Per 1000	Number	Per 1000	Number	Per 1000	Number	Per 1000
Vagrant Women (N =2.513)	41	16,32	15	5,97	21	8,36	77	30,64
All women (N = 1.693.244)	27.946	16,50	1.087	0,64	813	0,48	29.846	17,63

Here we can see that the number per 1000 of vagrant women that were sterilized under all three sections was nearly double the number for all women, i.e. 30.64 compared with 17.63. After World War II, the number of sterilizations of men and women under the 1 June 1934 law followed a pattern similar to that described by Allison Carey in the United States. The type of body that was impacted the most, after the introduction of birth control, was the poor female body.[573]

Several groups made note of the taterne and their lifestyle but it was the work of what became known as the Norsk misjon blant hjemløs (NMBH). Originally the group was known as "The Association to fight against the Vagrant" and was a "Christian philanthropic group" and its first efforts were at assimilation of the taterne.[574] This was similar to how various religious and charitable groups in the United States tried to assimilate Native American children. The NMBH group made several assumptions. They believed that a "mobile lifestyle" was more or less criminal and the life style itself was at least partially biologically pre-determined. In addition, the background

571 Per Haave, *Sterilisering av tatere*, 165.
572 *Ibid.*, 168. This table is mistakenly labeled and should be Table 6.12.
573 *Ibid.*, 162.
574 *Ibid.*, 180.

of the group had "an association with the politics of criminality and the racial hygiene viewpoint."[575]

While the NMH made the taterne a focus for its work it was psychiatric institutions that led the way in submitting applications for all vagrants who were sterilized. The NMH led the way in terms of applications for young vagrants, i.e. vagrants between the ages of 17 and 24. During the emphasis on human rights in the 1980s the role of various groups in their use of the 1934 sterilization law was scrutinized by the Storting; remuneration was paid to those still living for having been sterilized and both right- and left-wing governments apologized to them, as did the Norwegian Lutheran Church.

Per Haave points out that Norway's treatment of the tarterne "did not happen in an empty room."[576] Many things could be said about different institutions that dealt with the tarterne. I will focus here on just one, the NMH and on two facets of their work. The first facet is how this group believed itself to be doing, at the very least, philanthropic work for the less fortunate. In 1931, Ingvald B. Carlsen, who was the NMBH General Secretary from 1918 to 1935, said in an informal radio lecture that:

> It's the Christian feeling of responsibility (or the human feeling of solidarity) that tells us that these are human beings and we must try to give them a sense of human worth.[577]

But despite this, the goal of the NMH was always twofold, to gain social control over the tarterne as well as to provide assistance to them. A private Vagrancy Committee was set up in 1933 which set into motion more repressive policies including registration of vagrants, their fingerprinting, charting of prisoners residences along with interning "asocial" vagrants and sterilization of "the lowest level of vagrants."[578] But the rhetoric of care, in this case – Christian rhetoric – is not unlike the rhetoric of the progressive movement in Indiana. In many cases, the progressive movement allied itself with American churches, mostly protestant, and had identical concerns as this NMBH in Norway, albeit to different minority groups.

Just as 1907 in Indiana, there were powerful professional men in Norway who represented the two institutions of medicine and law whose interests intersected with the interests of political parties in Parliament. Although fewer attorneys and medical

---

575 *Ibid.* "Bakgrunnen var en orienteringmot kriminalpolitiske or rasehygieniske synspunkter; grupper med mobile livsformer ble antatt å være mer eller mindre kiminelle, og deres levemåte ble former som delvis biologisk bestemt."

576 Per Haave, "NS-Regimets 'taterpolitikk' – en minoritetspolitikk i utakt?" in Per Ole Johansen (ed.), *På Siden av Rettsoppgjøret* (Oslo: Unipub Forlag, 2006), 180, (my translation).

577 *Ibid.*, 185.

578 *Ibid.*, 187. Omstreiferkomiteen, "...foreslo komiteen en omsteifer- og løsgjengersentral, registrering, en trykt fortegnelse over omsteifere, kartegging av innsattes hjemstavnsforhold samt internering av 'utpreget asosiale omstreifere' og sterilisering av 'de laveststående omsttreifere'."

doctors were elected to the Storting than in the case of Indiana, this was likely a function of the relative prosperity of the two countries, even accounting for the passage of time. Even in 1934, Norway had not yet "caught up" with where Indiana had been in 1907 in terms of the number of doctors who could leave a practice for politics.[579] Another possible explanation was the type of education needed in each country to identify oneself as a "doctor." "Quackeri" (charlatanism) in Norway was a major issue in 1934 and, although the same phenomenon appeared in Indiana in 1907, the state Pure Food and Drug Law, passed in 1907 as a precursor to the national law, helped to relieve that situation.

On 22 August, *Aftenposten* reported on the Jurists' meeting that had begun on the Thursday the 16th in the packed Aula Auditorium at the University of Oslo.[580] Thematically, the issue of the attorney-client privilege and protection of this right was to be discussed but another major impetus for the meeting was that the group was celebrating its 200th year of existence. Various attorneys and dignitaries attended including Professor Fredrik Stang (1867–1941), Supreme Court member Hagerup Bulls and attorneys from Denmark, Sweden, and Finland. King Håkon VII (1872–1957) entered the hall at about noon and Professor Ragnar Knoph (1894–1938), who had been nominated for the Nobel Peace Prize four years earlier by Norway, gave the plenary session speech on "the protection of the personality."[581]

Jurists in Norway were facing not only fundamental epistemic uncertainty about the nature of law itself as revealed in Scandinavian debates about legal realism – which stretched into the 1970s – but practical problems also concerned them. The pace of civil litigation had been increasing in Norway and courts were congested, especially at the appellate level. Lawyers were aware that Norway's civil procedure was in need of revision. This issue, among others, had been up earlier in the year at the annual meeting of jurists in one of Norway's northern-most cities, Tromsø. About 40 jurists[582] from around the country plus 3 chief administrative officers, judges from rural districts, the Mayor of Tromsø and various authorities as well as members of the Trial Lawyers Association attended the meeting.[583] While a number of topics occu-

---

579 Please see, Jonathon Moses, *Norwegian Catch-Up: Development and Globalization before World War II* (Aldershot and Burlington: Ashgate, 2005).

580 *Aftenposten* (p.m. Edition), August 123, 934, 2. The Aula is in use today and is also a tourist attraction. It contains paintings on the walls by the artist Edvard Munch and is used for awarding Nobel prizes as well as for doctoral defenses, public lectures and concerts.

581 In common law countries the "protection of personality" is seen as the basis for tort law and rights of privacy.

582 In 1934, various types of attorneys existed in Norway. The location of knowledge in a society has been addressed by lawyer and sociologist Vilhelm Aubert (1922–1988). He also wrote his PhD dissertation on the subject of attorneys, their class origins, etc.

583 *Aftenposten,* (p.m. Edition), January 5, 1934, 1. Attendees included sorenskrivers Bonnevie and Falch, overrettssakførerne Falck, statsadvodkat Fjalstad and Oslo Chief of Police Jensen.

pied the attention of the attendees, the appellate system in Norway was under review and was subjected to heavy criticism at this meeting. As Vilhelm Aubert later noted, between 1815 and 1950, "the number of attorneys increased by a factor close to 20" while the "number of judgeships was not more than doubled."[584] Sorenskrive (Notary Public and lower-court Magistrate) Bonnevie wondered if the lower courts needed a new appeals process.[585] And, Attorney Falch hinted at the possibility of a circulating Court of Appeals that would travel throughout the country.[586]

One of the most significant legal reforms that were considered in the months of 1934 in the Norwegian media was that of abortion. Eight months after the jurists' meeting referenced above, state's attorney Sunde and a good number of the same jurists convened in Oslo to consider the issue. An extensive article in the *Aftenposten* summarized the speech made by Swedish Cabinet Minister K.J. Schlyter who was featured along with Norwegian state's attorney Sunde.[587] Schlyter, a respected Swedish jurist, who had published a complete collection of old laws as well as participating in the modernization of Swedish law, spoke on induced abortion and its criminal penalties.[588] He began by quoting statistics from Sweden for 1922, 1926 and 1930 that had been gathered by Associate Professor John Naeslund and governmental Bureau Chief K.A. Edin. Their research showed that 15,299 abortions had been performed in Sweden in those particular three years within all hospitals.[589]

The national population of Sweden during those years was 5,987,520 (1922), 6,074,368 (1926) and 6,142,191 (1930).[590] During these three years, about 15,299 abortions were performed; 359 were for "medical" indications and 502 for "criminal" indi-

584 Vilhelm Aubert, *Professions in Norwegian Social Structure*, 254. The number of fathers' of attorneys who themselves were attorneys, businessmen or other academics was in the process of decreasing while the number of attorneys whose fathers were "functionaries", farmers, artisans and workers was increasing. *Ibid.*, see Table II.

585 *Ibid.*

586 *Ibid.* His "hint" was specifically detailed enough to include the fact that it should be composed of lower court judges and a Presiding Judge and proposed a procedure whereby the court might not become overburdened, i.e. letting the Presiding Judge streamline some litigation. In 1915, two new important codes had already been been enacted by the Storting – the Code of Civil Procedure (Tvistemålsloven av 13. August 1915 nr. 6) and the Courts Code (Domstolloven av 13. August 1915 nr. 5) – but this does not seem to have offered any relief in his opinion.

587 *Aftenposten* (p.m. Edition), August 24, 1934, 5.

588 Please see, Jan-Olof Sundell, "Karl Schlyter: A Swedish Lawyer and Politician" in *Stockholm Institute for Scandinavian Law* 40 (2000), 505–514.

589 *Ibid.* This number is very large when one compares it to the number of abortion laws were liberalized in 1938. For example, in 1939 the number of reported legal abortions in Sweden was 439. Please see, http://www.johnstonsarcchive.net/policy/abortion/ab-sweden.html, accessed July 5, 2009. For an overview of abortion liberalization in Europe, please see Christopher Tietze, "Abortion in Europe" in the *American Journal of Psychiatric Health*, 57 (1967), 1923–32.

590 Please see, Statistiska centralbyrå at, http://www.scb.se/Pages/List___25377.aspx last accessed on July 5, 2009.

cations. Among these 502 women who had abortions, 38, or 7.6 percent died. Of the remaining women[591], 3,182 developed fevers and 121 or 2.8 percent[592] died. In 1930, statistics showed a total of 10,445 abortions and 95,000 live births. This meant an average of 10.9 abortions for every 100 live births.[593] But in Stockholm alone, this rate increased significantly to 25.6–33.8 for unmarried women and 15.8 for married women. Edin indicated that he believed the number to be "at least" 30 abortions for every 100 live births in Stockholm. In Germany, the number was said to be 33 per every 100 births. Scandinavian women were not being seen by competent medical doctors or midwives for any number of reasons including the abortion law and perhaps as many as 100 women died every year because of this.[594]

This meeting, which took place after the passage of the sterilization law, demonstrates the on-going articulations between the medical and legal institutions as regards body-law. This is important because the discourses about the revision of the then-current abortion law in Norway clearly over-shadowed the discussion of the sterilization law in 1934 if one considers frequency of discussion in the Norweigan press.

The bodies of those with disabilities and the bodies of criminals carried no particular power vis-a-vis the two major institutions of law and science, but we might expect that the bodies of women would be of some concern since the national birth rate was ostensibly a problem.[595] There was also a concern that women themselves have a degree of participation in decisions regarding reproduction, although this idea is also tied, as we see below, to ideas of the nation's legal "modernization."

---

591 Aftenposten (p.m. Edition) August 24, 1934, 5. The reporter who wrote this article was not specific as to what "of the remaining women" referred to.

592 If we assume that 121 women out of 3,182 died, this gives us 3.8% not 2.8%.

593 Aftenposten (p.m. Edition) August 24, 1934, 5.

594 *Ibid.* The issue of abortion had previously been addressed many times in Oslo newspapers, but in June, in the *Aftenposten*, a signed letter to the Editor was printed. The signators were Dotors Kristen Andersen, Hj. Schelling, Kristen Skajaa, Sofus Widerøe, Supreme Court Judge Thomas Bonnevie, Carl Hartmann, Attorney J.M. Lund and Harold Nørregaard. The question this group posed was whether or not abortion should be permitted if indicated for "humanitarian" or "social" reasons? The letter provided some guidelines; women would be required to apply for the abortion and to meet with three advisors, i.e. the hospital physician, the city or district doctor and a third doctor named by the county commission, all of whom had a duty of confidentiality. (*Aftenposten* (p.m. Edition), June 29, 1934, 1.) The authors of this §245 letter – §245 of the criminal law forbidding abortion – began their argument with statistics. In Germany for the year 1924 there had been over 800,000 abortions. In Oslo's Ulleval Hospital, the number of abortions from 1920–1929 was said to be around 3,800. (*Ibid.*, 2.) The doctors mentioned that they themselves had no wish to be at odds with the criminal law; it was their desire to have an abortion law passed by the Storting that would be punishment-free but yet not imply some moral acceptance of abortion itself. Irrespective of the fact that abortion was to a greater or lesser degree morally reprehensible, the only way to free people form the abuses of "quack-doctors" was to allow legitimate doctors to do the procedure without fear of punishment, or so this group reasoned.

595 *Aftenposten*, (a.m. Edition), May 9, 1934, 3.

For Schlyter, whose support for the changing of laws against abortion seems to be rooted in practicality, there appeared to be "quite a large degree of agreement" on the issue – at least in his social and work circles. He said that the reasons which "can be summarized as ethical and eugenic, should give a right to the termination of pregnancy. There need be no other more exhaustive motivation."[596] He cited cases of rape or incest, or where the mother or father was mentally ill, as obvious candidates for abortion but also mentioned the fact that should a young woman become pregnant and not be afforded the option of an abortion she might become dependent on the man for economic reasons.

Norwegian Medical Director Heitmann was quoted as saying that he would make use of the expression "a violation of a woman's sexual freedom" instead of an offense (crime) against a woman's sexual freedom "so as not to tie the right to abortion to a certain criminal law's perhaps antiquated chapter on sexual offenses."[597] Comparing the proposed Norwegian law to the equivalent Swedish and Danish laws, he said that Norway's law was more like the Swedish law on abortion but with a goal similar to the Danish.[598]

Schlyter then discussed the various "indications" which had been proposed as reasons for an abortion. As to "eugenic" indications, he was very clear about the legal wording for abortion that had been proposed. He said that the "eugenic reasons" for abortion "agree with" the corresponding "eugenic indications" in the new Norwegian and Swedish laws regarding sterilization.[599] Where there is a difference between the two laws – in accordance with the first draft where a reason for sterilization was the transmission of a dangerous bodily sickness – Schlyter preferred to follow the Norwegian law. As regarded the "social" indications in Sweden that existed as a reason for abortion, Schlyter wanted first to rescind the current contraception law, which stood in the way of on-going work on anti-conception methods. "We" are "late-comers" to the modernization of law, he said, and despite having a welfare state and having the information, all types of distressing situations still existed.[600]

Schlyter's idea for the reform of abortion laws also had connections with the new sterilization law. He commented that it had been suggested that, "with the new Norwegian sterilization law as a model", one could reduce the explanation needed for an abortion and that a woman herself could simply ask for the abortion based on a "reason which could be respected." Schlyter thought it impractical to detail all of the reasons that could be given for an abortion. He reasoned "Life is so varied and

596 *Aftenposten* (p. m. Edition), August 24, 1934, 5.
597 *Ibid.*
598 *Ibid.*
599 *Ibid.*
600 *Ibid.*

richer in situations than any theory."[601] In a choice between the previous suggestion and some other language, Schlyter would have chosen language such as "for highly respectable reasons" for the Norwegian sterilization law.[602] But it is clear that he also has some concerns about the language of "respectable reasons" becoming so vague as to encompass too many situations not really worthy of respect. Could a law with this type of wording become meaningless because of its vagueness? As with all drafting of legislation and legal codes, the wording must be detailed enough to mean something and produce the result that is wanted and nothing more – or less.[603]

Schlyter discussed the meaning of "need" in which he placed an emphasis on "economic" need. Should a woman be "condemned" to a pregnancy despite many other births and difficult work as the provider for the children? This type of situation could be similar to the "medical" indication if the mother's health were damaged as a result of carrying the pregnancy to term. But various types of distressing situations in a family could be imagined – for example, when a seaman returns home after a "long" voyage, i.e. more than nine months, and finds his wife pregnant. As the speaker said, we "obviously cannot have a common legal principle that allows for abortion in cases of marital unfaithfulness."[604]

On the other hand, Schlyter reasoned, should a family be allowed to throw a daughter out of the house "onto the street" when it becomes known that she is pregnant – and unmarried? It is possible the only option for her in that situation would be to make a living through prostitution. Often it was the fate of young women who approached a doctor for an abortion and were refused that they went from the doctor's office "into the ocean." Was this not really a "medical" indication or at least an "expanded" medical indication?[605] But he could not accept abortion for unmarried women as a general rule. And, he queried, what if the woman seeking an abortion is a teacher or a nurse? Which hospital supervisor would permit a woman to work as a nurse if she had a child? Obviously, there were societal norms that pertained to women at this time who worked in hospitals or classrooms, i.e. that they be unmarried and childless.[606]

This was neither the first nor the last time that legal reform of abortion laws in Norway would be considered. However, it is significant that it, rather than the sterilization law, was considered more seriously in the pages of both the political right and left media. A hierarchy of bodies was at stake, some more important than others. The

601 *Ibid.*
602 *Ibid.*
603 *Ibid.*
604 *Ibid.*
605 *Ibid.*
606 On August 25, 1934, the second half of the Schlyter's summary was printed in *Aftenposten*. One of leading discourses regarding women during 1934 was the ability of married women to continue working as teachers. Another discourse was the position of young girls who worked as "mothers' helpers."

issue of abortion for women will be revisited in Case Two herein, where yet another dynamic will be investigated, one that proceeded at a slower pace but surfaces when the ideographs, social movements, and rhetorical framing bridgeworks are examined.

4.6 Norwegian Parliamentary Masterframes: Legislating for National Health

While the major discursive masterframe in Indiana was to legislate "against sin", the major discursive masterframe in Norway was to legislate "for health." This is discussed here with reference to the transcript from the committee meeting where the sterilization law was debated.

The "healthy body" rationale was seen in Norway just as in Indiana but the emphasis on sin was not so obvious in Norwegian media. Norway greeted exhibitions from Germany, and one entitled "Healthy mothers – healthy people" made its way to Oslo in March 1934. Not only was this exhibit brought north but it was also welcomed by members of the elite, including members of most powerful political institutions, i.e. the Royal Family (HRH Håkon VII), legal (States Attorney Sunde), and scientific (Medical Director Heitmann). Members of powerful social institutions also welcomed the exhibit. Marie Michelet, the leader of one of the largest women's group in Norway the Norwegian Housewives Association (NHF) and her lieutenants made an outing to the exhibit during their national convention, also held in Oslo. We find that at least two other national women's organizations had also made the same decision to visit the exhibit.[607]

During the autumn and spring of 1907, the focus of politicians in Indiana was first, on the election of the Governor since this determined the party-affiliation of the Speaker of the House. Representative Emmett Branch, who was eventually elected Speaker of the House, determined which bills would ultimately be considered since they depended a great deal on the Speaker's assignment to a specific Committee and the work of that Committee. The success or failure of a particular bill also depended on exactly when the Speaker put the measure to a vote. Rep. Branch was, in essence, the "switch"[608] for a legislative motor, someone who could turn a proposed bill "on" or "off."

---

607 *Aftenposten* (p.m. Edition), March 10, 1934, 7. The other two groups were the "Hjemmenes Velslandsforbund og Norges Røde Kors landsforening" (HVF and NRKF).

608 Reporter Blodgett often referred to the Speaker's platform as "the switch" and, amid numerous cartoons alluding to "special interest" lobbyists, announced that the "Guardians of the Switch" were more "restless" than usual on 7 March 1934 near the end of the session. As Blodgett wrote, "They are afraid that something of benefit to the people instead of the corporations and whisky element will get by them." But Blodgett also gives insight into the actual machinations that the Legislature witnessed.

In Norway, where coalition building was more the model than was rule by a single party as in Indiana, the process was somewhat different. Many issues were of concern to the Storting including forced sales of businesses and farms, sale of effective or dangerous medicines, criminality - even whether or not women should be allowed to become priests in the Norwegian national church.[609] Suffice it to say that, based on the space given to such types of stories in major Norwegian newspapers, the Storting was more concerned with these matters than with the proposed sterilization law. In addition, unlike in Indiana, we have the actual printed record of the Committee Meeting where the sterilization proposal was debated and it is to that meeting that I turn in this section.

On 9 May 1934, a little after noon, a Storting Committee took up the matter of the Report from the Justice Committee on the proposed sterilization law. President Eiesland called the Committee to order and the Chair of the committee was Bjørnson (Bondepartiet, B). Members who spoke about the bill were Bonde (SP), Bonnevie (Ap), Fjalstad (H) and Cabinet Minister Sunde. In all, this Committee handled 8 items that afternoon, of which the sterilization law was number seven and it did so in 2 hours and 10 minutes, or, on average, it considered each matter for about 15 minutes.

The persons who spoke on this record were a unique set of individuals elected in 1934 and serving until 1936. Perhaps, the most interesting was an engineer, Gjert Edvard Bonde, from Bergen, the sole representative of the Society Party in the committee. He was one of two substitutes[610] for the actual representative, Bergen sociological author and founder of the Society Party, Bertram Dybwad Brochmann (1881–1956) who had been unexpectedly elected in late 1933.[611] The Farmers' Party was the

Sometimes when the clouds were the darkest and the air was heavy with gloom, and the Guardians of the Switch felt like going out to get a drink but were afraid to leave, Mr. Floyd Wood would enliven things with his famous song:

> Carl Wood he had a little gas bill
> Sam Murdock he laid it on a shelf
> And every time it tried to move
> It spanked its little self.

("Right in Among Legislators." *Indianapolis News*, 8 March 8, 1907.) What this appears to say is that Speaker Branch and his subordinates had to literally stay in place in order to defeat bills that the Hanley administration did not favor.

609 The last issue failed by one vote but was revisited again in the 1970s. In the translated transcription of the debate at Appendix E, Bjørnson makes mention of his vote for women priests. This gives a clue as to how fluid "progressive" politics was in Norway as well as in Indiana.

610 Although not elected, Bonde would substitute for Dybwad when he was unavailable.

611 The other substitute ("suppleanter") from the Samfundspartiet, also from Bergen, was a Resident Chaplain ("residerende kapellan"), Hans Bauge. http://exxtweb3.nsd.uib.no/data/polsys/Index.cfm?ArkivNr=18&Institutionsnummer=1...., accessed March 7, 2007. The term "supleanter" or "vararepresentant" meant that Bonde and Bauge were substitutes for the elected representative if he was unable to be present.

third largest party in the Storting and its representative on the Committee was Erling Bjørnson, a farmer from Opland County, one of 21 representatives and 7 substitutes. Carl Emil Christian Bonnevie (1881–1972), who was a rural magistrate from Lofoten as well as an Ap representative from Nordland District, was the third member of the committee.[612] The final member of the Committee was a state's attorney, Olaf Fjalstad, a Conservative representative also from Nordland County. He was first elected to the Storting in 1928 and would remain in that seat until occupation and afterwards until 1945. While representing this county he was also the Mayor of Tromsø in 1927 and a member of that city council from 1923 -1937.[613]

The Society Party (SP) was a very small party, organized by Brochmann in the early 1930s; the party disbanded itself in 1940 with Nazi Germany's occupation of Norway. Brochmann began his career by creating The Free Society Press[614] in 1929 and the newspaper *Samfundsliv* (*Societal Life*)[615] in 1931 and finally, organized the Society Party in 1933. There was little structure to the party and this gave Brochmann great latitude in the formation of policy. While in the Storting, he refused his salary saying he did not want to be a "parasite"[616] on society. But Farmers' Party member Bjørnson also used the word "parasite" in this debate since it referenced Brochmann's SP philosophy. The debate itself has been translated from the original and can be found at Appendix E.[617] Despite his refusal of a salary, Brochmann later aligned himself with the economic policies of the Quisling government and, after the war, was convicted of treason. The last time a Society Party member stood for election in Norway was in 1949. Robert Lalla describes Brochmann's ideas as a "a combination of Christianity and depth psychology."[618] In 1936, Bonde himself described Brochmann's economic politics as a "total economy", one in which the

---

612 I have interpreted the Norwegian word "fylke" as "district." Bonnevie was "egnens stortingsrepresentant" from 1934 to 1936. Please see, http://no.widkipedia.org/w/index.php?title=Carl_Emil_Christian_Bonnivie&printable=..., accessed June 20, 2009. He was also stationed as part of the Norwegian legation in Berlin and Vienna from 1919–1923.

613 *Ibid.*, 183. The composition of the 1934–1936 Storting can be seen at Appendix D with regard to party composition and livlihood.

614 Det Frie Samfunds Forlag.

615 Sanfundsliv.

616 "Snylte" in Norwegian.

617 The word "parasite" was also in circulation in both race-hygiene materials as well as in the Samfundpartiet rhetoric. The most that can be said is that Bjørnson may have used the word in his opening remarks as an intentional brace thrown at the feet of Bonde.

618 Robert Lalla, "Henimot nullpris! Samfundspartiet økonomiske tanker" in *Diskusjonsnotat #D-11/2004*, p. 4 at http://www.umb.no/ios/Publiskasjoner/d2004/d2004-11.pdf, accessed December 7, 2007. "...en blanding av kristendom og dybdepsykologi." The term "depth psychology" was coined by Swiss psychiatrist Eugen Bleuler (1857–1939) and, today, refers to a combination of theories and therapies usually attributed to Sigmund Freud, Carl Gustav Jung and William James.

most important elements were "...decapitalization, a national accounting [system] and decentralization."[619]

S.R. Bjørnson (B) started his comments by proudly endorsing the sterilization bill. Saying that it "fell to a farmer" who understood the workings of nature to speak first in advancement of the bill, Bjørnson was enthusiastic about all things scientific. Science and the will of the people, striding "hand in hand", had increased the average life expectancy of Norwegians. If this was to continue, then "powerful, genetically sound and productive stock" had to be produced, and "parasites" had to be eliminated just as weeds on farm had to be eliminated. However, those in society who were "capable workers" had, he argued, been "saddled" with a broad range of taxes and fees since, by 1934, it was no longer a matter of being "disgraced" if one went on welfare. This was a situation that made the capable, productive workers lose their own "will to live."

Bjørnson did mention the German forced sterilization law, but only in passing. He mentioned that the then-current German government took the condition of future generations so seriously that it disbursed "hundreds of millions of kroner" to help "new marriages." But he moved on rather quickly to say that future generations of Norwegians might well criticize the Storting later for not acting sooner and in a more fundamental manner. He also argued that the law "also gives an opening to go a bit further and open for admission to forced sterilization...[to other persons]."[620] I think it is fair to conclude from this that Bjørson probably hoped that this law would be only a first step towards a more comprehensive law since he added, if a such a bill were to be introduced, he would vote for it. Then, Bjørnson analyzed the strategy of why the bill was not as far-reaching as "we" would have liked. It was written as it was for fear that, if broadened, it would not be acceptable to the Lagting in much the same way as the recently failed law on women priests was not acceptable, a measure which he had also supported. Bjørnson was a man who clearly considered himself as a "progressive", supporting both the sterilization law and the law allowing women to become priests in the state Church. Bjørnson ended his remarks by thanking Minister Sunde for the "splendid" bill and the Norwegian Advisory Committee for Race-Hygiene and its "indefatigable leader", Dr. Alf Mjøen, who might at that point – finally – receive the recognition in Norway that he had achieved in other nations.

Representative Bonde was the next to speaker and called the bill "...on the whole, one of the most dangerous proposals that has seen the light of day."[621] From his remarks we know that Bonde believed that the law would obviously – and was intended – be extended to include "sexual criminals", a term never really defined by

619 *Ibid.* See also, Gjert Edvard Bonde, 3rd ed.*Totalitetsøkonomi: En oversikt over Samfundspartiets ideologi og retningslinear* (Bergen, 1966).
620 Appendix E.
621 Appendix E.

anyone in the Committee, thus raising the specter of homosexuals grouped together with pedophiles and sexually violent persons. Bonde's argument, as we will see, was one that has not changed much over the time span of these two cases. His opinion clearly favored "nurture" as opposed to "nature" since it was "societal influences" that he believed were the cause of crime. Bonde brought powerful themes to his remarks and used religion, saying that the Storting had not learned its catechism lessons and was "casting stones" just as in the Bible parable. He also accused the bill of being "barbaric and medieval" in its functioning, i.e. letting the innocent suffer for the sins of the guilty since it would be criminals who would suffer for the failure of society to change itself. Calling to mind more "modern" lines of argument, he said that if one wanted to be absolutely sure to create criminals, then jail was the place to do this. Finally, he challenged the Committee to consider the "new science" of psychoanalysis as a substitute measure for actual sterilization in the case of criminals.

Committee member Judge Bonnevie calmly rejected all of Bonde's arguments, saying Bonde had "missed the mark" in his argumentation, i.e. that the bill was not intended to sterilize "this third group", i.e. criminals. Where Bonde relied on religion in argumentation, Bonnevie instead spoke of political theory when he argued that the "right[s] of the individual must be weighed against the right[s] of society...."[622] But Bonnevie also thought that he and like-minded supporters of the bill had achieved " a **deeper insight** both into the interests of society and a deeper feeling of responsibility for generations to come."[623] What he meant by this deeper insight is unclear. In closing, he made sure to distance what the Committee was doing from anything that had happened in Germany, saying that whatever Germany had done was neither "partly" nor "totally" of any consequence in the Norwegian debate. In Bonnevie's mind, the prepatory work on the bill done by other Scandinavian countries as well as work done by Dr. Johann Scharffenberg was of more importance.

At that point in the discussions, Bonde handed a motion to the President that the 1934 Odelsting not consider the bill during that Session. Representative Fjalstad (H), a second-tier player in the debate, spoke next and merely echoed the importance of the consent provisions in the bill, echoing what both Bjørnson and Bonnevie had said. Cabinet Minister Sunde then spoke, essentially taking the debate in another direction in what amounted to an *ad hominum* attack on Bonde. Minister Sunde said "...before a person uses such types of expressions, he should take the trouble to read the bill and preferably, the entire preparatory work."[624] In other words, Bonde's competence as a diligent and careful representative was, at that point, on the table in much the same way as the bill itself.

622 Appendix E.
623 *Ibid.*
624 *Ibid.*

Bonde spoke accusing Bonnevie of claiming the same opinions that he, Bonde, was defending saying this was "typical" for Bonnevie. Bonde railed, as much as one could "rail" in about 15 minutes of debate, against the "system" in the Storting that allowed only for the "party opinion" and nothing beyond it. The fact that Bonde represented an entire party, the Society Party, was of no moment, or so he said. Other "scientific" work, at odds with the need for sterilization of criminals, was well known throughout the world and none of this had been taken into consideration in the preparation of the bill. Bonde challenged Sunde to deny this.

Bjørnson then spoke, taking his cue from Sunde, and advancing Sunde's accusation that Bonde had not even read the bill, much less the preparatory work. However, the Storting debate was conducted in 1934 and whatever the written and unwritten rules of conduct were, Bonde was accused of an "attack" on the Committee.[625] Bjørnson simply reiterated previous arguments, but also mentioned the birth rate in Denmark where "healthy...responsible families" were not having children while "defective families" were; this appears as a typical "race suicide" argument, reminiscent of the same arguments in Indiana in 1907. By his remarks, we can see that Bjørnson was quite involved in the passage of the bill. This stemmed, at least in part, from the fact that he and Bonde had crossed swords before since, since Bjørnson said, "this is not the first time that I have fought against this reactionary line."[626] Bjørnson ended by saying that the Society Party advanced "a type of freedom that the rest of us do not understand."[627]

Bonnevie spoke for the last time, again accusing Bonde of not reading the documents associated with the bill. And it is here that we find that other, unprinted documents had been read by the Committee that were not included in the record of the Storting; Bonnevie says that if Bonde had read everything, "and, in addition, more of the unprinted documents", Bonde would have seen the necessity for the law.[628] Exactly where these "unprinted" documents came from was not mentioned. However, given the nature of the debate, I suspect they were most likely from Professor Ragnar Vogt, Medical Director Scharffenberg and others, as well as Dr. Alf Mjøen.

Bonde's last remarks were directed at countering the accusation that he had not read the bill. He asserted that he has read the documents and said, "I treat this matter quite simply from the spirit of the law and the meaning that lies in the law and which will lead to the castration of sexual criminals as one of its goals."[629] Calling the law a "brutal" and a "violent" intrusion on the individual, Bonde ended by saying that

---

625 Appendix E.
626 Appendix E.
627 Appendix E.
628 *Ibid.*
629 Appendix E.

the branch of psychology that Vogt and Scharffenberg represented had nothing to do with the science he had in mind.

Finally, a vote was taken on Bonde's attempt to postpone the bill and this was defeated. A second vote was taken on the law, with one vote against it. After a suggestion from the President, a unanimous vote was taken agreeing to send it to the Lagting.[630]

These 10–15 minutes of Norwegian parliamentary history are informed by a number of values/norms and normative processes discussed in Chapter 2. If we apply Tamanaha's model, then we must examine the social norms and societies from which the law originated. The use of the words and phrases such as "parasite", "capable workers", "innocent suffer for the sins of the guilty" and "brutal and violent intrusion" in rhetoric taps into a very powerful epistemic level, a resting place for such norms/values sometimes espoused during moral panic and epistemic uncertainty.

4.7 Reactions to the Norwegian Sterilization Law

In 1938, Harald Bjelke issued a directive from Oslo regarding the "supervision" and "treatment" of sterilization cases.[631] It sought to clarify various situations and was incorporated by reference into the Norwegian sterilization legislation. It also added sections such as the fact that permission would no longer be needed if the medical reasons for the operation were themselves lawful.[632] Although the 1934 law was modified after its passage, the biggest changes were yet to come after Nazi occupation.

German forces entered Norway on 9 April 1940 and completed their occupation approximately one month later, on 8 May 1940. The Storting was disbanded and instead, a "Riksting" was set in motion as a law-making institution. The Nasjonal Samling (NS) government also instituted a leadership role for a person whom they considered had natural leadership capabilities, i.e. Vidkun Quisling, and set about to administer the nation. Since the normal prepatory work usually done in advance of the passage of a law was not done after this, preparation was "correspondingly reduced, both in quantity and content."[633] The Justice Minister during the Nazi

---

630 Appendix E. Those who were appointed to the Sterilization Advisary Committee under paragraph 2 included Medical Director Heitman who was the "Chairman", prof. Ingebrigtsen, prof. Ragnar Vogt, Supreme Court judge J. Rivertz and dr. Nic. Hoel." (*Aftenposten* (a.m. Edition), July 27, 1934, 2.)

631 Haave, *Sterilisering av tatere, 1934–1977,* 394. Note 510. "Veiledning i behandling av steriliseringssaker."

632 *Ibid.* Paragraph 2.

633 Henriette Sinding Aasen, *Rasehygiene og menneskeverd* (Oslo: Insititutt for offentlig rettskriftserie nr. 4, Kvinnerettslige studier nr. 28 (A), 1989), 5.

occupation of Norway was Sverre Riisnæs[634] and the Medical Director was Thorleif Østrem.[635]

The "Lov nr. 1 til vern om folkeætten av 23 juli 1942 med tilhørende forskrifter av 1 oktober 1943" (hereafter, "Protection Law of 23 July 1942") held that any person who had a "genetic sickness or defective condition" could be forcibly sterilized.[636] The point of the legislation was to prevent persons with "bad"[637] genetic material from reproducing. Briefly, the changes expanded the ways in which the 1934 law could apply to a person. §13 annulled the 1 June 1934 law on sterilization. §8 changed the composition and size of the 1934 law's Advisory Committee under its §2. Whereas previously the Committee had 4 members in addition to the Medical Director as Chair – 1 woman, 1 Judge and 2 medical doctors – the committee would, in 1942, consist of 6 members named by the Ministry of the Interior and was composed of 2 doctors, 1 eugenicist, 1 Judge and 1 woman with the Committee empowered to elect the Chair.[638] §5 allowed suggestions for whom to be sterilized. These could be put forward by a doctor, the head of a prison, force work institution, school, hospital, or reformatory.[639] In addition, the Police Chief, the Welfare Board, the Guardianship Committee or the Sobriety Committee of the place where the person lived or was currently located could also make the recommendation.[640] Finally, what Representative Bonde had feared during the Storting debate of 1934 eventually became a reality. §3 allowed removal of the desire to reproduce if the individual was found guilty of a crime under Chapter 19 of the Criminal Code and it was presumed that this conviction was the result of an "abnormal" sex urge. Forcible sterilization could also take place if the person was mentally ill, developmentally delayed, had permanently impaired mental faculties or there was a danger that the person would commit some crime under Chapter 19 of the Criminal Code.

The regulations enacted on 1 October 1943 ennumerated the types of hereditary conditions that were presumed to be included in the 1942 law. These included mental illness, and "developmental disability", "serious" forms of psychopathy including antisocial individuals, "serious" forms of alcoholism, schizophrenia, epilepsy, St. Vitus Dance, blindness, deafness, "serious" forms of bodily malformation. What was actually in this list was, however, almost inconsequential since it also included a

634 It would be interesting to know if this man Riisnæs was the same policeman
who testified at the Mrs. Tilka hearing. Both the Mrs. Tilka and Mrs. Aagot Hansen cases are mentioned below.

635 Appendix E, §2

636 *Ibid.*

637 [638] Haave, *Sterilisering av tatere, 1934–1977*, p. 394. Note 510. "Veiledning i behandling av steriliseringssaker."

638 *Ibid.*

639 *Ibid.*

640 *Ibid.*

catchall phrase whereby all serious forms of other sickness or defective conditions that were not mentioned could be a basis for inclusion under the 1942 law.

After the Nazi occupation, the law of 1 June 1934 law was again in full force and effect in Norway. It wasn't until 1950 that then Medical Director Karl Evang added another directive to the use of the sterilization law.[641] Certain IQ requirements were set in place and three types of situations were discussed. If a person was between 9 and 12 years old and had an IQ of 56–75, then this was "often" seen as a case of developmental disability, especially when combined with some psychological problem.[642] If the same person had an IQ of 75–90, s/he was presumed to be "normal" so long as there was no psychopathology or mental illness that complicated the matter.

Finally, forty-three years later, on 3 June 1977, a new law was passed that replaced the 1 juni 1934 sterilization law. The new law (3 juni. Nr. 57, 1977 Lov om sterilliser-ing) provided for sterilization or castration of a person living in Norway if the person was 25 years and applied for permission for it to take place.[643] The medical indications used to set the law in motion were limited and it was not applicable to cases of "medical or other reasons" for the operation. Furthermore, the law was not seen as commonly applicable to persons with serious mental problems or to the developmentally delayed or to psychological impairment.[644]

Henriette Sinding Aasen has made an evaluation of the 1934 law in light of the changes made later in 1942. She found that in the prepatory work of the 1934 law, there was contact with German authorities regarding the Norwegian sterilization legislation.[645]

> Among other things that were said about the German sterilization law of 1933 was that it was "alleged" to have been used as a pattern before the decision in the Committee's proposed bill was drafted. (Medisinalavdeligen 1941, s.5)[646]

Her final evaluation of the two laws is very interesting. After having studied both laws and the entire racial hygiene debate in Norway prior to World War II, she says that

---

641 *Ibid.*

642 *Ibid.*

643 Hans Flock and Birger Stuevold Lassen, Henrik Bull, Anne-Marie Tronslin (eds.), *Norges Lover 1687–2003* (Oslo: Det Juridiske Fakultet at the University of Oslo, Hos Glyldendal Akademisk, 2004), 1073.

644 *Ibid.* §2 "Dette gjelder ikke person som har en alvorlig sinnslidelse eller en psykisk utviklingshemmet eller psykisk svekket." This phrase however, is footnoted with reference to Jfr. §3. "Lovens område" is translated as "jurisdiction."

645 Aasen, *Rasehygiene og menneskeverd*, 55. Note 820.

646 *Ibid.* Blant annet ble det sagt at den tyske steriliserings-lov av 1933 "formentlig" hadde tjent som forbillde for vises bestemmelse i komitéens forslag.

> I am left with the image of a long process starting with medical and biological research, that built up towards the insane climax represented by National Socialism. Throughout, the goal all along was to change the fact that even "lesser" individuals, people with symptoms of deviance, were part of society as a whole.[647]

Consequently, she asserts that there was no "fundamental" separation between the 1934 law and the 1942 law in how those in control viewed society, whether or not the basis for the implementation and reinforcement of them was different.[648]

Representations of what good science could produce were combined with legal representations in an on-going process that was reflected in the laws themselves. The sterilization law of 1934 was preceded by a great deal of work by numerous people in Norway and it did not appear from nowhere. The representation by science that it could promise "progress" was both implicit and explicit. This provided yet another untested assumptive articulation with the law. If science could produce "progress" in a socially and politically unstable time for the majority of people in the country, then one could assume that the always-delicate balance between individual and societal rights and duties might also shift.

One problem with previous evaluations of the eugenics movement and its legal manifestations has been to assume that it was confined to a time period before and during World War II. However, some of these laws remained in effect, for example quietly sterilizing people that were not so obviously "defective" and usually due to their body status, i.e. female, poor and/or non-white. This is seen in both the American and Norwegian halves of Case One. The number of women who were sterilized continued to increase after World War II in both countries.[649]

4.8 Jasanoff Fields Reflected in the Norwegian Media

On Monday 8 January 1934 *Aftenposten* produced a large article on Gregor Mendel (1822–1884) entitled "The Founder of Genetics Research – Gregor Mendel."[650] Since the Austrian monk Mendel was born on July 20 (or 22), 1822 and died in January 1884, the article was meant to coincide with the anniversary of Mendel's death. Written by Fridthøf Økland, the article goes in predictable directions describing Mendel's work and its importance for science and society in 1934. However, two interesting uses of language did appear. First, is that Økland uses the word "tragedy" to refer to the

---

647 *Ibid.*, 62.

648 *Ibid.*, 62–63.

649 Carey, "Gender and Compulsory Sterilization, 74–105. Note 2008.

650 *Aftenposten* (a.m. Edition), January 8, 1934, 8. Norwegian newspapers of all political orientations did, on occasion, carry "educational" articles. *Arbeiderbladet* would normally do this in their Saturday afternoon edition while *Aftenposten* might do it at any time but more normally in the morning edition.

fact the laws of genetics were not discovered sooner. Second, it was also a "tragedy", according to Økland, that Darwin was unaware of Mendel's work since, if Darwin had been aware of that body of work, the history of Biology would have been written differently. In addition to the announcement of the new German Race Hygiene Law on 2 January and this article, we can see that within the first 8 days of newspaper production in 1934, all the elements of competing discourses and values/norms were already in place, ready to be played out over the next period to time.

Normatively inspired representations of what human sexuality meant took place in Norwegian newspapers in 1934. Dr. phil. Richard Eriksen wrote a feature article entitled "Sexual Fears" on 25 August.[651] He began his editorial admitting that sexual information in society was necessary. However, "the sexual problem" could not be solved with information alone. What this "sexual problem" actually was remained undefined and only insinuated but one possibility is that it may have focused on masturbation, just as that also was a major reason for sterilization according to Indiana's Dr. Sharp. According to Eriksen, the problem was so interwoven into the personal, social, cultural and religious life of society that physiological and hygienic knowledge alone would not be adequate to solve it. Eriksen wrote in his editorial against what he considered one of the fallacious arguments against sexual abstinence that was circulating at that time. The argument was that the male sexual organs needed to be emptied from time to time just as the urine bladder was emptied and that not to do this was unhealthy. Setting one's urges free as psychoanalysis suggested was also no solution according to Eriksen, who mentioned Jung, Adler and Freud and the fact that he was uncomfortable with their work.[652]

Also in August, Lektor Harald Amundsen wrote a feature article entitled "The Feminine Direction in the 'New' Genetics."[653] Amundsen cited to author Adolph Mathias of Germany on the discovery of the sex-linked XY chromosome concept, the Y from the father and the X from the mother, which, when united, produced a male

---

651 *Aftenposten* (a.m. Edition), August 25, 1934, 2. This type of article was a regular in *Aftenposten*. I use the term "feature article" for what is the norwegian word "kronikk" which is a submitted op-ed piece. It is not the quivalent of an editorial; it was a solicited piece or one sent by a professional in the community for inclusion in the newspaper. It was usually a political or scientific-educational article, located at the bottom of the second page.

652 *Ibid.* A Richard Eriksen defended his PhD dissertation in Christiania in December of 1915. The thesis was entitled "The Psychological Basis of Thinking" ("Tænkningens psykologiske utviklingsbetingelser") Eriksen's disapproval of "modern" psychology, in combination with Bonde's comments in the Storting Justice Committee meeting, indicates a split of opinion within the scientific and political communities on the worth of psychiatry, a split possibly by one's party affiliation. We find a repeat of this issue in the 1970s with the issue of treatment for a young girl supposedly possessed by the devil. Should the Church or a psychiatrist treat her?

653 "Den feminineretning i den 'nye' opdragelse" *Aftenposten* (a.m. Edition), August 1, 1934, 2. The title "Lektor" is used for the highest teaching position in secondary schools and for some positions at the university level.

offspring (XY).[654] Amundsen was not pleased with this development, whether based in accurate scientific research or not, since "this double-influence" had made its mark in both school and at home in Norway. He said that the "womanly element has become over-balanced."[655] He complains of Fru Stang from the Norwegian Feminist Association, saying "Before fru Stang and modern psychology gave us an explanation, we didn't know how the reduction in the number of children – all children – has now come to be." Amundsen also cited to Adalbert Czerny (1863–1941), a Berlin medical doctor, who was prominent in the specialization of what is now known as pediatrics but one sentence in particular leaves little doubt as to the political – rather than scientific – nature of his editorial. He says:

> What is needed now is resolute action against the destructive activity of the last generation if the mind of the nation is not to be destroyed.

Whatever Amundsen perceived the influence of the feminine and of psychology on children to be, it was to him a most serious matter. His first editorial was continued the next day when he cited to educational psychologist Henri Bouchet complaining that there is a "real individualism" and a "false individualism", the latter leading to "egoism" and a "lack of discipline."[656]

In this brief compilation of science-related articles that circulated in the media in Norway 1934, we see that the representations from experts ranged from what we now view as absurd to articles that now seem standard or even about the cutting edge of science work on genetics. But we should remember that, to the persons living at the time, it might have been "absurd" that the physical sex of an individual was determined by chromosomal input from both the male and the female. Only since 1934 has this been accepted as good science. It was good science in 1934 too, except that Amundson's interpretation of it politicized the scientific fact. Otto Mohr feared "objective" scientists entering into problems "not strictly scientific", and Amundson's article demonstrates how Mohr's fear could be played out in society.[657]

In this society and this time, what type of treatment could a person with no money or influence expect to be treated? I present two examples here – one "Tilka" and Aagot Hansen.

654 *Ibid.*

655 *Ibid.*

656 It is difficult for a non-Norwegian to understand the meaning and importance of this charge of "egoism." At this time especially, but even today, the word is used to mean something more than simply being self-centered.

657 Library of Congress (Washington, D.C., U.S.A.), *Papers of Margaret Sanger*, Accession Number 16,700, Vol. 29 Reel 19. Letter dated 11 May 1926. Letter dated Oslo, 8/11, 1927 by Otto Mohr, end page two and begin page three.

Unemployment and homelessness in Oslo presented a problem and the actions of those that were charged with keeping order articulated with both the medical and legal institutions. And, as I will point out, neither of these institutions could be counted on to resist non-normative behavior, thus unwittingly adding to the categories of people who could be forcibly sterilized. This was seen in the judicial machinations surrounding two women – Aagot Hansen and Tilka. The equivalent articulation occurred in the United States in the Henry Thaw case although the precipitating factors were different.

Of these two cases, the Tilka case is the easier to summarize. She had stolen a pair of pajamas and Officer Riisnæs testified against her, despite the fact that her competence was clearly an open question. On 3 January 1934 *Aftenposten* reported that Judge Juelsrud had refused to jail Tilka for lack of evidence.[658] Tilka was put on a stool before him and the Court tried to take testimony from her. Her defense attorney was playwright and defense attorney Vilhelm Dybwad (1863–1950). The ultimate goal of the hearing was to decide if she should be forced to undergo a psychiatric observation. What was known was that she was 60 years old and had been born in Danzig. As the newspaper reported, she appeared nervous and "broken." Her testimony was "unclear" and her memory was "very bad." She did not remember how many children she had or where she had been and when. From other testimony we learn that, between 3 June and 26 December 1933, she had been "disorderly" and had finally been jailed under Criminal Law §148 and §257 for stealing some pajamas. Police Officer Riisnæs[659] testified that she had also served 40 days some sixteen years earlier for shoplifting. No decision was made and the entire matter was revisited in the newspaper throughout 1934. Here we have the intersubjective category of gender implicated along with the facts for being older, poor and from another country.

The articulations in Tilka's case were standard but Aagot Hansen's case is notable because she had spent a number of years confined in a mental institution – without actually being mentally ill. Headlines from *Aftenposten* on 16 January declared that there were "strong" allegations of misconduct against the doctor involved in that case. Hansen had as her attorney, a Mr. Fuglesang, who was on that day in the process of taking the testimony in court from Hansen's doctor, also named Hansen.[660] According to Fuglesang, the doctor had shown "gross inattention" to the patient and her situation.[661] We read of Attorney Fuglesang's accusation and yet, the state's doctor, Dr. Hansen, had provided for the Court a lengthy document outlining his compliance with all the pertinent rules and regulations. Fuglesang's retort was reported as "dramatic" and to the effect that if the state-employed doctor had only used the printed

658 *Aftenposten* (a.m. Edition), januar 3, 1934, 1, continuing to 2.
659 Riisnås is only identified as "politifullmektig", i.e. assistant Chief of Police or Desk Sargeant.
660 *Aftenposten* (p.m. Edition), January 16, 1934, 1.
661 *Ibid.*

form, then he might not have had "enough space to write his (numerous) erroneous notations."[662] Was Aagot Hansen merely a petty, female troublemaker who must be mentally defective since she did not fit into the normative social structures held by the medical and legal institutions of that time and place?

Dr. Hansen was eventually charged with unlawful detention of Aagot Hansen under Criminal Law §226. Claims were brought against him not only for damages done to Aagot Hansen but also for the costs of Fuglesang's work. Fuglesang also examined the Director of the Lier Asylum, Dr. Christian Grimsgaard (1868–1939). Fuglesang emphasized that Grimsgaard should have refused to admit Hansen from the start after an examination of the papers which accompanied her to the asylum. Using a phrase that has become a classic in American tort law, Fuglesang said that Grimsgaard "should have known" by looking at the papers that she was not to be admitted. Fuglesang quoted from the State Attorney's brief that essentially admitted that Grimsgaard should have released Aagot Hansen, especially since both Professor Ragnar Vogt and Doctor Evensen had not found her to be mentally ill.[663]

Aagot Hansen testified as to the details of her handling at the Lier Asylum but there is not a great deal of this testimony in the newspaper. However, Fuglesang produced the initial observation of Aagot Hansen's presenting characteristics as "frigid, and with feelings of inadequacy."[664] Within the presence of the patient, Grimsgaard was reported to have said, "One gets all types of folks here." When trying to substantiate this and other facts, Fuglesang was denied a meeting with the workers and nurses at the Lier Asylum. He also reminded the Court that the Mental Health Asylum Control Commission required the patient to be examined within 7 days of admittance and, if this had been done, it would have been obvious that she was not mentally ill.[665] As the reporter noted when ending the article, absolutely nothing had been said to discredit Aagot Hansen's behavior. And, at that point, the case had only begun.

On 3 February, newspaper reporting of the case continued.[666] Fuglesang's adversary was statsadvokat Jak E. Anderssen (b. 1882). The use of Anderssen in this case is interesting since Anderssen had been an Assistant Chief of Police in Oslo for many years and according to *Aftenposten* "had a great concern for cases involving the mentally ill."[667] In fact, he had written a handbook for their treatment in 1921. Anderssen argued that, since Police Chief Bang's choice had been to put Hansen in administra-

662 *Ibid.* From these newspaper accounts, Fuglesang appears to have been a seasoned attorney and knew how to use a moment in the courtroom to his advantage. It was clearly one of those "dramatic" moments when he addressed the state's witness Dr. Hansen and asked – rhetorically – if if he would have had enough space to write everything about the case if he'd used the required form.

663 *Ibid.*

664 What these two indications have to do with mental illness is unstated.

665 *Aftenposten* (p.m. Edition), January 16, 1934, 1.

666 *Aftenposten* (a.m. Edition), February 3, 1934, 5.

667 *Ibid.*

tive observation, a choice he could make, her detention was completely lawful. In that sense, her detention was more "considerate" than the issuance of a Commitment Order to Prison.[668] When Officer Riisnæs testified at the Tilka hearing, it probably also had something to do with the number of unemployed out on the streets of Oslo rather than simply dealing with a "disorderly" older woman. One way for the Oslo police to cope could have been to use other institutions such as those for the "insane" to deal with the problem of overcrowding in the Oslo jail; this also made these people someone else's financial problem.

A number of legal questions were addressed during the hearing. The question arose whether or not a declaration of observation had been written. There had been interference with a citizen's liberty; this would have been the best method to use in order to avoid criticism. The newspaper commented, "It appears, nevertheless, that no place is it written that the observation document should be written and that this form can obviously in simple cases be ignored."[669] Should Chief of Police Bang have demanded a court order to take Aagot Hansen into custody at the hospital? The state's attorney answered in the negative saying that many cases were handled in Oslo which could, in fact, have been prosecuted as criminal cases but which were handled as an administrative matter. He gave the example of a man who had begun firing his rifle in his house and the occupants reported that they had been concerned for his mental health; this case had been handled administratively rather than criminally.

Fuglesang asked if, in another case where a man had shot the rifle, was it reported to the police? The answer was "No" but with regard to the Aagot Hansen case, Bang had a police report to consider and which he depended upon to become involved in the case. How one decided to become involved Bang said, "It [the decision] must be based on [the] discernment/understanding [of the authorities]."[670] But Fuglesang was not deterred. He asked, "On the Police Chief's discernment alone?" The witness answered, "It could be. It depends on the situation and circumstances."[671]

In response, the state's attorney had the witness testify that a policeman did not have the psychological insight needed to appraise the detainee's mental condition, that only a qualified doctor could do so. The witness said it was impossible to have a working knowledge of everyone and that one had to rely on reports given by people who knew the unruly – and possible ill – person. If there was a sense of urgency, one could rely on the police doctor for an observation as to the detainee's mental condition.[672]

668 *Ibid.*
669 *Ibid.*
670 *Ibid.*
671 *Ibid.*
672 *Ibid.*

Fuglesang continued and suggested that not out of respect to Aagot Hansen herself but out of respect for the larger municipality where Lier was located, shouldn't the judicial path have been chosen? The witness answered that one couldn't really say that it was a mistake to have chosen the administrative solution. He did not know if the doctor's information resulted in the request for admission to the asylum but the state's attorney statements were enough since there actually were numerous documents, which the Chief of Police had no need to see, and should rather be in a closed envelope. There was a form for this type of information, but it wasn't necessary to use it. All the information could have been written on another paper. Fuglesang asked the witness if there were forms available and the witness answered that the police station as "full up" with them.

Later, in the courtroom, the Administrator posed a question to which the state's attorney explained that, when a mental illness declaration was not done, such as was the case at the with Aagot Hansen, then a dangerousness declaration should be requested and that this could be grounds for admission to the asylum even if the patient was later found not to be dangerous. The state's attorney also said he would have, in retrospect, followed the same course of action in conjunction with the decisions taken by Chief of Police Bang. When one was concerned with presumably mentally ill persons, the most appropriate choice was the administrative choice, out of respect to the people involved.[673]

Professor Ragnar Vogt was present and asked the state's attorney a question about "dangerousness." Vogt took the opportunity to comment that, in his experience, dangerousness was less of a concern and was unnecessary for an administrative detention in an asylum. In response to another question the state's attorney reiterated that Aagot Hansen did not have some sort of sentence to do and her detention was not to be characterized as an arrest. The assumption was that a mentally ill person was being taken in for safekeeping. The last witness was the Ward Nurse from Lier Asylum, Agnes Berge. She testified that Aagot Hansen was difficult to deal with the entire time she had been at Lier. Aagot Hansen was not satisfied with the food and often swore. At that point, the case was adjourned and would be continued at a later date.

While this may seem like a diversion from my discussion of Norway's sterilization law it is here to show that a woman, a petty thief at most, who had been admitted to an insane asylum, even though not insane, could have been forcibly sterilized. Neither the institutions of medicine nor law could have been relied upon to review her situation. While in the institution, the only thing a nurse had to say about her was that she cursed and didn't like the food. With the passage of the new sterilization law, a new category of persons – vagrants – was included under it, whether admitted or not. Also, whether or not the Autonomy Theory of Law (AT), a philosophical device

---

673 *Ibid.*

that seeks to separate social norms from legal norms existed was of no moment in the life of Aagot Hansen.[674]

As I wrote at the end of the first half of Case One (Indiana 1907), Jasanoff's model of co-production allows an evaluation of how the Indiana sterilization law was enacted. The same model can be applied to the Norwegian sterilization law of 1934. As I pointed out at the end of the section dealing with Indiana, both science and the law created representations – in response to other social representations – of what was "defective", of what was "sane" or "insane" and of what was the "normal" manner of being a woman. As Henriette Sinding Aasen writes, quoting NS jurist Per Melsom, that "the [legal principle] rested on the biological "demand" which then formed the right to sterilize, and this was that

> the fundamental idea that the National Socialist right to develop rests upon, is biology. This right should serve life....The right has no goal in itself but it is at the center of a people's right to be secure in their life and development.[675]

Aasen writes that this must be regarded as "a new 'tradition' in Norwegian jurisprudence and legal philosophy." Aasen notes that the beginning point for any legal rules was no longer the "need to give the individual her rights and duties in a society ruled by norms and the division of authority."[676] As Melson put it, the principle he advanced "was [designed] so that its usefulness to the people must be the decisive point in both theory and practice."[677] While it may seem that I am over-stating the argument by the use of Melsom's words, it would be just as simple to argue using Representative Bjørnson's words. The point is the same; representations by both law and science dovetailed with overlapping schemas and structures to produce a law that, at a particular moment in history, chose the good of the group ("people") before that of the individual. The body became an epistemic index for the social stresses at work in Norway.

The legal and medical institutions, as both social structures and as a place for social networking articulated to help produce the sterilization law of 1934 as well as define the contours of sanity and insanity, what was acceptable and unacceptable for males and females, what was "normal" and not "normal." The law and science negotiations that were taking place in Norwegian society at this time provided "a site were social order and scientific knowledges [were] mutually constituted."[678] During

---

674 I will discuss this theory more fully in Chapter 7.

675 Aasen, *Rasehygiene*, 29. Note 820.

676 *Ibid.*, 55.

677 *Ibid.*, 29.

678 Gary Edmond, "The Law-Set: The Legal Scientific Production of Medical Propriety" in *Science, Technology & Human Values*, 26 (2001): 191.

the interwar period, not only knowledge about genetics, but also about psychology entered Norway and was processed in a dynamic and evolving manner.

We can see the impact of new scientific knowledge in the law in Norway in both the parliamentary and the judicial arenas, in the sterilization law and the Aagot Hansen case. Another way of seeing this process is what Gary Edmond calls the "'seamless web' between scientific and nonscientific forms of knowledge and life."[679] Through the interactions in the legal settings of either a Storting Chamber or Judge Juelsrud's courtroom, a law-science hybrid is produced. This hybrid is a contingent artifact of the time, place and society. The hybrid, in turn, both draws on and reinforces " a range of normative behaviors, commitments, and relations."[680] As Edmond points out, the life of these hybrids would be "compromised" if they were either evicted from their formal settings or the law were somehow changed to consistently reflect a social justice. Without the hybrids, the flow of reciprocal legitimation between the two spheres would be slowed to a trickle.[681]

Edmond has used the idea of a "law-set" to focus on controversies that involve this legal hybrid. The term "law-set" is taken directly from H.M. Collins' use of the term "core-set", meaning "a range of scientists linked in a web of interests and associations, conceived as important to understand a particular controversy and its outcomes."[682] The law-set has basically the same meaning but within the legal arena. While Edmond examines trial transcripts and does not extend his analysis to legislative or parliamentary hearings, I do.[683] Members of the law-set "are linked in a legal web" where the goal is to decide a controversy, to provide closure.[684] One difference between the law-set as defined by Edmond's and my extension of his idea is that his is usually backwards looking within the courtroom while mine could also be used to look forward.

In conclusion, if we look at the variables in this pair of comparative studies that compose Case One, and not simply at the Eugenics Movement, I believe that 1907 and 1934 might not have been the best of times to pass this type of legislation. In more

679 *Ibid.*, 192.
680 *Ibid.*
681 *Ibid.*, 193.
682 *Ibid.*, 194. Please see further, H.M. Collins, "The place of the 'core-set' in modern science: Social contingency with methodological propriety in science" in *History of Science*, 18 (2001): 6 -19.
683 My experience as an intern with the Washington State Legislature demonstrated that hearings prior to passage of any legislation were not only a venue for the staking out of normative positions but also a place where staff lawyers voiced their concerns about the legislation as written. For example, what would the "standard of proof" be in a new law? For this, one had to be conversant in previous case law and lawyers were routinely called upon for written materials prior to hearings. Politicians who cater to various constituencies rather than thinking about "the common good" often ignore these materials.
684 Edmond, *Law-Set*, 194. Note 866.

modern times, proactive closure on certain bio-medical proposals in the legislature or the parliament might be indicated for a period of time. This would make sense since the same "law set" or, or "core-set" if you will, is involved.

> Lawyers, police, scientist, judges and lay people converge to produce legally sanctioned outcomes designed to support their various and invariably competing interests and social visions.[685]

In fact, one could argue that the new "epistemic" hybrids that are produced in the legislative/parliamentary arena need to be examined even more closely than "Findings of Fact" from a courtroom at the appellate level. But this discussion also implicates the form that democracy now takes which is the subject of some other investigation, i.e. because a democratic society *can* legislate, *should* it legislate?

As I have shown, in both the American and Norwegian halves of Case One, the same intersubjective categories were implicated as subjects/objects of the new laws. The law-set in Norway in 1934 produced a sterilization law for "defectives", began work on amending the abortion law, and considered how to administer a process of admission to an insane asylum where "sane" people were not inadvertently locked up for months. The identities that were constructed in Norway and of which we see evidence of in 1934 are not very different at all from those we saw in the first half of this case in Indiana. The only obvious difference is the use of African Americans in Indiana and taterne in Norway, one a racial group and one an ethnic group. In both Indiana and Norway, these identities plus the identity of a person as "defective" by virtue of mental or physical disability were the main identities that were constructed on a daily basis. They were the "parasites" that cost Norway millions of dollars a year, in a time where that nation's economy was perceived as endangered and in which the majority perceived it as being in the middle of a political "crisis." These were the same type of people implicated in the Indiana law. The one consistent identity that we see as a type of bulwark against the demise of the population was that of "woman as mother." The point is, albeit in retrospect, that the population was not seriously endangered and that the role of women as mothers served as a smokescreen to reinforce comfortable, ages-old ideas of who and what a woman is and what she can and cannot do.

685 *Ibid.*

5 CASE TWO: Reversals of Negatiave Body-Law in the United States

5.1 Introduction

If the events in Indiana in 1907 and in Norway in 1934 represent one set of social norm inclusion into legal norms, can we find an antithetical set of events in order to compare them with Case One, in order to test my theories in that case? In other words can we find the "worst" and the "best" examples of body-law – or at least two very different examples – that the United States and Norway have to offer? Can we find a moment when the intersubjective categories in Case One changed configurations and/or gained in strength so that the "strong we" and the "weak we" occupied significantly different societal positions? Or, as Bourdieu might have asked, can we find a time when the "double naturalization" of bodies changed, when the "silent and invisible agreement between social structures and mental structures" changed so that the "law of the social body" was not converted into the "law of the physical body"? [686]

In the United States, the legal discourse that was ultimately linked with the idea that, within the realm of married life, heterosexual couples could legally use birth control was the discourse of "privacy" articulated in the Supreme Court case of Griswold v. Connecticut, 381 U.S. 479 (1965). Griswold stood on a socio-legal foundation consisting of a number of failed legal cases as well as various political strategies by activists, and strategic framings that stretched back to the turn of the century. But after Griswold was decided, it would take only eight years before the right to reproductive privacy for married couples would develop into the right to an abortion for any woman, pregnant less than 12 weeks, as outlined in Roe v. Wade, 410 U.S. 113 (1973).

However, during the eight years between Griswold and Roe the concept of privacy would itself undergo a metamorphosis, developing into the framing discourse of "choice."[687] The idea of "choice" would thereafter blossom, despite the fact that legal precedents undergirding Roe would undergo a persistent battering, and reduction, that not only contorted the common law tradition of *stare decisis*[688] but also brought

686 *Ibid.*

687 Most recently, the "right to choose" has been used quite effectively by advertising agencies to encourage consumerist activity. Money, power and privilege equate to "choice"; the U.S.S.C. has even equated "money" as a form of "speech." Please see Buckley v. Valeo, 424 U.S. 1 (1976). This development – among others – has called into question the use of this strategy among women's groups as well as in legal and political philosophy circles.

688 The Latin phrase *stare decisi* means, literally, "the decision." It means the holding in a case. In practice, it means that holdings in different cases, each based on a different set of facts, should be

the United States to the brink of overruling Roe.[689] The rhetoric of "choice" would also expand, leaving the bedroom and moving towards all things commercial. It would become entrenched in American social and cultural life and schemas, glorifying the individual within American political theory.

In Norway, by contrast, the right to use birth control was in place much earlier than in the United States. Another point of departure between the two countries was that the right to an abortion was legislatively – not judicially – decided and linked very quickly with the right to a "self-decided abortion." As in Case One, the Norwegian debate took place after the American debate; while Norway's sterilization law needed 27 years to be seen in Scandinavian societies, in the second case, the time period was only about 5 years. In 1978, the Norwegian Storting passed legislation allowing abortion throughout the first trimester without having to appear before a committee of officials. A woman was also able to have an abortion after 12 weeks, under specific circumstances and through the use of specific administrative procedure and an appearance before this committee. This law was passed in the midst of profound social and cultural changes similar to those that occurred in the United States. Access to birth control had also been a struggle but it had been won earlier in Norway's history than in America. Thus, in Norway the essential issue – abortion – was seen to crest in 1978, earlier than the assaults on Roe were seen in the U.S.

Case Two is also unique because it allows a dissection of the advantages and disadvantages of a legislatively created right versus a "judge-made" right to privacy. It also allows us to compare laws that were said to benefit women, and ultimately families, and which were initially advocated by women for women. In Case One, no "defective" had any voice in the legislation that was enacted, aside from perhaps the rare individual or institution.[690] The venue was one of legio-scientific paternalism

---

unified so as to present a precedent. If one moves beyond the precedent, the facts will need to be distinguished from the previous cases.

689 Please see an analysis of "partial-birth abortion" case in which Kennedy wrote the majority opinion, joining Roberts, Scalia, Thomas, and Alito at http://222.womensenews.org/article.ccfm?aid=3139, accessed February 19, 2008. The only woman on the bench, Justice Ruth Bader Ginsburg, issued a biting dissent from the bench against the male majority. Most Supreme Court pundits would agree that only Justice Kennedy stands between a wholesale overruling of Roe by that Court. Kennedy, born in 1936, began his political life by volunteering to draft a tax-cutting referendum for the California Republican Party for then Governor Reagan. Conversant with international law and continental life styles, Kennedy joined Souter and O'Conner in Planned Parenthood v. Casey in 1992, and also became a "visible defender" of gay rights on the Supreme Court. For an analysis of Kennedy's life, temperment and influences, please see, Jeffrey Toobin, "Annals of Law: Swing Shift" in *The New Yorker*, September 12, 2005, 51.

690 As one might expect, religious groups did become involved. In the years following 1880, the Roman Catholic Church was busy "struggling to absorb and accommodate" the huge number of Catholics who had immigrated to the United States. The issue of race degeneration through immigration provided only an "indirect confrontation" between the church and eugenicists. But, after 1910 theo-

and essentialism, combined with factors such as high unemployment and a decrease in the population in Norway. The same could be said of Indiana three decades earlier for slightly different reasons – high unemployment with rapid urbanization and immigration – factors that exposed societal problems, which were then interpreted as "race suicide." Case Two gives an opportunity to analyze what appears to be an opposite case in terms of representations, institutions, identities and discourses as well as the framing of the debates. These two cases, which use countries that are at first glance quite different from one another in terms of country population, history and politics, provide a basis for comparison for legal norm formation. In both cases, I examine the same four co-productionist fields of Jasanoff and how they intersect with the Tuori and Tamanaha models.

Both the United States and Norway, with nationally elected Congress/Parliament and legal systems, are categorized as liberal democracies. Through engaging with the issue of sexual reproduction, these institutions have ultimately made several assumptions about the facts of reproductive biology. These normative assumptions, on the surface, represent the science of reproduction but, by necessity and below the surface, also include normative assumptions about who and what men and women are and should do in life. I need to mention one important assumption here. In the United States and in Norway, a woman is considered to be an autonomous actor. By this, is meant that both men and women, at all times and at all places, until proven otherwise, independently decide whether or not to have sex – without any sort of coercion. Sex is assumed to be a voluntary act. Legally, sex is conducted in a socio-political, economic and emotional vacuum. Aside from rape in western legal systems, the responsibility for the possibility of pregnancy usually rests with the woman. One problem with this assumption is, however, that for a woman "sexuality and reproduction are inseparable from each other and from gender."[691] Gender roles and economic factors are entirely absent from the legal calculus.

Another obvious phenomenon is that the concept of "motherhood" changes from time to time and from place-to-place and this is done at the same time as competing discourses also arise within a given society.[692] As Allison Diduck notes, a kind

---

logians began to discuss the moral nature of vasectomies in the pages of the *American Ecclesiastical Review*, at the same time as birth control became a major issue in American life. In 1916, John Ryan of the Catholic University of America formulated the Chruch's natural law argument against birth control. In 1927, prompted by the USSC's decision in Buck, Ryan also wrote against sterilization saying it was not only "unscientific and bad policy" but also conflicted with the social justice vision of the 1891 encyclical, *Rerum Novarum*, written by Pope Leo. Please see, Sharon Mara Leon, "Beyond Birth Control: Catholic Response to the Eugenics Movement in the United States, 1900–1950." unpublished PhD diss., University of Minnesota, 2004, pp. 1, 51, 30, 52, 34.

691 Catherine A. MacKinnon, *Towards A Feminist Theory of the State* (Cambridge, Ma.: Harvard University Press, 1989), 184.

692 Anthropologist Sarah Franklin has written about this phenomenon with regard to modern for-of "shifting hierarchy" emerges and the "dynamics of interaction often include both domination and resistance, so that discourses such as feminism, modern rationality, science, social work and psychology are imbued with race, class and sexuality."[693]

> The ultimate tapestry [that] emerges is a law infused with constructs of motherhood interwoven with many different strands. The ideological significance of these dominant constructs and the law which supports them is that they then appear to be natural normal and legitimate.[694]

The stability of this normative legal tapestry is only an illusion, however, as each generation constructs its own dominant ideology that may be "imported and incorporated into law."[695] For example, in 1907, discourses existed which talked about the duty **not** to have children if they could not be properly cared for or were likely to be somehow "defective."

One hundred and eighty degrees later, the dominant legal ideology in the United States changed into that of a conflict between fetal rights and women's rights. What type of home a child grows up in is rarely discussed; race and class play no role whatsoever. To paraphrase the phrase conjured by Anatole France and later referred to by Justice Frankfurter in Griffin v. Illinois, 351 U.S. 12, 23 (1956), poor children have the same right to sleep or play in sewage under a bridge as rich children. The only discourse that seems **not** to have changed is the demand for better, more "perfect" children from women in a "traditional" (code for married, white, heterosexual, religiously conservative) family setting with "traditional", i.e. patriarchal values.[696] To an extent, this type of legally abstracted thinking has been made more contextualized in Norway, linked with relationships and experiences. A woman's social and economic situation is brought to the fore, especially since marriage is not the only basis for parental legal rights in Norway.[697]

---

mulations of kinship. Please see, Sarah Franklin, "Making Representations: Parliamentary Debate of the Human Fertilization and Embryology Act" in J. Edwards, et al., *Technologies of Procreation: Kinship in the Age of Assisted Conception* (Manchester: Manchester University Press, 1993), 96–131.

693 Alison Diduck, "Legislating Ideologies of Motherhood" in *Social and Legal Studies*, Vol. 2, no. 4 (1993), p. 462. This idea supports my use of those same categories in my analysis of the framing of discourses at the micro-level of a state/society.

694 *Ibid.*

695 *Ibid.*, 480.

696 This 1894 quotation by Anatole France surfaces again and again and was most recently referred to in Linda Lewis v. Grinker (Tommy G. Thomspon), a 2000 case decided in the U.S. Second Circuit Court of Appeals. The case dealt with medical care for pregnant women who are undocumented workers.

697 In Norway, any two persons who co-habitate without benefit of marriage have legal rights similar to those who are married. Today, about 50% of all births in Norway are born to parents who are not legally married; only 7% of this number refers to single mothers, living alone. This was reported by Christian Knudsen Sture, researcher for NOVA in his report "The Family in the Norwegian Society", 2006, available online at http://www.uio.no/studier/emnec/hf/iln/NORINTO500/v07/Family-Norwe-

Case Two is assembled in roughly the same way as Case One with one exception. The Griswold case was not the beginning but at the end of a long line of legal efforts by a social movement organization in the United States. That social movement is a key to an understanding of Griswold. The movement was very active in Connecticut, in the very same area from which Griswold would emerge. It also includes some of the very same actors. With that in mind, I examine the Comstock Law and the Chase Dispensary case before I move onto Griswold. The point is that the structures, schemas and resources that were in place in 1939, the year of the Chase Dispensary Case, had changed by 1965, the year that the Griswold case was decided by the United States Supreme Court.

5.2 Phase One: The Comstock Law (1873) and its Proponents

The American portion of Case Two begins and ends – in terms of geography – within a span of nine miles. Estelle Griswold and Dr. Lee Buxton, who were arrested in 1961 for operating a Planned Parenthood Center, lived in New Haven, Connecticut. New Haven is only nine miles from New Canaan, Connecticut, where Anthony Comstock (1844–1915) was born on 7 March 1844. Comstock and his social network were responsible for what are now commonly referred to as the "Comstock Laws", and which was the very same law, albeit in state form, under which police would first arrest members of the Chase Dispensary in New Haven in 1935 and Estelle Griswold and Dr. Buxton in 1961.

Anthony Comstock essentially set the arrest of Griswold and Buxton in 1961 in motion some ninety years earlier. Comstock was an extremely religious person – even for his own day and age. He spent his life in a personal crusade for moral purity – as he defined for himself and as a movement of like-minded citizens also did. Comstock and these citizens claimed to base their opinions, primarily on the Bible. And, there was one type of woman in particular that offended Anthony Comstock. This was a woman who believed in the right to plan the size of her family through the use of contraceptives, or in the right of women to engage in discussions and debate about matters involving sexuality, which inevitably included contraception and abortion. The type of woman who might launch a newspaper entitled "The Woman Rebel"

---

gian, accessed December 29, 2007. If a woman has a child and is unmarried, she is entitled to state benefits. The father of the child also has legal rights and duties as if he were the married husband of the woman. The basic law on married and unmarried heterosexuals who live together and have children can be found in the Law concerning children and parents ("Lov om barn og foreldre (barnelova)") of 8 April Nr. 7 1981 and its various amendments. The basic law on "partnerskap" for homosexuals is formulated in the Law of Registered Partnerships ("Lov om registrert partnerskap") of 30 April Nr. 40 1993. It is true that the paternity of a child is also legally independent from marriage in the United States, but cohabitation is not as socially sanctioned or the subject of law.

where, on the masthead, was printed the motto "No Gods, No Masters." The woman who actually did launch this newspaper was Margaret Sanger, whom we have met above in Chapter 3. She was the most visible female crusader for reproductive rights at the same time when Comstock sought to enforce his vision of "purity." In short, Sanger embodied the type of woman Comstock considered to be "impure" and as a consequence of that impurity, involved in illegal activates.

Anthony Comstock routinely used the American judicial system to advance his own personal moral belief system. In 1914, Comstock had Margaret Sanger arraigned on eight counts of obscenity for publishing newspaper articles on birth control. He also obtained a conviction against Margaret Sanger's husband, William Sanger, in 1915, for selling a single copy of a pamphlet on birth control entitled *Family Limitation.* But Margaret Sangerr was a force to be dealt with and would actually survive Comstock to see the birth control movement flourish. Early in life, Sanger became involved in public health nursing and concluded that "poverty, debility and big families went together."[698] In 1914, she founded *The Woman Rebel* to advance this idea. Not pleased, churchmen and politicians agitated for the police to swear out a warrant for her arrest, whereupon Sanger traveled to England. In England, she met Marie Stopes (1880–1958), author of the book *Married Love* and a major force in the British birth control rights movement. Upon her return to the United States, Sanger founded the American Birth Control League (ABCL) in 1921.

Anthony Comstock did not conduct his fanatical movement single handedly. His crusade was empowered by a number of private organizations as well as by the Congress of the United States, both groups possessing varied and numerous resources and expressing belief in the same schemas. Congress allowed Comstock onto the floor of the House of Representatives in January 1873, where he remained nearly all day. Carrying a satchel full of books and pictures he claimed were pornographic, he showed them to every member of Congress he could buttonhole, and lobbied for a bill that would give him the legal authority to carry on his campaign of persecution and censorship in the name of fighting obscenity. One biographer notes that tears flowed from his eyes as he addressed Congress, begging for a law to stop the "hydra-headed monster" of vice.[699]

Congress was impressed with Comstock's personal lobbying and passed what was known as the Comstock Act. This act made it a crime to advertise or mail not only "every lewd, lascivious, or filthy book, pamphlet, picture, paper, letter, writing, print, or other publication of an indecent character", but also any information "for preventing contraception or producing abortion." Congress passed this law with virtually no

698 *Time Magazine*, "Birth Control's 21st", February 18, 1935 at http://www.time.com/time/printout/0,8816,748484,00.html, accessed February 6, 2007.

699 Helen J. Self, *Prostitution, Women and the Misuse of the Law: The Fallen Daughter of Eve* (New York and London: Routledge, 2003), 46.

discussion, acting by unanimous consent in the Senate and under suspension of the rules in the House. The Comstock Law, in pertinent part, read:

> **Be it enacted....** That whoever...shall sell...or shall offer to sell, or to lend, or to give away, or in any manner to exhibit, or shall publish or offer to publish in any manner, or shall have in his possession, for any such purpose or purposes, an obscene book, pamphlet, paper, writing, advertisement, circular, picture, drawing or other representation, figure, or image on or of paper of other material, or any cast instrument, o other article of an immoral nature, or any drug or medicine, or any article whatever, for the prevention of conception, or for causing unlawful abortion, or shall advertise the same for sale, or shall write or print, or cause to be written or printed, any card, circular, book, pamphlet, advertisement, or notice of any kind, stating when, where, how, or of whom, or by what means, any of the articles in this section...can be purchased or obtained, or shall manufacture, draw, or print, or in any wise make any of such articles, shall be deemed guilty of a...[700]

Punishment for a conviction under this law was a misdemeanor and, as such, a Court was allowed to give a sentence from 6 months to five years at hard labor and a fine of from $100 to $2000.

The Congressional Committee on Appropriations then set aside several thousand dollars for a special agent to carry out the Comstock Act, and on 6 March 1873, 1 day before his 29th birthday, Anthony Comstock was commissioned as this special agent of the United States Post Office, vested with powers of arrest and the privilege of free transportation on all mail lines. This enabled him to travel the country arresting and prosecuting those who dared to send any information about contraception or abortion or, for that matter, anything that Comstock himself deemed to be lewd or indecent, through the mail.

As a result of Comstock's crusade, publishers were forced to censor their biological and physiological texts, druggists were punished for giving out information about contraception, and the average American had to live with censorship of his or her mail, without access to reliable information about contraception. Ultimately, the Comstock Laws were overruled at the federal Circuit Court of Appeals level. On 7 December 1936, the U.S. Court of Appeals for the Second Circuit upheld a district court ruling in the case U.S. v. One Package, 86 F.2d 737 (2nd Cir.) (1936). One Package held that the 1873 Comstock Law could not be used by the government to seize birth control devices shipped to doctors.[701] But the Comstock Law would still live on at the

700 U.S. v. One Package, 86 F.2d 737, 739 (1936). A copy of the entire Comstock legislation can be found at Appendix F.

701 See David J. Garrow, *Liberty and Sexuality: The Right to Privacy and the Making of Roe v. Wade* (New York: Macmillan Publishing Company, 1994), pp. 41-42. The United States is divided into 11 Circuit Courts of Appeal and the second circuit includes the three states of New York, Vermont and Connecticut.

state level until the 1960s when the demise of Connecticut's little Comstock would mean the demise of it in all other states.

After moving to New York, Comstock began working with the local Young Men's Christian Association, (YMCA). The YMCA had also been active in the same areas Comstock was concerned about and was instrumental in passing an ineffectual anti-obscenity law in New York in 1872. Comstock began an investigation of 165 obscene books and found that they all came from four publishers, three in New York and one in Brooklyn.[702] In order to buy the plates from one of the publishers, Comstock wrote to the Director of the YMCA, R.R. McBurney, asking for money.[703] The first paid President of the YMCA, Morris Ketcham Jessup (1830–1908), happened to see Comstock's letter on McBurney's desk and, as a result, Jessup then went to visit Comstock. This meeting produced the "most important and longest standing friendship" in Comstock's life. It also gave him access to men with money and power whom he might otherwise never have known and who eventually formed the New York Society for the Suppression of Vice (NYSSV).[704] After their second meeting, Jessup, through McBurney, sent Comstock the $650 that he needed to buy the obscene plates. The dramatic flourish with which Comstock delivered these unsavory plates and books impressed the YMCA and set a theatrical pattern, devoured by newspapers of the time, that Comstock repeated until the end of his life. Comstock worked on a number of fronts to achieve his goals, mainly prevention of "obscenity" through censorship and preservation of "purity" in society at large through a special type of morality in the family. Public censorship and private purity/morality both in the public and private spheres were two sides of the same coin for him.

Just as Dr. H. Sharp and his associates in Case One, Anthony Comstock had access to various, polysemious resources. These resources were tied to the social, religious and financial networks of other men, who like Comstock, had strict (public) schemas of what was "normal" and "not-normal" and who were tied to the institutional structures of the day. However, unlike the local Indianans who supported Dr. Sharp's work, the network that supported Comstock had a larger reach than the band of brother Hoosiers in Case One. I need only mention one member to emphasis this point, i.e. John Pierpoint Morgan (1813–1890).

J.P. Morgan was one of the original founders of the Society for the Suppression of Vice. Morgan was also extremely wealthy; he financed the U.S. Steel Corporation and later arranged a merger of the Edison General Electric and Thomson-Houston

702 Anne Louise Bates, *Weeder in the Garden of the Lord: Anthony Comstock's Life and Career*, (Lanham, New York, London: University Press of America, Inc., 1995), 59.

703 McBurney's position within the YMCA is ambiguous. He may have been a "director" but he may also have been the treasurer from 1870–1873.

704 *Ibid.* Please see Appendix A for a list and short biography of some of the original founders of the NYSSV.

Electric Companies to form the General Electric Company. If that were not spectacular enough, his company bought and reorganized 4 of the 5 major American railways between 1869 and 1899. If Case One demonstrated the social movement at the local level and a society in transition from pre-modern to modern according to Pescosolido, then Case Two demonstrates the effects of a social movement at a national level and in a modern society, using the same dynamics of activity as in Case One.

The wealth of Morgan and the zeal of Comstock combined to both change old societal structures and norms and to create new ones. If Anthony Comstock was anything, he was a zealot of whom the Anabaptist Puritans who landed in the New World would have been proud. In 1892, he was proclaimed to be the "bravest man in New York" by the *New York Evangelist*.[705] As Secretary of the NYSSV, it was on his shoulders that "the brunt of all the hard work in breaking up the dens of vice in this city" had fallen. He was portrayed as a hero in the war on vice.

> He bears on his face a scar which is to him a badge of honor, as much as the wound of a soldier received in battle, as it was made by the savage cur of a desperate villain whom he was conveying to the place of trial and punishment.[706]

Comstock wrote that there were "three Juggernaut cars of destruction driving through the community, with glittering blades attached to each wheel."[707] He envisioned these three cars of destruction as aimed at the corruption of "boys and girls of to-day (sic)", aimed at the defilement of American youth.[708] The three Juggernauts were "evil-reading, gambling and the liquor traffic."[709] To combat the first demanded one search out and destroy obscenity. The second and third Juggernauts demanded abstinence from alcohol and all games of chance, including state lotteries. Comstock himself and the NYSSV advocated this for about fifty years (1850–1900).

While Comstock himself did receive quasi-state legitimation in his job as a Postal Inspector, most of the activity of the NYSSV seems to have been extra-judicial.[710] As to the NYSSV itself and its goals, its arenas of engagement, the *New York Evangelist* notes:

> But a Society which is a sort of supplement to the Police, and whose agents have seldom to do so as policemen do, literally to knock down and drag out scoundrels, cannot always stand on

---

705 *New York Evangelist*, February 25, 1892 (APS Online), 4.

706 *Ibid.*

707 Anthony Comstock, "The Extirpation of the Crime-Breeders of the Day a Public Necessity" in *Belford's Magazine*, June 1880 (APS Online, col. 25), 64.

708 *Ibid.*

709 *Ibid.*

710 Anthony Comstock, "The Suppression of Vice" in *The North American Review*, CXXXV (1882), (APS Online), 484. Comstock was a "special agent" or "inspector" of the U.S. Post Office Department, without compensation, beginning in March 1873. As mentioned above, he later received compensation.

> ceremony. It is to be said to its honor that, in spite of all criticism and all opposition, it has gone ahead for twenty years, in the course of which it has suppressed an amount of evil that it is frightful to think of, breaking up gambling dens, policy shops, and the vile holes for the printing and distribution of obscene publications, which have been, in spite of the police, smuggled into the mails and set over the country.[711]

Of course, this religious publication might have been expected to support Comstock and we should consider this opinion with a critical eye. Nonetheless, it demonstrates the three battlefronts on which the NYSSV fought its battles for purity and morality in young souls.

The NYSSV was incorporated by the state of New York on May 16, 1873.[712] Nicola Beisel has researched the social backgrounds of supporters of the NYSSV and its sister organization, the New England Society for the Suppression of Vice (SSV).[713] She challenges the assertion that the moral reform movements, as exemplified in the SSV, were "the province of segments of the middle class experiencing erosion of their position in the hierarchies of wealth or social status."[714] Instead, she shows that it was the "high white collar" class such as "merchants, businessmen, financiers and professionals" that supported the SSV. Archived articles of the *New York Times* support this conclusion and the various interconnections among the original sixteen individuals who incorporated the NYSSV. The work of the group was not only carried out at meetings but at the opera, at religious services and at private social events.

It was the rhetorical message of these social structures operating on "several different levels" that supported Comstock's work.[715] An ideographic analysis of this rhetoric, focusing on "single words, characterizations, narratives, and myths" shows that the word "obscenity" had an extensive and broad meaning that impacted speech about sexuality. In addition to art schools, medical texts did not go unaffected. For example, a Mr. Sherman was arrested no less than three times for publishing his text on the hernia; a jury acquitted him twice but after a Judge instructed the third jury not to consider previous acquittals, Sherman was eventually convicted of circulating obscenity. A previous decision had held that it was "immaterial" if the information was "true and scientifically correct."[716]

---

711 *Ibid.* Adhering to the Fourth Amendment of the Constitution, prohibiting unreasonable searches and seizures, was perceived as "standing on ceremony" in the minds of these zealots. This attitude is mirrored in the current provisions of the so-called Patriot Act.

712 *Ibid.*

713 Nicola Beisel, *Imperiled Innocents: Anthony Comstock and Family Reproduction in Victorian America,* (Princeton: Princeton University Press, 1997), 49.

714 *Ibid.*

715 Marouf A. Hasian, Jr., *The Rhetoric of Eugenics* ,13–14.

716 Theodore Albert Schroeder, *"Obscene" Literature and Constitutional Law: A Forensic Defense of Freedom of the Press* (New York: Privately Printed, 1911), p. 338. This book can be accessed at http://www.archive.org/stream/obsceneliteratu01schrgoog#page/n343/mode/1up, accessed August 17,

Comstock's original linkage to the YMCA "and to its leaders by church and neighborhood connections" made Comstock almost invincible.[717] Horowtiz maintains that without

> the New York YMCA behind him, Comstock would have been merely a young clerk informing the authorities about wrong doing, and his career would have been inconsequential.[718]

For example, Comstock's minister was activist William Ives Budington (1815–1879). His neighbor was H.B. Spelman, the father of the wife of John D. Rockefeller.[719] Comstock also had ties to both temperance and eugenics supporters. In 1897, we read about the Women's Christian Temperance Union plans for a campaign against prize fighting in Buffalo, New York. We find that the Conference on Purity would precede the WCTU sessions in Buffalo by a matter of a few days. At the Purity Conference, under the charge of Dr. Mary Wood Allen, none other than both Comstock and Dr. and Mrs. Kellogg of Battle Creek, Michigan, would assist in the conference.[720] Sometimes these groups had common members who attended both conferences since they had similar agendas and values that were espoused by one group overlapped with values in another.

While the social movement may have been, as Beisel writes, initiated by white collar elites, the problems that the movement addressed were seen at all levels of society, whether acknowledged or not. Erich Goode and Nachman Ben-Yehuda write that social problems can be manifested at three levels, the grass roots level, the elite level and within an interest group.[721] The elite-engineered model, according to them, uses major institutions – law, medicine, religion – to "generate and sustain moral outrage" against the deviant group."[722] The grass roots and interest groups, however, while probably well-intentioned, are used by the elites, according to Goode and Ben-Yehuda. According to these researchers, the intention of the elite group is not actually to solve the "problem." The intention is to "divert attention away from real problems

---

2009.

717 Helen Lefkowitz Horowitz, "Victoria Woodhull, Anthony Comstock, and Conflict over Sex in the United States in the 1870s" in *The Journal of American History*, 87 (2000), 419.

718 *Ibid.*

719 *Ibid.* Please see footnote 37. Buddington was also a Christian Commission Delegate.

720 *New York Evangelist*, (1830–1902), May 6, 1897 (APS Online), 18. The Kellogg breakfast cereal was a peripheral manifestation of the positive eugenics "health" movement. It was touted as having an anti-masturbatory effect. Please see, John Harvey Kellogg, Plain *Facts for Young and Old* (Battle Creek, Michigan: Good Health Publishing Co., 1892), pp. 320–64. I thank Prof. Sætnan for bringing this to my attention.

721 Erich Goode and Nachman Ben-Yehuda, "Moral Panics: Culture, Politics, and Social Construction", in *Annual Review of Sociology*, 20 (1994): 149.

722 Jeffrey S. Victor, "Moral Panics and the Social Construction of Deviant Behavior: A Theory and Application to the Case of Ritual Child Abuse", in *Sociological Perspectives*, 41 (1998): 547.

in a society, the solution of which would threaten the economic and political interests of the elite group."[723] A cursory look at the names and connections within the NYSSV vis-à-vis the economic problems facing the United States in the early twentieth century, including the power of corporations, would seem to support this notion.

The eugenics movement in the United States had always had a connection with the issue of birth control. Eugenics reformers and birth control advocates tended to belong to the same associations. But, the type of issues that both groups supported appealed to the adherents of some religions and not to others. For example, at the American Eugenics Society and the Eugenics Research Association combined annual meeting in New York on 19 May 1930, Rev. Kenneth C. MacArthur, who was the rural secretary of the Massachusetts Federation of Churches, said that the church needed eugenics.[724] MacArthur's comments demonstrate two concerns; the burden on churches that had to deal with poverty due to families having too many children as well as the production of a "super race, free of prejudice, ignorance and emotional instability."[725]

By contrast, some women in the Roman Catholic Church disagreed with birth control, whatever the social price or impact on the individual woman. Denver, Colorado, was the site for the 1930 National Council of Catholic Women where a number of issues were taken up and were passed. One resolution opposed "sterilization of the mentally deficient" and also urged "intensive study of family education to counteract the teaching of birth control and companionate marriage…."[726] The group also opposed beauty and endurance contests for women since they were "unworthy of the high dignity and noble functions of womanhood."[727] It also announced its support for a ruling of the Supreme Court that gave parents the right to decide if their children should attend public or private schools.

But the position of the Roman Catholic Church toward eugenics and birth control had not yet so solidified as to be some sort of a moral tollgate. John G. Murray (1877–1956) was made the first auxiliary Bishop of the Roman Catholic Church of Connecticut in April of 1920. Not surprisingly, in 1923, he opposed the efforts of the Connecticut reformers to change its little Comstock Law at that time. He testified in the Connecticut Legislature on the bill to allow a "medical exception" for the use of birth control where the life of the women might be endangered should she become pregnant. These remarks have a distinct eugenic edge. He "called for the preservation of the race" and

---

723 *Ibid.* What were the problems that SSV work sought to deflect attention from? One need only look to many types of reformist legislation in the 1930s, which ranged from labor laws to pure food and drug laws.

724 *Chicago Daily Tribune*, May 19, 1930, 19.

725 *Ibid.* Clarence G. Campbell, of New York, was elected president of the research association at this meeting. MacArthur also advocated the sterilization of alcoholics.

726 *Chicago Daily Tribune*, October 2, 1930, 31.

727 *Los Angeles Times*, October 2, 1930, 13.

said that, unless everyone had at least four children per family, the "races from northern Europe...the finest type of people, are doomed to extinction."[728] He eventually followed the Roman Catholic policy on birth control set by the then Archbishop of New York, Patrick Cardinal Hayes. As is sometimes common with various forms of extremism, Hayes set in motion a set of unintended consequences. In 1921, he had the power, even though he was a religious figure, to have the ABCL's first convention raided by police and, in doing so, gave the [American Birth Control League] "a big boost...."[729]

5.3 Phase Two: Challenges to Comstock in New Haven (1939)

Many in the United States felt a climate of dread during the summer of 1939. Despite the fact that the Neutrality Act had been passed by Congress in 1937, on 21 September, six days before Nazi forces crushed the Polish resistance, Franklin D. Roosevelt called a special session of Congress to repeal the arms embargo to allied countries. Earlier, on 14 June, after remarks by the President that Germany's neighbors felt "threatened", Germany offered a mutual non-aggression pact to Baltic and Scandinavian countries which Finland, Sweden and Norway rejected. The United States would eventually become an active combatant two years later on 8 December 1941, after being attacked by the Japanese at Pearl Harbor.

Despite the fact that it would take two full years and an unprovoked attack by Japan to move the United States to enter the war, there was, in 1939, a growing sense in the United States that war was inevitable. Indeed, the Roosevelt government had taken steps to prepare for that eventuality. The first of Winston Churchill's six-volume history of World War Two is called *The Gathering Storm* and this is exactly the sense one has when reading newspapers from New Haven, Connecticut, in the summer of 1939. In New Haven, the local Italian and Polish immigrant populations received news of the advancing German front throughout Europe, especially in the pages of the *The Waterbury Democrat.*

In a state that had once been considered mostly the province of Protestant and Congregational churches, Roman Catholic Church membership had doubled in Connecticut between about 1900 and 1930.[730] On 28 April 1910, Catholicism "came of age" in Connecticut, as John J. Nilan was installed as Hartford's seventh bishop. During his tenure, he concerned himself "with the fostering of many ethnic parishes which

728 Susan C. Wawrose, *Griswold v. Connecticut: Contraception and the Right of Privacy* (New York, London, Hong Kong, Sydney, Danbury, Connecticut: Grolier Publishing, 1996), 33–34.

729 *Time Magazine*, "Birth Control's 21st", February 18, 1935, at http://www.time.com/printout/0,8816,748484,00,html, accessed February 6, 2007.

730 Please see Appendix G for data on this.

would serve Connecticut's diverse population."[731] In the 1930's, these Catholic parishes in Connecticut were still divided along ethnic lines.

But ethnically based parishes were not new, even in 1910. Work on St. Patrick's Church in New Haven County began under the reign of Bishop O'Reilly and Rev. Edward O'Brien in the mid-1800s. As early as 1851, the new pastor of St. Patrick's was Rev. James Lynch, a graduate of All Hallows College in Dublin. Lynch built a convent in Middleton for an Irish order of nuns, the Sisters of Mercy, whom he brought from Ennis, Ireland to educate generations of American Catholics.[732] Germans, on the other hand, gravitated to St. Boniface's Church under Fr. Wendelschmidt in 1868.[733] The first Italian community began at St. Michael's under Rev. Vincent Asterri. An Italian religious order, the Apostolic Sisters of the Sacred Heart, were "welcomed in New Haven in September, 1906" to begin their work.[734] Polish Catholics began the church of St. Stanislaus, along with priests of the Polish branch of the Vincentian Order.[735] Even Lithuanian Catholics had a Church, St. Casimir's, established in 1912.[736] Since post-bellum times, these parishes had all split into numerous other parishes, especially in response to additional immigration and the birth rate.

Catholic colleges and universities were also founded during this time in New Haven and the vicinity. Jesuits founded Holy Cross College in neighboring Worcester, Massachusetts, in 1843 and Boston College in 1863. Albertus Magnus College, a Dominican college was founded in 1925 in New Haven and the Sisters of Mercy founded St. Joseph College in 1932 in Hartford.

Connections between the Roman Catholic community and the birth control debate in Connecticut are not difficult to find. Some of the leading figures involved in judicial proceedings in 1939 – just as would again happen in 1961 – were Catholic. This is not to say that other religions were not involved, pro or con, but that this religion, more than others, played a major role in the issue. For example, on 4 May 1939, the *Waterbury Democrat* reported on Father Richard J. Dowling, S.J. the Dean of Education at Holy Cross, giving a lecture to alumni "making a plea for Catholic principles in a world of confusion and upheaval" since only those religiously-based ideas could conquer all problems.[737] In the audience were State's Attorney William B. Fitzgerald, Attorneys John E. Whelan, Frank MacDonald, Joseph Alishausky, Vincent Scully, Frank Summa, Frank Healy, Judge Edward J. Finn, State Senator Edward P. Egan, Deputy Coroner William B. Hennessey, and Doctors Joseph Reynolds, C.E. Dwyer,

731 *Ibid.*
732 Right Reverend Thomas S. Duggan, *Catholic Church in Connecticut* (New York City: The States History Company, 1930), 233–34.
733 *Ibid.*, 336.
734 *Ibid.*, 338–39.
735 *Ibid.*, 350.
736 *Ibid.*, 351.
737 *Waterbury Democrat*, May 4, 1939, 3.

Walter Keefe, Thomas Welch, Joseph Burke and Alfred Finn. Also in the audience was the Rev. Eugene F. Cryne who would eventually take a leading role in the impending Chase Dispensary battle.[738]

The *Waterbury Democrat* reported on the activities of Catholic priests with some frequency, in contrast to the *New Haven (Evening) Register*. Rev. E. Cryne was, in 1939, the pastor of St. Patrick's Church and also the Director of the Waterbury Office of the Diocesan Bureau of Social Service, one of ten such bureaus. He was reported as heading a local delegation to a session of the Diocesan Bureau of Social Services in New Britain in order to hear a speaker, Katherine Lenroot, of the United States Department of Labor.[739] Edna Mae Maloney, Agnes C. Fitzpatrick and Margaret Tehan would accompany Cryne. The local advisory board for Cryne's Bureau included State's attorney William B. Fitzgerald, who had also been in the audience above. Other board members were attorneys John Gaffney and Frank Healy, Judge Frank P. McEvoy and Doctors Richard Hinchey and Raymond J. Quinn. This would mean that, within the space of 7 days, it is possible that Rev. Cryne would have had contact with Fitzgerald and others twice, first at the Holy Cross alumni dinner and then at the Bureau meeting. If this was a matter of routine, we can assume that the Roman Catholic Church had regular access to members of both the judiciary and the medical profession.

Catholic women had on-going contact with Cryne. Almost every parish had a local equivalent of the of Council of Catholic Women, including Waterbury. Cryne's Bureau of Social Services was located at 56 Church Street where the Women's Council regularly met. In each parish, the local priest would be the Chair of the Committee, which allowed for supervision – and presumably, influence – over the women in the parish and their charitable work.[740] Members of the Catholic Bureau of Social Services were also well connected in New Haven. For example, attorney Vincent A. Scully, mentioned above, shared offices with John F. McDonough who was elevated from the Naugatuck Burough Court to the local Court of Common Pleas in June.[741] Judge Edward J. Finn had retired and Governor Raymond E. Baldwin had replaced Finn with John McDonough, perhaps keeping the Irish ethnic group satisfied with his gubernatorial appointments.

Since the early 1920s, the Connecticut Birth Control League (CBCL) had been agitating within the state legislature for a number of years to obtain a "medical exception" for the health of the mother to their "little Comstock law." In 1923 at the Parson's Theater in Hartford, over "800 supporters, mostly women, listened to Margaret

738 In 1930, Fr. Cryne was the second resident pastor at St. John of the Cross parish in Middlebury where he was described as watching "with paternal care over the interest of his flock, devoting his spare time to the care of the cemeteries in Waterbury." Apparently, between 1930 and 1939, Cryne also did organizational work in addition to his care for cemetaries.

739 *Waterbury Democrat*, May 11, 1939, 3.

740 *Waterbury Democrat*, May 15, 1939, 7.

741 *Waterbury Democrat*, June 3, 1939, 3.

Sanger's call to free women from the burdens of childbearing and for legal birth control under medical supervision."[742] In 1925, these reformers again brought their demand to the Connecticut legislature and gave testimony at hearings on the bill. Along with Sanger was Katharine Houghton Hepburn, a powerful speaker in support of birth control and women's suffrage.[743] The only opponent of the bill to speak in 1925 was a woman from the Connecticut Council of Catholic Women.[744]

The years 1927 to 1929 were disappointing for birth control advocates. Membership in the national ABCL fell from 13,000 in 1923 to 2,800 in 1926 and the *Birth Control Review* "had only 47 subscribers in all of Connecticut."[745] But, in 1929, after the ABCL had used grass roots organizing to "set up local birth control committees in small towns" the 1929 legislative hearings on the subject were again "raucous, with nearly 1,000 people in attendance."[746] In addition, the Conference of Congregational Churches in Connecticut also supported the reformers' legislation. The bill was defeated without debate in the Connecticut Senate.

The House was another matter, however, and Representative Epaphroditus Peck, an attorney, forced debate to be held. One female representative spoke against the bill. Her reasoning was that if it passed "only immigrants would contribute to the population growth and girls could become prostitutes."[747] It was her view that 75% of girls would become prostitutes. At this remark, there was a "swell of hissing" and she was "silenced as she stood."[748] Despite all this, the bill failed in the House by an overwhelming vote of 226 to 18.[749] Clearly, legislators were not ready to commit to the idea that a doctor should be able to practice medicine as s/he saw fit when it came to female patients.

In 1930, a decision from the Second Circuit encouraged reformers. In Young's Rubber Co. v. C.I. Lee & Co., Inc., 45 F.2d 103 (1930), the Second Circuit Court of Appeals[750] had ruled that, where local laws made it permissible for a doctors to prescribe them, it was not illegal to transport condoms over state lines.[751] A "doctor's bill" was therefore introduced during the 1931 Connecticut legislative session. Although the Judiciary Committee supported this bill, in an amended form, it was still defeated

---

742 Wawrose, *Griswold*, 33. Note 917.
743 *Ibid.*, 34. Hepburn was the mother of the well-known actress.
744 *Ibid.*
745 *Ibid.*
746 *Ibid.*
747 *Ibid.*, 37.
748 *Ibid.*
749 *Ibid.*
750 The Second Circuit includes the states of New York, Connecticut and Vermont.
751 Please see, *University of Chicago Law Review*, 6 (1939), 260.

in both houses of the legislature despite the fact that the Connecticut Birth Control League had gotten the support of 400 doctors prior to the legislative session.[752]

Given the fact that the Judiciary Committee had supported the bill, there was "renewed enthusiasm and an increase in CBCL [Connecticut Birth Control League] membership."[753] Dr. A. Nowell Creadick, a gynecologist, became leader of the CBCL at this time, and a few days after his assuming leadership, pushed the Connecticut State Medical Society to make a statement of "unanimous support" for the 1931 bill.[754] However, unlike in Rhode Island, where a birth control clinic had been opened in July 1931 "without incident", Creadick advised against this type of "nullification" tactic[755], perhaps fearing direct confrontation. In 1933, the CBCL tried again and the House passed the bill with one amendment and that was that the law applied to married women only. The vote was 169 for the measure and 80 against it. However, the Senate rejected it "soundly."[756] In 1935, a "wealthy supporter" made it possible for a Maternal Health Center to open in Hartford; this center treated women who fit within certain strictly defined criteria and "tested the limits of the statute without outwardly aggravating the authorities."[757] Also, in 1935, Sally Pease replaced Dr. Creadick as president of the CBCL, thus signaling a change in CBCL strategy.

Connecticut authorities did, however, watch the Chase Dispensary, also known as the Hartford Maternal Health Clinic. Despite a report in the press that it had closed, the Clinic did not shut down and even established a number of these Maternal Health Clinics in Connecticut. The CBCL chose not to involve itself in the 1937 legislative session. Consciously or unconsciously, nullification of the law was indeed taking place. Polls in 1936 indicated, "70% of Americans favored legalizing birth control."[758] Additionally, one journal "reported that the mailing of contraceptives was as common

752 Wawrose, *Griswold*, 38. Note 917.

753 *Ibid.*

754 *Ibid.* On the national level, February 1935 saw the sixth attempt by Margaret Sanger to have a federal law passed that would allow doctors to give their patients advice on birth control defeated. As the federal Comstock Law still read, doctors could not give this information without facing the possibility of arrest and/or fine. *Time Magazine* published a story that included Sanger's reaction to the defeat. Here, it described her as "plump Mrs. Sanger" and noted that, instead of bowing to the will of a male Congress, she held a party to celebrate the 21 years of the birth control movement. Attending the party were "powerful names" such as Mrs. J. Borden Harriman, Mrs. Harold L. Ickes and Mrs. Frederick A. Delano, an aunt to then President F.D. Roosevelt.

755 Here, use of the word "nullification" means that despite the illegality of an act, public support is so strong that the move is supported and is allowed to exist. A similar meaning exists in the law. For example, despite evidence in a trial and despite the Jury Instructions that are given by a Judge, a jury may decide to do the exact opposite of what it is instructed.

756 Wawrose, *Griswold*, 39–40.

757 *Ibid.*, 40. Women clients had to be married, living with their husband, have at least one child or be "physically or economically unfit for pregnancy" and unable to pay for private care.

758 *Ibid.*, 41.

as 'the use of gummed postage stamp'" and even the Sears and Roebuck catalog, a staple in American homes at this time, advertised "preventatives."[759]

In early June 1939, a birth control clinic was reported as operating in the Chase Dispensary.[760] At first, there was some doubt as to just what exactly the services it provided were. Jeannie Heppel, Superintendent of the Dispensary, told the *Waterbury Democrat* "a birth control clinic had been operating there since last October."[761] Meanwhile, Dr. B. Henry Mason, Superintendent of the Hospital to which the Dispensary was attached, and Dr. Charles Larkin, head of Gynecology, were quoted as saying it was a gynecological clinic and **not** a birth control clinic. Both stressed that advice was given to women on a "medical basis" when questions were asked; advice was not given to "healthy, normal women." Hepple had also noted that women were seen only upon written referral from their family doctor. But A. "Sally" Morgan Pease of West Hartford had informed the Connecticut Birth Control League on Thursday, 8 June, that there **was** a birth control clinic that had been operating at the Chase Dispensary. The *Democrat* noted that Catholic clergy "may" call the event to the attention of Maurice F. McAuliffe, Bishop of Hartford, since "several clinics are reported operating in the state."[762]

What had actually happened was that the Waterbury Maternal Health Center had begun operation on 11 October 1938 when Nurse Clara McTernan had asked to use two rooms of the hospital for one day a week. The "usual" restrictions on birth control work had been in use, all funding for the work was private and "[m]ost important, the hospital and the center would be distinct entities with no connection."[763] In fact, with Sally Pease directing the work, field worker Leah Cadbury and nurse Clara McTernan, had set about to open a birth control clinic in Waterbury at the Chase Dispensary building, attached to the Waterbury Hospital. Two doctors were enlisted; a friend of the McTernan family, Dr. William Goodrich, who had already worked in the Hartford Maternal Health Center and Dr. Roger Nelson were to be the medical team at the Dispensary along with the women.[764]

Sally Pease was enthusiastic about the Clinic. When she spoke to the annual meeting of the Connecticut Birth Control League (CBCL) at the Farmington Country Club, she characterized the new Chase Dispensary at the Waterbury Hospital as one of

---

759 *Ibid.*

760 *Waterbury Democrat*, June 10, 1939, 1. Susan Wawrose notes that the *Waterbury Democrat* was the "newspaper of choice for much of Waterbury's substantial Roman Catholic population...." Wawrose, *Griswold*, 46–47.

761 *Ibid.*

762 *Ibid*. McAuliffe was ill at this time.

763 Wawrose, *Griswold*, 46. The restrictions were that birth control services would be given only to married women, living with their husbands who did not have money for private care.

764 *Ibid.*, 45–46. Goodrich was a graduate of Columbia Medical School and Nelson of Cornell Medical School.

the CBCL's "most important achievements of the previous year."[765] The main speaker at the CBLC meeting had been Dr. Woodbridge E. Morris, then General Director of the Birth Control Federation of America where he noted that birth control had had a slow acceptance in America because "apparently we are still mid-Victorian in our thinking."[766]

Inevitably, the Roman Catholic Church became involved in the matter. Rev. Eugene P. Cryne, whom we have already encountered, was also President of the Catholic Clergy Association of Waterbury. He called a meeting of priests in that group for Saturday morning, June 10, 1939 and by the next morning a proclamation that this group had drafted was read from every Catholic pulpit in Waterbury.[767] Catholics were told that birth control was against the moral law, that the spread of birth control information was illegal and that they should avoid the clinic. And, on Monday 12 June, this proclamation was printed on the front page of the *Waterbury Democrat*.[768]

While we cannot know for certain, one Catholic who might have been sitting in one of those pews on 11 June was William "Bill" Fitzgerald, the State's Attorney in Waterbury, whom we have encountered a number of times. If he was anything, he was a quick understudy and had learned that not enforcing a law, however outdated, could be professional suicide. In fact, Larry Lewis, Fitzgerald's predecessor, "had been forced to resign for failing to enforce the state's gambling laws."[769] Within less than 24 hours after perhaps hearing the sermon, Fitzgerald approached Judge Frank P. McEvoy, also a Roman Catholic, for a search warrant for the Chase Dispensary located on Field Street, and the warrant was granted.[770] One colleague had described McEvoy as "wildly Irish Catholic" who had "grown up with the teachings of the Church and who was married to an outspoken opponent of birth control."[771]

The search warrant was executed and within the hour that the search took, numerous "unidentified" articles were confiscated.[772] County Detective Roland G. Alling and Deputy Sheriff Albert Francis searched the dispensary on Monday morning. In the afternoon, Fitzgerald conferred with Assistant State's Attorney Walter W. Smyth

765 John W. Johnson, *Griswold v. Connecticut: Birth Control and the Constitutional Right of Privacy* (Lawrence: University Press of Kansas, 2005), 21. The meeting was held on June 8, 1939, a Thursday.

766 *Waterbury Democrat*, June 12, 1939, 4.

767 The text of this proclamation can be read at Appendix H.

768 *Waterbury Democrat*, June 12, 1939, 1.

769 Wawrose, *Griswold*, 47.

770 *Ibid.*, 23. According to Johnson, McEvoy's wife was a "leader in blocking a pro-birth control statement by the Connecticut League of Voters several years earlier." Wawrose apparantly describes the same inident when, in 1932, at the convention of the League of Women Voters, Mrs. Frank McEvoy, had threatened to leave that organization with all her Catholic sisters if it voted to endorse birth control.

771 Wawrose, *Griswold*, 47.

772 *Waterbury Democrat*, June 12, 1939, 1. Detectives made the surprise search shortly before 10:00 A. M.

and Alling.[773] Meanwhile, Doctors Larkin, Foster and Goodrich, who had previously refused to characterize the clinic as a "birth control" clinic, did admit that information was given to women whose health "would be 'endangered or seriously impaired' by child-bearing."[774]

On 17 June 1939, one week after Deputy Sheriff Francis and County Detective Alling had searched the Chase Dispensary Clinic the *Democrat* reported that Sallie Pease "welcomed" a court test of the legality of the local clinic. Pease reiterated the League's stand that the laws were "medieval" and that "changing times" required they be reevaluated. Pease issued a statement, which, in part, read:

> We are convinced after reading the history of the passage of these laws that they were designed to prevent immorality, and that they in no way touched birth control clinics, which promote the health of families under the supervision of qualified physicians.[775]

Pease ended her statement saying that medieval laws could not "halt the march of progress and health."

On 17 June a hearing was also held before Superior Court Judge McEvoy, the same Judge who had issued the warrant. This was probably a "show cause hearing" in which Dr. B. Henry Mason and all other "interested parties" were summoned to explain why the seized materials should not be destroyed. Mason did not attend. In his stead, attorney J. Warren Upson (1903–1992) appeared on behalf of the Waterbury Maternal Health Clinic and the Connecticut Birth Control League. He identified the items as the property of the clinic and contested their destruction. Upson asked for a continuance in order to prepare his case and the matter was set over until 3 July. Along with Upson was another attorney, Lawrence L. Lewis, the man who had preceded Fitzgerald in the same job. Upson also identified the officers of the Waterbury Maternal Health Center as Clara McTernan of Columbia Boulevard (President), Mrs. Henry C. Griggs of Tower Road (Treasurer) and Mrs. R.W. Goss of Columbia Boulevard (Secretary). Upson identified this group as "informal in character – with no particular organization." While this group was not incorporated, the Birth Control League itself was a corporation, whereupon its financial assets and the assets of the Board members could come into play.[776]

The *Democrat* had reported various aspects of this story for one entire week, on the front page of the paper, with nothing but numerous repetitions of the same facts, making transparent pleas for prosecution and a statewide investigation. But on the

773 *Waterbury Democrat*, 12 June 1939, p. 1.

774 *Ibid.*, 4. This entire account was indirectly challenged by the *Democrat*, which reported that Rev. John S. Kennedy, associate editor of the *Catholic Transcript*, had received a complaint from a Hartford woman, saying that she had been sent unsolicited circulars on birth control work in the area.

775 *Waterbury Democrat*, June 17, 1939, 1.

776 *Waterbury Democrat*, June 17, 1939, 4.

twelfth of June it had new facts, one of which was potentially more interesting than others. Not only had Alling and Francis seized "devices", they had also seized some records from the clinic.[777] A list of all the seized items had been returned to Judge McEvoy and the items were delivered to the Show Cause Hearing in paper bags and piled on a table in the courtroom. Fitzgerald explained the procedure through which the Clinic had been served with notice of the hearing but also said the Waterbury Hospital had "disclaimed any interest in the articles" at that time. He also cited §6246 and §6562 of the General Statutes of Connecticut, as those laws that were violated by the items. Section 6246 found it illegal for "any person to prevent conception "by the use of any drug or medical instrument" and Section 6762 found it illegal for anyone to assist in contraception.[778]

As a State's Attorney, Fitzgerald had wide jurisdictional powers. He also had several potential defendants to choose from for his indictment. Why did it take him six days to reach this decision as to whom to prosecute? At the time Fitzgerald may have been sitting in the pews of his neighborhood Roman Catholic Church and listening to the proclamation denouncing the birth control clinic on Sunday, June 11, he may not have known that his next-door neighbor – and friend – on Columbia Street, nurse Clara McTernan, was involved with the clinic.[779] Fitzgerald eventually chose to set any consideration of friendship aside and eventually chose two staff doctors, Roger B. Nelson and William A Goodrich, as well as Clara Lee McTernan as defendants.[780] The three were arrested on Friday, 23 June after 2:00 P.M. when Fitzgerald obtained warrants for their arrests from Judge Wynne, in Superior Court. All parties orchestrated the time and date of the arrest.[781] What is interesting about the arrest warrants is that they were obtained so late in the week. Friday afternoons in any Superior Court are likely to be a slow time. Was it possible that Fitzgerald thought he could keep them in jail over the weekend for the lack of a Judge? What we do learn in Monday's *Democrat* is that Fitzgerald, being a zealous prosecutor, did ask the court that

777 After the first – and only – mention of "files" seized at the clinic, all mention of them stops in the newspaper and the confiscated evidence is described as actual birth control items. One is tempted to wonder if the "files" confiscated implicated some – or even many – working class Catholic families or even of the police officers themselves and upper class Catholics? Any mention of "files" or documents simply disappears.

778 *Waterbury Democrat*, June 23, 1939, 8.

779 *Waterbury Democrat*, June 23, 1939, 8. McTernan, said the Democrat, is "identified with the exclusive McTernan School for Boys, on 106 Columbia Boulevard."

780 *Ibid.* As it turned out, Fitzgerald soon discovered that he and McTernan were literally neighbors and friends.

781 *Waterbury Democrat*, June 24, 1939, 3. "Mr. Lewis informed Judge Wynne that the proceedings had been agreed upon." Dr. Goodrich lived at 138 Grove Street, Dr. Nelson at 161 North Mayn and Clara McTernan at 106 Columbia.

each post a $500.00 bail. But Judge Kenneth Wynne denied Fitzgerald's motion and the three were released on their own recognizance.[782]

We may never know what the personal politics of the Editor of the *Waterbury Democrat* were or what his idea of unbiased reporting was. Nonetheless, we can make a fairly reasonable supposition about its sympathies on the Chase Dispensary case. On the front page of the *Democrat* directly adjacent to the birth control clinic story of 23 June, which was the headline story, was an inset of the "Stork Stamp." It showed a woman with children on either side of her. She was looking down lovingly at a newborn child. Apparently, the French government, worried about the declining birth rate, had issued the stamp to depict "the joys of motherhood."[783]

Superior Court Judge Kenneth Wynne made a decision in the Chase Dispensary Case in early August 1939. The younger Judge Wynne sustained the demurrer[784] that Upson had filed, which could have ended the case then and there. What we do find out in the newspaper report of these events is that it was attorney Fitzgerald, who wanted to make this a test case and that Wynne, by his upholding of the defense demurrer, gave a "tacit recommendation" to Fitzgerald to take the case to a higher court.[785]

The *Democrat* cited a lengthy section from Wynne's 25-page memorandum that accompanied his decision. Wynne cited to the Massachusetts Gardner case in which that state's statute, similar to Connecticut's, was upheld by that state's highest court. Wynne also quoted from Chief Justice Rugg of Massachusetts "whose opinions are universally valued and respected."[786] Wynne said:

> No decent person would deny the laudable objective of morality and chastity, which...[the Gardner case decision] sought. It is, however, common knowledge that many legislators voting against the recognizing of the medical aspect of the problem, appease intellectual integrity by a specious argument that reputable doctors and a respectable married women will not be affected. It is against this easy doctrine of inconsistency that high-minded members of the medical profession have inveighed. Now comes the test.[787]

---

782 *Waterbury Democrat*, June 24, 1939, 3.

783 *Waterbury Democrat*, June, 23, 1939, 1. Placement of the stamp story was, most probably, not an accident. For a more detailed account of the legal maneuvers in the Chase Dispensary Case, please see Appendix I. The stamp cost 80 centimes, 10 centimes of which would go to support the National Alliance for the Increase of the Nation's Population.

784 To sustain means to to uphold as correct after objection by the opposing party. A demurrer is essentially a legal signal meaning "So what?" Upson was saying that if everything the State was complaining of was true, where was the harm?

785 *Waterbury Democrat*, August 7, 1939, 1 Flush left. It is probable that all parties involved in this case had the same intention, i.e. to make this a test case.

786 *Waterbury Democrat*, August 24, 1939, 1.

787 *Waterbury Democrat*, August 7, 1939, 4.

The very next day, the *Democrat* reported that sources close to Fitzgerald's office had "hinted strongly today that an appeal would be taken to the Supreme Court of Errors"[788] of Judge Wynne's decision. The orchestration of the Chase Dispensary Case was almost complete.[789] This appeal would stop the defense motion, to be heard in September, to discharge the three defendants. Once the appeal of Wynne's decision had been heard, the entire issue could be decided "once and for all."[790]

Birth control activists who were part of the larger social movement knew what this strategy meant. Congratulations on Wynne's decision came from all quarters despite the fact that his memorandum basically found that the dispensary had been organized to violate the existing statutes. The general director of the Birth Control Federation of America, Dr. Woodbridge E. Morris, was quoted referring to the "outworn laws" implicated in the case, and said "Physicians of the state are now free to practice medicine." Mrs. A.W. Pease, President of CBCL, was reported as saying that Wynne's decision was "a great triumph of common sense over a ridiculous Connecticut law." The Vice President of the Hartford league, Mrs. Thomas Hepburn, praised Judge Wynne's decision as "wise and humane" and the three defendants as having "moral courage in the face of embracing accusations against them when they were performing a valuable service to the City of Waterbury."[791]

Legal strategy aside, Nelson, Goodrich and McTernan were eventually convicted. Fitzgerald's appeal of Wynne's Demurrer was upheld at the appellate level. Upson appealed the conviction of the two doctors and nurse, which was a decidedly reasonable move, especially in light of the earlier federal decision in United States v. One Package. In a split decision in State v. Nelson et. al., the Connecticut Supreme Court signaled it was in no mood to listen to what the federal government had to say on the issue and, in a 3-2 decision, upheld the conviction. This decision established that the long sought after medical exception in Connecticut could – or would – not be read into the 1879 statute and the conviction of the Chase Dispensary workers was upheld.[792] But Upson had, if anything, whittled away at the confidence of the Con-

788 The Supreme Court of Errors is the older name for what is now simply ccalled the Supreme Court of Connecticut.

789 Waterbury Democrat, August 8, 1939, 3.

790 *Ibid.* This is Wynne's language for his memorandum.

791 *Ibid.* In this case, a great deal of emphasis was focused on the destruction of items that County Detective Koland G. Ailing and Deputy Sheriff Al Francis had taken into evidence when they raided the Chase Dispensary. Included in Wynne's decision was an authorization for the destruction of the items, although McEvoy stipulated that their destruction should wait until after the criminal case had been finished.

792 *Waterbury Democrat*, June 14, 1939, 1, 26. Please see State v. Nelson, 7 Conn. Supp. 262 (New Haven County Court, 1934), followed by the appeal at 126 Conn. 418, 11 A.2d 859, 129 Conn. 84, and 26 A.2d 582 (1942).

necticut Court. In his brief he had used as precedent a 1888 Wisconsin Supreme Court Case, for the idea that:

> ...any citizen of Connecticut may deal with **his own body** in any way **he** wants to and it is his natural right to do so if he does not impair any similar right on the part of another citizen. (Emphasis mine.)[793]

Whatever was, or was not, a legal "natural right" would have to wait twenty-six years to be defined.

5.4 Phase Three: Legal Norm Production and the Right of Privacy

After the 1939 Chase Dispensary case, the Supreme Court of the United States heard two cases, concerning the same troublesome Comstock law and from the same (troublesome) state – Connecticut. The first centered on a Dr. Wilder Tileston, an obstetrician, whom the Court said had no "standing" to bring his legal action; this was because there was no actual "case or controversy" demanded by Article III of the Constitution. The Tileston v. Ullman, 318 U.S. 44, 63 S.Ct. 493, 87 L.Ed. 603 (1943) case had been legally flawed from its inception since Tileston had asked that court for a "Declaratory Judgment", i.e. for the trial judge to declare the Comstock law invalid. Procedurally, this would have been a "quick and dirty" end to the law from which the state could take an appeal if it wanted. However, nothing related to Tileston's right to practice medicine as he saw fit or as to the patient's right under the 14th Amendment was presented in the pleadings at the trial level. Civil and criminal procedure at that time made more demands on practitioners and the rules demanded that if arguments were not "front-loaded", the higher Courts would not – could not – supply any remedies at the "back-end."

The legal attempt to "fir[e] a heavy broadside" at the Comstock Laws took time and determination – and, the right set of facts and the right combination of Supreme Court Judges.[794] The next attempt came from three joined cases; they were Poe et. al. v. Ullman, 367 U.S. 497 (1961) (No. 60), Doe v. Ullman (No. 61) and Buxton v. Ullman (No. 62). All three were heard before the Supreme Court in 1960 with a decision issued in 1961. While all three had pretensions at this "heavy broadside", none of them succeeded.[795] But a "heavy broadside" begins quietly with a great deal of planning and,

---

793 Obituary for J. Warren Upson, online at http://bronsonlibrary.org/filestorage/33/upson.bmp, accessed January 7, 2008.

794 *New Haven Register*, 29 January 29, 1961, 31.

795 Poe was argued March 1–2, 1961 before the USSC. Attorneys for appellants were Fowler V. Harper, Harriet Pilpel, Morris L. Ernst and Nancy F. Wechsler for Planned Parenthood Federation of America, Inc., (amicus curiae), Whitney North Seymour for Dr. Willard Allen et. al. and Osmond K. Fraenkel

in this respect, these three cases helped to prepare for Griswold by teasing out the issues to which members of the Supreme Court might – ultimately – be receptive.

The first case involved a Jane Doe, a New Haven housewife, for whom another pregnancy would be "perilous to life"; the second involved Paul and Pauline Poe, a New Haven couple, who had had three children, each with an congenital abnormality that died soon after birth; and the third case was by Dr. C. Lee Buxton, Professor and Chair of the Obstetrics and Gynecology Department at Yale Medical School as appellant. The first two cases argued that the statutes infringed on their liberty and "put their lives and health in jeopardy" and Dr. Buxton argued that the laws prohibited him from "practicing his profession according to the scientific principles upon which it is based and according to his conscience" thereby depriving him of protection under the 14th amendment.

The Planned Parenthood League of Connecticut (PPLC) was disappointed by the results of the earlier Tileston case, but Estelle Griswold, who became director of the PPLC in 1953, along with New York attorney Morris Ernst, refused to be so pessimistic. Along with assistance from the American Civil Liberties Union plus the energy of thousands of women during what could be called the "winter" of the women's movement – the 1950s – and the willingness of Dr. Lee Buxton, another challenge was brought in May 1960. This second Connecticut challenge brought on board the experience of Yale law school professor, Fowler Harper, and the PPLC counsel, Catherine Roraback. Having "cut his teeth" on the authoritarian antics of Eugene McCarthy, Fowler Harper was ready and able to contend with the government and the Roman Catholic Church hierarchy. Hull and Hoffer make the following assessment from the period after the unsuccessful Buxton challenge.

> Even though times had changed in Connecticut, and liberal Roman Catholics called for an end to the church's political campaign against birth control – it pit Catholic against Protestant and made the church into a political actor instead of a guardian of private conscience – the church's hierarchy continued to lobby [against repeal of the Comstock law in Connecticut]... [Fowler] argued, as much against the Roman Catholic church hierarchy as against the state, that the law violated "the right to engage in normal marital relations", which meant the right of married people in their own bedrooms to exercise "a personal freedom or privilege to procreate or not procreate as the individual may desire or as medical factor may dictate."[796]

On 2 March 1960, oral arguments had taken place before the Supreme Court in Buxton, et. al. v. Ullman, 367 U.S. 497 (1961). The *Waterbury Republican* carried an UPI wire report about the event and it is here that we get the flavor of the arguments. This report characterized the Justices as "cool" to Dr. C. Lee Buxton's challenge to the

---

and Rowland Watts for the American Civil Liberties Union (ACLU), et. al., and for the appellees, Raymond J. Cannon, Assistant Attorney General of Connecticut with Albert L. Coles, Attorney General. The case was decided on June 19, 1961.

796 *Ibid.*

1879 Comstock law.[797] Buxton, who had received his medical degree from Columbia in 1940, had joined the staff of the Department of Obstetrics and Gynecology at Yale University Medical School in 1954. He was known as a "gentle crusader" who talked "quietly, often sprinkling his conversation with droll comments." His research concentrated on problems of sterility and he found it ironic that he'd gotten into so much trouble over the problems of fertility.[798] Unlike many researchers in general, he was reported as liking to spend time with his patients.[799]

In terms of strategic legal procedure, Yale Professor of Law, Fowler "Chick" Vincent Harper (1897–1965), had filed a declaratory judgment action on behalf of Dr. Buxton in which Harper claimed that the Connecticut law did not allow Buxton to practice medicine in that he could not prescribe contraceptive devices for the two woman participants in the case. During the oral argument, the Justices "showered" attorneys with questions, some producing "outbursts of laughter in the usually sedate courtroom." Two things appeared to worry the Justices, one of which was the fact that no one had ever been tried and convicted under the law, according to Connecticut Assistant Attorney Raymond J. Cannon. The other was a problem of proof since, according the Justice Felix Frankfurter, under Connecticut law, wives could not testify against husbands and vice versa, so the likelihood that there would ever be proof that the birth control prescription had ever been used was zero.

Justice John M. Harlan, asked Cannon if the state of Connecticut would use search warrants to see if married couples were using contraception, to which Cannon answered "I don't know." Frankfurter followed up with the statement that it was important for the Court "to know if there can be prosecutions." Harper Fowler tried to make the point that a doctor could be punished for giving advice alone, but some of the Justices "expressed doubt on this point."[800] There was reported to be "some confusion" as to how contraceptives were sold in Connecticut. Chief Justice Earl Warren asked if they were sold in the "ordinary course of trade" and Cannon replied that they were sold in a surreptitious manner. Justice Frankfurter asked if they were sold in a similar fashion to the way liquor was sold under the Volstead Act where one had to belong to club and give "a pass sign." Again, Cannon had to confess ignorance, saying he had "no personal knowledge."[801] Rather than be misunderstood, Justice Frankfurter retorted, "I wasn't drawing on that."

Confusion also seemed to exist on whether or not the sale of contraceptives was legal depending on the purposes for which they were sold. Harper argued that they

---

797 *Waterbury Republican*, March 3, 1961, 1.

798 *New York Times*, June 8, 1965, 34.

799 *New York Times*, July 8, 1969, 43 (Obituary).

800 Absent a look at the original pleadings, we are left to wonder if Fowler had included a First Amendment challenge.

801 The Volstead Act, the popular name for the National Prohibition Act, was in effect between 1919 and 1933.

were legally available for the purpose of preventing disease. But, in response to Justice Charles E. Whittaker, Cannon said that they could not be legally obtained for any reason. Frankfurter, who seemed to be rather engaged in the argument, then asked if they could be bought for a collection since "People collect all sorts of queer things." This apparently introduced a meandering conversation of reminiscences where Frankfurter told Cannon he knew a man who collected matchboxes and another who collected sausage containers. Cannon then retreated to the position that they could be collected "for scholarly purposes."

The Chief Justice again tried to get a succinct answer from Cannon as to whether or not there was a "direct law prohibiting the sale of contraceptives." The state's attorney responded that a man was once fined for selling them from a vending machine but Cannon was not sure what law that was. Frankfurter than asked whether or not the law was based on the "assumption that procreation is the only justification for conjugal relations?...Increase and multiply is the inarticulate[d] purpose of your legislation[?]"[802] To this rather engaged Judge, Cannon gave the rather feeble answer of, "I suppose so."[803]

It was Frankfurter who eventually authored the majority opinion in what was a 5-4 decision in favor of the state. Frankfurter ruled the action did not present a genuine case since no one had actually been prosecuted under the Connecticut law. The case was dismissed but it was Harper who later brought his battle expertise to the Griswold case. There, he argued that the 9th and 14th amendments to the Constitution protected a "right of privacy" and that this right also protected other interests in the 1st, 2nd, 3rd, 4th and 5th amendments.[804] This was – finally – a winning argument.[805]

5.5 Scientific Discourses and the "Throbbing Uncertainties of the Cosmos"[806]

Dr. Alan Guttmacher (1898–1974), Chief of Obstetrics and Gynecology at Mr. Sinai Hospital in New York, was pictured in the book section of the *New Haven Register* early

802 *Waterbury Republican*, March 3, 1961, 1.
803 *Ibid.* It appears that Cannon was not ready for this oral argument. I was unable to discover if he was a young state's attorney and had been sent as a lamb to the slaughter or if the state thought the case didn't need a seasoned, effective, attorney since it was so confident it would win the case.
804 Harper died on 8 January 1965 before the decision in Griswold was handed down. His was a life dedicated to civil rights, attacking the McCarthy hearings as well as debating right wing politician, William F. Buckley, at Yale in 1954. He held the Simeon E. Baldwin Chair at Yale University Law School.
805 Fowler Harper synthesized a number of currents in American jurisprudence in his argument. However, and this is not meant to detract from his work, it was ultimately a number of liberal judges who would decide – or be persuaded – by the arguments.
806 *New Haven Register*, January 1, 1961, 10.

in January. Doubleday had published his new book, *Babies by Choice Not Chance,* the same month. Guttmacher would become a familiar face in New Haven throughout this period, advocating for the right of contraception. Guttmacher himself had joined the birth control movement in the 1920s as an intern after witnessing the death of a woman from a botched abortion. By 1960, he had already written three other books, *Life in the Making*, (1933), *Into This Universe*, (1937) and *Pregnancy and Birth*, (1957).[807] Finally, in 1962 he became President of the National Planned Parenthood Federation.

On Friday, 1 January 1960, Mayor Lee of New Haven gave his inaugural address, reported as "appropriately ceremonial and understandably vague" by the *Register*. The newspaper made less vague statements, saying that the largest problem looming for New Haven was to "return to solid and stable financial standards at City Hall."[808] The municipal budget had to "be put on an even keel." Lee's political career actually began in 1939 when the Democratic chairwoman of the 17th Ward asked Lee to run for alderman in New Haven.[809] Lee won and joined forces with Max Schwartz "to sponsor many New Dealish proposals, most of which were promptly voted down by older members of the board."[810] His first job had been as a reporter for the *Journal-Courier* and he was later elected as alderman. Although his manner of practicing politics was a bit unorthodox, it earned him the support of voters. He walked into the job of Mayor in a city he described as "a decaying community." He had publicized the fact that "10,000 disease-carrying rats infested a single street in the center of the city."[811] In addition to talking about public health problems, he

> embarrassed and angered many voters – including some prominent citizens and at least two red-faced city officials – by having the police tow away their automobiles for illegal parking.[812]

---

807 "Alan F. Guttmacher 2898–1974) at http://www.guttmacher.org/about/alan-bio.html, accessed May 30, 2006.

808 *New Haven Register*, 3 January 3, 1960, p. 18.

809 *Saturday Evening Post*, 19 April, 19, 1958, p. 115.

810 *Ibid.*

811 *Saturday Evening Post*, April 1958, 31.

812 *Ibid.* The *Saturday Evening Post,* portrayed Lee as a man on a mission. The *Post* showed a picture of him in front of a new construction site that had been a former New Haven slum. What Lee had inherited politically from the federal government was the National Housing Act, designed to "lend money to buy and clear blighted areas for resale to private investors and [which] would make grants to cover two thirds of the net cost." Lee also "hounded" property owners for back taxes, abolished "patronage jobs", fired some city workers for "loafing" and "waged a long running battle with the town's only newspaper owner, John Day Jackson".... In November, 1960, he had won re-election by a "record breaking plurality" of 23,000 votes. The 42-year-old Lee, who had never attended college, was described as "tightly wound" but with an "informal manner." Lee was Roman Catholic and during his political career, the *New Haven Register* ccontinually fought his reforms. Nonetheless, in April 1958, he looked quite "impressive" to the *Post* which claimed he was "[s]aving a 'dead' city."

Given the corruption scandal associated with Mayor Hayes in 1939, the fact that one could no longer "fix" a parking ticket signaled a new era for New Haven residents who had experienced the earlier periods.

The editorial page of the *New Haven Register* wished its own Governor Abraham Ribicoff well as he left Connecticut to join President Elect John F. Kennedy's Cabinet. It predicted a "problem-strewn path" for the Lt. Governor, John M. Dempsey, who would succeed Ribicoff as Governor of Connecticut.[813] Kennedy himself faced a "politically divided government" with the Democratic Executive and Senate matched by a Republican House of Representatives. The newspaper called for "political honesty" and the "need for statesmanship above party maneuver." But the tone of the New Year's Day editorial in the *New Haven Register* was a bit subdued and the voice was inward looking as it said:

> But lofty musings about the condition of men and alarmed analyses of the political, the economic, or the spiritual failings of this generation are unlikely to produce more results than could be produced through a greater self-knowledge on the part of each of us. So let us today put aside the madness of governments, the contradictions of science, the paradoxes of geography, and the throbbing uncertainties of all the cosmos, to think a moment about ourselves – to weigh the measure of good that we achieve, the measure of love that we dispense, the measure of truth that we defend.[814]

The lofty rhetoric this Editor uses could mean s/he was still under the spell of the national election held in November of 1960, a hard-fought battle that most citizens, particularly in the South, instinctively knew would begin a social revolution.

The social character of the New Haven community in the early 1960s can be analyzed in various ways. However, one interesting detail is found in early January, with a Westbrook dateline.[815] A woman was reported as shopping in a New York department store and gave her mailing address to the clerk as "Westbrook, Connecticut." The clerk responded "not THE Westbrook?" Westbrook had apparently developed a reputation as a "Peyton Place."[816] A Westbrook sailor, stationed at the Great Lakes Naval Base in Illinois, corroborated the reputation by reading a "lurid account" in a Chicago paper about his hometown.[817] The report hypothesized that the suicide of a First Selectman in March and the discovery of embezzled municipal funds in April of the previous year accounted for the reputation. In short, the social fabric of schemas

813 *New Haven Register*, January 1, 1961, 10.
814 *Ibid.*
815 Westbrook, Connecticut is less than 30 miles east of New Haven.
816 The reference to Peyton Place, a city located in New Hampshire, may be from the 1957 movie by the same name, staring Lana Turner, Lee Philips, and Hope Lange. Later, in 1964, Peyton Place became a TV series and the name is generally associated with places where the inhabitants have two types of values, one set in private and one set in public.
817 *New Haven Register*, January 1, 1961, 1.

claimed to be unchanging and immutable was unraveling as the hypocrisies of that time were being reported. On the other side of the Atlantic, Norwegians would candidly call this type of activity, the "double morality."

On 24 January Dr. Alan F. Guttmacher whom we have encountered above, gave a talk at the Yale-New Haven Medical Center to a capacity audience. Guttmacher was reported as advocating that "'contraception should be taught in high schools and colleges' along with other sex instruction in order to have an informed populace."[818] Guttmacher had a dual appointment and was also at that time a Clinical Professor at Columbia University. He urged the United States to adopt "legal programs" such as those "undertaken in countries such as Sweden and Japan" so that the population problem might be addressed. The health of the mother should, according to Guttmacher, "serve as a ground [for an abortion] as well as her life" and that additional grounds such as "eugenic consideration, pregnancies occurring from rape, and socio-economic reasons." He also noted it was "most illogical" to provide for public health services such as immunizations while doing "nothing about conception control." As for religion, Guttmacher said that the attitude of one religious group toward the issue of contraception should not be "forced upon another [group]."

The *Register* made information about legal assaults on Connecticut's 1879 birth control ban well known. In late January, it reported on the challenge brought by Planned Parenthood, the ACLU and a group of university obstetrics and gynecology professors; this was the Harper and Rorabeck team mentioned above who would soon challenge State Attorney General Albert Coles.[819] While Protestant church authorities approved of artificial contraception, the Roman Catholic position was that this was "contrary to divine law." The *Register* did report that one – more liberal – "Catholic publication" had written that a "Catholic can justifiably favor repeal of the Connecticut and Massachusetts anti-contraception laws, or breathe happily if they are declared unconstitutional."[820]

Furthermore, Comstock's ghost was still present and active in Connecticut. For example, in 1961, two women's groups, the West Haven Junior Women's Club and the Connecticut State Federation of Women's Clubs, Inc., resurrected the fight against "obscenity." At the head of this drive was Mrs. Roger Addil of Orange who urged public support for a U.S. Senate Bill that would create a "Federal Commission on Noxious and Obscene Matters and Materials." The bill had been introduced on 4 January with the support of 22 Senators. The 17-member Commission was envisioned as an "investigative agency" with subpoena power that would report directly to the President.[821]

---

818 *New Haven Register*, January 25, 1961, 6.

819 This case was Griswold v. Connecticut.

820 *New Haven Register*, January 29, 1961, 31.

821 *New Haven Register*, February 5, 1961, p. 16. In the same issue of the *Waterbury Republican*, the issue of women being allowed in bars to drink alcohol was discussed. Miss Margaret O. Gray of the

5.6 The "Usual Suspects", the Institutional (Religious) Field and Griswold

The annual meeting of the Advisory Board of the Catholic Diocesan Bureau of Social Services was held on 12 March 1961 in Hartford. The speaker was the assistant executive secretary, Richard Mastronarde, a graduate of the University of Connecticut's School of Social Work, who spoke on the topic "Trends in Family and Child Care."[822] From the list of those attending, we can see that at least some of the individuals who had been involved in the 1939 Chase Dispensary case were there. The Rev. Eugene P. Cryne was still involved with the organization, this time as Associate Director of the Bureau and Frank T. Healey was President of the Board. The intervening 23 years had been kind to both men; Cryne had been elevated to Monsignor or "Rt. Rev." and Healey had become a Judge. The Bureau was also having financial problems at this time.[823]

Women's Christian Temperance Union (W.C.T.U.) of Connecticut claimed to want to "keep a feeling of respect among our fellow citizens" by arguing against women being allowed into bars. She advanced her particular version of the history of previous years saying, "I saw plenty of what went on in those days." (*Waterbury Republican*, March 1, 1961, 13.) What was at issue was, literally, a matter of physical distance. In 1961 a woman could drink at a table, if tables were present, but was not allowed to drink at the bar. Women who did drink at the bar were commonly referred to as "B-girls", "usually working on a commission from the management, and encouraging male patrons to buy her and themselves more drinks than they actually intended to buy." (*Ibid.*) The legislature had heard arguments, pro and con, on the question of "Is it right for women to do their drinking at a bar?." The review of the entire issue was possibly due to support from the Associated Restaurants of Connecticut and the Connecticut Hotel Association whose lobbyist, attorney Stephen Sweet, said that the law was "an old blue law that's been on the books long enough." (*Ibid.*) On Sunday, the *Republican* ran a cartoon by "Mort" on the editorial page with the caption "A Bar Flyess." At the bottom of the cartoon was the sentence "Bill in Legislature Would Allow Women To Sit at the Bar." (*Waterbury Republican, The Sunday Republican*, March 5, 1961, 6.) The cartoon itself pictures a man and a woman at a bar with a bartender behind the bar. The man is dressed in hat and coat and is smoking. He is turned to look at the woman, who is clearly meant to be drunk. Her purse is on her arm but open. Her glass is in the process of being tipped over. One shoe is off and one is curled around the barstool. She is saying, "My husband doesn't understand me." My interpretation of this is that "Mort" is saying women should be allowed to be bar "flyess's" and repeat the same self-pitying phrases that male bar flys are often hear to say.

822 *Waterbury Republican*, March 11, 1961, 2.

823 *Ibid.* Assistant Associate Director Rev. John G. Fanning and Attorney James F. Henebry, Chair of the Finance Committee discussed these problems. James F. Henebry (1913–1992) was also born in Waterbury and practiced law there after receiving his law degree in 1940. He served as a trial judge from 1967 to 1992; he was elevated to the Court of Common Pleas in 1975 and to the Superior Court in 1977. (Please see, Obituary Sketch of James F. Henebry at: http://www.cslib.org/memorials/heNEBRYJ.htm acessed on January 7, 2008. His "most memorable case" was the jailing of 70 Bridgeport teachers involved in a 1978 teachers' strike.) Others at this meeting included several staff members, the Chairman of the Nominating Committee and the President of the Waterbury Council of Catholic Women, Mrs. Charles A Wolisschlager.

Superior Court Judge Frank T. Healey had again been elected President of the local Diocesan Bureau of Social Services at the meeting mentioned above. Also elected were James F. Henebry, First Vice-President, Carmen Donnarumma, Second Vice-President, Miss Mary Schmidt, Secretary, Rt. Rev. Msgr. Eugene P. Cryne and Assistant Treasurer, Rev. John G. Fahning.[824] Mastronarde had concluded in his talk that the trend in Catholic childcare was to treat fewer children but ones with more specialized needs, such as the emotionally disturbed. In 1959, the Bureau had given services to 566 children; in 1960 that number had increased to 618. According to Dist. Secretary Agnes F. Brovick the increase was due to "troubled family relationships", such as divorce, separation and mental problems.[825] The number of unwed parents had also increased. She noted there had been an increase in "applications around prenatal and postnatal services for mothers of out-of-wedlock children."[826]

Judge Healey was a very active in Catholic organizations in the county. In May, he was re-elected to the Board of Trustees of the Diocesan Bureau of Social Services for the Archdiocese of Hartford at its annual meeting.[827] In 1939 during the Chase Dispensary Case, Healey had been an attorney working at a general practice in Waterbury. He worked there for 14 years after having graduated from Yale Law School in 1925 and before he was elevated to the bench. According to his obituary, Healey always remained a hometown boy.[828] He was a "representative of an old and respected Irish Catholic family." As the reporter wrote:

> This fact is mentioned because Judge Healey would have wanted it so. He never left anyone in doubt about the fact that he was of Irish descent, and he was an almost militant Roman Catholic. He was proud of both distinctions.[829]

Jesuit priest Robert F. Drinan (1920–2007), at that time Dean of the Boston College of Law, also spoke at this meeting on the high divorce rate and methods of lower it.[830] Rt. Rev. Msgr. George M. Grady noted that, in 1960, the Bureau had served 3,944 families using expenditures of $782,672. Hard-to-place children were discussed as well as the fact that the Bureau "continued to work closely with public agencies both at the local and state levels."[831] The Board of Charities was facing different schemas such as more

---

824 Spellings of of the surnames Cryne and Fahning vary from article to article.
825 *Waterbury Republican*, March 12, 1961, 12.
826 *Ibid.* The agency also had 15 boarding homes at its disposal during 1960.
827 *Waterbury Republican*, May 8, 1961, 3.
828 *Connecticut Reports* 150, 733–35 as found at http://www.cslib.org/memorials/healeyFT.htm, accessed on April 23, 2014.
829 *Ibid.*
830 Drinan would go on to be elected as a Representative to Congress from the state of Massachusetts, serving for ten years between 1971 and 1981. Pope John Paul II then forbade him to continue as an elected Congressman.
831 *Ibid.* Those attending included Attorney James Henebry and members of the Waterbury Bureau.

babies born "out-of-wedlock" and a rising divorce rate, even among Roman Catholics. That society in general, and Catholic society in particular, had changed, was obvious.

These two authoritative figures had been at the same (figurative) table in 1939. In 1961, in terms of the Roman Catholic Church as an institution, the same normative institutional structures were still in place as had been in 1939; women did the day-to-day administrative work while the male hierarchy held decision-making positions within the group. But this would soon change. It would not be long before another generation of Roman Catholic faithful would occupy those chairs, a generation that had felt the winds of change in the Roman Catholic Church set in motion by Vatican II (11 October 1962–8 December 1965) as well as the Civil Rights Movement and the Women's Movement, among others.

Between the major "failed" birth control cases, social structural and schematic changes of tectonic magnitude had taken place. Decades of grass roots organizing combined with experience gleaned from less fruitful legal action, plus the energy of Estelle Griswold and Lee Buxton and the strategic legal insight of Fowler Harper combined to finally create a successful legal case from Connecticut. The method of change would be different from Case One; this time, the law would be "judge-made" rather than legislatively formed.

The set of facts underlying Griswold were set in motion in July of 1961 when Estelle Griswold, executive director of the New Haven Planned Parenthood Clinic signed a lease for 79 Trumbull Street in New Haven on behalf of the Planned Parenthood League of Connecticut.[832] The hopes of these progressive women who had rented the New Haven Planned Parenthood Clinic were to be tested when one James Morris, a Roman Catholic by religion, and the married father of five children, complained to the police about the clinic.[833] Pictures exist of Morris – alone – picketing the Clinic with a sign reading "ThE Law is The Law OR is it? *Morality is in danger*!"[834] It took only five months for events to unfold so that, after the issuance of a warrant on 10 November, Estelle Griswold and her clinic medical director, Dr. Lee Buxton, presented themselves to detectives John Blazi and Harold Berg to be arrested with warrants that had been procured by circuit court prosecutor Julius Maretz.[835] Estelle Griswold was the energetic executive director of the New Haven Planned Parenthood Clinic who had signed a lease for 79 Trumbull Street in New Haven on behalf of the Planned Parenthood League of Connecticut in July of 1961.[836] Dr. C. Lee Buxton remembered that he and Mrs. Griswold had been called by the prosecuting attorney and asked "how we'd like it done", in reference to the arrest. He was asked if he'd like a paddy wagon

832 Wawrose, *Griswold*, 82–83. Note 917.
833 *Ibid.*, 10, 85.
834 The typographic irregularities reflect Morris' own spelling and punctuation.
835 Wawrose, *Griswold*, 85.
836 *Ibid.*, 82–83. Note 917.

sent "with policemen and photographers...or would we prefer to turn ourselves in quietly."[837]

Meanwhile, Griswold, worked its way through the state courts to the federal Supreme Court and on June 7, 1965, Justice William O. Douglas issued the opinion of the Court, which declared the law under which Griswold and Buxton had been arrested as unconstitutional.[838] Reactions to the Griswold decision differed. Rather flippantly, Dr. Buxton remarked to a friend that, "considering all the trouble that the [Griswold] case had caused him, the judge who convicted him could have at least fined him more than $100."[839]

Griswold v. Connecticut, 381 U.S 479 (1965) was a 7–2 decision of the United States Supreme Court and the author of the decision was Mr. Justice William O. Douglas. At the time, Douglas had been a Supreme Court Justice for four years, having been appointed by J.F. Kennedy on 1 October 1962 as a replacement for F.D. Roosevelt's appointee, Felix Frankfurter, of One Package fame. Justice Tom Clark, who had followed all things concerning birth control over time as a Clerk of the same Court, joined Douglas in the majority decision. Concurring in the outcome, but not necessarily the reasoning, were Justices Goldberg, Warren, Brennan, Harlan and White. Justices Stewart and Black cast the two dissenting votes.

Griswold had come before a Court that was mainly liberal in its leanings. Arthur Goldberg, a labor lawyer, had been added to the Court in September 1962 serving until 1965. Earl Warren (s. 1953–1969), unlike in Poe, had a transcript of the trial of Griswold and Buxton and could not therefore claim there was no "real controversy." He "would have preferred" that the Connecticut legislature had done its own work and had struck down the statute, but he did think it was "overly vague – the narrowest possible grounds for voiding it."[840] Justice Harlan was in ill health but vigorously opposed the birth control law and Brennan, a devout Roman Catholic, was of the same opinion. Byron R. White, who had been a Deputy Attorney General under J.F. Kennedy, had replaced Justice Charles Whittaker. Only Justice Potter Stewart had qualms. In Poe, he'd been willing to base a reversal on the 14th Amendment[841]; it was

---

837 *New York Times*, July 8, 1969, 34 (Obituary).

838 *Ibid.*, 99.

839 *New York Times*, June 8, 1965, 34. The fact that Estelle Griswold and C. Lee Buxton were convicted and fined is history that some have forgotten, never learned or conveniently overlooked. On *Fox News' Special Report*, 24 October 2005, host Brit Hume claimed that no one had ever been prosecuted under Connecticut's "little Comstock Law" before Griswold was decided, to which Douglas W. Kmiec, constitutional law professor at Pepperdine University, responded "That's right. This was largely a test case, although it was a criminal statute, and they could have been subject to fine and imprisonment." Please see, http://mediamatters.org/items/printable/200510270006, accessed January 7, 2008.

840 N.E.H. Hull and Peter Charles Hoffer, *Roe v. Wade: The Abortion Rights Controversy in American History* (Lawrence, Kansas: The University Press of Kansas, 2001), 83.

841 The 14th Amendment to the Constitution, ratified after the Civil War in 1868, includes 5 sections.

one thing to declare a statue illegal based on an actual, existing Amendment but it was another to find a right that didn't even exist in plain language in the Constitution.

William O. Douglas had two problems that he had to deal with in the writing of his decision. The first was that the federal Constitution includes no reference to marital (or any other form of) privacy as such. The second was that there was a long-standing policy that the Court would not interfere in a state's attempt to regulate "public morals." This had been so with regard to the use of alcohol, gambling, homosexuality and sex crimes. Douglas took his cue from Fowler Harper's briefs. In fact, according to some, Harper was the "author of the right to privacy."[842] This is not unreasonable, as Harper, along with his Yale colleague Fleming Jones, had written a multi-volume treatise on torts, the subject where speculation about a right of personal privacy would most likely take place. However, the development of the "right to privacy" is a bit more complicated.

Since Fowler Harper was terminally ill when the briefs had to be submitted to the Supreme Court, his Yale colleague, Thomas Emerson, "framed the final brief and argued it before the Court."[843] A law review article written by law professor Norman Redlich had influenced both Harper and Emerson and they chose to make the right of privacy the centerpiece of the brief on behalf of Griswold and Buxton. One could say, as Hull and Hoffer do, that Emerson's final brief "waffled" as to where the right could be found; one could also say Emerson gave the Court a choice, overlooking no possible source.[844] This approach garnered support from some quarters, even within the Catholic Church. The Catholic Council on Civil Liberties filed an *amicus curiae* brief in support of Griswold and no less than Cardinal Richard Cushing of Boston agreed to the move.[845] This again supports the notion that the Roman Catholic Church of the early 1960s was not the monolithic institution with one, absolute, singular interpretation on issues that the Vatican, largely during the papacy of John Paul II

It was a fundamental addition to the Bill of Rights and provides a definition of citizenship (Section 1), ante-bellum representational apportionment (Section 2), exclusion from office for those involved in an insurrection (Section 3), payment of debts incurred during an insurrection (Section 4) and a promulgation section (Section 5). The most salient feature of the 14th amendment lies in Section 1, providing "due process" and "equal protection" under the law to all persons – not only citizens of the United States. Section 1 has been used to overturn the Dred Scott case as well as argue against segregation in Brown v. Board of Education. (But see Roberts in Parents Involved in Community Schools v. Seattle School District No. 1, 551 U.S. 701, 127 S.Ct. 2738, 75 U.S.L.W. 4577 (2007).) It was used in Roe v. Wade as well.

842 Please see: http://www.law.onu.edu/about/Fowlerharper.html, accessed on January 7, 2008. Homepage for the Ohio Northern College of Law.

843 Hull and Hoffer, *Roe,* 83.

844 *Ibid.*

845 *Ibid.* Cushing went so far as to support a Massachusetts bill that would repeal their anti-birth control legislation. Hull and Hoffer, *Roe*, 83.

(r. 1978–2005), and Benedict XVI, and later imposed on the American Roman Catholic hierarchy as well as devout believers.

Douglas argued that the right of privacy is created by the 1st, 3rd, 4th and 5th Amendments to the Constitution. The 1st Amendment is commonly referred to as the granting the "right of association", the 3rd prohibits the State from housing soldiers in one's house in time of peace, the 4th Amendment protects citizens against unreasonable searches and seizures and the 5th Amendment does not allow the State to compel testimony against oneself. Because Douglas worried about a "plain meaning" or "specific intent" argument, he leaned on the 9th Amendment which says that "The enumeration in the Constitution, of certain rights, shall not be construed to deny or disparage others retained by the people."

Justices Goldberg, Warren, Brennan and Harlan, in the main, agreed with Douglas on the first issue of where a right of privacy can be derived. When writing about the second issue, they found the right of privacy as "fundamental" thus demanding the highest level of scrutiny, "strict scrutiny." Justice Potter Stewart, a Republican appointee to the Court, dissented; he could find no such language in the Constitution as a "right to privacy." Nonetheless, he called the Connecticut law "asinine", "unwise" and "uncommonly silly." In other words, the state was free to pass as many silly laws as it wanted, and they may be legal, as long as the Constitution said nothing about it. Stewart's reasoning is a perfect example of a contextualization or, the view from nowhere. The fact that women had died as a result of just such abstract reasoning was of no moment to an "originalist" Justice such as Stewart.

The precedents that Douglas used were more than forty years old and did not even use the word "privacy." These were Pierce v. Society of Sisters (1923) and Meyer v. Nebraska (1923). Pierce dealt with an Oregon law that sought to compel every child to attend public school. Meyer dealt with a law forbidding the teaching of any other language than English to schoolchildren below the eighth grade. At issue was the teaching of German. What Douglas was doing was using legal reasoning to argue that "confidential relationships" in Pierce and Meyer were similar to the confidential relationship between a husband and wife.[846] While it might be difficult to imagine that what language one speaks or where one's child goes to school could be similar to the communication between husband and wife in the marital bed – aside from their location in a "private sphere" – it demonstrates two things: first the lengths to which Douglas was willing to go to find precedent to support his unique argument and second, the paucity of cases with facts that dealt with husband-wife communication on sexual matters.

When it came time to vote on Douglas' opinion, there were only four votes – Douglas himself, White, Goldberg and Harlan. If the opinion had five votes, it could be said to be the "decision of the (entire) Court." Brennan and Warren chose instead

846 Hull and Hoffer, *Roe*, 84.

to concur with Goldberg's opinion since it embraced the 9th Amendment as a source of the privacy right. Goldberg had assigned a clerk, Stephen Souter[847], to research the origins and purpose of the 9th Amendment. Souter found that James Madison, the "principal architect of the Constitution as a whole", had written the amendment and it had been passed by both houses of Congress with little debate and no changes.[848] Congressmen were afraid that the first eight Amendments might not have been "comprehensive enough to secure the rights and liberties of Americans."[849] The 9th Amendment, according to Goldberg, made allowance for additional rights that the original framers had not envisioned. Goldberg wrote that "the language and history of the Ninth Amendment reveal that the framers of the Constitution believed that there are additional fundamental rights, protected from government infringement, which exist alongside those... specifically mentioned in the first eight constitutional amendments."[850] Despite Goldberg's citation to James Madison for the 9th Amendment as a source for legal privacy, Justice Black found no such right in the same set of words.

Justice White's argument is worth noting. He thought in larger concepts – but not as large as "privacy." For one, he was concerned that he had often "berated his colleagues for reintroducing substantive due process" in criminal matters.[851] For another thing, White was concerned about the subject matter of the Connecticut law itself, "its interference with marriage."[852] States had to show, if their laws were to intrude upon a "fundamental" constitutional right, that their law was based on a "compelling state interest", and not "merely related to a legitimate government interest." States would often argue that their laws against birth control were related to the deterrence of "illicit sexual relationships like homosexuality, adultery, and incest", as if combining all these groups together would make the arguments too loathsome to listen to and thereby produce a knee jerk reaction – against proposed birth control law.[853] Justice White had a problem with such reasoning, however. He saw no relationship between birth control information and deterring adultery or homosexual activity.

In the end, Justice William O. Douglas' opinion was published but it was not a decision of the entire court. Accompanying it were three concurring opinions.[854] The

847 Souter was appointed to the Court in 1994.

848 John W.Johnson, *Griswold v. Connecticut* (Lawrence Kansas: University Press of Kansas, 2005), 171.

849 *Ibid.*

850 Hull and Hoffer, *Roe*, 85.

851 *Ibid.*, 86.

852 *Ibid.*

853 *Ibid.*

854 A "concurring" opinion is one that agrees with the holding of the case by the Justice who writes the opinion for the majority. A concurring opinion usually approaches the legal problem presented somewhat differently, oron other legal principles, but nonetheless agrees in the holding.

first, by Arthur Goldberg, was joined by the Chief Justice, Earl Warren, and William Brennan. Harlan wrote the second concurrence; Byron White wrote the third concurrence while Black and Stewart wrote the two dissenting opinions.

5.7 Rapid Social Change and Intersectional Categories

What changes were occurring in and between the larger social structures in the United States at this time? As the United States Congress convened on 6 January 1960, eleven months before the national presidential election, the two most "explosive issues" were civil rights and federal aid to education, according to the *New Haven Evening Register*.[855] One might have thought that World War II and its aftermath might have prompted changes in normative practices as regards racial minorities. Women had taken the jobs of men in various industries during the war and one might also have thought the normative attitudes towards women would have been sifted. Nonetheless, the Vice President of the Democratic National Committee, Katie Louchheim, who addressed The Women's National Party said that women needed to "win for ourselves the acceptance of the fact that [we] are people [too]."[856] The group was reported as "dedicated to the passage of a constitutional amendment to guarantee women equal rights with men." Women, she said, just like men, had "varying interests" and men "with a social conscience" thought like "women with a social conscience." The problem, in Louchheim's view, was "over-domesticated women in their thinking about public affairs."

Political changes were not as opaque social transitions. On 2 January 1960, the *New Haven Evening Register* noted that then Democratic Senator from Massachusetts, John F. Kennedy, was "set to make it [bid for the Presidency] official."[857] This was of importance for a number of reasons, one of which was the fact that he was Roman Catholic and, if elected President, would be the first President who was a member of that faith. Later that year, on 6 November 1960, Kennedy had visited Waterbury, Connecticut. Approximately 40,000 people waited until 3 A.M. on a cold winter night to hear him speak from the balcony of the Roger Smith Hotel.[858] Kennedy's Press Secretary, Pierre Salinger, was to later recall that this "was the greatest night of the campaign."

On January 21, 1961, Democrat John Fitzgerald Kennedy was sworn in as President of the United States. The inauguration was held in "the freezing aftermath of driving

855 *New Haven Register*, January 6, 1960, 1.

856 *Ibid.*, p. 6.

857 *New Haven Evening Register*, January 2, 1960, 1.

858 Please see http://en.wikepedia.org/wik./Waterbury, Connecticut, accessed on February 27, 2008.

snowstorm" that enveloped the east coast of the United States. New Haven recently re-elected Mayor Richard C. Lee declared a state of emergency as "a blizzard whipped the state, shutting schools, banks, business and industry and keeping most people indoors."[859] Kennedy became the 35th President of the United States at 12:51 P.M. ten minutes after Lyndon B. Johnson was sworn in as Vice President. The *New Haven Register* used the UPI story of the inaugural that reported "World Peace Top Goal of New Leader." Kennedy's 1300 word speech addressed not only Americans, with its classic challenge to "ask not what your country can do for you, but what you can do for your country" but also to "my fellow citizens of the world" who should ask "not what America will do for you, but what together we can do for the freedom of man." As to Cuba, Kennedy said, "Let every other power know that this hemisphere intends to remain the master of its own house." As temperatures continued to plunge, John M. Dempsey, originally a native of Ireland, was sworn in as the Democratic Governor of Connecticut, a clear sign that the state had changed from its 1930s attitude toward immigrants.[860]

As with the previous case, it is important to establish what socio-cultural conditions existed that may or may not have contributed to a sense of "moral panic" in the country. Although local economic indicators may not have been bright, Associated Press reporter Jack Lefler filed a report, reprinted in the *Register*, which noted that the nation's 1959 business activity exceeded experts' expectations. Although a steel worker strike of 116 days had taken place in 1959, the December industrial production was "near the all-time highs of the pre-strike period in steel."[861] On 4 January 1961, the United States and Cuba severed diplomatic ties and the *Register* noted this was a "genuine misfortune."[862] But it minced no words, calling Fidel Castro a "megalomaniac" and said, "there was no other choice." It predicted "difficulties ahead" and said Guantanamo was a "problem of explosive proportions", whether the United States chose to keep the base or not.

The economic situation might not have been a problem but race relations were significantly troublesome; desegregation in America's South was finally becoming a reality. In 1954, the Warren-era Supreme Court of the United States in Brown v. Board of Education, 347 U.S. 495 (1954) (Brown I) had decided that "[s]eparate educational facilities are inherently unequal."[863] In 1960, African-Americans Hamilton E. Holmes

859 *New Haven Register*, January 20, 1961, 1.

860 *New Haven Register*, January 24, 1961, 1.

861 *Ibid.*, p. 16.

862 *New Haven Register*, January 4, 1961, 26.

863 Laurence H. Tribe, *American Constitution Law* (Mineola, New York: The Foundation Press, 1978), 1019 -1020. Brown v. Board of Education, 349 U.S. 294 (1955) (Brown II) addressed the issue of appropriate relief pursuant to Brown I. Brown I reviewed the "separate but equal" rationale found in Plessy v. Ferguson, 163 U.S. 537 (1896). There, "equal but separate accommodations for the white and colored races" met with the Court's approval; if they were unequal it had nothing to do with "anything found

(age 19) and Miss Charlayne Alberta Hunter (age 18) were refused admittance to the University of Georgia in Athens and challenged that decision in Holmes v. Danner. On 4 January 1961, Federal District Court Judge W.A. Bootle (1902–2005) ruled that the university had discriminated against the two on the basis of race and ordered their immediate admittance. Demonstrators hung an effigy of Holms from an arch at the university and burned a "small cross" near a freshman dormitory after the ruling. Georgia's state law prohibited the use of state funds in the operation of either integrated educational institutions or those ordered to be integrated. However, it was pinned under another order to desegregate Atlanta public schools that September.[864]

Four days after his first order to admit Holmes and Hunter, Judge Bootle again had to issue a temporary injunction ordering the Governor of Georgia, Ernest Vandiver, and the State Auditor, R.E. Thrasher, from obeying Georgia state law and cutting off funds or withholding operating funds from the University of Georgia at Athens. On the front page of the *Register*, over the headline "U.S. Judge Bars Governor From Closing Georgia U.", appeared yet another harbinger of tense days to come, "U.S. Will Continue Maneuvers Despite Protests of Castro."[865]

In mid-January a full-page advertisement appeared in the *Register*, with 6 x 3 ¾ inch pictures of Presidents Eisenhower and Kennedy side-by-side under the banner "We are challenged as a people. We are summoned as a nation."[866] Under the pictures the text noted that there existed "worldwide unrest" and a "precarious peace." It was an advertisement a book, *Goals for Americans*, which came out of the *Report on National Goals*, a report that advocated public involvement in the "decade of decision ahead."[867] The *Report* set as major goals at home, among others, to "Improve educa-

---

in the [state] act [mandating racial segregation of railroad passengers]" and if there was any badge of inferiority it was "solely because the colored race chooses to put that construction upon it." Tribe, *Constitutional Law*, 1019–1020. This is another example of a type of legal "relativity" where the reality held by some is blamed by those holding another reality for "non-existent problems" the first group says it has.

864 *New Haven Register*, January 7, 1961, 2. Dwight D. Eisenhower appointed William Augustus Bootle to the Federal District Court in Georgia in 1954. Three days after ordering the two students to be admitted to the University, he stayed (blocked) his own order since the University had appealed it to a higher court. Until the end of his life he maintained that the stay of his own order was "business as usual." Finally, he revealed to Professor Robert A. Pratt that he did so in order to get the case before the Fifth Circuit and the Supreme Court as soon as possible. Donald L. Hollowell (1917–2004) and Constance Baker Motley (1921–2005), attorneys for the two students, then petitioned Judge Elbert P. Tuttle of the United States Court of Appeals for the Fifth Circuit, who overturned Bootle's stay. On 10 January 1961, the University took its case to Justice Hugo Black, a former Klu Klux Klan member, who turned it over to the full Court. The Court upheld Tuttle's ruling but on 11 January when Holmes and Hunter tried to attend classes, rioting broke out at the university and the university suspended them, ostensibly for their own safety. On 12 January, Judge Bootle ordered them reinstated.

865 *New Haven Register*, January 10, 1961, 1.

866 *New Haven Register*, January 19, 1961, 3.

867 *Ibid.*

tion so that every child is educated to his full capacity", to "Reduce the last barriers to full respect for every individual – especially that of race" and to "Bring high quality medical care within every American's reach." Abroad, the goals included the fight against Communism, arms stabilization and a strengthening of the United Nations as well as confining "outbreaks of violence anywhere in the world."

The "space race" was narrowed by Americans, who on 1 February, made a fourth successful launch from Cape Canaveral in which a "space chimp" named "Ham", riding inside a Mercury capsule, survived the launch of a Redstone Minuteman missile and its 420 mile journey.[868]

Normative political practices as regards the techniques of social movement organizations (SMO)[869] were changing in major ways. On a spring day in March, the *Waterbury Republican* used a term in its first editorial that most Americans had little familiarity with but which, in retrospect, became a fixed political tactic of the 1960s and beyond. The Republican's editorial titled "Passive Resistance" noted how interest in the idea had "surged" in the "past two years."[870] The editorial mentioned the boycott of segregated buses in Montgomery, Alabama, sit-in demonstrations at lunch counters and "pray-ins" against racial segregation. William S. Nelson, then Vice President of Howard University, was teaching a course in the philosophy of nonviolence and was especially suited to the job since he "has visited India and once knew Gandhi personally."[871] The editor of the *Republican* was insistent in giving credit to American transcendentalist writer, Henry David Thoreau, however

> It is remarkable that in all the references to Gandhi as an example to the American Negro's passive resistance against segregation credit is never given to the prototype of the idea: Henry David Thoreau....It is an American idea, after all, and Gandhi freely acknowledged the inspiration he gained from reading Thoreau as a youth in South Africa....It is part of American heritage.[872]

Ascribing "passive resistance", in light of the work and success of Gandhi, to American heritage, while technically true to a point, tends to undermine the work Gandhi did and minimizes the successes he achieved, i.e. the liberation of a nation. Thoreau's time in jail for refusal to pay a poll tax that indirectly supported slavery is not a fair comparison. The resistance of feminists aimed at protesting against their lack of civil rights in Britain is a fairer comparison, especially since some died, but it comes nowhere near to Gandhi's use of and success with the strategy.

868 *New Haven Register*, February 1, 1961, 1.
869 SMO is an acronym for social movement organizations. Please see Chapter 2.
870 *Waterbury Republican*, March 1, 1961, 6.
871 *Ibid.*
872 *Ibid.*

In the *Suburban Section* of the *Waterbury Republican* on Sunday 22 March was a full-page advertisement by the Shell Oil Company.[873] The headline read "Bulletin: Shell Research scientists reveal how they got 168.47 miles per gallon." Using a "highly modified" 1924 2-passenger coupe that Shell "rescued from a junkyard for $35", Dave Berry and Fred Schuette won a marathon competition, using tires that were a yard in diameter plus other significant changes. Shell's message was that its new "mileage booster" Platformate released "11% more energy than the finest 100-octane aviation gasoline."[874] Whether or not Shell had some knowledge of international oil reserves is unknown; the point is that many of the issues seen in the *Republican* resurfaced a mere 30 years later, be they state vouchers for private education or the fuel efficiency of carbon-based machinery. Even the gas crisis of the 1970s in the United States would be all but forgotten by the media by the turn of the century.

Late in March, President Kennedy warned Russia that the United States and her allies would "have to consider their response" to the fact of "armed attacks by Communists rebels" in "war-scourged Laos."[875] Kennedy later opened a news conference with a statement on Laos and "huge maps" charting the "progressive communist conquests of Laos since late August." Kennedy's thesis was that the fall of "the little mountain kingdom" would "endanger the security of all Southeast Asia" as well as affecting the security of United States. Kennedy hoped that that Russia would agree to a British-backed proposal for a cease-fire and start to negotiations.[876]

Pacifists were again on the front page of the *Republican* when the New England Committee for Non-Violent Action was pictured with placards passing "through Waterbury yesterday on their 300-mile route from Kittery, Maine to the U.N. building, New York." Pictured in the lead was Richard Zink, age 20, who had boarded the nuclear submarine USS George Washington in October 1961 before being pushed into the water by "defending sailors." In the picture that accompanied the story was one of first uses of what has since become known as the "peace sign" but which the Republican reported as a "semaphore language for 'nuclear disarmament'."[877] The marchers gave lectures and movies at the local YMCA before moving on to New York. The leader had been Robert Swan who had spent two years in jail during World War II "for his pacifist views." Swan had become ill and his wife had to replace him as leader of the group and she had herself spent six months in jail in Omaha, Nebraska for illegally entering a missile base there. The *Republican* described the marchers as

---

873 *Waterbury Republican-American*, March 22, 1961, Suburban Section, 2.

874 *Ibid.*

875 *Waterbury Republican*, March 24, 1961, 1. Flush Left.

876 *Ibid.*

877 Gerald Holtom designed the "peace sign" in 1958 for the anti-nuclear march from London to Aldermason. It is based on the semaphore signals for "N"(nuclear) and "D" (Disarmament). I am grateful to Prof. Ann Sætnan for this information.

> A curious blend of the old and the young, the beaten and the defiant, bearded and the clean-shaven, the zealous self-admitted anarchist and the college boy just out to get away from classes.[878]

In this report there is a bit of bemusement about the entire episode, the type of episode that would eventually become common fare for television viewers across the United States during the late 1960s and early 1970s. But one should note the reference to anarchy, a contributing factor to the "moral panic" that we have already seen in the previous case.

A major reason that this would become a status quo practice at this time was the earlier Civil Rights Movement; this social movement organization produced changes that women's groups would then take as models for changing social norms for women. For example, we read that after one group of black and white "Freedom Riders" had been arrested upon their arrival by bus in the Mississippi capital of Jackson, Attorney General Robert F. Kennedy issued a plea for them to slow down the pace of desegregation actions saying, "A mob asks no questions."[879] Twenty-seven people from two buses were eventually arrested and put in jail for "breach of peace, disobeying an officer and attempting to incite a riot." Jackson city police ringed the bus station, some with dogs, and arrested the group when they entered a "white only" waiting room. They were asked to leave but refused and were "accommodated" by Jackson Chief of Police, W.D. Reyfield. A $500 bail was set for each charge, which none managed to obtain until the N.A.A.C.P. (National Association for the Advancement of Colored People) posted the $1500 bail for each person. The incitement to riot charge was dropped and the cases were to come before Jackson Municipal Court the following day. About 100 national guardsmen with rifles maintained a vigil at the Meridian bus station in anticipation of more Freedom Riders. Paul Dietrich, a 29 year old white man from Washington D.C. and the Rev. James M. Lawson, a "Negro minister from Nashville" were arrested along with the group.

This was also time of an unsettling "moral panic" in the United States. Schemas and structures were clearly changing and the outcome was, as yet, unknown. If anything, we saw the same set of Pescosolido factors present in Case One in Indiana (1907). Social life was again being transformed, this time from the "modern" to the "after-modern" (postmodern) just as Indiana had previously experienced the beginning of a change from "pre-modern" to "modern" societal structures and articulations. In this new social arrangement, membership in any given social circle could be both chosen and inherited, i.e. chosen, for example, by one's work but inherited as in the case of membership in a family. The "moral personality" of the individual

878 *Waterbury Republican*, Sunday, March 26, 1961, 1. Flush Right.
879 *Waterbury Republican*, May 25, 1961, 1. Flush left.

was "circumscribed in a new way."[880] More choices were included in the life of the individual and religion will lose its former dominance.

5.8 Denouement: The Equal Rights Amendment

As we shall see in the Norwegian half of this Case, an Equal Rights Amendment was also considered during this period of social change. In the United States, the politics of birth control issues essentially culminated with women winning the right to have an abortion through "judge-made law" in 1973 in the Supreme Court case Roe v. Wade (1973) 410 U.S. 113, 93 S.Ct. 705, 35 L.Ed. 147. But, at the same time, women failed to win any legislatively enacted law directly related to the equality of the sexes. The Equal Rights Amendment (ERA) had been revived during the 1960s. Originally, Alice Paul (1895–1977) had first been proposed it in 1923 at the 75th anniversary of the 1848 Seneca Falls Women's Rights Convention. Then, it was called the "Lucretia Mott Amendment", after Quaker abolitionist and suffragette Lucretia Mott, and it read; "Men and women shall have equal rights throughout the United States and every place subject to its jurisdiction."

The Congress of the United States passed the ERA on 22 March 1972; however, as a matter of procedure, because it was passed as a proposed amendment to the Constitution, it also had to be subsequently passed by two-thirds of the states. This meant that 38 of 50 states had to pass it within their own legislatures. The amendment had a seven-year deadline for passage of the proposed clause. Within a year of its proposal, the amendment was passed in 22 states. In 1973, 8 states ratified the amendment, in 1974, 3 states, and in 1975, 1 state. Opposition came from states' rights quarters, business interests such as the insurance industry, and right-wing fundamentalist religious organizations.

In 1977, Indiana ratified the amendment, the last to do so to date. The seven-year deadline soon became a serious impediment and in 1979, only after a march of 100,000 citizens in Washington D.C., did Congress extend the deadline for passage until 20 June 1982. Despite concerted effort by proponents, no other states ratified the amendment. In 1980, the Republican Party removed it from its platform as Ronald Reagan was elected President.

On 14 July 1982 the Equal Rights Amendment was again proposed in Congress. In the 107th Congress (2001–2002) Senator E. Kennedy of Massachusetts re-introduced it as S.J. Res 10 and Representative Carolyn Maloney of New Jersey as H.J. Res 40, both of which contained no deadline for ratification as the previous amendment had, and it has been re-introduced during every Congress since then.

880 *Ibid.*, 56.

For the time being, in the United States at the level of the Supreme Court, the rulings in Griswold and Roe seem to have been the culminating point for women's rights, reproductive or otherwise. While it is true that various states have undertaken to protect women workers in various ways, in terms of reproduction and equality, these cases remain the limit of legal self-determination over reproduction by women. What is also important, as we shall see in the next chapter, is that – by comparison – Norway's enactment by its Parliament of both an abortion law and an ERA in 1978 has produced far better results in terms of societal acceptance and practice.

5.9 Jasanoff Fields, Changes in Scientific and Institutional Discourses

How had the Jasanoff fields worked to introduce new paradigms in American society making both Griswold and Roe possible? A number of discourses and representations, as well as institutions and identities, had changed between the 1930s and the 1960s. One such discourses was of "women as workers." For example, in July 1939 the *Democrat* ran an article on the Massachusetts Women's Club President, Florence Birmingham. Birmingham had challenged Eleanor Roosevelt to a public debate on the proposition "Should wives be permitted to hold jobs outside the home?"[881] Eleanor Roosevelt declined the offer but Edwina Austin Avery, a suffragette and member of the National Association of Women Lawyers, took up the "cudgel on behalf of the Working Wife."[882] Both were afforded space in the *Democrat* along with John T. Flynn who was to "view the question through the unprejudiced eyes of an economist."[883] What was ultimately at issue wasthe current national legislation outlawing married women the right to work. By 1939, 30 legislatures had seen such attempts.

But in the early 1960s, other ideas of what was the proper place and role for women were in circulation. Feminist Betty Freidan was not the first woman to question her role as a wife and a mother in American society. Her analysis of these roles, however, did have an energizing effect within the women's movement at this time. One important thing to note here is that parts of a typewritten manuscript as well as reprints of some of her lectures can be found in Justice Douglas' files in the Manuscript Room of the Library of Congress.[884] Despite theory to the contrary, what Douglas read and had

---

881 *Waterbury Evening Democrat*, July 14, 1939, 22.

882 *Ibid.*

883 *Ibid.*

884 In the summer of 2006, I reviewed the files of Justice William O. Douglas at the Manuscript Room at the Library of Congress in Washington, D.C. Several copies of corrected and re-corrected page copies of the Griswold text could be found there, as well as some memorandums about Griswold. More interesting, however, were several items from or about Betty O. Freidan. Included in those files were a paper copy of remarks she given to the Cornell University Intersession on Women, Ithaca, New York

experienced did affect his thinking and his willingness to “find” or “discover” the law of privacy in the penumbra[885] - that vague, shadowy are around the Constitution.

Discourses on the nature of what it meant to be a “real” woman had also changed dramatically in the intervening years between Case One and this Case. The “American Mother of 1939” was Otelia Compton, highlighted in the *Waterbury Democrat.* Mother of four, including Nobel winner in Physics (1927), Arthur H. Compton, she credited her parenting success to prayer. She worked her way through college and earned her degree after ten years; she then married her teacher, Elias Compton, who eventually became President of Wooster College. She was chosen Mother of 1939 by the Golden Rule Foundation as “representative of the best there is in womanhood”, the “[u]narticulated voice of millions of mothers throughout the nation.”[886] Rev. Dr. John C. Walker, pastor of the Second Congregational Church, echoed this sentiment in his sermon of 14 May 1939, saying that motherhood was the “best...noblest and most inspiring of all earthly vocations....”[887] The Christian mother was not only the strength of the church but also of the state.

In 1961, the New Haven Register ran an interview with social psychologist, Mack Hanan. He urged women whom he saw as “the sex which still retains rights to non-conformity” to prepare the nation for change by preparing their children “to dare.” The review tagged Hanan’s book *The Pacifiers* as an “angry new book about America’s soft-soap self-image.” Saying that women were still allowed to different, “emotional, intuitive, even frivolous”, they should encourage their child to be independent thinkers. He suggested mothers encourage children to get pen pals from different countries, visit different Churches on Sunday or join a dramatics club. Hanan was quoted as saying that the country was “a society in detour.” America was “neither in favor of very much nor against very much, we are mostly just going through life

January 22/25, 1969, entitled “Tokenism and the Pseudo-Radical Cop-out: Ideological Traps for New Feminists to Avoid.” I also found an unidentified magazine text of a two-part article, part one entitled “Television and the **Feminine Mystique**” and part two entitled “The Monsters in the Kitchen” and several pages of corrected typewritten text. Although this text could have been part of Friedan’s manuscript for *The Feminine Mystique*, published in 1963, it has more the sound of another book by Friedan, “The Second Stage, It Changed My Life: Writings on the Women’s Movement.” There is also a business card from Charlotte L. Mayerson of Random House in Douglas’ files and it is possible that Mayerson sent Friedan’s materials to Douglas.

885 The use of the word “penumbra” is taken from the Griswold decision itself in which Douglas wrote: “The foregoing cases suggest that specific guarantees in the Bill of Rights have penumbras, formed by emanation from those guarantees that help give them life and substance.” The dictionary definition of “penumbra” is that it is “a partial outer shadow that is lighter than the darker inner shadow (umbra), for example, the area between complete darkness and complete light in an eclipse.

886 *Waterbury Democrat*, May 15, 1939, 14.

887 *Ibid.*

together, conditioned to accepting the symbol for the substance, the bypass for the thoroughfare."[888]

By 1965, medical technology also offered women new choices regarding if and when to become pregnant. Medical institutions in the United States represented to the American public that the oral contraceptive was safe and a prudent way to control the number of children a husband and wife decided to have in their family. In August, 1960 the Food and Drug Administration in the United States had approved sale of the birth control pill to the public after a submission by G.D. Searle & Co.[889] Trade-named "Enovid", credit was given to two men for its development, Dr. Gregory Pincus, Ph.D. (1903–1967) of the Worcester Foundation for Experimental Biology at Harvard and Dr. John Rock (1890–1984) of Harvard Medical School. Approval was given for women to use the pill for up to two years, although Dr. Alan Guttmacher, of Planned Parenthood of America's Medical Committee was quoted as saying that no adverse side effects had been noted with use up to 44 months.[890]

Ironically, Dr. Rock, who had been born in Marlborough Massachusetts, had been raised a committed Roman Catholic. As a young man of 14, his parish priest told him to "Always stick to your conscience. Never let anyone keep it for you. And I mean anyone else."[891] After taking a job after his high school graduation where he was exposed to the living conditions of banana plantation workers in Guatemala, Rock decided to attend Harvard University in 1912. In 1915 he went on to Harvard Medical School and began working as an obstetrician. In 1922, he was appointed an Assistant Professor of Obstetrics at Harvard Medical School where he was able to conduct research on human fertility. In 1939, he opened the first "rhythm" clinic at the Boston Free Hospital for Women. His intention was to assist infertile women so that they could identify the best time for conception.

Dr. Gregory Pincus, who would work with Dr. Rock, had been appointed Assistant Professor at the same university in 1931, where he conducted research on ways to prevent conception by working on the effect of progesterone on rabbits. It was Margaret Sanger who introduced Pincus to Katharine McCormick, heiress to the McCormick threshing machine fortune. McCormick quickly gave Pincus $40,000 to support his work. Pincus, however, was not a medical doctor and this restricted the type of research he could conduct. Pincus approached Rock, who was then nearing retire-

888 *New Haven Register*, January 3, 1961, 15. Or, see also, Mack Hanan, *The Pacifier: The Six Symbols We Live By* (Boston: Brown, Little, 1960).

889 *Marriage and Family Living*, August 1960, 242.

890 Ibid.

891 Malcolm Gladwell, "John Rock's Error: What the co-inventor of the pill didn't know about menstruation can endanger women's health" in The New Yorker, Department of Human Resources, March 13, 2000, 52. Also see, Loretta McLaughlin, The Pill, John Rock and the Church: The Biography of a Revolution (New York: Little, Brown and Company, 1982) and Lara V. Marks, Sexual Chemistry: A History of the contraceptive Pill (New Haven: Yale University Press, 2001).

ment. Although Rock was socially conservative and still a faithful member of the Roman Catholic Church, he nonetheless believed in population control. With McCormick's money, Pincus and Rock started drug trials on 50 women which they labeled a "fertility study" to avoid any problems. By 1955, they realized that the science was available for what we now call the birth control pill.

Six years earlier, in 1949, Rock had collaborated with David Loth and written a book entitled *Voluntary Parenthood*.[892] Christopher Tietze, a reviewer for*The Quarterly Review of Biology*, pronounced the book "verbose" and with too much emphasis on technical detail for the average reader. One chapter was entirely devoted to the Catholic point of view that, according to Tietze, was "fairly represented by the Rev. Francis J. Carroll of the Catholic University of America." Of this chapter, Tietze wrote, the "implications of this point of view are only hinted at, and are not discussed."[893]

Eventually Rock, the father of five children, realized that the Vatican needed to be convinced and he and population control supporters both emphasized the "natural" use of hormones to mimic a woman's monthly fertility cycle. Rock wrote a book outlining his work entitled *The Time has Come: A Catholic Doctor's Proposals to End the Battle over Birth Control.* The book was published in 1963, two years before Griswold was decided. This time, Carl G. Hartman reviewed Rock's book for *The Quarterly Review of Biology*.[894] Hartman wrote that Rock worried equally over both his "fecund and his infertile" patients. Rock's own Bishop was Richard James (Cardinal) Cushing (1895–1970). From 1944 to 1970, Cushing served as auxiliary Bishop of Boston and was elevated to the College of Cardinals in 1958 by then Pope John XXIII (r. 1958–1963). Cushing was also a "close friend" of the Kennedy family and had married John Kennedy and Jacqueline Bouvier in 1953. In 1963 Cushing was Archbishop of Boston and was quoted as saying about Rock's book that:

> In this book there is much that is good...[The author] has clearly demonstrated that the Church is not opposed to birth control as such, but to the artificial means to birth control.[895]

Cushing's statement is an elusive one, especially in view of the current position of the Roman Catholic Church on the subject. It can be read as demonstrating that even the Church, in addition to society at large, was in the process of developing an opinion about birth control. But, it can also be read as indicating that Cushing was of the

---

892 John Rock and David Loth, *Voluntary Parenthood* (New York: Random House, 1949).

893 Christopher Tietze, "Voluntary Parenthood" in *The Quarterly Review of Biology*, 25 (1950): 122.

894 Carl G. Hartman, "The Time Has Come" in *The Quarterly Review of Biology*, 38 (1963): 286–87.

895 Hartman, *Time Has Come*, 287. Please see, http://www.en.wikipedia.org/w/index.php?title=Richard_Cushing&printable=yes, accessed on February 28, 2008. This article also makes the following observation, *without footnoting any source* that "Cushing was essentially tasked with making the Roman Catholic acceptable to the general American population in preparation for then Senator John R. Kennedy's run for the White House."

opinion that the use of the body's natural hormones was a "natural" means of birth control.[896]

Opinions by Rock and Cushing aside, Hartman wrote in his book review "Rock's theology is not up to his medicine." The Church had actually already decided that Rock's method was unnatural. With no little prescience, Hartman wrote that the Church's negative reaction to the use of progesterone:

> is but one illustration of decisions which the Church will have to make in the future, decisions perhaps more difficult and doubtless more fateful for humanity than the rejection in the days of Copernicus of the geocentric theory of the universe.[897]

Hartman took time to address the issue of over-population and contrasted President Eisenhower's "cold, laissez faire, negativistic attitude" of encouraging population control to the attitude of the new President, John F. Kennedy, his State Department and his new Secretary of Health, Education and Welfare, Anthony J. Celebrezze. Both Kennedy and Celebrezze, despite being Roman Catholics, were much warmer toward the idea of population control.

Rock did include in *The Time Has Come* a "vivid picture of the battlefield" between Catholics and Protestants on the issue of birth control. Rock held out hope and included in his book an entire chapter devoted to "arguments for conciliation and peaceful coexistence."[898]

But attitudes within the Roman Catholic Church routinely change at glacial speed. Telling the Vatican "the time has come" was of no moment to those who walked the halls there. On 25 July 1968, the encyclical *Humane Vitae*[899] was issued by then Pope Paul IV (1897–1978) (r. 1963–1978). This document, relying on the 7 dissenting votes of the 72-member Committee that studied the issue of birth control, refused to allow the use of synthetic hormones to regulate births. The encyclical merely noted, without giving the number of votes in the Committee, that there had not been "complete agreement" about "the moral norms proposed."[900] *Humane Vitae* analyzed numerous ideas including that of "responsible parenthood" that, it said, "concerns the objective moral order which was established by God, and of which a right conscience is the true interpreter."[901] Despite this fig-leaf bow to the supremacy of conscience, thereby

---

896 *Ibid.*

897 *Ibid.*

898 John Rock M.D., *The Time Has Come: A Catholic Doctor's Proposals to End the Battle over Birth Control* (New York: Alfred A. Knopf, 1963). See Chapter 11.

899 "On Human Life" and subtitled "On the Regulation of Birth."

900 Paul VI, "Special Studies" in *Humanae Vitae*, 2 at http://www.vatican.va/holy_father/paul_vi.encyclicals/documents/hf_p-vi_enc_25071, accessed on November 17, 2006.

901 *Ibid.*, 4.

avoiding its own problems with Vatican II and *stare decisis*, the document ultimately said that:

> We are obliged once more to declare that the direct interruption of the generative process already begun and, above all, all direct abortion, even for therapeutic reasons, are to be absolutely excluded as lawful means of regulating the number of children.... Equally to be condemned...is direct sterilization.... Similarly excluded is any action which either before, at the moment of, or after sexual intercourse, is specifically intended to prevent pro-creation – whether as an end or as a means.[902]

None other than the Bishop of Kraków, Karol Wojtyla, later Pope John Paul II, contributed a major portion of the wording of *Humanae Vitae*. Wojtyla later supported the encyclical with his own 1993 encyclical, *Veritatas Splendor.*[903]

In the end, timing may have been everything for the issue of birth control and the institution of the Roman Catholic Church. Later research, especially that done by medical statistician Malcolm Pike between 1980 and 1981 and oncologists Darcy Spicer and John Daniels, would have allowed Rock to argue that, in essence, the pill was an anti-cancer drug, saving the lives of women from breast cancer.[904] This is the argument of Malcolm Gladwell makes when he writes that this entire scenario was neither the fault of Rock nor of the Church. As Gladwell writes:

> It was the fault of the haphazard nature of science, which all too often produces progress in advance of understanding. If the order of events in the discovery of what was natural had been reversed, [Rock's]...world and our world, too, would have been a different place.[905]

Perhaps this is too generous of an interpretation of the facts by Gladwell in light of the overwhelming number of members who were on the Vatican commission on birth control had voted to approve use of it. In 1968, an aging Dr. Rock finally followed his conscience as his parish priest had once encouraged him to do and stopped attending the Church to which he had belonged his entire life.

The institutional Roman Catholic Church was also weakened throughout the 1960s. This "secularization" of Catholics living in the United States did not start with John Kennedy's election. Second-generation American Catholics had been at least

---

902 *Ibid.*, 5. It is interesting that the encyclical begins with abortion, moves to sterilization and then – finally – to birth control. One would think that the reverse, if anything, would have been the logical construction. This begs the question that is this was written as a moral "shot-gun" approach to all matters of sexual intercourse. Offended in the extreme by abortion, that approach then "rolled down a hill" to hit birth control at a bottom wall.

903 "The Splendor of Truth", an encyclical issued on August 6, 1993.

904 Malcolm Gladwell, "John Rock's Error: What the co-inventor of the pill didn't know about menstruation can endanger women's health" in *The New Yorker*, March 13, 2000, 63.

905 *Ibid.*

partially assimilated, and were "wealthier, better educated and [more] geographically diversified" than their immigrant mothers and grandmothers.[906] Between 1940 and 1960, the Catholic population of the U.S. had doubled.[907] Despite the fact that the pre-Vatican II Church still retained a tight hold on its flock, the GI bill had made it possible for more Catholics, veterans of World War II, to get a higher education. This post-war Catholic culture had no doubt what its answer would be to whether a Catholic could be a good citizen. In 1956, William J. Brennan had been nominated to the Supreme Court and, in a statement foreshadowing Kennedy's own statement said "What shall control me is the oath that I took to support the Constitution and laws of the United States and so act upon the cases that come before me for decision. [T]hat is the oath and that alone which governs [my actions]."[908]

The Roman Catholic Church may have assumed, based on earlier religious schemas that all its followers were in accord with Vatican pronouncements on sex, sexuality and birth control. But this was an untenable belief. Already in 1936, *Fortune Magazine* conducted a poll of the adult population and asked "Do you believe in the teaching and practice of birth control?"[909] A total of 66% of all those who were polled answered "yes" and a total of 42.8% of Catholic women who were polled answered "yes." Two years later, in 1938, a total of 79% women who answered the poll said "yes" and 51% of the Catholic women who answered said "yes."[910] By 1943, the percentage of Catholic women with a grammar school education who answered "yes" had risen to 70.2% and of those who were college graduates, the number was 92.6%.[911] Clearly, had the hierarchy been listening to its educated female membership, other assumptions about institutional Church strength might have been made.

While social and legal representations about the essential character and proper domain for the human body are at the core in this work, another interesting representation that emerges from in Case Two is the change in representation about what was the "public" realm and what was the "private" realm in American society. Progressive reformers had had no problem intruding into the reproductive lives of criminals, immigrants, ethnic and racial groups and women at the beginning of the century. These groups were not in the ascendancy in terms of political and social power and, as the "weak we", were acceptable targets of public policy, informed by a science that was often wedded to ideology. In addition, limitation of the offspring of those who were considered "degenerate", who did and would no-doubt continue to cost the state enormous amounts of money was also an acceptable, even noble, goal. This was

906 *Ibid.*, 77.
907 *Ibid.*, 76.
908 *Ibid.*
909 Harriet F. Pilpel and Theodora S. Zavin, "Birth Control" in Marriage Counseling Section of *Marriage and Family Living*, May, 1952, 119.
910 *Ibid.*
911 *Ibid.*, 120.

so, in part, because the implicit assumption was that somehow the "germplasm" of those who were citizens belonged to the nation and not the individual.

As a consequence, in terms of the body of the "other", it would become "private" vis-à-vis the state during the intervening years between Case One and Case Two. Finding that bit of privacy took form within the shade of the "penumbra" of the American Constitution.[912] In short, law came to reflect the normative values of the "strong we" in the late 1960s and early 1970s. But to do this, the issue of judicialized reproductive somatechnics was placed back into the private sphere, away from any contextualization. In this respect, the outcome may have been positive and what generations of birth control supporters may have wanted, but the foundations were nowhere as near as solid as in Norway, as I will demonstrate below.

In the 1960s, after decades of organizing and twenty-five or more failed attempts in the Connecticut legislature to bypass its equivalent of the Comstock law, women and men were beginning to frame their personal reproductive health as a private matter; the body had been taken out of the public arena of the Indiana state legislature and put back into the private arena under the rhetoric of "choice."[913] This was also the outcome in Norway, albeit with a different rhetorical basis, as we shall see in Chapter 6.

---

912 This is no doubt incomprehensible to originalists, such as Antonio Scalia of today's Supreme Court. Originalists interpret facts in light of what words meant at the time of the writing of the Constitution. But it goes without saying that no founding father had ever seen a packet of birth control pills. The founding fathers had probably never considered a human sterilization procedure either, but this had not provided any problems for the Buck court.

913 Please see, Rohan Hardcastle, *Law and the Human Body: Property Rights, Ownership and Control* (Oxford and Portland: Hart Publishing Company, 2007) for an update on the issue of ownership detached parts of a living and/or dead body such as tissue, DNA and cell lines. The ownership of one's own living body was thought as laid to rest with the issue of slavery.

6 CASE TWO: Reversals of Body-Law in Norway: Birth Control and Abortion

6.1 Introduction: Same Issues, Different Direction, Different Result

Both the United States and Norway underwent social movements that advocated for the right to birth control and to have an abortion within certain parameters; but those paths took different forms and eventually led to significant differences. Effectively, the Storting became the arena in which the debate on these measures took place in Norway. In America, reformers worked at both the state and federal levels within their individual state legislatures, all the while attempting various arguments at the Supreme Court level. In contrast to the American case law resulting from the facts in Griswold v. Connecticut, 381 U.S. 479 (1965), the Norwegian Storting had, at various times, passed laws on birth control and abortion from the late 1950s to 1978, in which accommodations on the issues had been reached and legally formalized within that body. But in 1978, the new Norwegian law was the result of a legislative consensus which itself was based on a larger socio-political upheaval. Norwegian women had tried for as long as their country had existed to extract the same reproductive rights as their American counterparts had also fought for, working consistently but also unsuccessfully on the other side of the Atlantic Ocean.

At the beginning of the Storting session in 1978, members of the Norwegian Storting who might have happened to read *Aftenposten*, could have read about protests by both the Christian-based Folkesaksjon (People's Action Against Abortion, FASA) and the Feminist Movement in Oslo and throughout Norway.[914] Segments of the national Lutheran Church (Den Norske Kirke, DNK) in Norway became the leading resisters to social change especially change with regard to the role of women in society and to any changes in sexual norms. The consensus that was eventually reached in the Storting was a difficult one and will be examined here as well as the politics and social movements surrounding the change in the law and the various social schemas and structures brought into play in the process.

The legal right to possess methods for birth control by women and to secure abortion rights in Norway was actualized incrementally, ending, for the purpose of this analysis, in 1978 in a new abortion law. As in the United States, the same two debates took place in stages alongside one another. In both cases, the right to birth control was perhaps more visible than the right to an abortion, although the two

914 For example, please see *Aftenposten* (p.m. edition), 19 January 1978, p. 1) and *Aftenposten* (p.m.) 8 March 8, 1978, 1 and continued throughout the year. Please see, *Aftenposten* (a.m. edition), 16 October 16, 1978, 3 and *Aftenposten* (p.m. edition), November 2, 1978, 7.

issues were joined – by necessity. The most proximate attempt to the new 1978 law to allow abortion had been introduced into the Norwegian Parliament during its 1974 session and had been voted down on 31 October 1974 by the non-socialist parties along with one SV Representative, Otto Hauglin. The result was an abortion law, passed on 13 June 1975, which would come into full force and effect on 1 January 1976. A year earlier, the Norwegian abortion law had been enacted, on 13 June 1975 and entitled *Law on abortion* No. 50; it superseded a law passed on 11 November 1960, nr. 1. which itself had changed the 1902 Criminal Law provision for punishment of abortion.[915] The 1975 law had allowed for abortion if a woman's pregnancy would lead to "an unreasonable or unfair physical or psychological burden for the woman" or put her in a "difficult life situation."[916] It was perceived as a serious setback to Norwegian women and their vision of self-decided abortion. It was not only considered unacceptable to progressive women but this law was considered to be unacceptable to all parties involved.

Women regrouped and launched another campaign, beginning with abortion hearings in the Parliament in 1976 and a women's political action movement in 1977. The goal of this action was to increase birth control information including easier access to it. The goal was, eventually, to force Storting representatives to pass another abortion law that allowed for "self-decided" abortion within the first 12 weeks of pregnancy. These demands were finally met and a new abortion law including these criteria was passed on 9 June 1978, after more than 65 years of political pressure, agitation and political maneuvering by Norwegian women.[917]

In both countries the debate over birth control and abortion took place in conjunction with a number of other issues; these included such things as a woman's right to work and to equal pay for equal work. But what is unique in the comparison between these two countries in this second case study is that Norwegian women – and men – obtained a gender equality law. The Norwegian Storting also passed the *Lov om likestilling mellom kjønnene* (*Law on the equality of the sexes*, No. 45 on 9 June 1978. (LLK) The act was actively supported by the Labour Party and the Socialist Left Party and was primarily meant to address inequality that women faced in their working life. Section 1 of the law states:

---

915 Hans Flock, Birger Stuevold Lassen, Henrik Bull, Anne-Marie Tronslin, eds., *Norges Lover, 1687–2003*, (Oslo: Utgitt av Det Juridiske Fakultet ved Universitetet i Oslo, 2004), 67, 1008. The 1978 law was not the first time the abortion law in Norway had been changed by legislation; it had been changed in 1964. However, for the purposes of this dissertation I will concentrate on the 1978 law.

916 *Ibid.*, 285.

917 Please see, for example, Elizabeth Lønnå, *Stolhet og Kvinnekamp: Norsk Kvinnesaksforenings historie fra 1913* (Oslo: Glydendal Norsk Forlag, 1996).

> This law shall concern equality between both sexes and is especially concerned with bettering the position of women. Women and men shall be given equal opportunities to education, work, and cultural and professional development."[918]

This language clearly envisions that some, if not a large role, be played by the law rather than through using some vague notion of "good will" within the workplace as a method for mandating equality.[919] Given that the law mentions equal opportunity in education, work, cultural and professional development, emphasis has been extended to these areas.[920] Particularly important was the establishment of oversight and enforcement bodies such as the Lov om likestilling mellom kjønnene (§§ 10–12), provided for in the 1978 Law.[921]

Again, in 1981, three years after the gender equality law was passed, the Parliament made another bold move, especially in comparison with the United States, and the gender equality act was amended to include a new provision, §21.[922] This section required a 40% representation of both sexes on all public boards, councils and committees. The intent of was to urge women from traditional female centers of influence such as health to enter the political realm and to increase their representation in what were traditional male strongholds such as defense, technology, agriculture and communications. This "Forty Per Cent Rule" was also incorporated into the Local Government Act of 1992.[923] By contrast, the issue of an ERA in the United States has become dormant.[924]

---

918 Flock, Lassen, Bull, Tronslin (eds.), *Norges Lover, 1687–2003*, 1085. Note 831.

919 That Norway has had a long history of a vigorous labor movement should be noted. Women were a part of this movement and had a great deal of experience with the "carrot and stick" approach to solving workplace problems. While the United States also had a labor movement, it seems it might not have had the momentum or a class-based consciousness that prevailed into the middle half of the 20th century. Norway had this momentum.

920 Some exemptions exist, e.g. for religious communities.

921 The Act is also enforced by the Equal Status Council, founded in 1972, as stipulated in law nr. 47 of 1972; both provisions are responsible for organizations that serve as a liaison with authorities, organizations and the public on matters of equality under the act. The *Lov om likestilling mellom kjønnene* of 9 June. No. 49 1978 can be found in *Norges Lover* at pages 1085–1089. §§10 and 11 were amended in 2003.

922 *Ibid.* Law nr. 59 of 1981. The 1978 law has been amended several times, including by nr. 12/1983, nr. 6/1988, and nr. 120/2003. The gender law must adapt to laws with which it interacts when these laws have been modified. The 1981 revision extends the reach of the law to elected and appointed political bodies.

923 The "40% Rule" requires that the balance of the two sexes in governmental positions, as outlined by law, must have a ratio between 40:60 (females: males) and 60:40.

924 In 1977, Indiana was the last state, the 35th of the needed 38 states to ratify the ERA. Each year it is reintroduced in Congress and the deadline for ratification has been extended at least once. To be passed, it needs three more states to ratify it and, at this point, the prospects of any three more states ratifying it are slim. This "bootstrap" philosophy combined with an other factors makes it unlikely any ERA will be successful in the United States until or unless some situation forces a reexamination

Before considering specific norms, actors, structures and events at work in 1978 in Norway, we need to examine how life had changed in Norway between 1934 and 1978; this includes a brief look at social schemas, demographics and the role of DNK. In 1956, the Norwegian Program for Electoral Research, which had been established at the Institute for Social Research in Oslo by Stein Rokkan and Henry Valen, collected data about Norwegian voters.[925] The representative sample was of voters between the ages of 20 and 80 years of age and was still being evaluated by researchers a decade later, including W. Martinussen. This year – 1956 – is exactly midway between 1934 and 1978 and I use the data from it as a means of giving some idea of the social currents moving within Norwegian society 22 years before the abortion and equality laws were passed.

By 1978, Norway was again experiencing a socio-political "crisis" much as it had in 1934, although in 1978, the economic life of most citizens was certainly better. My use of the word "crisis" here is meant to imply that an imbalance in societal relations makes stasis nearly impossible, i.e. that some sort of change may be imminent, and this seems to exactly be the case. As I noted above, Martinussen studied the Rokkan/Valen data, focusing on a significant question, i.e. could one "detect a decreasing effect of the sex role norms and sex discrimination" or, were those norms and discrimination "just as powerful today as they were in previous generations?"[926] To answer this, he analyzed political alienation as it is related to sex, age and education. As a general rule, differences between men and women in political alienation were "greatest in the younger age groups" and these differences decrease with age, perhaps as result of marriage, which tended to increase security for a woman.[927]

Martinussen found that women were "to a certain extent" more politically powerless and indifferent than men but were not particularly more detached from the political process."[928] He concluded that the higher a woman's education and the more politically relevant her organizational membership, the less a woman might label her experience as politically alienating. This was true, of course, for men as well as women at this time. But Martinussen also found that "sex differences are still extensive" and could be summarized as follows:

1. Women are to a certain extent more politically indifferent and powerless than men within the categories where they are equal with men with regard to education and degree of political organization. The exceptions to this general trend are insignificant, but we note that for the politically organized with primary school or less, both men and women are of 'average' indifference, and among the experts

of priorities and institutions.

925 Willy Martinussen, *The Distant Democracy: Social inequality, political resources and political influence in Norway* (London and New York: John Wiley & Sons, 1977), 14, ii.

926 *Ibid.*, 164.

927 *Ibid.*

928 *Ibid.*, 161.

who are nonpolitically organized, the men are insignificantly more powerful than women.[929]

2. Women are more subjectively detached from politics than men in the group 'politically organized with a low level of education', while the opposite is the case among the nonpolitically organized: women more than men believe that politics affect their everyday life. This standpoint is most often taken by politically organized experts of both sexes.
3. Politically organized women at the two lowest levels of education are more suspicious of the political parties than men, and those with the lowest level of education have the least confidence in the conduct of the public authorities.[930]

The opposite situation was to be found among those who were not members of unions; to a greater extent, more men than women believed that authorities practiced discrimination.

How did political alienation relate to party affiliation? Martinussen relied on responses by those who had voted in the 1969 Parliamentary election and looked at three factors – the lack of opportunity, the lack of motivation and the lack of political participation experiences – with relation to political affiliation. A few simple conclusions can be noted here which help to highlight how the 1978 abortion legislation came into being. Across the political spectrum in 1969, from the extreme political left (Communist) to the extreme political right (Conservatives), the highest percentage, with regard to a lack of motivation as measured by "indifference" rested in the Agrarian party. The perception of "powerlessness" was highest in the Labour Party and "detachment" was highest – again – in the Agrarian Party followed closely by the Christian People's Party. The least detached were members of the Communist Party, followed by four parties at essentially the same level, the Social Democratic Party, the Labour Party, the Liberal and Conservative Party. Those who felt the least powerless were in the Christian People's Party, followed by the Conservatives and the Social Democratic Party. By occupation, the same study found that fishermen, followed by manual workers experienced the most political poverty.[931] Those with the least political poverty were high ranking public officials followed by high-ranking private executives.

Based on these conclusions, the nine years from 1969 to 1978 were nothing short of turbulent – especially with regard to the issue of gender and political alienation. The perception of sex discrimination was prominent among younger people, especially women. If we look at the group of 20 to 30 year old citizens, who would be in the

929 *Ibid.* The three levels of organization were politically organized, non-politically organized and not organized.

930 *Ibid.*, 161–62. The three levels of education investigated were primary education, vocational education and professional education.

931 *Ibid.*, 204. Table 9.5.

30 to 40 year group ten years later in 1978, we find the following differences between men and women. (In bold lettering below.)

Table 6.1: Political alienation related to sex in specific age group[932]

Women and Men, 20–30 Years of Age in 1969	**Primary Education**		**Vocational**		**Professional**	
Form of political alienation	Women	Men	Women	Men	Women	Men
Indifference	72	46	66	38	36	18
Powerlessness	78	70	70	47	26	38
Detachment	50	46	51	44	32	45
Distrust of parties	75	54	62	57	48	64
Belief in discrimination	55	36	90	80	46	63
Average N =	13	13	90	80	30	40

The above table is but one small piece of the 1969 survey mentioned above done by the Institute for Social Research in Oslo. But, from this table we can see that, assuming little change, an engine that drove socio-cultural changes in the decade prior to 1978 could be related to the discrimination that women who had a vocational education felt as well as the feelings of both men and women who had a professional education. It is difficult to argue with these numbers; clearly there was a feeling that discrimination based on sex was present in Norway. While professionally educated men and women felt less powerless and were less indifferent than the other two groups, both men and women in the other two groups, with the possible exception of men with a primary education, could have supported the women in their views on discrimination. But this sense of unfairness was not the only force at work. As we will see, the decrease in DNK attendance, i.e. religiosity, also played a major role in both the abortion and sexual equality laws that were passed in 1978.

The table also shows that feelings of indifference, powerlessness, detachment and distrust of parties ran across the spectrum of differing levels of education. This, in combination with how the degrees to which different major political parties felt "powerless" lends credibility to the idea of a social crisis in the making or already in place.[933] As we saw above, the KrF felt the most powerful while Ap felt the least powerful. But KrF also felt more "detached" than a combination of the Labour Party along with Liberals and Conservatives. KrF's detachment is seen in full bloom 10 years later during the abortion debate in its ideologically directed debate. The sense of "powerful" that the KrF felt was realized when the Ap lost the 1969 election. However, at

932 *Ibid.*, 165. This Table is extracted information for the 20–30 year old group. The original 3 tables on page 165 also had figures for 31–50 years of age and 51–80 years of age.

933 See Lønnå, *Stolthet og kvinnekamp*, 223. Note 1106. Lønna calls the year 1968 the "quiet before the storm." My thanks to Ellen Andenæs for bringing this book to my attention.

the Ap's national convention in 1969, it endorsed self-decided abortion for women and did not withdraw from that position until, after other parties joined, the law was changed in 1978.[934]

Martinussen argues that five factors play a role in the extent to which citizens do nor do not seek political change. These are that, 1. individuals and groups who have unequal access to "values", and therefore it is possible to speak of inequality of conditions in which people live, 2. these inequalities are socially recognized and citizens believe themselves to have a common interest with people in similar groups, 3. the inequality of circumstances and recognition of this create differences in political beliefs and orientations as well as in attitudes toward the then current political system, 4. the inequality of circumstances means systematic differences in access to material, social and intellectual political resources, and 5. the differences in access to political resources and political motivation leads to inequality of actual political participation.[935] Given these five factors, we could say that there was a crisis looming on the horizon for Norway in the decade following 1959 when this research data was collected.

During 1978, statistics about various intersubjective groups[936] and about families in Norway were seen in the pages of a number of papers, including *Aftenposten*. Statisk Sentralbyrå (The Central Bureau for Statistics, SSB) in Norway had published a report in July of 1977 with statistics on family life in Norway. Norway had approximately 1,630,000 families as of that date. Of this number, 39% or 633,000 married couples were living with children in the home while 19% or 306,000 married couples did not have children living with them. Seven per cent of the 1.63 million families, or 116,000 families, consisted of a mother or a father, but not both, as heading the household.[937] The remaining 35% were living alone – 15% men and 21% women.[938]

In addition to relying on newspaper data, we can turn to the area of Fertility Studies which has recently given us a more complete idea of what was happening in Europe in the years leading up to the industrial revolution and the development of the

934 *Ibid.*, p. 242.

935 Martinussen, *The Distant Democracy*, 12. Note 1114.

936 Noteworthy are those differently abled and the mentally ill, especially at Trondheim's facility, Reitgårdet.

937 *Aftenposten* (p.m. Edition), 3 March 1978, 6.

938 *Ibid.* Three definitions of a family were given. There were, 1. one which must be registered as living in the same house and consisting of a man and hustru (housewife) with or without unmarried children, or 2. either a mother or a father with unmarried children, or 3. a single person, regtistered as living in a house, living without unmarried children and without a spouse or a parent. (Familienenheten er definert some en ren familiekjerne, og personene innenfor en famliekjerne må være registrert bosatt i sammen bolig. En familile kan bestå av mann og hustru uten eller med ugifte barn, mor eller far med ugifte barn, eller enslig person some er registrert bosatt uten ugifte barn og ikke sammen men ektefelle eller foreldre.)

birth control pill. Two different types of demographic studies have given us a picture of Europe; they are micro-level family reconstitution studies and macro-level studies based on published census and geographically defined vital statistics.[939] Knodel and van de Walle make four observations of marital fertility between 1800 and 1970,[940] keeping in mind that nuptuality patterns in Western Europe played a key role in pre-industrial Europe as opposed, for example, to developing countries today. These four conclusions are:

4. Fertility declines took place under a variety of social, economic and demographic conditions.
5. The practice of family limitation was largely absent (and probably unknown) among broad segments of the population prior to the decline on fertility, even though a substantial proportion of births may have been unwanted.
6. Increases in the practice of family limitation and the decline of marital fertility were essentially irreversible processes once underway.
7. Cultural setting influences the onset and spread of fertility decline independently of socioeconomic conditions.[941]

Knodel and van de Walle looked at 10% increment declines in marital fertility between 1800 and 1970. The demographic and socioeconomic indexes that they considered were the marital fertility before the decline, index of proportion married, overall fertility, infant mortality (per 1,000), per cent of male labor force in agriculture, percent rural, percent in cities over 20,000 and per cent illiterate. For Norway, the date of decline in marital fertility by 10% was 1904. The date of that same 10% decline phenomenon in Sweden was 1892, Denmark, 1897 and Finland, 1908.[942]

In their study, Knodel and van de Walle fix Infant Mortality (per 1,000) for Norway in 1904 as 76, the Percent of Male Labor Force in Agriculture was 37%, percent rural was 72%, the Percent in Cities over 20,000 was 18% and the percent illiterate was "low."[943] The ranking of countries in terms of the date of this 10% decline in marital fertility, beginning with France (1800) was, Belgium (1882), Switzerland (1885), Germany (1890), Hungary (ca. 1890), England and Wales (1892), Sweden (1892), Scotland (1894), Netherlands (1897), Denmark (1904), Austria (1908), Finland (1908), Italy (1910), Bulgaria (1912), Spain (1918), Ireland (1929), Costa Rica (1962), Taiwan (1963), Chile (1964) and Thailand (ca. 1970). In other words, this was a trend not only in the Scandinavian countries but also throughout Europe and throughout the world

---

939 John Knodel and Etienne van de Walle, "Lessons from the Past: Policy Implications of Historical Fertility Studies" in *Population and Development Review*, 5 (1979), 217–18.

940 While this may seem like a very long period of time, I thought it necessary to balance the picture in the first paragraph from only 1977.

941 *Ibid.*, 219.

942 *Ibid.*, 221, Table 1.

943 *Ibid.*

at the turn of the century which the advent of accessible contraception would change further.

Knodel and van de Walle also calculated three indices; they were Ig (level of marital fertility before the 10% decline, Im, Index of Proportion Married and If, overall fertility. They also examined a time series for the index of family limitation, a value they labeled "m." In all the countries studied, once the m value rose above a minimal level and once the Ig index started to fall below the predecline level, the fertility trend toward decline "continues virtually uninterrupted until radically different levels are achieved."[944] This observation confirms "the fertility transition results from a new form of reproductive behavior rather than from an extension of previously established patterns."[945]

As was seen in Case One, the lowering of a nation's population can also be the harbinger of debates about the role of women and her role in the family or as a worker as well as about those who were unable to work, as well as immigration or racial/ethnic participation in civic life. On New Year's Day, 1978, the *Aftenposten* began the New Year with an article on global population. The SSB had, for the first time ever, joined in an investigation with the World Fertility Survey,[946] to investigate why the number of children in Norway had decreased.[947] Three groups were to be investigated; one survey would be answered by everyone in the survey group, one by married co-habitating couples and one by a group that had never been married or had co-habitated. Women would be asked a number of questions about their living situation, how they had been raised, their education, income, professional work history, and pregnancy history. Their pregnancy history would include how many, if any, of their pregnancies had ended in an abortion. If the pregnancy was carried to term, they would be asked the possibilities of help with the child, the amount of time they devote to the child, and if they had a modern or traditional attitude toward their quality of life.[948]

This research was based, in part, on theories held by Professor Richard A. Easterlin, who was based in the United States. An SSB consultant, Helge Brunborg, had studied Easterlin's population predictions, already considered controversial. Easter-

944 *Ibid.*, 233.
945 *Ibid.*
946 This survey is described as a global survey, meant to investigate why there were consistently fewer births in industrialized nations. Please see "The World Fertility Survey" in *European Demographic Information Bulletin*, Vol. 4, No. 1 (March, 1973). Also see the on-going work of the survey at the Office of Population Research at Princeton University, http://opr.princeton.edu/archive/wfs/ last accessed 10 August 2009 and at the U.S. National Institute of Health, http://www.ncbi.nih.gov/pubmed/12311520?/og$=activity, last accessed 10 August 2009.
947 *Aftenposten*, 2 January 1978, p. 9. Author, Trine Hay. Please see, Richard Easterlin and Eileen A. Crimmins, "Exploratory Study of the 'Synthesis Framework' of Fertility Determination with WFS Core Questionaire Date" in *WFS Scientific Reports*, No. 40, (London: World Fertility Survey, 1982).
948 *Ibid.*

lin hypothesized that people's preferences toward how many children they had and toward their material consumption were based on the conditions in which they themselves had been raised. If their expectations were not fulfilled as adults in relation to what they had as children, they would reduce the number of children they had. Since those born in Norway in the 1930s became adults in the 1950s, at a time of comparatively better economic conditions, it was thought that Easterlin's theory could be tested in Norway. The reporter noted that in the middle of the 1960s birth control had become available in most industrialized countries, including Norway.[949]

Even if controversial, Easterlin did provide an analytic framework for the study of fertility that continues to this day. The use of statistics is paramount in his work and he sometimes uses fertility as an independent variable to "help explain some intractable aspects of social life."[950]

In Norway in 1978, it was not concern over the "right" type of population as in Case One, where large numbers of immigrants had resettled in the United States and were having large families. The "moral panic" that fueled this crisis contained fewer factors. It was a leaner "moral panic" than we saw in Case One in both countries, devoid of any "progressive" aspirations, without an observable eugenics movement and mainly concerned with the intersection of gender role schemas and religious structures, i.e. DNK and members of the FASA who were members of DNK or another Church with similar dogma regarding sex and sexuality.

If it was possible that abortion might be allowed in Norway, then it made sense to know exactly how many applications for an abortion had been made in the recent past and to analyze them. In March 1978, Psychiatrist Berthold Grünfeld (1932–2007) wrote an article for *Aftenposten* about this issue and its implications in which he analyzed this data from the Ministry of Health for the last 4–5 years.[951] The number of live

---

949 This article in *Aftenposten* was accompanied by four other articles on one page, situated later in the newspaper; they were entitled "Fewer Norwegians at the Turn of the Century?", "Two Children are Enough No children not an option", "Eight Children, One Dog, Cat and Turtle" and "Fewer and Fewer Births." (*Aftenposten*, January 2, 1978, 17.)

950 *Aftenposten* (a.m. Edition), March 7, 1978, 2. Grünfeld wrote his dissertation on abortion and was awarded a doctorate in medicine in 1973. In 1993 he was made Professor of Social Medicine at the University of Oslo. He was born in what was then Bratislava in Czechloslovakia and in 1939, along with 34 other Jewish children was taken by train to Norway by The Nansen Help ("Nansenhjelpen") and Women for Peace and Freedom ("Kvinneligaen for fred og frihet"). Please see, http://www.wikipedia.org/w/index.php?title=Berthold_Gr%C3%BCnfeld&printable=yes, accessed Sept. 19, 2007.

951 Nicholas Townsend",Reproduction in Anthropology and Democracy" in David I. Kertzer and Thomas Fricke (eds.), *Anthropological Demography: Toward a New Synthesis*, (Chicago: University of Chicago Press, 1997), 98. Since 1978, however, features of this framework have been questioned, for example, that "fertility" is taken as "unproblematic" and that these models are "directed at the left hand, independent variables or causal side of the model[s]." (*Ibid.*) As Townsend argues, the underlying definition of "fertility" in Easterlin's work is not questioned by such factors as cohort, period, age and parity-specific measurements. The second feature of "fertility" in these frameworks that can

births per year in Norway had fallen since 1973 after staying "surprisingly stable" at 65,000–69,000 prior to that date. This trend was also mirrored in Sweden. The number of abortions had also begun to stabilize in 1974 with approximately 15,000 each year. Eight of one hundred women between the ages of 14 and 44 became pregnant in 1977; two of those eight ended in abortion and six of eight pregnancies resulted in a live birth. Grünfeld noted that this "confirmed one thing", i.e. that Norwegian women were "very diligent, responsible and conscientiously using birth control."[952] In 1977, 100,000 women used the birth control pill as their primary form of birth control, with another 150,000 women using intra-uterine coils and another 100,000 using condoms. Grünfeld interpreted this to mean that 2 of 3 Norwegian women had access and used "good and effective birth control."[953]

If this were in fact true, then why, *Aftenposten* asked, was there still a need for abortion? Grünfeld answered that in 1976, one of every four abortions that took place involved young women in their teen-age years. Still, 60% of all teen-age pregnancies ended in births. Technical failure also accounted for a number of unwanted pregnancies. The failure rate for an intra-uterine coil accounted for 2,000 to 5,000 pregnancies in 100,000 women per year. If 150,000 women used that method of birth control, then one could calculate 3,000–7,500 unplanned pregnancies per year, some of whom may want abortions. Human failure was also a factor in unwanted pregnancies. Regarding the population as a whole, Grünfeld's opinion was that, on an average, every Norwegian[954] had 1.1 children during the course of a lifetime, unlike Sweden where the number of pregnancies was "sinking drastically."[955]

Just as in both the American and Norwegian section in Case One, the role of women in society was a matter for debate in 1978. The issue of whether or not women should work outside the home had never really been settled for some members of either society with the exception of contributing to the home front war effort in World War II. That more and more women either chose to or were forced to work outside the home either through economic difficulties or death of a partner was, however,

be questioned "is the feedback from fertility as the dependent variable to fertility as an independent variable"; the feedback loop may have a causal arrow from "cumulated family size" to "reproductive history" or from "fertility" to "institutions, social and economic structure, norms; external conditions, etc." (*Ibid.*, 99.)

952 *Ibid.* The population of Norway 1977 was approximately 4,035,200 million. (http://www.populstat.info/Europe/norwayc.htm, accessed November 6, 2009). If 50% of that population were women, then we have 2,017,600. In general a population has women in the proportion of 1 -14 yrs. Old (19%), 15–59 yrs. old (60%) and 60+ yrs. old (21%), then the number of Norwegian women between the ages of 15 and 59 in 1977 would have been approximately 1,210,560. (http://www.popuplstate.info/Europe/norwayg.htm, accessed 6 November 6, 2009.)

953 Ibid.

954 This statistic presumably means 1.1 child for every male and female. Norwegian citizenry were procreating to the point of keeping the population stable.

955 *Ibid.*

a reality.[956] That more and more women were becoming better educated was also a social fact.[957] That the number of female voters nearly equaled male voters in Norway was a fact.[958] Nonetheless, a conflict inherent in the issue of women working outside the home again came to the surface in 1978. This nature of the conflict was in the question: If women work outside the home, then who will provide the social care that women had provided for centuries that included care for the young and the old as well as the domestic work?

In mid-January in 1978 in the pages of *Aftenposten*, Sissel Dahl took up the issue of gender equality that most supposed would soon become a legal reality in Norway along with self decided abortion. She was surprised to find that within the business community fulltime jobs for women had increased only 4% in 1977; her opinion was that they should occupy between 35 and 40% of fulltime positions.[959] She was supported in this opinion by Kari Vangsnes, of the The Equality Commission,[960] who voiced concern over the tendency for married or previously married women who were hired for "part-time jobs", defined as less than 30 hours per week. Between 1974 and 1976, there had been a noticeable increase in this type of work in the "service" industries – hotel and restaurant workers – as well as in the banking and insurance sector and in the health and social services sector.

The issue of women in the national work force had not gone unnoticed and had been researched. *Arbeiderbladet* ran a review of Harriet Holter's book, *Women's Life and Work* in its Culture section on 4 January 1978.[961] The review, written by Ruth Johnsen, was entitled "Sex Roles and the Development of Society", something that seemed to be a new concept for newspapers of the day. In addition, Johnsen, who was a women's consultant at the District Work Office in Oslo and Akershus, had not just one, but three articles published by *Arbeiderbladet*. They focused on gender stereotyping, women and work possibilities and the politics of women's employment.[962] One of her articles dealt specifically with the Resolution of 5 August 1977, which said that all citizens between the ages of 16 and 60 had a right to paid work.[963]

---

956 Lønna, *Stolthet og Kvinnekamp: Norske Kvinnesaksforenings*, p. 159. Note 1106. Also see, Arnlaug Leira, "Kvinner i lønnsarbeid og ulønt arbied" in Thordis Støren and Tone Schou Wetlesen (eds.), *Kvinnekunnskap* (Oslo: Gyldendal Norsk Forlag, 1976), 119–37.

957 *Ibid.*, 287.

958 Thordis Støren and Tone Schou Wetlesen, eds., *Kvinnekunnskap* (Oslo: Gyldendal Norsk Forlag, 1976), 201.

959 *Aftenposten* (a.m. Edition), January 14, 1978, 36.

960 Likestillingsrådet, see http://www.kampdager.no/arkiv/forskning/artikkel_haavind.html, accessed April 4, 2010.

961 *Arbeiderbladet*, January 4, 1978, 14.

962 "Kvinnersvalg av yrke og utdanning", *Arbeiderbladet*, January 5, 1978, 14 and "Fylkesarbeidskontoret", *Arbeiderbladet*, "Kvinnene i sysselsettingspolitikken", January 6, 1978, 13.

963 *Ibid.*

One sector of society that quickly derived benefit from the agitation for gender equality was the military. In early March, Erling Norvik indicated in a speech at Haugesund that women reserve personnel in the military would henceforth be paid on a differentiated scale according to her rank rather than of a fixed sum for participating in courses and exercises.[964]

6.2 Cascading Intersections: Parliament, the Law, Abortion and the State Church of Norway

As was seen in the American half of this comparison, religious institutions played an important political role in policy making.[965] It is perhaps easier to see the role of religion in the abortion issue rather than in the use of birth control methods, since – if the Roman Catholic Church is an example – it took a period of time before its "official" position on synthetic hormone birth control technology coalesced. Norway's state church and other conservative forces had already been involved in working against abortion during the inter-war period. At the end of the 1950s the liberalization of Norway's abortion laws became an issue – again. Finally, in 1960, the Norwegian law was changed to allow for abortions if there were sufficient "social-medical" indications that one was needed. However, a woman needed to apply to a panel of doctors and this situation continued until 1978. DNK and the "free churches" advanced the most strident opposition to this legal situation.[966]

Between 1960 and 1978, the reasons for liberalization of the Norwegian abortion law were very similar to those used in the United States. Whatever abortion laws were in force in the individual states within the United States were no deterrent for women with money. If a working class woman wanted an abortion she was subject to unpre-

964 *Arbeiderbladet*, March 1, 1978, 8.

965 It is often difficult to extract the role of religion in political affairs. Nonetheless, we do have historical cases that are instructive. What the Weimar Republic and apartheid-South Africa are to legal history and jurisprudence, the actions of the Roman Catholic Church in Nazi Germany are to the interaction of religious and political ideology about reproduction. The Third Reich and the Church clashed over control of reproduction – among other things. As Paul Weindling notes with reference to the January 1, 1934 law, "Law Against Compulsive Criminality", that when the draft law was presented to the the German cabinet on July 14, 1933, Franz von Papen "objected that the state of [...sexual] diseases was curable and that the Catholic Church could not allow the state to usurp control over reproduction." Paul Weindling, *Health, Race and German Politics Between National Unification and Nazism, 1870–1945* (Cambridge: Cambridge University Press, 1989), 254. This issue of who controls reproduction is often a matter of patriarchal and patriarchal-type power, whether comes from political or religious quarters – or a combination of both.

966 "Free churches" refers to what might be called "low-church" chapels. The physical trappings of DNK are not present and they are more "protestant" in appearance and in style. They are also, generally, more fundamentalist than the majority within the DNK itself.

dictable treatment at the hands of a person who may or may not have had any medical education and who was not regulated by any market forces since s/he could charge what s/he wanted for the illegal procedure. In other words, unequal access to medical care was an issue. One type of treatment could result in a full life, well lived and productive and the other in death. But the fact of abortion clashed with what churches believed was the worth of the human (fetal) being which could be traced to both the Christian and the humanistic tradition.[967]

In 1978, the Parliamentary session that reconsidered the abortion issue also – implicitly – reconsidered the relationship between the state and the state Church. The Norwegian Constitution §2 granted freedom of religion, but the DNK remained the official state Church in 1978. Section 2 of the Norwegian Constitution read:

> All inhabitants of the Realm shall have the right to free exercise of their religion. The Evangelical Lutheran religion shall remain the official religion of the State. The inhabitants professing it are bound to bring up their children in the same.[968]

But when the new abortion law was passed, some DNK priests felt that they could not continue as priests and agents of the state Church. An indication of the impact of societal shifts on DNK and its relationship to the state was seen in the protest by Børre Knudsen (b. 1937), a vicar in Balsfjord, as well as in the resignation of a Storting representative who was also a priest, Per Lønning.

After the new abortion law came into effect on 1 January 1979, Knudsen refused to carry out certain duties of his official state office.[969] Knudsen continued as the priest in the local church but, as part of his campaign against the state, Knudsen renounced his oath of office, broke all communication with anyone who had connections with the official state church, and neglected to carry out consecrations – mostly marriages – all the while refusing to take his salary from the state.[970] Knudsen's reasoning for his refusal to yield to state authority was that the new abortion law was in conflict with the common idea of the worth of human beings and with DNK as the state religion under §2 of the Constitution. He reasoned that the state had deprived itself of the right to undertake the administration of the church and his goal was to use the abortion law in a legal challenge in order to clarify the state church relationship.[971] He proposed a "strike" of bishops and priests wherein they would relinquish their official status – and salary – from the state. However, only one priest, Per Kørner, joined ranks

967 Bernt T. Oftestad, Tarald Rasmussen and Jan Schumacher, *Norsk Kirkehistorie* (2nd ed.) (Oslo: Universitetsgforlaget, 1993), 284.

968 Flock, Lassen, Bull, Tronslin, eds., *Norges Lover, 1687–2003*, 1. Note 831.

969 Bernt T. Oftestad, Tarald Rasmussen and Jan Schumacher, *Norsk Kirkehistorie*, 285.

970 *Ibid.*

971 Oftestad et al., *Norsk Kirkehistorie*, 285. Note 1156.

with Knudsen.[972] Essentially what Knudsen managed to do was to bring major events in the social life of Balsfjord to a halt. Couples could not be married and neither could their marriages be registered with the state. This inability to register marriages went beyond halting social life however since it also had economic implications.

Knudsen's strategy in pursuit of his goal was in direct opposition to that used by the College of Bishops and Oslo Bishop, Andreas Aarflot (b. 1928). Their position was that the relationship between the church and the state should be changed, but it should be changed through a common political process, rather than through the more militant Knudsen model. What was at issue was the type and measure of force that DNK could bring to bear against the state; Knudsen believed he could force the state to abandon the new abortion law whereas, in a more moderate fashion, Aarflot felt DNK could only "instruct" the government as to the right and wrong of its law-giving function by having it consider the rulings passed by Bishops on various issues.[973]

Eventually, in 1983, Knudsen had his legal case come before the Supreme Court.[974] The state wanted Knudsen removed from his office on the grounds that he had renounced his oath of office and had failed to provide services for the citizens of Balsfjord by taking the official seal used to register marriages, etc.[975] The Supreme Court squarely faced the issues presented by Knudsen as to §2 of the Norwegian Constitution saying that §2 of the Constitution could not be understood as to "create barriers for the state's law making ability."[976] The state's only duty was to provide for the administration of the Church. There was no need for a judge of the Supreme Court to rule on the abortion law since the Parliament had lawfully passed it.[977]

Knudsen's reaction should be seen in the structural and schematic contexts of the day. The 1970s were a time when people were ready to explore other forms of belief, even including Eastern religions. The membership of virtually every Western denomination declined, except for perhaps those involved in the evangelical movement. In 1938, the membership of DNK was 96.5% of the total population. In 1960, that figure had not changed much; by 1991 the figure was 90.5%. A 6% drop in membership may not signify as serious a change in religiosity as I allude to here, but membership and

972 *Ibid.*, 285–86.

973 *Ibid.*, 286.

974 Rettstidende 1983 s 1004. Knudsen's legal challenge also relied upon the Norwegian Constitution §4 (The King's duties toward DNK), the European Convention on Human Rights (20 January 1966) Art. 4 (No slavery, forced or compulsory labor) and the United Nation's Declaration on Human Rights (December 10, 1948), Art. 3 (Right to "life, liberty and security of person").

975 Bernt T. Oftestad, Tarald Rasmussen and Jan Schumacher, *Norsk Kirkehistorie*, 286. The official seal must appear on a document for it to be considered legal. When Knudsen took his his seal, which was used as part of his position out of circulation, this interfered with the operation of government.

976 *Ibid.*

977 *Ibid.* Knudsen lost his challenge but, through use of a resolution, he was allowed to remain an ordained priest.

attendance are two different phenomena. Chaves and Cann argue that a state Church is a "source of a low degree of religious pluralism and, therefore, of low participation in organized religion."[978] While DNK was used for memorializing various life passages, attendance after World War sunk and remained low. In 1958, 2.9% of the population routinely attended Sunday services; in 1978 that figure was 2.5% and in 1990, 3%.[979] During the 1970s, DNK also lost about 60,000 members and Church membership, as measured by the number of children baptized in the DNK, had decreased.[980]

Another indication of religiosity in Norway is the number of Norwegians who were leaving DNK around 1978. Figures of DNK membership were inflated in any event since all Norwegians who were not registered with another faith, were presumed to be members of DNK. In 1970, a record number of Norwegians (7,205), presumed to be members of DNK, followed an administrative procedure, and opted out of the Church.[981] The next peak of Norwegians leaving DNK was in 1978 (11,230).[982]

These figures show that while structures and schemas supporting the DNK were in place before World War II, by the late 1950s, they had, to a small but significant extent, changed. Membership that required church attendance is not practiced in Norway. However, even though regular attendance was not a rule, Norwegians continued to use DNK and DNK rituals to memorialize significant life passages, i.e. for birth (Baptism), adulthood (Confirmation), commitment (Marriage) and death (Funerals). This was a new practice in light of pre-War II schemas and indicated a significant change in what the structural entity of DNK meant in the lives of Norwegians. Flocks of believing worshipers began to absent themselves from regular attendance in DNK. By 1978, they would appear in DNK when a member of their family was born, came of age, married or died, although the number of families engaging in these rituals was also decreasing.[983]

As important as some felt the equality issue was, it was not equal rights that occupied the political center stage in Norway in 1978. The abortion debate was the main issue in 1978, just as it had been in 1934, in large part through the work of a grass roots religious movement that had formed in response to the passage of the 1975 abor-

---

978 Robert J. Barro and Rachel M.McCleary, "Religion and Ecocnomic Growth across Countries" in *American Sociological Review*, 68 (2003): 761 citing to Marck Chaves and David E. Cann, "Regulation, Pluralism, and Religious Market Structure" in *Rationality and Society*, 4 (1992): 272–90.

979 *Ibid.* p. 298.

980 *Ibid.*

981 Knut Lundby and Ingun Montgomery, eds., *Statskirke i etterkrigs samfun: Kirkehistorie og sosiologiske synspunkter på Den norske kirke etter 1945* (Oslo Bergen Tromsø: Universitetsforlaget, 1981), 71. Whether or not the factor here, that fewer Norwegians attend DNK church services, means that fewer Norwegians are religious is another question. What it does mean is that fewer Norwegians were routinely exposed to official DNK doctrine.

982 *Ibid.*, 73.

983 *Ibid.*, 80.

tion law, a law aimed not only at abortion. This group, FASA, was very active in the debate over whether or not a woman had the right – for herself – to choose to have an abortion. Beginning in the spring of 1974, this group had already collected 610,000 signatures against the new abortion law that they believed would come before the Parliament in the fall of 1974.[984] Hans Olav Tungesvik, a KrF Representative in Parliament from 1977 to 1985 from Hordaland, had been the Chairman of FASA from 1974 to 1975. By January, 1978, it was his opinion that Norway had assumed the contours of a totalitarian state.[985]

The abortion law had been given a great deal of support from Norway's Labour Party. However, the Labour Party, as the traditional party of workers, also supported what might be called a "conscientious exemption" for health workers who did not want to participate in the actual performance of an abortion. While normally to the left of center, the Labour Party had to consider those members of its constituency who were workers in medical facilities.[986] It should be remembered that the Labour Party was not the only party that supported "self-decided" abortion in Norway. By contrast, it was the Norwegian Christian People's Party, the KrF, which provided the "most energetic opposition to the liberalization of the abortion law."[987]

Tungesvik and his KrF supporters maintained a high level of activity as the 1978 Parliament sat to consider these issues. In January, Tungesvik found out that Health Director Torbjørn Mork had sent a letter to the Chief Administrative Doctor[988] in Sogn and Fjordane in which he had asked that the abortion committee there "see that the law is practiced in accordance with its intentions."[989] Tungesvik's rhetoric was laced with sarcasm when he wondered if Mork was not satisfied with the number of abortions already being done.[990] This question of the intent of the law versus its practical applications also engaged the Minister of Social Affairs, Ruth Ryste, She said that it was not Mork's intent to overrule the committee's decisions there, since he, as national Minister of Health, oversaw all abortion decisions made by local committees.[991] She reiterated the government's precautions against too many abortions, highlighting the 12-week limit within which to have a legal abortion. She also underscored that the government's strong commitment to birth control as a way of reducing the number of abortions.

984 Oftestad, et. al., *Norsk Kirkehistorie*, 284. Note 1156.
985 *Aftenposten* (p.m. Edition), January 16, 1978, 4.
986 *Aftenposten* (p.m. Edition), February 7, 1978, 3 and *Arbeiderbladet*, January 18, 1978, 5.
987 Oftestad, et al., *Norsk Kirkhistorie*, 285. Note 1156. "...den skarpeste motstander av liberalisering."
988 I have translated "Fylkeslage" as Chief Administrative Doctor" since a "fylke" is a "county" or a "district" in Norway.
989 *Arbeiderbladet*, January 18, 1978, 5.
990 *Ibid.*
991 *Ibid.*

DNK was not the only religious institution to become involved in the abortion debate in 1978 in Norway. For example, *Arbeiderbladet* ran a letter to the editor from Magnus Tausja, director of the group, Norsk pro vita (Norwegians for life, NPV) on 12 January.[992] Although the group used Latin in its name, Tone B. Jamholt described this group as a "Christian" rather than a "Catholic" health personnel organization, clearly against any form of abortion and also with strong criticisms of birth control.[993] Not surprisingly, Tausja supported the right of reservation based on individual conscience. Referring to Mork's press conference of 2 January, in which the Minister of Health asked for all health workers, no matter what their personal opinions, to "show responsibility", Tausja maintained that he had personal knowledge that no catastrophes had occurred for the "few" women who had sought abortions at "so-called peripheral hospitals", and thus, that there was no need for concern.[994] NPV had fought "beak and claw" against abortion and in February was reported to be starting up an "information office for pregnant women."[995]

The "conscientious exemption", also called the "right of reservation" for health workers, was a heated subject in Norwegian newspapers, as we have seen above. Not only had religious personnel and politicians become involved in the abortion issue but doctors also added the weight of their profession to personal opinions. Mork was constantly in the spotlight and it was his opinion, or lack of consistent opinion, to which many doctors directed their most biting comments. On 3 January, Director Mork had indicated in the press that there would be "many difficulties if the new abortion law includes a right for health personnel to refuse to take part in an abortion."[996] Dr. Per Arne Norum of Oslo responded to Mork's comments by saying "the [real] problem is to be found in Mork's stand on the issue…."[997] Norum's problem was with Mork's remarks in an article published earlier on 11 May 1974 in which he said first, that the right to an abortion had to take precedence over the conscience of a doctor and second, that any person applying for a medical job had the duty to inform any potential employer of his or her ethical objections to assisting in an abortion.[998] Norum's questioning of Mork's proposal ended with the intentional use of a German word, when he asked, "In a true democracy, can such a solution ever be taken in the face of those who think differently such that we risk coming nearer to "*berufsverbot*" (black listing)."[999] Here is an example of the "cultural stock" that can be used in a social

992 "Norsk Pro Vita",*Arbeiderbladet*, January 12, 1978, 5.
993 *Arbeiderbladet*, February 4, 1978, 7.
994 *Ibid.*
995 *Ibid.*
996 *Aftenposten* (p.m. Edition), January 20, 1978, 14.
997 *Ibid.*
998 *Ibid.* "…for *opplysningsplikt om etiske holdninger ved søknader* – for at man skal unngå problemer med avviklingen av fri abort."
999 *Ibid.*

movement; through an indirect reference to the occupation of Norway in World War II, Norum invoked a broad – and deep – schematic understanding of that oppression.[1000]

But Norum wasn't the only one who could plumb the depths of politically emotional rhetoric with the use of the German language. The same day as his article, *Aftenposten* published a letter to the editor from Brita Siljan Vogt who asked if women were some type of threat to men who were living a truly Christian life. She was annoyed with the Geilo meeting and wrote that many theologians had interpreted Paul's various and sundry admonitions to women differently from those who attended the Geilo meeting. She closed her letter by asking:

> Could we women get concrete information on which fatal and negative consequences would be caused by having women priests?... What if we rebelled against *Kinder, Küche und Kirche.*"[1001]

While abortion was perhaps the most difficult of issues, it was one of many ancillary issues that dealt with women's equality. Women clergy, the rights of women workers, and fears of what reproductive empowerment meant for the decreasing Norwegian population at large were some of the many other questions attached to abortion and gender equality. For example, how were babies to be categorized if they could not be immediately assigned a notation "born inside marriage" or "born outside marriage."[1002] What would be their standing in society should this piece of information not be officially noted? Kirsten Mathesen of Kristiansund voiced her deep frustration in late January in *Aftenposten* when she made reference to the Norwegian White Paper, NOU 1977:35. Here, it was suggested that the only information on a child's birth certificate should be that it was born outside of marriage "until the opposite was proven."[1003] She called for a protest of this idea, which she said, was a "development that would only make marriage hollow and diminish respect for it as an institution." It was her opinion that to do so would destroy the "natural and correct framework of home and family."[1004]

The rhetoric of movement framing and re-framing attached to the abortion and gender equality laws had reached the point where German words were being employed, with everything that that implied for this country that had been occupied during World War II. A non-Norwegian observer might well have asked "What next?"

1000 Mayer N. Zald, "Culture, ideology, and strategic framing" in Doug McAdam, John D. McCarthy, Mayer N. Zald, eds., *Comparative perspectives on social movements: Political opportunities, mobilizing structures, and cultural framings* (Cambridge: Cambridge University Press, 1996), 273.

1001 *Aftenposten* (p.m. Edition), 20 January 1978, p. 14.

1002 *Aftenposten* (a.m. Edition), January 24, 1978, 26.

1003 *Ibid.*

1004 *Ibid.*

Since it was the state Church that felt attacked, perhaps it was the penultimate religious enemy that was at work?

6.3 The Return of Witches: Social Stress and Competing Discourses about Abortion

Anthropologists have shown that societies under stress often resort to supernatural occurrences to help solve issues, laying them to rest.[1005] Norwegians no doubt thought themselves to be a modern country in 1978, but this did not prevent the devil from making an appearance during this period, in the Vestlandet region. Just as had happened in 1934 when the Church had fought against a less restrictive abortion law and birth control, this exorcism pitted DNK against current scientific knowledge held by medical institutions in Norway, specifically the discipline of Psychiatry.

William Sewell has written about religion and social stress and asks if, when schemas and structures are undergoing stress, is there any way of determining the depth to which societies are under stress or how the stress will be manifested? Sewell notes that structures are at risk "to some extent" every time they shape a "social encounter."[1006] This is so, he says, because "structures are multiple and intersecting, because schemas are transposable, and because resources are polysemic and accumulate unpredictably."[1007] Structural schemas that are "deep" are "pervasive... in a wide range of institutional sphere, practices and discourses...[and] tend to be relatively unconscious..." In general, religion has such a deep structural schema that it can "mutually tune a people's conceptions of the real with their conceptions of the appropriate way to live."[1008] Citing to Clifford Geertz, Sewell writes that religion is also about "unsettling human emotions...[and]...the threat of chaos."[1009] In answer to the question posed in the beginning of this paragraph, the "depth" of the stress that structural schemas are undergoing might be determined by the appearance of religion's main chaotic force and its main adversary, the devil. It should also not be surprising that religion and science should – again – come into conflict in 1978, just as in Case One in the discipline of psychiatry.

In the spring of 1977, a young female student in the town of Os was thought to be possessed by the devil. She had undergone therapy of some type, but, in the end, had also undergone an exorcism under the auspices of the Home Mission for Evan-

1005 Please see for example, Maya Green, "Witchcraft Suppression Practices and Movements: Public Politics and the Logic of Purification" in *Comparative Studies in Society and History*, 39 (1997): 319–345.
1006 William H. Sewell, Jr., *The Logics of History*, 143. Note 410.
1007 *Ibid.*
1008 *Ibid.*, 181.
1009 *Ibid.*, 188.

gelism (HME).[1010] In late January 1978, *Arbeiderbladet* published an editorial cartoon showing what appeared to be a priest holding a woman upside down in his hands. Where the head of the priest should have been, however, were flames and, coming from behind the priest's body, was a serpent-like tail. In the far distance was a crucifix with the body of Christ turned away from the priestly-devil figure.[1011] The editorial was titled "Cruel treatment of human beings." This was in reference to an interview in another newspaper, *Dagbladet*, of the young woman who had undergone the exorcism. The information contained in that interview successfully convinced *Arbeiderbladet* editors that there was very little need for exorcisms but that there was a great deal of influence by the devil on the men in DNK. *Arbeiderbladet* plainly stated that these adventures by the state church amounted to spiritual charlatanism. It was difficult for the editor to believe that a majority of Church members would defend such a primitive and anti-human behavior. The editor wrote:

> If one wanted to protect the victims of these exorcisms from the public, then exorcisms are the most questionable form of protection one can think of. The truth is that it is really the activities of certain agitators in the darkest backrooms that cannot tolerate the light of day."[1012]

In February, a public apology for the exorcism was said to be ready and would be issued from the administrative Board of Directors of the Home Mission since the exorcism had taken place under its auspices. The organization had taken criticism not only in such forums as the *Arbeiderbladet* but had also been criticized from within; the lead article in the Home Mission's magazine, "For Poor and Rich", had taken a stand against the form of the exorcism. The author of the article, Rector Even Fougner, wrote in *Arbeiderbladet* that, "Under the circumstances, I would warn against foolish activities when one is dealing with psychiatric problems."[1013] But this caution came only after the disclosure that the organization's Youth Ministry Secretary, Oddvar Søvik, had been involved in the incident. *Arbeiderbladet* reported further that it was "possible" that Sovik's own actions should also be examined by the Board of Directors.[1014]

Arbeiderbladet again took up the issue of exorcism in late April in an interview with Cand. theol. Ebbe G. Reicheit. The "demon-debate" may have been over, for the time being, but in its wake Reicheit had strong opinions about the future of the Norwegian Church in Norway. He wondered if it could be that Christian narrow-mindedness found in a certain type of "piety" that undermines human development was

1010 I have translated "Indremisjonen" as "Home Mission for Evangelism."
1011 "Mishandling av mennesker", *Arbeiderbladet*, January 31, 1978, 4.
1012 *Ibid.*
1013 *Arbeiderbladet*, February 3, 1978, 1, 7.
1014 *Ibid.*, 7.

itself a form of demonology.[1015] He noted that a type of piety that finds its expression in wanting what is best for others is quite different from choreographing humans by patterns of commands and forbidden action. For Reicheit, the latter type of piety was a dangerous demon. Reicheit had no time for what Philip Houm had called "church justice."[1016] If Christians in Norway were to continue to treat those of different opinions with "cruelty", then this would lead to the fall of the Church, thought Reicheit. As an example, he discussed the abortion debate. It should be the exception rather than the rule, he said, that church folk should try to give their opinions and insights to pregnant women. Rather, it would be better that Christians not take from women themselves the responsibility to make a decision by enacting a law that forbade abortion. Norway should have a law that "acknowledges" this, but church folk must also help the pregnant woman to bear her responsibility.

In the mid-1970s, Norway was again undergoing a period of deep structural and schematic crisis. The exorcism episode supports my argument that state sponsored legislation during chaotic times in the history of a country can be literally inscribed onto and embodied in those invading, and/or foreign, and/or female, and/or non-white, and/or lower class and/or disabled bodies. In this case, the Church, the "strong we" impressed its reality on the body of a young female student, a member of the "weak we." The threat of chaos and significant unsettling emotions that the Church hierarchy and membership was experiencing were transferred in the form of the devil into this woman, putting the structure of DNK and the medical structures of the day at odds with each other. Eventually, the medical structures proved more powerful, as we will see below.

In February 1978, a priest named Helge Aarflot wrote an article on the weaknesses inherent in the new abortion law and, in passing, criticized Bishop Georg Hille[1017] for having said that Aarflot's ideas would split the religious community in half.[1018] Aarflot was concerned with documents which had come out of the Bishop's meeting in 1977 that made no distinction between protection of both the life in being – of the mother – and the unborn life. Aarflot alleged that some bishops, including Hille, had not continued to support the 1977 declaration and, because of their statements, a split within the church was to be expected. This is not a new idea since what appeared to be a split between rural and urban parishes on the issue of abortion already seemed to be taking place. In general, Bishops from the Oslo, Hamar and other urban areas, had decided against supporting the more radical FASA. But Aarflot felt he had to urge

1015 *Arbeiderbladet (Kultur)*, April 26, 1978, 14.

1016 *Ibid*. "kirkedommen."

1017 Bishop Georg Hille, Bishop of Hammar from 1974–1993.

1018 *Aftenposten* (a.m. Edition), February 9, 1978, 3. Helge Aarflot was only described as a "Menighetspresten" which is a priest for a specific DNK congregation.

the more liberal in the Church hierarchy to "correct themselves" and join FASA as well as align themselves with the Bishop's 1977 statement.

Social Minister Ruth Ryste said in early February that her department "hadn't discussed" changes in the 1 May 1975 abortion law that had already been accepted by the Odelsting and which did include the "right of reservation" for health personnel who had ethical problems with participating in an abortion procedure.[1019] She said that she and her department were still in the process of working on a draft of the new law. Again, she commented on Torbjørn Mork's year-end remarks as "dangerous" in which Mork had said that to create a "right of reservation" would "create, among other things, different treatment and practical problems at hospitals." A "right of reservation" clause had been an element in the 1975 law and had already created a great deal of conflict. The Norwegian Doctors Association, the Norwegian Nurses Association and FASA had all supported this clause. In addition, Secretary of State Nyhus had commented to *Vårt Land*[1020] that no one would be forced to participate in an abortion under the new law.

The issue of a "right of reservation" was the subject of the entire program *Short Notice*[1021] on Norwegian television in February. In addition to this NRK-produced television program, an abortion film, produced by a French group, had been imported into Norway by NPV and debate followed as to whom and in what forum the film should be shown, if at all. Questions persisted about its value and even Church and Education Minister Kjølv Egelund said that the film was so "unbalanced and atypical" that it was not suitable as an educational film at all.[1022]

Through the process of framing, social movement organizations hope to achieve both resonance and salience with the general public. But resonance depends on both empirical credibility and the credibility of the framers. And salience depends on a narrative fidelity with the public; in other words, how good is the fit of the frame with the national culture?[1023] Beginning very early in 1978 both the resonance and the salience of the anti-abortion networks in Norway were under pressure, not only because of the actions of their opponents but also due to the actions of their own members. For example, in February 1978 Bjarne Slyngstad criticized the FASA as an attack against the Labour Party itself. Slyngstad wanted the KrF to stop its "moralizing" since it had been accused by the Labour Party of "combining the abortion issue with politics." Nonetheless, as Slyngstad also noted, there were Christians who were

1019 *Aftenposten* (p.m. Edition), February 9, 1978, 1.

1020 "Vårt Land" means "Our Country." It is a newspaper produced by conservatives and has a Christian perspective.

1021 I have translated "På Sparket" as "Short Notice." It has the flavor of "off the cuff" political debate.

1022 *Aftenposten*, (a.m. Edition), February 15, 1978, 3.

1023 Robert D. Benford and David A. Snow, "Framing Processes and Social Movements: An overview and assessment" in *Annual Review of Sociology*, 26 (2000): 618–622.

members of the Labour Party and the abortion debate did not follow strict party lines at all times.[1024] In addition, the fact that NPV had imported the type of movie which Egelund, the Church and Education Minister, would call "unbalanced" only served to undercut Pro Vita's own credibility. In short, in the midst of this extremely emotional political debate, at least one faction started to go beyond what society found acceptable.

But the rhetoric of the abortion debate only reached new levels of fury. In early February, the Oslo Arbeidersamfunns opplysingskontot (Oslo Workers Society Information Office) was threatened. A staff member, midwife Ellinor Fylling, and others in the office who supported the right to abortion received stenciled threats from a man; the threats were mostly of a biblical nature. But the threats were unique in that the workers were threatened with a combination of fire and brimstone as well as the more modern equivalent – atom bombs.[1025] Part of the reason for the anger may have been that this office had gathered statistics during the 7 years that the group had been in existence. These numbers directly contradicted the logic of FASA and Rø, who claimed that abortion would become a means of birth control. In 1977, for example, this Oslo office had 2622 consultations, 205 of which were for abortion counseling and 2,417 for birth control information.

The group NPV was not to be reasoned with since their first priority was to protect the physical "unborn life" and not the on-going life of the mother or the quality of her family and their lives. To that end, the group had imported the French film, mentioned above, that purportedly had a Christian perspective on the issue. On Friday, 10 February, the male KrF Parliament representatives, a few Labour Party women and others, previewed this movie on the initiative of Labour Party member, Sissel Rønbeck.[1026] The movie, which was intended for young people, provoked a "sharp reaction" among the viewers. Keeping in mind that the NPV group exceeded even the KrF position on abortion, this could have been expected and, as Tone B. Jamholt reported, the film was purely propagandistic in nature. The film began with an "idyllic" portrayal of pregnancy and birth, accompanied by calm soothing music. Focusing only on the child, the mother was portrayed as smiling while giving birth. The second part of the film was a dark, "grotesque" contrast which showed the abortion of a fetus which doctors considered was over four months old. Blood flows from the woman as viewers see an "arm, a bone and a head" being removed from her. According to Jamholt, the movie was clearly meant to scare young girls. That the movie showed nothing about the particular situation of the mother – or father – went without saying.

1024 *Aftenposten* (p.m. Edition), February 7, 1978, 3.

1025 *Arbeiderbladet*, February 4, 1978, 7.

1026 *Arbeiderbladet*, February 11, 1978, 6. "Jeg mener filmen kan virake som vold på sjela. Den er ikke saklig, og propaganda har ingen ting i skolen å gjøre. I f.eks. NRK ville man aldri kunne sende en slik film, i alle fall ikke isolert."

Sissell Rønbeck made the initiative of showing the film as part of her efforts to question the Department of Church and Education as to whether or not the film was suitable for showing in schools. Her opinion was that the film was propaganda and that, with regard to the national television network, NRK, "it should never release such a film, especially in isolation [without context or rebuttal]."[1027] Even KrF-member Hans Olav Tungesvik, who viewed the movie along with Rønbeck, felt the first part of the film was fine, but 17-18 year olds should be alerted beforehand as to the content and should make a decision whether or not to see the second half of the film. The rest of the male contingent from the KrF could not understand what Rønbeck meant when she said the portrayal of pregnancy and birth was too "idealistic." For their part, a member of NPV simply said that they wanted to portray pregnancy and birth as "something positive."

In late February, Chairman Magne Roland of the Norwegian Christian Doctors Association and four members of the governing board sent an appeal to the government to withdraw the new abortion law as they believed it broke with medical, legal and ethical principles and 1000 years of legal tradition.[1028]

While DNK, KrF, FASA and NPV strategized as to how to win the war in which they saw themselves involved, tolerance was the theme of an *Aftenposten* editorial by Haldis Nilson Scarborough on 14 March 1978. Scarborough admitted that tolerance was necessary in a democracy and that it was growing stronger in Norwegian society through pluralism. But, as a Christian, what did this mean for her? Aware of the literature on the subject, she quoted passages from Locke's *Letter on Religious Toleration* as well as from Martin Luther. The passages she had selected set up a fundamental contradiction between tolerance in a liberal democratic society and Christianity and to understand it differently would be a "misunderstanding of both tolerance and democracy."[1029]

6.4 Scientific Discourses and the Challenges to (Religious) Institutions

The Norwegian Church had clashed with the medical profession at the very beginning of 1978 over the issue of abortion but in March, it became apparent to readers of the *Aftenposten* that DNK was also on a collision course with modern Psychiatry. Psychiatrist Njål Madland, who had treated the above-mentioned young female student in Os, openly refuted DNK's official version of events that had been given by Bishop Thor

1027 *Ibid.* Little was Rønbeck to know that eventually the film would be shown on national television.

1028 *Arbeiderbladet*, March 1, 1978, 8.

1029 *Aftenposten* (a.m. Edition), March 14, 1978, 6.

With. Bishop With maintained that he had appreciated how serious the student's condition was and had directed her minister to have a good working relationship with the girl's psychiatrist. That minister understood that the girl needed psychiatric help and made an appointment for her. He continued to discuss this with her in his therapy sessions with her and even made contact with the psychiatrist and asked for advice. But Madlund had a different account of events.

Madland recalled that he had not had contact with either Oddvar Søvik, the National Youth Secretary of the Home Mission for Evangelism or the girl's minister, academic Lecturer and Pastor, Ols Øystese.[1030] The girl's situation had come to Madland's attention through a request for treatment from the girl's male cousin who had recently moved to Bergen. Øystese had had contact with Madland earlier, after Øystese met with the girl and he became afraid she might commit suicide. At that point Øystese brought her to Madland but at the end of the therapy session, Øystese took her home, which all found to be a reasonable course of action – at that time. But how Bishop With could then maintain that there had been "cooperation" between Øystese and himself was a bit of a "mystery" to Madland.[1031] That Øystese had made contact with Madland prior to the exorcism was absolutely not true, according to Madland. When he later heard the girl's story, he was "appalled." He was also "astonished" that they would bring her in for treatment and then take her out of treatment without any warning.

Søvik and his superiors at the Mission Association for Evangelism maintained that both written and oral communication had been made with the girl's relatives and that everything that had happened was with their full understanding. Madland reported, however, that he knew the Bishop had not had any contact with the family until they themselves learned of the exorcism in a letter the girl had written to them after everything had become a matter of public record. As for the male cousin in Bergen, he said he had no idea that there was some sort of demonic presence attached to the events as late as the night before the "séance" in Os.[1032] As for any "understanding" among the parties, the cousin said he had refused admission to both Søvik and Øystese who had came to his house after the girl had sought refuge with him.

With regard to the assertion that the girl had undergone the exorcism voluntarily, Madland referred back to the fact that Søvik and a "known preacher of the gospel" had sat in one room with the girl, both putting forward the hypothesis that she was possessed. This hypothesis had been confirmed since she would not, or could not, repeat the phrase "Jesus is my Lord." That was in the spring of the previous year (1977) and a first exorcism was performed. The second exorcism then took place in June 1977,

1030 *Aftenposten* (p.m. Edition), March 3, 1978, 2.
1031 *Ibid.*
1032 *Ibid.*

even though she had felt better after the first.[1033] She recalled that after these, she had " a good deal of anxiety and nightmares."[1034] Søvik had written to the young woman the following:

> I don't know what you believe or think about me and you probably feel that it is terrible of me to say you are possessed of an evil spirit. But you also know all the signs of this... The question for you now is, will you be free?[1035]

When the young woman later wrote to the General Secretary of the HME, Gunnar Prestegaard, she was referred back to Søvik, essentially meeting a wall of silence from the religious community that had originally sought to help her.

For Madland, the lack of respect that the priests who were involved in the exorcism had for Madland's profession was telling. Also telling was that – according to Madland – they put the "fault" for the exorcism on the girl herself, which was supposedly "voluntary" – after they had sent her a written diagnosis. Madland had himself tried to engage the Bishop in a discussion of the matter but had no luck in doing so. Had the student herself and her family not made contact with Madland, the entire matter would have gone unnoticed and the clergy not questioned about their actions.

This exorcism experience was addressed by the full political spectrum in Norway and HME's behavior was found wanting. That this branch of DNK was receiving such stark criticism signaled a demise in the more moderate DNK population, not liberal but not as conservative as FASA. The more radical factions within DNK, such as FASA and those in an alliance with NPV were also losing credibility with society at large by adopting a "win at any cost" attitude. The religious structures in Norway were shifted and rearticulated into more pluralistic structures with other-than-religious schemas. The questions that remained for DNK at large were varied and difficult and would eventually determine how DNK would enter the twenty-first century.

6.5 Abortion and the Strength of the Women's Movement in Norway

March 8th is traditionally celebrated as International Women's Day around the world. It had been almost 70 years since German socialist Clara Zetkin (1857–1933) and other women attending a conference in Copenhagen in 1910 had demonstrated for women's rights. Every year since then, women had decorated the statue of Norway's first feminist, Camilla Wergeland Collett (1813–1895), with flowers in the Castle Park

1033 *Ibid.* The first exorcism cost 700 NOK; the second exorcism was free.
1034 *Ibid.*
1035 *Ibid.*

in Oslo. While this may have been an annual event, 1978 was especially note-worthy. As Eva Bratholm of *Arbeiderbladet* announced, the day would be "celebrated as never before!"[1036] What had become "more and more clear" was that this particular International Women's Day was not simply a day for quiet reflection and modest demands. Demonstrations were planned and Norwegian women were ready to show what concerned them as well as "other central political questions" of the day.[1037]

Pictures of seven women accompanied *Arbeiderbladet* article of March 8, 1978. Those seven women depicted a range of political parties in Norway at this time. Conservative Party-member Mona Røkke said she would support events in Drammen by talking to people about what the day meant while Turid Varsi would go with her daughter to the Labour Party demonstration in Oslo. Kirsti Grøndahl would give a lecture in Drammen on the national and international aspects of the day. KrF member Eli Kristiansen, however, reported that she would not take part in the demonstration in Oslo and took the opportunity to wonder what women would do if they had two separate demonstrations to choose between, which was in fact the situation. Ambjerg Sælthun for the Center Party said she had so much to do for her work as a Member of Parliament that she would be working at home. While not being against the idea, Labour Party member Mary Eide wasn't sure if she had time to attend the demonstration and Conservative Party member Karla Hafstad said that she would be giving a lecture for women party members in Oslo on the background of the day, i.e. why they should participate and what there was to be gained from doing so.

The demonstration did not begin exactly on the morning of the 8th as planned. Beginning already on the night of March 7th, some women took part in a demonstration against sex discrimination in advertising. Throughout the underground train stations in Oslo, graphically nude advertisements had appeared and women, armed with spray paint, defaced the advertising or tore it down. The women had visited every station in Oslo with the exception of upper Groruddalen. Despite requests from Oslo government officials to the advertising company prior to International Women's Day to avoid problems by not putting the posters up, they had been put up anyway and advertised American pornography in a Norwegian magazine. Odd Øren in the Olso Public Transport's advertising office opined that the appeal from the government hadn't been "right" but also admitted that, in this case, the Norwegian magazine that was involved had "gone over the line."[1038]

As was noted above, Oslo did indeed have not one, but two women's demonstrations on International Women's Day, 1978.[1039] Kvinnefronten (The Women's Front), Norsk Kvinneforbund (The Norwegian Women's Association), Oslo Kvinnesaks-

1036 *Arbeiderbladet (Reportasje),* March 8, 1978, 6.

1037 *Ibid.*

1038 *Ibid. Also see Arbeiderbladet (Reportasje),* "Til aksjon med spray boks", March 8, 1978, 6.

1039 *Arbeiderbladet,* March 8, 1978, 6.

forening (The Oslo Women's Legal Rights Association) and Communist groups had organized one demonstration while the Oslo Women's Equal Rights Association had organized another demonstration. The first group was to gather at Youngstorvet and was supported by the groups mentioned above as well as individual members of the Lesbisk bevegelse (Lesbian Movement) and the Nyfeministene (New Feminists). The second group also included representatives from Brød og Roser (Bread and Roses), Nyfeministene and again, the Lesbisk bevegelse. This group marched, beginning from Fridjof Nansens Plass. While both groups had women's equality as a goal, it is safe to say that differences in ideology and strategy had a big part to play in the perceived need for two demonstrations.[1040] As Elizabeth Lønnå writes, Kvinnefronten and Nyfeministene had "emancipation from capitalism and patriarchy as their main goal" while the Kvinnesaksforening's main objective was equality between the sexes.[1041] How did Oslo's largest newspaper, *Aftenposten,* describe International Women's Day activities in Oslo? The afternoon edition ran headlines such as "Women's Demand: Six Hour Workday" and "Women's Slogan: Self-Determined Birth."[1042] The next day it reported that 3,000 people had taken part in a Bergen and that men had also taken part in the Oslo demonstration.[1043] While equality might have been the theme for all the demonstrations, the immediate concern of both demonstrations, was captured in a placard which said "Self-Determined Abortion – down with 'the committee'."[1044]

This demonstration can be seen as the high point of the women's movement at this time in Norway. The fact that there were not one but two marches indicated that – already – the movement was coming unraveled, a victim to radical politics and insider debates. What it did do at this time and place, however, was to demonstrate that the women's movement could put thousands on the street and, as such, had a great deal of political power and that this power was focused on the abortion and gender equality laws that soon would be passed in the Parliament. The same type of Women's Movement occurred in the United States, a bit earlier. However, it too fractured, becoming dormant. After the USSC issued its decision in Roe and the ERA had come close to passing, the women's movement seemed to have lost some of its salience within the every-day life of Americans.

1040 In the three groups – "Kvinnefronten", "Norsk Kvinneforbund" and "Oslo Kvinnesaksforening" – we see a range of reformist versus confrontational styles, in addition to the range of right-left within the left wing itself. This accounts for some of the differences among the groups. In addition, the thesis of the "United Front" split the two groups. Kvinnefronten was a Maoist's (AKP-ml) "broad front" group.

1041 Elizabeth Lønnå, *Stolhet og Kvinnekamp: Norsk Kvinnesaksforenings historie fra 1913* (Oslo: Gyldendal Norsk Forlag, 1996), 288.

1042 *Aftenposten* (p.m. Edition), March 9, 1978, 26.

1043 About 20,000 took part in Oslo. Please see http://www.kamgdager.no/index.html, accessed November 5, 2009 for details relating to the founding of the different groups.

1044 *Aftenposten* (a.m. Edition), March 9, 1978, 56.

In and of itself the "right of reservation" for medical personnel might have been a minor issue in the abortion legislation debate except that Norway had a very strong labor movement as part of its history. The political equation that emerged from this had been that workers, be they medical doctors or others, were workers and workers deserved rights. How would the Labour Party, a home to many in the women's movement, address this problem if doctors insisted on a "right of reservation" not to assist during abortion procedures? Doctors continued to employ *Aftenposten* as a means for discussion of their rights under the impending legislative scheme.[1045]

The struggle over a "conscientious exemption" was debated with intensity not only among health personnel but also within the Ap itself in the Women's Secretariat. Labour Party women made a decision in early April and publicly announced that they were against the right of medical personnel to refuse to participate in an abortion because of personal moral objections. But it soon became obvious that definitions of "worker" within the Ap were changing in light of the broader Women's Movement in Norway. In a letter to the government, the Secretary for the Labour Party Women's Affairs, Aud Blegen Svindland, asked the government not to support such a reservation clause in the soon-to-be-enacted abortion law.[1046] Svindland, released information to *Arbeiderbladet* that that group had sent a letter to the government saying that the "right of reservation" by health personnel to refuse to take part in an abortion should not be included in the new abortion law.[1047] Cabinet minister Kirsten Myklevold told *Arbeiderbladet* two days later that a clash had indeed taken place within the Labour Party on the right of reservation.[1048] Myklevold said that there was no consensus whether or not the reservation right would pose problems for women and that "this is discrimination we have now and must work with."

Myklevold was correct about a clash. Arbeiderparti women had found themselves divided on the issue of health personnel refusing to take part in abortions. It was the first time in memory there had been a voting battle in the Ap Women's Secretariet with a final vote of 4-4 on the right of reservation.[1049] The double vote of the Director – Svindland – was used to create the group's policy against the reservation right. Eventually, the right of reservation was included in the new law and Aud Blegen Svindland announced that she was happy over the new law but not about the right of reservation.[1050]

1045 *Aftenposten* (p.m. Edition), February 9, 1978, 1. After the election of fall, 2013, the FrP and the Høyre joined forces to again debate the right of reservation.

1046 *Aftenposten* (p.m. Edition), April 3, 1978, 2.

1047 *Arbeiderbladet (Reportasje)*, April 3, 1978, 11. Apparently, this meant that the women of the Labour Party differed with some men in the party on the issue of a "right of refusal" clause.

1048 *Arbeiderbaldet (Reportasje)*, "Abortloven in Statsråd fredag. Ingen endringer i reservasjonsretten", (continued from page 1), April 5, 1978, 7.

1049 *Ibid.*

1050 *Arbeiderbladet (Raportasje)*, April 5, 1978, 8.

In mid-March, a communication by FASA to Social Minister Ruth Ryste brought the abortion issue again to the front page of newspapers. In this announcement, FASA said:

> There is a clear relationship between experimenting with artificial life, the demand for self-decided abortion, the death of infants and mercy killings because the worth of humans has become reduced according to its worth as an object of utility.[1051]

The communication itself was signed by Otto Christian Rø and contained six questions. These were:
1. Is the fetus a life different from that of the mother?
2. Is the inducing of an abortion a matter of taking a life?
3. Does the fetus have independent human rights?
4. Does the Director of Health maintain that an abortion performed on demand according to the wishes of the mother is an ethical conflict between the right of the fetus to [the protection of] law and the demand for abortion?
5. Is the duty of society to protect life also implicated with respect to the unborn life?, and
6. How should the fetus' right to life be protected if the woman alone has the decision [to undergo an abortion]?[1052]

The reaction from Health Minister Torbjørn Mork to FASA's communication was especially blunt. He called the communication the "most demagogic that I have heard yet."

Hans Olav Tungesvik, a Parliament representative and FASA sympathizer whom we have encountered above, said that he also was a bit surprised to see the linkage between self-decided abortion and test tube babies. Apparently, the FASA material had also made mention of the fear of a Nazi-holocaust situation to which Tungesvik replied:

> To have these ideas in the picture now is the work of insane people with sick thoughts and it is not really especially helpful in relation to today's issue.[1053]

Bergliot Børresen, who was described as both a "Christian and an abortion supporter" by *Arbeiderbladet*, said she saw the FASA comments as "grotesque" especially when making a connection between abortion and *in vitro* fertilization at the "same time as they were totally silent on the issue of atomic power and the neutron bomb."[1054] Børresen was careful to point out that abortion did show respect for life, the life of the

1051 *Arbeiderbladet (Reportasje)*, March 15, 1978, 9.
1052 "Seks spørsmål til Mork", *Arbeiderbladet*, March 18, 1978, 5.
1053 *Ibid.*
1054 *Ibid.*

woman! She wrote that FASA had a historical misunderstanding about abortion as not being permitted during the Third Reich since the point was to produce as many children as possible.

While one of the things that the government did at this time was to respond to frequent attacks by FASA such as the above, another strategy proceeded more quietly – without the hysteria provoked by themes of Nazism. Tone B. Jamholt reported in *Arbeiderbladet* that all cities with 15,000 or more inhabitants would provide education on the use of condoms. To that end, 44 offices were to be set up with additional funding by a supplementary grant of 3.3 million kroner. The State Association for Sexual Information ("RFSU") had, in 1976, sold 10 million condoms through its 3,000 outlets, the most – 30% - being sold at gas stations.[1055] The government, the RFSU and the Directory of Health had combined to review a five-year period ending in a 3.3 million kroner grant for this condom campaign. Health stations would also have the duty of providing birth control information and supervision. While in 1976, 94,000 women had relied on the birth control pill with another 90,000 on the coil (IUD) and 4,000 using diaphragms, more outlets were needed to prevent sexually transmitted diseases. The logic in this, the government pointed out, was that pregnant women, whose pregnancies came to term, would have uncomplicated births if they were healthy and not burdened by sexually transmitted diseases.

The new abortion legislation ultimately included a right of reservation for health personnel on the grounds of conscientious objection. Nonetheless, this paled in light of the biggest change in the law as proposed which, when passed into law at paragraph 2, would read:

> If the woman finds, after she has received information and counseling, that she cannot go through with the pregnancy, then she herself may make the decision to have an abortion provided that the surgical procedure takes place before the 12th week of the pregnancy and that serious medical reasons do not mitigate against it.[1056]

Essentially, this was a significant change from the earlier law. This law allowed the woman herself to decide what "indications" were present that pointed toward having an abortion. No longer would a woman have to convince a committee why she should be allowed to have an abortion. As Eva Bratholm wrote, the previous system was prone to "over-dramatization" and was essentially a shame-filled practice. From the Department's point of view the practical work that needed to be done was to organize districts so that women would have the opportunity to practice this right regardless of the staffing in any individual hospital. The law also addressed birth control. After

1055 "3 millioner til kondom kampanje", *Arbeiderbladet (Reportasje)*, April 1, 1978, 8.
1056 *Arbeiderbladet (Reportasje)*, April 5, 1978, 7.

an abortion, if a woman requested information, she must be given instruction on the prevention of pregnancy.[1057]

Parliament members found a letter signed by 60 gynecologists in their mailboxes later that week.[1058] The letter, in essence, argued that, should the abortion proposal be passed by the Parliament, a "totally new principle of medical practice" would be instituted, i.e. that the patient herself could decide what course of (medical) action was appropriate. The editorial cartoon used irony regarding this notion; it showed three tall men, coats not unlike white laboratory jackets, bending over a much smaller woman standing naked, clothes strewn on the floor, in the center of their small group. The letter urged the continuation of the committee system. The doctors allowed that abortion would continue in Norway but that the "central" question was not abortion but who decided whether it took place – a woman or the committee members, i.e. medical doctors.[1059]

If the Parliament passed the new abortion law as suggested by the government, what would become of FASA? Otto Christian Rø answered that question by reminiscing that the movement began as a spontaneous reaction against the 1974 abortion law. When Eva Bratholm, perhaps in jest, asked Rø if his group might not join in the anti-neutron bomb group, Rø simply said that, while it was fine that groups opposed the neutron bomb, his group needed to "concentrate" on the abortion issue.[1060] Bratholm asked Rø if there were any medical indications that he and his group would accept as reasons for abortion, to which he replied, rather evasively, "This is not something to which we can give a concrete answer."[1061] By answering as he did, Rø failed to address issues of rape, incest or serious medical complications as a reason for an abortion, again displaying an "all or nothing" approach. Bratholm asked Rø about a previous statement Rø had made, where, in principle, he had said he had no problem with having the issue of whether to allow an abortion submitted to a court of law. Bratholm asked him if this meant that women would be legally forced to carry through with a pregnancy? Rø confessed that he really hadn't meant that; however, there did seem to be a conflict of interest – in his mind – between the fetus and the mother when the mother wanted an abortion.[1062] The mother was her own attorney but the fetus had no defender. But Bratholm persisted and pressed Rø as to whether or not a woman could be legally forced to have an unwanted child? To this he replied "These are your words, not mine."[1063]

In its summary of legislative activity in Week 14, *Arbeiderbladet* noted that the government had finally produced its proposal on abortion. It reported that there was,

1057 *Ibid.*
1058 *Arbeiderbladet,* April 6, 1978, 4.
1059 *Ibid.*
1060 *Arbeiderbladet (Reportasje),* April 7, 1978, 7.
1061 *Ibid.*
1062 *Ibid.*
1063 *Ibid.*

for some, a measure of "joy" in the legislative "breakthrough" but that this had been disturbed by the inclusion of the right of reservation for medical personnel.[1064] KrF had also responded to the government's proposed law. As *Arbeiderbladet* reported KrF position, the rape of a woman or incest within a family should not "automatically" give a woman the right to an abortion.[1065] That this followed from that party's point of view wherein life began at conception and should only end "naturally" was no surprise. At his press conference, Olav Tungesvik, the "main person" behind the Party's proposal took time to give his opinion that the birth control device known as the "spiral" also induced abortions. Lars Korvald added that there had been a "tightening" of KrF's position since 1975 on rape and abortion was not to be "automatic" in cases of rape except if it would create serious permanent illness of a psychological or physical nature. Apparently, in the mind of KrF, a woman who underwent rape and who had managed to "cope" with it without serious mental or bodily damage could be forced to carry the pregnancy to term. For some politicians such as these, the issue of abortion was a single issue. For others, the issue had many facets, including the perceived need for abortion. Although the KrF Party excluded consideration of birth control, other parties did not.

In Vestfold, Dr. Georg Bentze[1066] wrote, it was "meaningless" to continue any discussion on the new law concerning the "right of reservation" for doctors. He analyzed the new law as based on the "Big Brother principle" and blamed Satan for the dictatorship of the Norwegian state over doctors.[1067]

The State Secretary for the Ministry of Social Affairs (1973–1977), Kjell Knudsen (Ap), had kept a lower profile during the March and early April debates but, in April, he began to talk about the issues. At that time, he became too radical for the Norwegian People's Action Against Abortion – or, at the very least, for FASA Chairman Rø. Rø had felt the need to send a letter to *Abeiderbladet* in mid-April outlining exactly what Knudsen's strategic relationship to that organization was. Prior to that time, FASA had nothing "against" Knudsen. FASA had joined with Knudsen in trying to induce feelings of guilt in politicians for the annual 15,500 abortions in Norway but it was Rø's opinion that Knudsen went too far when he tried to do the same with the People's Action itself.[1068] In the beginning, FASA had not concerned itself with the issue of birth control. But, in the meantime, it had decided that use of the "spiral" was a means of abortion and not birth control. Rø wrote, in an open letter to *Arbeiderbladet*, that:

1064 *Arbeiderbladet*, April 8, 1978, 5.

1065 *Arbeiderbladet (Reportasje)*, April 8, 1978, 8.

1066 Dr. Bentze had moved from Hungary and was an acupuncture enthusiast. His experience with Communism may account for some of his views.

1067 *Aftenposten* (a.m. Edition), April 19, 1978, 9.

1068 *Arbeiderbladet*, April 19, 1978, 5.

> He [Kjell Knudsen] asserts that resistance against effective family planning can often be found among People's Action participants. Where did he get this from? (New paragraph) Where have People's Action members tried to instill a feeling of guilt in women who use the spiral? You see, the People's Action has – from its start – not accepted the idea of concerning itself with questions relating to birth control. But the People's Action is fully informed that the spiral cannot be said to be a form of birth control but, instead, as a method of abortion....Knudsen has several assertions that he hasn't bothered to document. Worse yet, in the meantime, he now tries to influence the undersigned [FASA] that [it] "intentionally concealed evidence of the fact that the number 15,500 represents the number of abortions that take place legally." (New paragraph) Absolutely not![1069]

Here we can see some harsh criticism within the ranks of those who opposed abortion. Fighting within one's own ranks is usually thought to be reserved for left-wing political circles or, it may also be that right-wing groups are more controlled about washing their dirty laundry in public. In any case, we see some cracks in the unity of the movement. And here, Rø is not only ideologically angry with Knudsen but is also personally angry at his statements and insinuations. That FASA had a policy of not concerning itself with family planning methods at the inception of the group was clearly changed after the release of certain claims about the use of the spiral.

Aftenposten tentatively entered the fray in late April. In what was a precarious position for a newspaper, *Aftenposten* took a position on the issue, saying in an editorial that, like some other debates in Norway, this debate was infused with "black and white thinking."[1070] The editorial first cited KrF-member, Per Høybråten (1932–1990), who had characterized the entire debate as one of "socialist parties" against his own party and its "defense of the unborn life" which was "based on fundamental Christian beliefs." The writer of the editorial found this characterization a "mystery" and wondered how the KrF could criticize the policy since it had never considered the abortion question, first and foremost, as a question of politics. The *Aftenposten* editorial said:

> We consider the abortion question an enormously important and difficult question. We have no difficulty in seeing that this has to do with the right and worth of unborn life. Nor do we have any problem when abortion must be considered a last resort. But we do have difficulties when one, in a manner like this, pretends that it is absolutely a case of an "either-or" matter. In addition, we are – to quote a well-known politician – "disappointed" when the need to stigmatize people with another point of view is given the greater part of the space in a newspaper.[1071]

1069 *Ibid.*

1070 *Aftenposten* (a.m. Edition), April 28, 1978, 2.

1071 *Aftenposten* (a.m. Edition), April 25, 1978, 2. Placed directly next to *Aftenposten's* lead editorial. "Vi gjenta at abortsaken er en uhyre viktig og vankselig sak. Vi har ingen vanskeligheter med å se at dette har å gjøre med det ufødte livs rettsvern. Vi har heller ikke problemer når det hevdes at abort må være en siste nødutvei. Men vi har altså visse vanskeligheter når man i en sak some denne later som om det skulle dreie seg om et absolutt enter-eller. Dertil blir vi en smule **"vonbrotne"** for å sitere en kjent politiker – når trangen til å stemple folk med et annet syn gis mesteparten av spalteplassen." The editorial in that edition of *Aftenposten* also talks about use of this word.

The use of the word "disappointed" in this editorial was a clear signal to those that followed politics in Norway. The Norwegian word used was for "disappointed" was "vonbrotne", a word not in normal circulation. But this single word lived on as a commemorative of the comment made by then Parliamentary group leader of KrF, Kjell Olsson Bondevik (1901–1983), when the negotiations he had been asked to lead in order to create a conservative coalition government broke down in 1971 – after just one day of talks – over the issue of admission to the European Union.[1072] That KrF's insistence on black and white answers for a delicate and serious problem should be its undoing and that the words of its own patriarch such be used against it in a conservative newspaper indicates exactly how tumultuous this issue was. Ideological breaks in conservative politics were beginning to show and show in the public editorials of a conservative newspaper. It could also be argued that the right wing did more damage with this attitude among the general population and may account for some with more conservative views abandoning the middle ground and supporting a more lenient approach to the problem.

Under the new abortion law, only women who were pregnant 12 weeks or less could legally decide on their own to have an abortion. Perhaps as an indication how frantic the political right was, we see a shift in strategy and an appeal to extreme cases that may or may not have taken place at all. Dr. Ola Didrik Saugstad wrote an article about the fact that the division between a fetus and a newborn child was often "blurred." For Saugstad, viewing the fetus as a "clump of cells" involved a scientific myth. As a neonatalogist, Saugstad's opinion was that a better theoretical understanding and better medical techniques were blurring the lines between what were fetuses and what was a new born. This all led to various ethical reassessments. It was also his opinion that allowing abortion was then being reconsidered in a number of countries, including the United States. He credited the American decision in Roe v.

1072 There was also another irony to the use of the word "vonbrotne" ("broken hope") by *Aftenposten.* When, on 8 March 1971, Kjell Olsson Bondevik, uncle of the later Prime Minister, Kjell Magne Bondevik, had used the word, he was basically acknowledging that his last chance to become Prime Minister had slipped away. He did not live to see his nephew, politician and ordained DNK priest, Kjell Magne Bondevik (b. 1947), become Prime Minister. Bondevik served inthat office from 1997 to 2000 and from 2001 to 2005. I am thankful to Prof. Sætnan for this insight.

Wade as creating more interest in the debate.[1073] Finally, Saugstad cited a book by G. Leech entitled "Biokratene"[1074] in which Leech says:

> By "child liquidation" I mean murder of a child where the parents have taken the alternative after having evaluated that the suffering of the child, a life in being, would be greater than the suffering if put to death. Perhaps one ought to insert two or three days or weeks as a "test life" so that the doctors can check for defects and where the parents take a decision as to whether they wish to keep the child and rear a damaged newborn or not.[1075]

This is interesting rhetoric; it is an attempt by Saugstad to use irony combined with his status as a neonatalist as a means of interjecting himself into the abortion decision-making process.

These two episodes demonstrate that at the macro-political level, the KrF was losing salience for individuals at the micro-level. Because dogmatic political positions, based in core religious beliefs, were not available for compromise, the framing discourse of the abortion issue had stopped at the micro-level. While an actual decision would later be taken at the Norwegian Parliament to legally allow "self-decided abortion", in one way, the decision had already been taken within society itself. The debate itself had exposed differences, large and small, within the ranks of both the right and the left, but society, as *Aftenposten* had so succinctly hinted at, was tired of "either-or" thinking.

In early May 1978, the FASA in Oslo increased its attacks on the Ap government. Attorney Gunnar T. Johannessen, who was part of the FASA leadership, took "large

---

1073 Saugstad himself became involved with the American judicial system. His testimony – predictably "anti-choice" – appears in the 8th Circuit Court of Appeals (from Norwegian settled Minnesota, North and South Dakota) in the case of Planned Parenthood v. Rounds (Planned Parenthood of Minnesota, North Dakota, South Dakota; and Carol E. Hall, M.D., Plaintiffs and Appellees, v. Mike Rounds, Governor, and Larry Long, Attorney General of theState of South Dakota,in their official capacities, Defendants and Appellants, No. 05–3093). To date the U.S.S.C. has not accepted *certiorari* of any case aimed at posing a frontal assault on reversing Roe, although this South Dakota case set up the premier opportunity for the Court to do so. A decision was issued on Rounds in early December, 2007. A 5-4 decision was issued with Judge Souter writing the opininon and joined by Justices Breyer, Kennedy, Stevens and Ginsberg. The basis for the decision was that the "compelled speech" mandated by a doctor to a patient in §7 of the South Dakota House law 1166 was unconstitutional. However, Justice Scalia took the opportunity to say that the decision ignored precedent and that Roe was wrongly decided. He would have been joined by Alioto and Roberts, but for this statement. Please see, http://sunn.wordpress.com/category/planned-parenthood-v-rounds/, accessed March 4, 2008.

1074 "Biokratene" can be translated as "de somstyer livet" or "those that govern/control our lives."

1075 *Aftenposten* (a.m. Edition), April 25, 1978, 2. Citation by Saugstad is to G. Leech, *Biokratene* (Oslo: Aaschehoug, 1971). "Med barnelikvev(r)dering mener jeg drap på et barn der foreldrene har kommet frem til dette alternativet efter å ha vurdert om lidelsen ved å beholde liver vil bli store en lidelse ve å avlive det" Og de innføre to eller tre dager eller uker some "prøveliv" slik at legene kan controllere om det hadde defekter og foreldrene ta stilling til om de ønsket å beholde og oppdrag et skadt spebarn eller ikke."

caliber shots" at the government's proposed abortion especially paragraph 2, which had also been in contention in the previous 1975 law. This section set out various grounds under which an abortion could be sought after 12 weeks of pregnancy.[1076] Johannessen's main concern was §2, subsection c. which allowed for an abortion after 12 weeks in cases where there was a "great danger" that the child could be sick due to a serious genetic illness or some illness that the mother had unwittingly contracted, such as rubeola during her pregnancy.[1077] What Johannessen did not mention was that KrF, in 1968, had indicated they had no problems with this. FASA also arranged for a conference in Oslo where it would present a document detailing reasons against the proposed abortion law to the government. The document was a series of articles by, among others, Per Lønning, author Sigbjørn Hølmebakk and Professor Dagfinn Fellesdal.

At a press conference, Otto Chr. Rø said that the government "no doubt conceived of this new law as an adjustment, from a [Committee consent rate of] of 98% to 100%" referring to the consent rate of the Committee who heard abortion petitions.[1078] But FASA saw the law as a shift in cultural values away from the protection of all life. Johannssen remarked that KrF's position was nearer to what FASA really wanted. But Rø strongly asserted that FASA was not aligned with any particular political party and would try to influence all parties alike. The new secretary for the movement, Anne Enger Lahnstein, spoke from a woman's perspective saying that the impending law accepted male thinking; she thought it true that most women did not want the law but that most men did.[1079] Lahnstein said the supposed demand for abortion rights "showed contempt for what it means to be a woman and for the desire to become a man."[1080] She thought that, in newer feminist literature, one got the impression that having a female body was a difficult destiny to bear. For Lahnstein, what was needed was to get away from this idea as well as to ensure that the "womanly function of bearing a child must be a part of gender equality." If this was not done, "then we are in danger of a new type of women's oppression."[1081] Ruth Ryste responded by claiming "shock" at these newest attacks.[1082] Although FASA had always used strong language, Ryste said the movement had reached new level of unreasonableness.[1083]

1076 *Arbeiderbladet (Reportasje)*, May 3, 1978, 7.

1077 Hans Flock and Birger Stuevold Lassen (eds.), *Norges Lover 1687–2003* (Oslo: Det Juridiske Fakultet at the University of Oslo, Hos Glyldendal Akademisk, 2004), 1008. 13 June No. 50 1975, Law on Abortion.

1078 *Arbeiderbladet(Reportasje)*, May 3, 1978, 7.

1079 *Ibid.*

1080 *Ibid.*

1081 *Ibid.*

1082 *Ibid.*

1083 *Ibid.*

The first weekend in May saw a meeting of the leadership of the women's movement. If the government thought that the right of reservation for health personnel was no longer an issue, they had only to listen to Aud Blegen Svindland, leader of the Labour Party's Women's Secretariet. Her message was practical, yet forceful. In her opinion, no one knew exactly what the right of reservation meant. In which exact arena of the health system did this right come into effect? For her, there were still too many places in the system where women could be brow beaten when seeking an abortion. The solution was, according to Svindland, to abandon the right of reservation for medical personnel altogether.[1084]

By mid-May, Parliament was divided into three factions regarding the abortion issue. The Department of Social Affairs had presented its report supporting "self-decided" abortion to the Government and, as expected, a majority of the Labour and left-leaning parties supported the report, although the position of two Socialist Left representatives was still unknown. The government's report agreed that women should have the right to decide to have an abortion within the first 12 weeks of pregnancy. Three cooperating political parties – H, KrF and SP – opposed the report with KrF proposing a more restrictive policy than that accepted by the other two.

The three-party faction mentioned above could not accept that the mother should be entrusted with decision-making regarding the fetus.[1085] To the Conservatives, the Christian People's Party and the Center Party, it was unthinkable that legal protection for the fetus should be removed during the first 12 weeks of pregnancy, for any reason. The Conservatives and Center Party held a common belief that the law was simply too liberal and "convenient." All three groups underscored the fact that the "indications" or reasons given for an abortion were troubling. The KrF party made it clear that under no conditions would it accept "social" indications as an adequate reason for an abortion. Along with the Center Party and the Conservatives, the KrF party believed that accepting statutory language such as "life-threatening or other circumstances" would only lead down a slippery slope, finally ending in "social" indications.[1086] It spent its time lobbying for the "right of reservation" by medical personnel. Some thought was given to requiring that women must have every abortion in the vicinity of her home but KrF party members believed this would conflict with the right of reservation.

Edda Espeland warned in the *Family Section* of *Aftenposten* on 19 May that the new abortion law could be undermined through the action of some women's groups in their eagerness to have the new law enacted. These groups had sent a letter to all the members of the Social Department that was handling the new law in Parliament. The law, as then written, imposed a responsibility on the doctor to inform the patient

1084 *Arbeiderbladet*, May 8, 1978, 5.
1085 *Aftenposten* (a.m. Edition), May 13, 1978, 3.
1086 *Ibid.*

about the abortion procedure and its "medical results."[1087] The women's advocacy groups that had sent the letter had interpreted this to mean that a doctor must tell the patient that a life would be ended by taking part in the procedure. They reasoned that doctors had a general duty to disclose the nature and extent of any medical procedure and how it would be performed. Their opinion was that nothing more should be needed for the medical procedure called an abortion. The groups also reasoned that this would be an opportunity for the doctor to use his authority, or even introduce subjective feelings on the subject in order to influence the women to another, different decision. The women's groups signing the letter were Bread and Roses, The Lesbian Movement, New Feminists, and The Women's Front.[1088]

Espeland made the case for how this type of activity could undermine the new law. The fact remained that the draft law had a clause that allowed the doctor to refuse to carry out the abortion if "weighty medical reasons" advocated against the procedure.[1089] Kristin Hodnekvam added the observation that if a woman was in such poor medical condition that she could not undergo an abortion, how was it that she could successfully undergo a nine-month pregnancy.[1090] These women's organizations were also clearly against the imposition of a 12 week cut-off date since, they argued, over 95% of women who sought an abortion already did so within that period. If a woman must seek an abortion after 12 weeks, forcing her to go through the application procedure, that would only serve to make a bad situation worse.[1091]

The new abortion law had ramifications beyond the obvious. Since abortions were a "necessary evil", state money for birth control and financial help for women with difficult pregnancies was considered a necessary accompaniment to the new law. These two items soon received 2.5 million kroner in aid from the government. Among the initiatives that would be taken, according to Ruth Ryste, was to encourage the use of condoms since, in the one year between 1977 and 1978, 13,000 new cases of gonorrhea had been reported. The KrF party would not support this latter measure. Kjell Bohlen of the Labour Party responded to them by noting that the incidence of gonorrhea in Sweden had fallen 35% when a campaign of the same type had been used there, but, during the same time period, the number of gonorrhea cases had doubled in Norway.[1092]

1087 *Aftenposten* (p.m. Edition), May 19, 1978, 6.
1088 *Ibid.*
1089 *Ibid.*
1090 *Ibid.*
1091 *Ibid.*
1092 *Aftenposten* (p.m. Edition), May 26, 1978, 4.

6.6 The Norwegian Equal Rights Amendment

In late May, the Parliament also began to grapple with the issue of a gender equality law. On the morning of 24 May, Josef Elias "Jo" Benkow (b. 1924) of the Conservative Party in Akershus began to chair hearings in the Odelsting Chamber of Parliament on a law that would protect the simple, yet legally complicated idea, of human equality. Benkow was reported as specifically addressing concerns of the KrF party and the Center Party, saying that the goal was to break up the deep-rooted inequality between the sexes that was no longer suitable for a neutral understanding of legislation.[1093] Two days later, Cabinet Minister for Administrative and Consumer Affairs, Kirsten Myklevoll (1928–1996), testified before the Odelsting Chamber and, in very moderate language, began by noting that both sexes have privileges and weaknesses. The purpose of the legislation would be, according to Myklevoll, to give women the legal right to earn a salary in the workplace and to give men the opportunity to engage in home and local life.[1094]

The gender equality law passed in the Odelsting by a vote of 72 to 40 despite an attempt by the KrF to add several paragraphs to an existing law, arguing the effect would be the same. *Aftenposten* noted that after many years of "rambling" and a "good deal of compromise" between the Labour Party and the Conservatives, they had finally made gender equality a legal fact to life in Norway. But questions remained, especially regarding what was called "positive discrimination", known as "affirmative action" in the United States[1095], or where women might receive preferential treatment in special cases. This still threatened the "big coalition" of right and left. To this, Kåre Willoch – Norway's "Mr. Conservative" – stepped forward to emphasize that discrimination itself was negative and "something other than equal treatment."[1096]

All those involved in this legislative debate recognized that practical questions remained to be worked out. One significant question was how would the law be operationalized within unions and professional organizations. Again, Myklevoll put the law in perspective and said that it had never been the goal of the government to create restraints on the handy man or kitchen helper but, by the same token, one had to realize that trade unions and other organizations had a big influence in society and

---

1093 *Aftenposten* (p.m. Edition), May 24, 1978, 6.

1094 *Aftenposten* (a.m. Edition), May 27, 1978, 3. Myklevoll was a LP member.

1095 The most famous case on this issue is Bakke v. Regents of the University of California. Mr Bakke, a white male, complained of the university's refusal to admit him to medical school there, i.e. the university had admitted a woman instead.

1096 *Aftenposten* (a.m. Edition), May 27, 1978, 3. Willoch began his elected career as a Conservative representative in 1954. He was in Parliament, continuously elected, from 1954 to 1989, a total of thirty-five years. He was also Prime Minister, serving from 1981–1983 and 1983–1986. His first term was as a Høøre member but his second term was in a coaliton made up of H, SP and KrF.

needed to incorporate the new law.[1097] Many such organizations had been more eager to protect their privileges than to encourage the process of providing equal rights during the Parliament debate. For his part, KrF party representative and ordained Lutheran minister, Kjell Magne Bondevik, found it "strange" that the courts would have to make a decision about what was an "ordinary theological" understanding.[1098] Despite this understanding, a *Law on the Equality between the Sexes* was passed on 9 June 1978.[1099]

6.7 Abortion as a Challenge to Institutional (Religious) Discourses

DNK Bishop and Høyre representative, Per Lønning,[1100] eventually resigned from his Parliamentary post after the abortion legislation was passed. He then authored a document entitled "Therefore...Documentation about the abortion debate and the abdication from office", in which he outlined the reasons for this dramatic step.[1101] During the abortion debate, Lønning had been extremely engaged in the running commentary that *Aftenposten* had presented to the public and was the "foremost spokesman" for DNK in the abortion debate.[1102] But since the abortion debate had essentially opened a Pandora's box of all things related to human sexuality, and since either Christianity or religions in general, and the Norwegian Church in particular, had views on this subject, Lønning also became caught up in a wave of issues surrounding the more general subject of sexuality. After an overwhelming majority had passed the new abortion law in Parliament, Lønning resigned from the Parliament in protest.

Before Lønning resigned, however, there were more immediate reactions by DNK to the new law since the debate among Church leaders in Norway, their followers and those who had supported the change in the law was not finished. The Lutheran Church in Norway had traditionally used what is referred to as a "pastoral letter" as a strategic maneuver to address what it believed was pressing social and political issues in Norway.[1103] A twentieth century example of this was the Bishops' letter

1097 *Ibid.*

1098 *Ibid.*

1099 Hans Flock and Birger Stuevold Lassen (eds.), *Norges Lover 1687–2003* (Oslo: Det Juridiske Fakultet at the University of Oslo, Hos Glyldendal Akademisk, 2004), 1085.

1100 Per Lønning was made Bishop of the Diocese of Borg in 1969. Later, he resumed pastoral duties as Bishop of Bjørgvin from 1987–1994.

1101 Please see, Per Lønning, *Derfor...:Dokumentasjon omkring abortdebatten og en embetsnedleggelse* (Oslo: Gyldendal, 1975). Also see, http://openlibrary.org/b/OL5005759M/Derfor-, accessed August 12, 2009.

1102 Oftestad, Rasmussen and Schumacher, *Norsk Kirkehistorie*, 284.

1103 The Norwegian word for this is "hyrdebrev."

of 9 February 1941, read in church pulpits to protest human rights conditions after Nazi troops occupied Norway. That letter was spread throughout Norway during the wartime occupation and was considered to have had a "very strong effect."[1104] It received nation-wide support from Christian organizations as well as from the Free Christian Churches in Norway.[1105] On 14 February 1942, Norwegian Bishops also sent a letter to priests and parishes on the education of children after it became painfully clear that the Quisling Administrative Office for Churches was determined to indoctrinate a new generation of adherents. These two occasions had been filled with both power and resistance during the occupation.[1106] This short review of how the pastoral letter had been used in the past only serves to underscore the concern that the Norwegian Church felt when presented with a new, and more liberal, abortion law. In 1978, DNK – again – decided to use a pastoral letter, to be read after the abortion law of 1978 had been passed.[1107] However, as events unfolded, it was actually read prior to the passage of the new law, creating even more accusations and counter-accusations.

From a structural and temporal standpoint, the pastoral letter – and reactions to it – were what Sewell calls an "act of signification."[1108] He writes about the storming of the Bastille as this type of event. At that time in France, the social and "political structures were massively dislocated."[1109] Storming the Bastille was an event that reformed social and socio-religious structures.[1110] The authority of DNK was placed in

---

1104 Ingar Hagan, *Den Norske Kirken i Storm* (Drammne: A.S. Lunde & Co's Forlag, 1967), 33. Also see, Chr. A.R. Christensen, *Norge Under Okkupasjonen*, 2nd ed. (Oslo: Fabritius & Sønners Forlag, 1965), 64.

1105 Hagen, *Storm*, 89. The phrase "Free Christian" group is a literal translation of "frie kristne" and refers to "low church" groups in Norway.

1106 DNK did resist the Nazis occupation. One such event is worth recounting. By Easter Sunday 1942, about 11,000 Norwegian clergymen had resigned their positions in potest against the Quisling regime; only about 40 remained in their posts. (Many of the clergymen who had resigned died in German concentration camps.) Norwegians were then forbidden to attend a church service in Trondheim's Nidaros Cathedral in February and "thousands" stood before the Cathedral in the freezing cold and sang "A Mighty Fortress is Our God" after Oslo's Bishop Eivind Berggrav had been "locked out" of the cathedral. Berggrav was hauled before Quisling who shouted "You vile traitor! You deserve to have your head chopped off." To this Berggrav replied, "Here I am." Please see, *Time Magazine*, April 13, 1943 at http://www.time.com/time/printout/0,8816,866504,00.html, accessed March 17, 2008. While the Nazi letter had an effect, other letters did not. For example, DNK also sent out what is commonly referred to as a "the culture letter" in September 1945. Written by a committee named by the Church, it "did not have the influence they had thought and hoped for." Please see, Torleiv Austad, "Kirkenkampen – en intermesso?" in Knut Lunby and Ingun Kongtomery (eds.), *Statskirke i etterkrigssamfunn* (Oslo Bergen Tromsø: Universitetsforlaget, 1981), 24.

1107 http://www.kampdager.no/arkiv/abort/abortkamp/hyrdebrev_aksjon.html, accessed, May 18, 2006.

1108 Sewell, *Logics*, 245.

1109 *Ibid.*

1110 The timing of the issuance of Church documents that demonstrate "rearticulated events" is not always straightforward. The Roman Catholic Church has also used "pastoral letters", encyclicals and

the breach in much the same way as governing forces were in France. The issuance of the pastoral letter in Norway and the reactions that followed signified "new meanings that, taken together, reshaped the political world."[1111] I think that how Sewell describes the Bastille can also be applied to this event.

> [The e]vents...signify something new and surprising. They introduce new conceptions of what really exists.... of what is good, and of what is possible....The most profound consequence of the taking of the Bastille was then a reconstruction of the very categories of French political culture and political action.[1112]

The taking of the Bastille was not simply or merely a physical event in the world; the persons who took part in it were "symbolically motivated" in that they saw the Bastille as an "intolerable barrier to their political hopes" and that symbolism and rhetoric later raced over the world. A cultural transformation had taken place in Norway just as in France. This cultural and social transformation was "both stimulated and locked into place" by "simultaneous shifts both in resources...and in modes of power...." and not even a pastoral letter from the DNK, trying to maintain control over its congregations, could stop these shifts of power.[1113]

The pastoral letter was read in DNK churches throughout Norway on 4 June 1978, although some priests did refuse to read it. *Adresseavisen*, a newspaper located in Trondheim, editorialized about the pastoral letter, noting that it had caused turmoil within and outside of the Church itself.[1114] The document was itself very short and read as follows:

---

agreements for much the same purpose and as a matter of diplomacy. For example, the *Reichskonkordat*, signed in 1933 by Eugenio Cardinal Pacelli, on behalf of Pope Pius XI, and Franz von Papen, on behalf of German President Paul von Hindenburg, can be contrasted with Pope Pius XI's later 1937 encyclical *Mit brennende Sorge*, authored by Pacelli. Very simply, these two documents were seemingly at odds with one anther; the first was an attempt to secure freedom of religion for Catholics in Germany and the other was a denunciation of Reich activities. Pacelli became Pope Pius XII in 1939 and is the main character in Rolf Hochhuth's controversial 1963 play, *The Deputy*. Pacelli is portrayed as a hypocritical pontiff, silent about the on-going Holocaust, the fact of which was well known to him. His silence as Pope stands in opposition to his authorship of *Mit brennende Sorge*. But, having said this with reference to the use of the pastoral letter by the Roman Catholic Church, it is difficult to reach any other understanding of Norwegian Church's issuance of its pastoral letter than that abortion was not a matter for compromise. Since its inception, the Norwegian nation had been conceived of as a liberal Democracy – albeit, with a state Church – and was built on many ideas including the ability to compromise.

1111 Sewell, *Logics*, 245.

1112 *Ibid.*

1113 *Ibid.*, 246.

1114 *Hvem, Hva, Hvor 1979: Aftenpostens Aktuelle Oppslagsbok* (Oslo: Chr. Schibsteds Forlag, 1979), 73. Here, *Aftenposten* commented "The new law on abortion has been passed that gives a woman herself the right to decide on the matter within the first twelve weeks of pregnancy. The law has raised

1. A law has now been passed on access to self-decided abortion in our country. There has, for many years, been conflict on this question, conflict in which the Church has also had a strong engagement, from time to time, but without making statements on this practice for which this law now makes allowances.
2. It is important for the Church to speak out about the situation, which has now developed, while not changing the position for which the Church has fought. The holy Gospel says that humans are created in God's image. This also pertains to unborn life from its inception. The Christian conscience is bound by God's word. A nation's law cannot interfere with this relationship.
3. The Church wants now, in its teachings and in its preaching, to uphold the Bible's view of humanity and the responsibility that implies for embryonic life. This life's need for sanctity and its right to worth must be upheld now more firmly than ever. Through its priests, the Church will seek to lead those who, in dealing with this new law and with those who might experience crises of conscience be they individuals, families, health personnel, and others are disturbed by it.
4. The Church will make every effort so that every single mother, without worry, can bear her child. We would hereby encourage everyone who shares the Church's views to participate in this attitude and action with true Christian compassion. And we will never cease to point out the elementary duty of society to care for adequate social security for all mothers.
5. Protecting the unborn life is not only a matter for the Church. It also concerns respect for human life and human dignity in the entire population of the country.[1115]

The letter was simply dated "June 1978" and was signed by ten persons – (Column One) Tord Godal, Dagfinn Hauge, Bjarne O. Weider, Kristen Kyrre Bremer, Erling Utnem, (Column Two) George Hille, Andreas Aarflot, Sigurd Lunder, Thor With and Gunnar Lislerud.[1116]

Just as its 1941 predecessor, the text was confiscated beforehand, not by SIPO (the secret police) but by feminists. Over 10,000 signatures were collected as a protest against the document in the week preceding the reading of the letter. When it came time for Bishop Aarflot to read the pastoral letter in the Ullern Church, situated near the University of Oslo campus, feminists were organized for an ensuing protest. What they either did not realize, chose to ignore, or may even have capitalized upon, was that that particular Sunday was the 75th Anniversary of the dedication of the Ullern Church and that both the King, H.M. Olav V (1937–1991), and the Mayor of Oslo would be in attendance along with a number of political figures. Because of the presence of the King and other dignitaries, there were a number of television cameras also present.

---

no little conflict, not the least of which has been in Church circles themselves. In June, ten Bishops of this country issued a pastoral letter, which was read in most of the pulpits in Norway. The contents of this letter caused resentment amongst many by those who saw it as reactionary and not friendly toward women. All of the Bishops and the majority of Christians in this country saw it, however, as important to make known concern for the lack of protection shown the unborn life which they saw as the meaning for the new law. We give here the pastoral letter in full."

1115 *Ibid.*

1116 *Ibid.*

The women and their supporters went ahead with the demonstration. A number of gay men went along to support the women and when Aarflot began to read the letter, the group moved up in the Church, chanting slogans such as "No to the Church's Misogyny" and "Look at the Church's Double Standard" and "Where is the pastoral letter against the [Vietnam] War?"[1117] The women unrolled a banner and started to play flutes. Some in the congregation put a "stranglehold" on many of the women and shoved them up against the stonewalls of the Church.[1118] In retrospect, Marte Ryste remembered that the gay men acted as a diversion for the women and the men received the brunt of physical damage from the Church attendees.[1119] Eventually, the police, who were waiting outside the Church, arrested the participants in the demonstration and took them into custody. They were each fined between 800 and 1,000 kroner for disturbing the peace, which they refused to pay. They pleaded "not guilty" and explained they had not disturbed a worship service but had demonstrated against Aarflot and his pastoral letter. The matter was set for a trial which, when it happened, was subverted through use of it as a type of "theater." Using total role reversal, men sat wearing dresses and women such as Aud Blegen Svindland, Chair of the Labour Party's Women's Section, wore suits. Svindland also testified as to how the Church had never really cared about women or their human rights.[1120] The group was eventually convicted and a concert to support the group and to pay their fines was put on at Club 7 by a number of artists who donated their time to the effort.[1121]

As part of the abortion debate that continued throughout the spring of 1978 in the pages of Norwegian newspapers, a parade of various experts with varying opinions throughout the pages of the newspapers took on the appearance of a "war" of experts. In late April, *Arbeiderbladet* reported that the number of abortion applications had decreased by almost 10% as had also happened in the same first quarter of the year in 1977. It was the first such decrease since 1964 when an abortion law had been first legislated. But consents for abortion during the same period had risen from 96 to 98.5%.[1122] Some 3,909 applications for an abortion had been handled during the first quarter, 408 fewer than the preceding period. So, despite fewer rejections of applications, the total number of abortions had decreased in Norway.[1123]

1117 Please see source, "Aksjonen mot Hyrdebrev" http://www.kampdager.no/arkiv/abort/abortkamp/hyrdebrev_aksjon.html, accessed May 18, 2006.

1118 *Ibid.*

1119 *Ibid.*

1120 *Ibid.* Aud Blegen Svindland would later be recalled as the "mother" of the new abortion law and is a medical doctor. http://www.nrk.no/programmer/radio/solvsuper/5250803.html, accessed May 19, 2006.

1121 *Ibid.*

1122 "Abort-tallet sinker. Trass i færre avslag", *Arbeiderbladet*, April 26, 1978, 7.

1123 *Ibid.*

In early May, more stories appeared about the Norwegian Central Statistics Bureau (SSB) and its calculation of the number of abortions. Although the SSB had used numbers from only the first quarter of 1978 regarding abortion figures, Dr. Ragnhild Halvorsen was quoted as saying that she "would not be surprised" if the number of abortion applications would continue to decrease in Oslo. The SSB had indicated that the number of abortions in the first quarter of 1978 in relation to the same period in 1977 and had decreased for the entire country. In fact, the number had decreased 10 percent.[1124] In 116 districts the number of abortions had decreased and in some cases, by as much as 20 percent. A total of 3,909 abortion applications had been handled in the first quarter of 1978 and were 498 fewer than during the same period in 1977. Throughout the entire year of 1977, a total of 15,941 applications were handled through the Primary Committee; of these, 15,303 or 96% had been approved and 638 denied. Of those denied, 344 appealed the decision and another 255 were approved, making a combined acceptance rate of 97.4%. Young women below the age of 20 filed the greatest number of applications, accounting for the 42.1% or the total number of applications.[1125]

6.8 Society and Institutional Changes: God, Politics and Abortion

Norwegian Bishops as well as many politicians could not remain silent after the abortion debate. In retrospect, the pastoral letter was only the opening salvo in a national "debriefing" within some segments of Norwegian society. Bishop Tord Godal (1909–2002), head of the Nidaros Diocese (1960–1979), responded to charges made by Labour Party member Geirmund Ihle on 7 June in *Aftenposten*.[1126] Godal addressed Ihle's "suggestion" about the timing and manner that the pastoral letter was presented within the DNK. It had been read from pulpits on 4 June 1978 but the law was passed nine days later, on 13 June 1978.[1127] Faced with this, Godal apologized for the timing of the letter. Despite his apology, Godal had an excuse. The matter had originally been set to come before the Lagting on Friday, 2 June 1978 but, on Thursday, 1 June, it had been postponed one week. Godel noted that it would have been "very difficult" for the Church to adjust its reading of the letter with this short notice.

Godal began his apology by reviewing the opposition the Church had to abortion throughout its history. A Bishop's meeting in 1934 had given serious consideration to

1124 *Aftenposten* (a.m. Edition), May 8, 1978, 6.

1125 *Ibid.*

1126 *Aftenposten* (a.m. Edition), June 15, 1978, 2. Tord Godal was Bishop at the Nidaros Cathedral in Trondheim for almost twenty years, from 1960–1979 and was succeeded by Kristen Kyrre Bremer, 1979–1990.

1127 Law No. 50 of 13 June 1978, "Om Svangerskapsavbrudd", as amended by law No. 66 on 16 June 1978, §4.

the Norwegian government's abortion liberalization and again in 1935, 1938 and 1960. The Bishops had also made a common statement in 1971, entitled "Abortion, human opinion and law."[1128] Throughout this time period, according to Godal, the Church's position had remained the same. "Unborn life" had also been of "essential concern" to the Church and this was the reason that all churches stood together on this point. The Church would never stop reminding society that unborn life was of value and had the right to life.

Ihle had suggested that the DNK's statements seemed to conveniently come out when the Labor Party was in power and that what the Church really wanted was to control Norwegian politics.[1129] To this Godal responded that the church had at all times paid attention to the issue of abortion regardless of party politics or personages. Contrary to Ihle's perception, Godal pointed out that the two most important documents issued by DNK in the twentieth century on the issue of abortion had been issued when non-socialist parties had been in power, in 1934 and 1971.

Godal continued his editorial four days later and again emphasized the point that DNK had maintained a consistent policy toward the politics of abortion. Indeed, he had to continue his editorial because Ihle's memory had apparently been better than Godal's as to which governments – socialist or non-socialist – had been in power when the Church had issued its more serious statements. In an article entitled, "The Same Abortion Position Irrespective of Politics", Godal – again – had to apologize in the opening paragraphs; the DNK's 1971 declaration had not come out under the Borten (non-socialist) government; instead, it had come out under the Bratteli (Ap) government. Godal maintained that all statements, as regarded the 1930s, had been issued without regard to the type of government in power. The 1971 statement had been required since the number of abortions had consistently increased throughout several years. This development was not tied to periods when the Labour Party had been in power, and because of this, Godal could not see how one could say that the Bishop's initiatives were unilaterally aimed at the Labor Party.[1130]

Yet another episode shows show fierce the debate in Norwegian society over the new law was, in contrast to the decade after Roe in the United States. In order to frame and re-frame how society should accept the new law, reliving old political battles – before and during World War II – became standard fare in this debriefing process. Willy Møller added his thoughts to the church's actions in an article entitled "What Anger about the Church's Pastoral Letter?"[1131] Calling the fury that DNK's actions had induced in the Labour Party "grotesque", Møller found this reaction difficult to under-

1128 *Ibid.* "Abort, mennesksyn, lovgivning."

1129 *Ibid.*

1130 *Ibid.*

1131 *Aftenposten* (p.m. Edition), 23 June 23, 1978, 4.

stand.[1132] It was true enough, he said, that the Labour Party had been "in general irritating and irritable lately" but the "magnificent salad" of problems that the Government had found itself in regarding a number of issues could not be laid at the feet of any one party. Møller thought the fury must have some other basis, perhaps in the person of Guttorm Hansen (b. 1920), the Labour Party President of the Parliament.[1133] Hansen had also said that the pastoral letter was a "special form" of Church communication from the bishops and drew a parallel with the letter that had been issued during the occupation in 1941. Møller wrote that Hansen was "obviously ...afraid" that the 1978 letter would have as deep an impact on opinions as the 1941 letter had previously had. Møller believed it could be said that the Labour Party alone could be assessed "full responsibility" for the new abortion law.[1134] And furthermore, according to Møller, it should be remembered that it was the same party that had the "main responsibility" for what the country had lived through beginning on 9 April 1940 when the Nazis began their invasion of the country. It was easy enough to understand how they would react now, in 1978, with such intensity to anything that "smacked of a pastoral letter."[1135] In other words, the Labour Party should be as embarrassed about the new abortion law as it should be embarrassed about how easily the Nazi invasion had proceeded!

The Labour Party retaliated to this type of debriefing by Møller and others. In a June editorial entitled "When Bishops Carry On Politics", Geirmund Ihle and asked why the Bishops had not issued a pastoral letter between 1963 and 1973 when the number of abortions in Norway had quadrupled. Ihle had argued that this had been a period of non-socialist leadership and so should not be blamed for that increase.[1136] But Møller then rejected Ihle's conclusion in that earlier article as nothing but "elementary childish thinking" on the part of Ihle.[1137] Møller said that the Labour Party had "blessed" Nowegians with a law on abortion on 11 November 1960 and all of the abortions that had taken place from then until 1 January 1976, when the Labour Party's abortion law of 13 June 1975 went into full force and effect, were by implication, its fault. Møller noted that the Bishops could have done little during that time.[1138]

Møller also returned to another of Ihle's statements from the same June article, in which Ihle had said that the Church's silence between 1965 and 1973 needed to be contrasted with the 1978 pastoral letter. The Church, according to Ihle, should simply not have involved itself in such an emotional issue. Møller sarcastically recom-

1132 *Ibid.*

1133 Guttorm Hansen was President of the Parliament from 1973–1981.

1134 *Aftenposten* (p.m. Edition), June 23, 1978, 4.

1135 *Ibid.*

1136 *Aftenposten*, June 7, 1978, 3.

1137 *Ibid.*

1138 *Ibid.* "All the abortions from then on until 1 January 1976, when the party's law of 13 June 1975 took effect, occurred under the then current law, about which the Bishops could do very little."

mended that, as soon as possible, Ihle consult with his fellow party member, Guttorm Hansen, who had said during the Lagting's debate that it didn't bother him if the Bishops became involved in "politics" since it was their right.[1139] Obviously cognizant of Labour Party literature on the subject, Møller also recommended that Ihle consult the party's editors who had said the Church could "be at hand and become involved and have the right as a democratic constitutional community to make a target of a law that is under consideration."[1140] Møller finished by saying that the Church had a right to become involved in the matter and that he was "surprised" that the press had reacted against the Church and the social problem of abortion since the Church had a long history of commenting on the problem.

As mentioned above, the Conservative Storting Representative and DNK Bishop, Per Lønning, had resigned after the abortion law had been passed. His interpretation of the episode appeared in the pages of *Aftenposten* in late June.[1141] In an article entitled "What the Pastoral Letter Disclosed", Lønning made it clear that he was not going to again revisit the Church's position on abortion but to "expose" what had taken place in Norwegian culture during the debate.[1142] Lønning wrote that a "church that is awake" would have things to learn from the over-heated debate that had just taken place in Norway.[1143] He admitted, and this gave weight to Ihle's argument, that the Church, although it had a "prophetic calling", need not enter every debate.[1144] Lønning was shaken not only by the intensity of the debate in Parliament, but also perhaps by the strident demonstrations, i.e. women "out of place" accompanied by others routinely kept out of sight and out of mind. How such slogans he had read about and had seen could have come into anyone's mind and had been voiced with such force was a surprise to the Bishop, obviously not familiar with some segments of Norwegian culture and society.[1145]

6.9 Openings for Changes in Other Body Laws

The use of religious dogma in political debate in Norway had not fared well in 1978 and DNK was keenly aware of this. It was almost unfathomable that the KrF, itself vehemently opposed to abortion in all cases, had indirectly caused the passage of the law itself. The FASA social movement, organized in the early 1970s, had tried numerous framings and reframings of the issue but had lost salience – this time – with the

1139 *Ibid.*
1140 *Ibid.*
1141 *Aftenposten* (a.m. Edition), June 23, 1978, 6.
1142 *Ibid.*
1143 *Ibid.*
1144 *Ibid.*
1145 *Ibid.*

Norwegian public. Instead, previously ignored intersubjective groups such as homosexuals[1146] and the "handicapped"[1147] used this opportunity to organize for their own human rights and push their issues into the public's consciousness.

Numerous body laws can become visible once the one in the body of law begins to take on the appearance of irrationality. The webs of these laws are connected and this is demonstrated by the fact that, at the height of the abortion debate, Per Lønning found time to write an op-ed piece for *Aftenposten* entitled "Concerning the Church and Sexual Hostility."[1148] The term "sexual hostility" referred to Øyvind Foss's edited book in which Foss raised significant concerns with the Church's then-current position on homosexuality.[1149] At a time when Lønning was as politically engaged as he was and perhaps considering his own resignation from the Storting, this response shows how important the connections among body laws can be.

There were at least two serious problems for Lønning and DNK with Foss' book. The first was the background of the various authors in the edited work. The book contained articles by Per H. Andersen, a hospital priest at the Ullevål Hosptial since 1975, Sverre Inge Apenes, a priest from Andøy and Drammen and since 1975, a Chaplain for Fagerborg Congregation in Oslo, Svend Bjerg, a lecturer in Systematic Theology at Århus University, Jens Brøndum, a student priest at Danmark's Tekniske Højskole and author of several books, Tor Edvin Dahl, a supporter of the Pentecostal Movement, and Karen-Christine Friele, General Secretary of The Norwegian League of 1948.[1150] Bitten Modal, editor of *Sirene* (The Sirens)[1151] (1973–1976), and who was also on the Board of Directors of the Oslo Women's Feminist Association (1977) and author of several books including "The ABC of an Abortion Application" and "The ABC of Birth Control" contributed to the volume.[1152] In addition, the editor of the book had been a priest in Oslo, Tønsberg and Drammen and was then a student priest at the University in Heidelberg.[1153]

1146 Please see, Øyvind Foss, (ed.) *En seksualfiendtlig kirke?* (Oslo: Gyldendal, 1978).
1147 In September, *Aftenposten* included a two-page spread on people with diabilities engaged in sports. (*Aftenposten* (p.m. Edition), September 23 1978, 18–19.).
1148 *Aftenposten* (a.m. Edition), May 10, 1978, 6.
1149 Øyvind Foss, (ed.) *En seksualfiendtlig kirke?* (Oslo: Glydendal, 1978).
1150 The Norwegian Association of 1948 ("DNF-48") was a previously secret organization, founded by and for homosexuals in 1950. From 1966 to 1971 the group agitated against Criminal Code §213 that made male homosexual acts illegal; these were decriminalized in 1973.
1151 *Sirene* was a feminist periodical, often portrayed as "pornographic" since it included frank discussions of sexuality.
1152 Foss, *Seksualfiendtlig kirke?* Information about the authors in unnumbered *Endpages*.
1153 *Ibid.* Foss' other books included "Report from Berlin and the Treason of the State Church" and "The Church and the Class Struggle." Øyvind Foss was the first gay theologian to "come out" during this time. Karin-Christine Friele and her partner would be the first couple to register in Norway under the Civil Union legislation of 1993.

The second problem was that Berthold Grünfeld, a well-known sociologist had also contributed to the volume.[1154] Grünfeld contributed salient observations about the role of DNK in Norway and the changes that had taken place in society as well as those that were still underway in Norway. The problem was that Grünfeld's observations were confirmed by the abortion debate and vote. He had written that members of DNK – i.e. Norwegian society – had developed an "open attitude" toward sexuality together with the occurrence of the "sexual revolution."[1155] Grünfeld wrote:

> The Church has, to a certain point, has been affected by the secularization process, by ideas from modern psychology and sociology. The Church can no longer attempt to control people's behavior in the area of sexuality by withholding from them knowledge of methods to prevent unwanted pregnancy, as it has done for the last 50–75 years. The intellectualization of society and its democratization make this impossible. Consequently, the Church's techniques of domination have been weakened, and also in this area where it has tried to expand its guardian empire by infiltrating the secular legislation with its system of norms.[1156]

Grünfeld's interpretation of what was happening within secular society had to be answered and Lønning accepted the challenge.

Lønning was given a great deal of space by *Aftenposten* to present his views. He continued his first article in a subsequent issue of the newspaper, finally finishing on the 16th of May. His final paragraph read:

> In short, I do not have enough of a perspective over all the consequences of this issue to make an unambiguous "yes" or "no" [regarding homosexuality]. But the question shall be re-viewed as a question and seriously so. When the Church draws up a vision of Charity based on Biblical faith in Creation, from the Bible itself and its creation story and when it has spread forth the truth on how human recklessness and egoism corrupt all of God's good gifts, can we then think that we can remain in a "no-man's land" such that a human's pressing need to live out his or her sexuality will be ethically legitimated, obviously with the reservations that lie in the sacredness of relationships with one's fellow human beings.[1157]

Lønning had conflicting thoughts on the issue of homosexuality. DNK had said, in 1977, that being a homosexual was not a problem in its eyes but same-sex sexual practices were a problem, i.e. sinful.[1158] Nonetheless, homosexuality was being publicly

---

1154 Foss, ed. *Seksualfiendtlig kirke?* Note 1336. Information about the authors in unnumbered *Endpages*.

1155 *Ibid*., 66.

1156 *Ibid*., 66–67.

1157 *Afternposten* (a.m. Edition), May 16, 1978, 6.

1158 Gro Lindstad, *Norway* in *International Gay Lesbian Human rights Commission Report*, 137 which can be found at http://www.iglhrc.org/files/iglhrc/reports/2OUR_Norway.pdf, last accessed 3 March 20008. The Roman Catholic Church still follows this type of analysis. In 1993, three Bishops in DNK were of the opinion that this thinking should be changed and that homosexuals, even those in relationships, should be allowed to become priests. As of 2007, all candidates to the Nidaros Cathedral

considered, not for the first time, but in an open manner, with real names and faces attached to the issue and with the hope of political power.

Other types of bodies were becoming visible. Life for the "differently abled" was beginning to change but challenges did continue. A handicapped woman, Liv Brandvold, wrote to *Aftenposten* to complain about the shortage of social services for the handicapped. Giving herself as an example, she explained that she had been moved into a special apartment in January 1976 and should have had access to help for 10 hours per week.[1159] Instead, the Røa health and social center had been unable to send any help at all and she had to rely on friends for help for the intervening two years.

While new energy had been used to advance rights for the handicapped, the stigma of being labeled "handicapped" had also continued, 44 years after the sterilization laws in Case One had been passed. In Oslo, mothers who were actively engaged in the care of their handicapped children faced the societal ramifications of governmental categorization of their children. The Norwegian government had set aside monies available to those children who attended childcare facilities. Appropriations of over 3.5 million kroner for extra help at these nurseries had been made available but the government had discovered that some parents had refused to register their children as "handicapped" and that more money was needed since the number of these children had been underreported. KrF was opposed to the idea, saying that, despite the requests for more information from some Oslo childcare centers, the numbers were correct as reported.[1160]

Despite the changes in societal structures and schemas, both DNK and the women's movement would emerge from their political encounters as broken, smaller and potentially less powerful institutions. For the time being, political party structures emerged the victor, better able to assimilate the societal changes that had been undergone. And, in retrospect, the law on abortion and equality between the sexes in Norway seemed to be better situated to handle future challenges than its American abortion counterpart and never completed ERA.

6.10 Changes in the Four Jasanoff Fields

Representations of what was "normal" and "abnormal" in Norwegian society were impacted by science in this case within the public domain just as in the previous,

Bishopric in Trondheim were asked this question, and all gave this same opinion accepting homosexual unions. Indeed, homosexuality was being publicly considered, not for the first time, but for the first time in a manner with real names and faces attached to the issue and with the beginnings of political power.

1159 *Aftenposten* (p.m. Edition), February 8, 1978, 13.

1160 *Aftenposten* (p.m. Edition), April 8, 1978, 8.

earlier case study. And science was lending the weight of its expertise to legitimize those representations. Medicine as an institutional force in Norway had been under social stress, including pressure from women to be medical doctors, for some time. In mid-February 1978, Ruth Remberg wrote an editorial about the history of women as medical doctors for *Aftenposten*; the events of 1978 seemed to beg comparisons with earlier times. Remberg began by contrasting the experience of Germany's first female medical doctor, Dorothea C. Erxleben who became a doctor in 1754 "without any major problems" with that of England's Elizabeth Blackwell who had to emigrate to New York in order to attend medical school. Closer to home, Emma R. Heikel had become a doctor in Finland in 1878 and legislation passed in Denmark on 3 June 1870 had sent "a clear signal" to women that the profession was open to them there. Nonetheless, Denmark was one matter and Norway was another.

Seven years after the Danish decision, Livius Smitt, a nephew of Johan Sverdrup, asked the Storting to "clear up" the matter of women doctors. Seven of the eight medical doctors on the Faculty of Medicine at the University in Oslo opposed the idea of women as doctors. Only Professor Jacob Helberg stood for gender equality. Later, in February 1884, E.H. Berner denounced the idea that women should be permitted to sit for university examinations or be permitted to work as civil servants, which he believed to be a natural consequence of the law of 15 June 1882 that allowed women a higher education.[1161]

As usual, variations that the law could never have foreseen came about. Dr. S. Holth married Marie Spanberg (1865–1942) in 1893. She had studied obstetrics in Germany and the two of them began a practice in Kristiania (Oslo). The Justice Department voted to permit this and the right of a woman to practice medicine was enshrined in K.r. 20/11 of 1897. Between 1893 and 1900, 410 men and 19 women sat for the medical examination in Norway.[1162] The law of 9 December 1912 gave women the right to work as district civil servants and women soon became district doctors. Between 1893 and 1942, the percentage of female doctors remained at approximately the same level – seven percent.

But the institution of medicine would soon be changed as more and more women began to attend university. More would eventually become medical doctors and be admitted to practice around the country. These women were the visible signs that this institution was changing. Women could be carriers of medical expertise. The change in the number of women doctors and student is demonstrated in the following chart.

1161 *Aftenposten* (a.m. Edition), February 14, 1978, 6.

1162 *Ibid.* Ramberg mentions 3 of these 19 "pioneers"; Alexandra Ingier, Alette Schreiner, the first woman to become a member of the Videnskapsakademnet, Elise Dethjoff who worked on TB, and Marie Hjølseth, who was awarded the Skjelderup gold medal for her scientific work.

Table 6.2: Members of the Norwegian Medical Association, 1996[1163]

	Physicians		Students	
Age	**Males**	**Females**	**Males**	**Females**
< 30	307	391	1,042	1,031
30–49	5,766	2,670	135	96
50–69	3,249	619	-	-
> = 70	980	156	-	-
Sum	10,302	3,836	1,177	1,128

An influx of women into medical school and into the profession of medicine began in the age group of 30–49 year olds as of 1996. This meant that these females would had entered school in the years 1976 through 1995, assuming they entered at least as a 20-year-old adult. By 1996, we can see the number of females and males who were members of the Norwegian Medical Association (NMF) who were less than 30 years old was essentially equal. The number of female physicians of all ages who were members of the NMF was also essentially equal with male members of all ages. The increase in female medical doctors less than 49 years old meant that, at least to some increased degree than before, the perceptions of women would be taken into considerations with regard to pregnancy. In addition, even though the work of the midwife had been replaced by hospital stays and medically supervised birth during the course of the early 20th century in the United States, this had not been the case in Norway, where midwives were still routinely used alone or in combination with medical doctors during pregnancy and birth.

DNK was overwhelmed with issues prompted by new scientific breakthroughs and the beginnings of biotechnology. Adding to this, the abortion debate only exacerbated the situation. Abortion as a individual matter, decided in the private sphere rather than in the public realm of the church was originally beyond the comprehension of DNK institutional hierarchy. True, the "defense of unborn life" seemed to have the rhetorical high ground. But the success of the women's movement had, however, been able to capitalize on the discussion about the role of women in society as never before. This movement was so powerful that it was able, as represented in the person of Aud Svindland, to change the thinking of Labour Party women from her identity as a "worker" to that of being of "woman." This was at a time when, in terms of economics, more women workers were employed outside the home than ever before. For Norway, this was a very important schematic and structural societal change.

1163 Øivind Larsen, "Doctors, Migration, and Professional Career" in Øivind Larsen and Bent Olav Olsen (eds.) *The Shaping of a Profession: Physicians in Norway, Past and Present* (Canton, Massachusetts: Science History Publications, 1996), 454.

While medical institutions had been becoming more egalitarian throughout the time period between 1934 and 1978, the institutional Norwegian Church had tried to sidestep the issue of women becoming priests. However, debate on the issuedid not stop. As well, there was a noticeable decline in participation in routine church activities. As Ingrid Bjerkås (1901–1980), the first woman to be ordained in Norway in 1961, so succinctly noted, the Church seemed to be acting in a comfortable isolation."Behind [their resistance to the idea of women priests] is an isolated churchunfortunately more concerned about its self importance and with [a type of] language that people barely understand."[1164] Her appraisal of the situation was that, "on the ground", people were not against the idea of women priests. The idea had not, however, received validation within the institution itself to the extent that some worried about the ERA as mandating acceptance of women as priests.[1165] But institutional change within DNK was not far off and that institution would eventually accept women as priests, indeed as bishops. That institution would not only change to the extent that gender equality extended into the sacristy but that DNK's position on sexuality would be rewritten within the next twenty five years. Persons, who were in committed homosexual relationships, would by 2008, be accepted as priests in DNK.[1166]

In the last quarter of the twentieth century one might have expected the last vestiges of Victorian sexuality to be laid to rest. Women's sexuality had been medicalized during that period in many forms; one way was to portray women as "hysterical." Yet, after all that time, in 1977, a book by Otto Weininger (1880–1903) was translated to Norwegian by Sven Kærup Bjørneboe (b. 1943) and was reviewed by Carl Fredrik Engelstad (1915–1996) in not one, but two articles for *Aftenposten*.[1167] In 1903, Weininger, an Austrian philosopher, published his main work, *Sex and Character,* in which he set out his thoughts on "the woman problem" among other things.[1168] Another consistent theme in Weininger's works is the idea of willing oneself a genius, aided by embracing celibacy. The book is often characterized as misogynist and anti-Semitic but there were some who still praised it.[1169] That Weininger remained an idol with regard to the "woman problem" and that, 75 years after his death, in the midst of agitation for gender equality, that his book should be re-issued is an indication of how strong patriarchal attitudes were. It was also an indication that these ideas are conveniently

1164 *Arbeiderbladet*, January 14, 1978, 16.

1165 *Aftenposten* (a.m. Edition), January 16, 1978, 23. In January, a secretary for the Consumer and Administrative Cabinet Minister, Bjørg Leite, had said that the women priest question was a "borderline" case and that, as the proposal was then written, there would be an exception of the beliefs of a faith community. However, this did not materialize in the law that was actually passed.

1166 Rosemarie Köhn was the first female bishop in DNK; Per Lønning ordained her in 1969.

1167 *Aftenposten* (a.m. Edition), February 6, 1978, 5.

1168 *Ibid.* "Geschlecht und Charakter" The phrase "the women problem" is from a comment by August Strindberg on Weininger's book.

1169 The Nazis used it in their propaganda.

re-cycled form time to time, often with the same type of political proponent and used for the same purpose.[1170]

Various models exist concerning institutional change over time. On such model is that of Stephen Krasner called "punctuated equilibrium." This enjoys "widespread acceptance among institutionalists"[1171] and theorizes that institutions enjoy a long period of stability which are then, from time to time, "'punctuated' by crises that that bring about relatively abrupt institutional change, after which institutional status again sets in."[1172] The problem with this model, is that,institutions explain everything until they explain nothing. Institutions are an independent variable and explain political outcomes in periods of stability, but when they break down, they become the dependent variable, whose shape is determined by the political conflicts that such institutional breakdown unleashes. Put somewhat differently, at the moment of institutional breakdown, the logic of the arguments is reversed from "Institutions shape politics" to "politics shape institutions."[1173]

As Thelen and Steinmo acknowledge, a "more dynamic model is needed to capture the interplay of the two variables over time."[1174] I believe that the dynamism that is needed to explain not only the two variables these editors mention but additional variables is the co-productionist idiom model that I have been using throughout this work. I also agree that the assumption that "institutions explain everything" is a limiting factor in light of how the Jasanoff model works at all levels of society. Granted, to look at all four fields – institutions, discourses, representations and identities – adds more "stickiness" than some researchers might like. But, as a tool for a comprehensive understanding of social change, I think that "stickiness" is well worth the effort.

Despite the fact that the Krasner "punctuated equilibrium" model has been criticized, the idea does fit well with the Pescosolido model that was mentioned in earlier chapters. But the idea of "stickiness", in which normative change factors are intertwinedat all levels works against the idea of any "pure" or "neat" Weberian types[1175] and toward the Tamanaha and the Tuori model for legal norm formation.

1170 *Aftenposten* (a.m. Edition), February 6, 1978, 6. The book reviewer was a well-known author, journalist and Director of the Norwegian National Theater in 1960–1961. To be fair,along with Englestad's second of two articles, another book review was printed and this was of Sissel Lange-Nielsen's book entitled *Hysteria or Sickness: On Women and Psychiatric Problems* published by Pax in 1977.

1171 Kathleen Thelen, Sven Steinmo, and Frank Lonstreth (eds.), *Structuring Politics* (Cambridge: Cambridge University Press, 1992), p. 15. Please see Stephen Krasner, "Approaches to the State: Alternative Conceptions and Historical Dynamics" in *Comparative Politics*, 16 (1984): 223–246.

1172 *Ibid.*

1173 *Ibid.*

1174 *Ibid.*

1175 Although Weber never meant for the "pure" type to be anything other than an abstract conception, it is usually used as leading to an existing reality.

To an extent, the four Jasanoff categories of institutions, discourses, representations and identities are "sticky" factors. They can and often do overlap and the discourse of "woman is worker" is one example of this overlap. In Norway at this time this discourse was particularly salient. For example, an editorial in *Aftenposten* explicitly discussed the essence of "womanhood" and implicitly, the nature of "feminism" when Nina Britt Berge's editorial entitled "Women's rights – quo vadis?" was published in early April.[1176] Berge found it "astonishing" that many women were of the opinion that they represented values other than those possessed by men, the "so-called meek values." Citing to statements by Kaya Irgen and Ingeborg Moræus Hanssen, Berge agreed that it may well have been that the essence of womanhood was different from the essence of male culture. But, for her, "the aim of real equality must be for men to go back to the home and for women in large numbers to go out into the world and make salaries."[1177] And, as noted above, this was what was happening in Norway.

Motherhood can also be seen as an identity, a discourse – even as a representation and institution. What is evidence of one category can and does reinforce other categories. For example, at Easter time, 1978, several articles in *Aftenposten* focused on the role of parents in the lives of children. These children said approximately what social researchers would only confirm later, through various methodological machinations. On the role of woman as cleaner, children wrote such things as "A mother is someone who washes [house/clothes/us]", "Momma washes dishes" and "Momma cleans up – pappa messes things up." When comparing roles in the family, children said, for example, "A mother must do everything – Pappa is good at repairing things." As to temperament, one wrote, "Momma is patient, pappa gets angry quicker." Finally, the role of women in the home was summarized, as "Momma doesn't have any time."[1178] The "patience" of women who were not only mothers but also workers is a classic representation of these meeker values but they also served to reinforce various political models of the institution of motherhood.

The idea that a women's place was primarily or only in the home yielded at this time to the idea that women themselves would decide whether or not to bear children, whether or not to work outside the home and whether or not to be married. As a clue to how institutional politics were affected by these changes, we find that Conservative Party women went on the political offensive in mid-March 1978, looking toward immigrant women for increased membership. With some chagrin, Eva Bull Lund reported that they had "missed a great deal" in not reaching out to immigrant women before. Lund went so far as to appeal to Pakistani families to "not try to become like us"

1176 *Aftenposten* (a.m. Edition), April 5, 1978, 6.
1177 *Ibid.*
1178 *Aftenposten* (a.m. Edition), March 22, 1978, 34.

but to “hold onto their family traditions and their culture.”[1179] The political calculus involved in this statement seemed to be that, rather than take a position against immigrants, as one might expect Conservative Party members to do, immigrants would be welcome, as long as these immigrants held onto their own patriarchal traditions and culture. The goal was to keep women’s status as it had been at any cost, even if this meant reaching out to various, non-white ethnic immigrant groups.

1179 *Aftenposten* (p.m. Edition), March 7, 1978, 4.

7 Comparisons and Conclusions

7.1 Normative Body Categories and Societal Changes

In Case One/Indiana, the two dominant ideological narrative discourses were supplied by science and politics. Science provided the idea of an "eugenics movement" while politics provided the "progressive movement." In some cases the two narratives merged to create the notion that sterilization was a kinder way to achieve Progress and that Progress itself was an ideological narrative that warranted this type of action. The progressive movement existed in a symbiotic relationship with the eugenics movement.

The Committee that held hearings on the sterilization bill in the Indiana Legislature was composed primarily of medical doctors. Even if this was the early days of the field eventually called Genetics, and the "fly room" at Columbia was three decades and half of a continent away,[1180] While I did find that some doctors were well read and up to date with on-going scientific research. These men knew exactly what was at stake. Others, like Dr. Read, were both political agents and medical professionals. Also, there was a network of eugenics supporters in Indianapolis such as Demarchus Brown, the librarian who translated eugenics works from German into English. A number of eugenics enthusiasts, such as Dr. Sharp himself, who traveled from meeting to meeting at regular intervals, bolstered the perceived need for the sterilization law. What Sharp added to the issue was a mentality less than scientific, however. He brought an outlook that was steeped in Victorian sexual norms that found masturbation disturbing and socially counter-productive.

Another dominant discourse at the macro- and meso-level was the fear of "race suicide." This is an old but very reliable phenomenon that is set in motion when some in a nation perceive that the "right" people are not reproducing, and reproducing depends on the "right" place for a woman.[1181] This is one of the reasons why religious institutions are often implicated in the phenomenon. Indeed, today we see signs of the same phenomenon, the "demographic winter" that Christian right-wing groups claim is in the immediate offing for Western Europe.[1182] In 1907, immigrants to the middle west of the United States were reproducing, but they could be from anywhere, and could include Italians or, worse yet, even southeast Slavs. Whites were seeing more African-Americans in what were becoming urban settings. Educated men criticized the on-going fact of lynchings but close proximity between the races was unsettling,

1180 This is a reference to Columbia University and the laboratory that used the common fruit fly (drosephilia melagaster) as a tool for genetic discovery.

1181 Slobodan Milosevic did this with regard to Albanian birth rates in the province of Kosovo prior to the war in Yugoslavia, 1991–1995.

1182 Kathryn Joyce, "Missing the 'Right Babies'" in *The Nation*, March 3, 2008, 11.

especially between white females and Black males. The world was indeed changing – in line with the Pescosolido Model that I used above. Indiana was moving from an agrarian and pre-modern societal structure of nested social and family connections to something else, as yet unknown. And, along with these changing circumstances, individual and societal norms were changing in virtually all levels of society.

Another macro-/meso-discourse was the fight by women for the vote in Indiana at this time and for emancipation in general in the United States. Again, that result was about 20 years in the future. But this social movement also added stress to the schemas (representations and identities) that Indianan society had taken for granted. That this social movement became grafted onto other narratives could have been predicted. In one direction, arguments were that to give women the vote was a "progressive" matter, a matter of fairness and equity. But, in another direction, these women who demanded the vote were often unpredictable. Some could be seen as "real" women and these were women who stayed at home and cared for children and their husbands. But others demanded to work outside the home. What was the proper role for women and who had the authority to tell society that?

These phenomenona, which I have called "intersubjectivity markers" help us to identify the processes that preceded the law that was passed in Indiana. As I have shown, they mediate the articulation and dis-articulation of societal schemas at various times in history. Social movements do their part in this process also, as I have shown through the framing and re-framing processes that went on over time in both countries. But social movements are at the meso-level of societal activity. Beneath those movements, mico-level markers undergird social phenomenon, the body being the most fundamental of all markers.

There also existed "laboratories" for the discursive machines of progressivism, eugenics and race suicide. These were state institutions such as prisons, poor houses and orphanages and private institutions such as wine halls that catered to "fallen" women, alcoholics and those who gambled. While these provided a huge amount of grist for these discursive mills, the amount of actual cause and effect data was very small. Statistics as a academic discipline was only beginning, regression analysis only a dim possibility. Eugenicists such as Galton were at the leading edge of trying to use statistics to prove various assumptions about heredity. These laboratories not only provided an opportunity to classify human beings but also to count them and classify them. Once counted and classified, as in scientific laboratories in general, they also provided an opportunity for experimentation. Dr. H. Sharp was eager to perfect the sterilization procedure and he had a population at his disposal. This population could be a willing population since gaining a measure of control over masturbation was linked to societal and religious schematics. Even eating the right type of cereal developed by John Harvey Kellogg might help one conform to what was expected of a proper citizen.

What was the role of the law and legal institutions? American jurisprudence was being formed in the likeness of the natural sciences at eastern universities. If one applied the right set of legal principles, often based on naturalistic notions, to the facts in a case, one could find the "right" answer to any case. But the social sciences claimed to have discovered certain new, even reproducible, facts. One such emerging discipline was psychology, and the law had to contend with new concepts of insanity. The Thaw trial provided a showcase for these new concepts, labeling the entire affair a case of "*dementia Americana*." But this period raised significant questions about how, or if, to incorporate social science data into legal rulings. Indeed, at a more basic level, was social science even a "science" at all?

The often-cited to ruling in Buck v. Bell, written by Justice Holmes, in which he writes that "three generations of idiots is enough" as supporting the sterilization of a young woman, Carrie Buck, would seem to be a good reason – in retrospect – for not incorporating social science, or even "hard" scientific data into decision-making by judges. Like many of the personalities involved in these two case studies, Holmes considered himself a progressive. The best scientific evidence available to him, i.e. eugenics and the classification of "idiots" through testing, led him and others to consider the decision in Buck as fair.

Later, in discussing Skinner v. Oklahoma, I described how the sterilization of a confirmed criminal male was voided for lack of due process requirements. True, this signaled a new era in American jurisprudence, to the detriment of *stare decisis*, but did this actually change anything "on the ground?" The answer is "No" and here we see how important the intersubjective markers are in the process of change and the ebb and flow of scientific "truths."[1183] Had Holmes considered the intersubjective markers of his day and age as compelling evidence of inequality, he might not have been so sure of his opinion even if hard science was telling him one thing and society another. Had those who decided Skinner looked at the status of women, they could not have been sure that it was properly decided either. Does this mean that cases cannot be decided only on the facts themselves? Does this mean that the meso- and the micro-levels of society are interconnected through the body of the individual, whether it be the body of Carrie Buck or of the chicken-thief Mr. Skinner? I will address this issue below.

In Case One/Norway, the same types of meso-level phenomenon were in play although not in with the same intensity. Progressivism was not as pronounced a phenomenon in Norway as in the United States, but the eugenics movement and the idea of "race suicide" certainly were paramount in the minds of those who legislated Norway's sterilization law in 1934, 24 years after Indiana. The idea that the body politic was at risk was also addressed, although not as often as the "race-suicide" notion in Hoosier newspapers. In *Aftenposten*, for example, one could read about "fewer

1183 Please see, Allison C. Carey, "Gender and Compulsory Sterilization Programs in America, 1907–1950" in *Journal of Historical Sociology*, 11, (1998) 74–105.

births in Oslo" in 1933, down to a level of 8.10[1184], "the lowest [level that] has been recorded."[1185] World War II also loomed on a very close horizon and Norwegian newspapers published articles about the German eugenics movement on a regular basis.[1186]

Perhaps the most significant propagandist for the eugenics movement in Norway was Dr. A. Mjøen who, like Demarchus Brown in Indiana, supplied legislators with an on-going source of eugenics materials. Mjøen's links to the German eugenics movement are documented here as elsewhere. Oslo doctor, Dr. Otto Mohr, who had done work at Columbia University with Thomas Hunt Morgan, was one of the persons who suspected Mjøen's scientific work. But, based on the written Storting record, none of the legislators – save Representative Bonde – nor the legal personalities involved, including the State's Attorney, seemed to doubt Mjøen and only applauded his work. In terms of the three Norwegian newspapers from 1934 that I reviewed, Dr. Mohr kept a rather low profile.

Dr. Mohr did confide his "fear" of what was taking place to American birth control activist Margaret Sanger. He wrote that he feared the "so-called 'objective' scientist" when s/he were dealing with subjects "not strictly scientific." I believe he had Mjøen in mind, or other scientific experts of the day who became involved in politics, when he made this rather prescient statement. The caste of medical experts in Norway was similar to that in Indiana. The main medical propagandists in Norway, Doctors Vogt, a psychologist, Scharffenberg, an institutional physician, and Mjøen had, as their American equivalents Doctors Butler, Hurty and Sharp.

But Case One/Norway was different in that it had its own set of intersubjective markers. Instead of African Americans such as in Indiana, Norway had its "taterne" and ethnic Sámi population. And, true to the pattern that was seen in the United States and, despite whatever group the original legislation had targeted, i.e. the handicapped and mentally ill in this case, the group that was legally "touched" was eventually expanded to include these ethnic intersubjective groups. At this same time, women in Norway were also demanding a less restrictive birth control and abortion legal atmosphere. The "Mothers Hygiene Clinics" had survived various legal hurdles but universal access to birth control information and/or materials or abortion was not on the legislative horizon. Women were also being fired from jobs just because they

---

1184 *Aftenposten*, (a.m. Edition), May 9, 1934, 3.The article does not give any information about how this number was calculated, only that in 1933, 2107 children were born in Oslo – 1105 boys and 1002 girls. There were 16 deaths within 24 hours of birth of the 2107 children. The article does say that, in contrast to the 8.10 figure for 1934, in 1925 that number was 10.44, in 1920 it was 18.65 and in 1915 it was 20.08. Given that the population of Oslo in 1925 was 255,700, I suspect that 8.10 is the number of births per 1000 citizens. But what I want to focus on is that the perception given in *Aftenposten* that births were decreasing, whether or not they really were.

1185 *Ibid.*

1186 For example, *Aftenposten*, (p.m. Edition), February 10, 1934, 3. The headline is "Is the white race doomed to extinction?" This article was based on the periodical *Norges Vern* (The Defense of Norway).

were married. While this made sense to some in the Labour movement in Norway, it was an issue that would not recede into the background very soon.

Also tearing at the fabric of social cohesion was the fact of unemployment in 1934 in Norway. Urban centers were beginning to grow, just as had happened earlier in Indiana. But the infrastructure could not accommodate the growth. In addition, strikes and labor unrest was rife, and as Dahl so succinctly puts it, Norway was "a picture of a society at war with itself and those who govern [were] not capable, or willing, to point out how to get out of th[e] mess..."[1187] People looking for work were on the street as well as people without a place to live. Social order was an issue for the police as well as for the government.

One of the ways to move vagrants, or of persons seen as a "weak we" body out of the capital was to put them in a legal or a medical institution. The two legal cases, of Mrs. Tilka and Aagot Hansen, demonstrate how these "weak we" bodies became the sites of articulation and disarticulation of these structures. Tilka had stolen a pair of pajamas and Officer Riisnæs testified against her, despite the fact that her competence was clearly an open question. Hansen, on the other hand, had actually been sent to an institution for the insane, and the doctor who had signed her assessment was charged with unlawful imprisonment.

The Norwegian legal system was overloaded and needed structural reform, as several practitioners noted. But Scandinavian Legal Realism seemed to be of little help to the Mrs. Tilka's of Norway – any more than American Legal Realism was of use against the Joseph Lochner's[1188] of the United States. Neither of these two legal systems, as distinct from one another as one could find at this time and place, could not accurately consider Aagot Hansen's competence or the condition of a baker's lungs who worked more than 60 hours week in a confined space with flour in the air. The law was too slow and theory laden, in both Indiana and Oslo, to be of use on a day to day basis, in light of the shifting social schemas that history presented.

In Case Two/Connecticut, a new reproductive technology emerged again in conjunction with social fragmentation and schematic disarticulations. The organization,

---

1187 Hans Fredrik Dahl, *Norge Mellom Krigene*, 15.

1188 Please remember that Lochner v. New York, 198 U.S. 45, 25S. Ct. 539, 49 L. Ed. 937 (1905) was a 5-4 decision USSC case and said that the freedom to contract had been violated by the arrest of Joseph Lochner, the owner of a Utica New York bakery. Mr. Lochner had allowed a baker to work more than the 60 hours per week in violation of the then 1895 New York "Bakeshop Act." This Act had set the working hours for bakeshop employees as 60 hours per week, 10 hours per day. USSC rejected the New York state law that was intended to safeguard public health and upon which the arrest was predicated since anyone was free to contract as he or she willed and circumstances outside the "four corners" of the contract could not be considered. Ironically, Oliver Wendell Holmes, Jr., who wrote the majority opinion in Buck, wrote the dissenting opinion in Lochner. To be fair, Lochner could never have been decided in Norway as it was in the United States, especially after the nascent Labor Movement took hold in Norway.

Planned Parenthood of Connecticut, could not have know at its inception that the research into synthetic hormones would eventually replace birth control methods of the day or increase the availability far beyond what it had been, mostly due to market influences. But as a part of a social movement, whose strength had waxed and waned for decades within Connecticut, as well as other states, it contributed to establishing a test case that would wend its way to the United States Supreme Court. Unlike in Norway, which also had a similar movement, this was a choice that Planned Parenthood of Connecticut made because the legislative route had been foreclosed to them. The Norwegian Parliament was metaphorically large enough for these discussions and for independent decision-making, unlike the state legislature in Connecticut. Even the medical institution in Connecticut could not influence the Connecticut legislature and this was because of religion in addition to the schematics attached to the role of the woman. The PPC had no option but to either wait for disarticulation while trying to educate society or move to legal institutions.

As I noted, the first Chase Dispensary case in 1939 was a prelude to the 1965 Griswold case. The year 1939 was one of dread within the United States as a war loomed on the horizon. The Roman Catholic Church in Connecticut had created alternative social structures for an immigrant population, educating children in Catholic schools, even importing various orders of nuns from different European countries as teachers for its ethnic immigration populations. In this respect, the Roman Catholic Churches actually catered to different national immigrant groups. But, an earlier set of immigrants had already been educated in the New World, and, for example, Irish-Americans in Hartford sat in positions of power in both the religious and secular arenas.

By the 1960s, the Roman Catholic Church still had a great deal of power in the lives of Connecticut Catholics. However, a more pluralistic society had been formed during those intervening thirty years. In addition, changes were being set in motion within the Roman Catholic institution itself. Reverend Cryne, Judge Fitzgerald and Attorney Healey were either dead or elderly and in the early 1960s and the generation of young Irish men in line to take their places would face a set of searing social movements, all seeking some measure of relief from the religious – and legal – institutions, schemas and resources that these men represented. While there would always be men such as James Morris, the devout Catholic who first instigated the police investigation of Estelle Griswold's clinic, and while the numbers of men and women like him would fluctuate over the next decades, it was unlikely that there would continue to be the obedient masses who listened to the Waterbury Proclamation written by Cryne and his council in 1939, especially in light of the Vatican II Council.

Dr. John Rock is an example of the embodiment of these social and religious disarticulations. From being a devout Roman Catholic and medical practitioner/researcher as a young and middle-aged man, he died as a non-Catholic. One could say his Church left him over the issue of birth control rather than that he left his Church. Sadly, his belief in individual conscience would be reintegrated by the Second Vatican Council, but too late for Rock as an individual Roman Catholic.

The genesis of the birth control pill and its testing on non-white women is also an intersubjectivity marker.[1189] It is similar, but not identical, to the now infamous "Tuskegee Experiments" in which black men, without any measure of informed consent, were used to track the medical effects of syphilis. The reproductive technology that the "pill" represented was marketed to first world women, who were ready for it, since at least two waves of the women's movements had lobbied for safe and reliable birth control methods over decades. These were decades that included Dr. Hannah Stone's importation of condoms from Japan and Judge Frankfurter wondering on behalf of his hypothetical "friend" if the friend's collection of sausage casings was illegal. It is clear that both areas of social analysis were changing – again – just as the Tamanaha theory might predict.

Estelle Griswold and the PPC had felt it necessary to switch pressure from one branch of government to another – from the legislative to the judicial branch of government. Thus, they began developing test cases aimed at securing birth control. Because no such similar case existed in Norway, other than perhaps the Knudsen Case, which is not exactly "on point", I was left with American case law to examine with Parliamentary legislation that gave Norwegian women themselves the right to decide to have an abortion within the first 12 weeks of pregnancy.[1190]

Adjudication in the United States has always been problematic in that it represents the intersection of political influences, claims of *stare decisis* and objectivity, as well as jurisprudential theory. These are major areas of influence, thought and exploration. At the appellate level, Americans are left with only "the black letter of the law", i.e. transcripts from the trial level. Law made above the trial level does not have the benefit of facial expressions, body language and neither does it have the intensity of legislative debate. Only abstract principles and the epistemic "Finding of Fact" remains from the earlier trial process. True, some Justices such as Frankfurter would use oral arguments for investigating those earlier events. In Buxton, he had asked the state's attorney whether or not the law was based on the "assumption that procreation is the only justification for conjugal relations?... Increase and multiply is the inarticulate[d] purpose of your legislation[?]"[1191] Despite Frankfurter's questions, he authored a decision in that case saying there was really no actual issue in play. But,

---

1189 For an overview of the development of reproductive technology, please see the four articles by Clarke, Kammen, Oudshoorn and Marks in Part 1, "Conceptions and Counterperceptions: User involvement in the Development of Contraceptive Technologies" in Ann R. Sætnan, ed., *Bodies of Technology: Women's involvement in repreductive medicine* (Columbus: Ohio State University Press, 2000).

1190 The phrase "on point" is American juridical phrase for whether or not the facts of one case are similar to another case. In this respect a case can be spoken of as on "all fours", meaning complete factual similarity, or on "all threes", not quite similar, etc.

1191 *Waterbury Republican*, March 3, 1961, 1.

as is common in American law, the concurrence that Justice Brennan wrote, "practically invited another lawsuit."[1192]

In Case Two/Connecticut, the judiciary was faced with a situation often described as "when law runs out." Would Justice Douglas use the deductive model, precedent or the policy model for adjudication of Griswold?[1193] Douglas, whom some claim as having been sloppy and/or lazy in Griswold, basically chose the policy model by finding law in the penumbra of the Constitution. The works of Betty Freidan in the Griswold file at the Library of Congress attest to this. As Duncan Kennedy writes, the policy model is often – intuitively – perceived as a "Trojan horse for ideology."[1194] This notion, taken together with the idea that within the "argumentative strategies (deduction, precedent, policy) that apply across the range of legal questions, there is a subset of rights arguments that are virtually identical to those used in political rights discourse", created the "right to privacy" in Griswold, a case "favorably disposed to [huge] ideological stakes."[1195]

Peter de Marneffe has written that Griswold cannot be "reconciled with the principle of popular sovereignty [but] how much should this worry us if we believe that Griswold is nonetheless a morally correct decision?"[1196] Today, Griswold remains as to left wing American politics as Parents Involved is to right wing politics, since ideology is also at the disposal of all citizens.[1197] But popular sovereignty is still not the bottom where the rock thrown off the Griswold cliff will eventually land. This ideological "virus", ideology being only one of these viruses, has been scrutinized by the CLS movement and has interjected into legal discourse I have outlined above. It speaks to a basic flaw in Liberalism as practiced in the United States; it "infects" on a regular basis. As Kennedy writes:

> It undermines the broad Liberal consensus not just about how society should be but about how it pretty much, with warts, is organized, namely, in accord with the principles of individual rights, majority rule, and the rule of law. It suggests that, appearances to the contrary notwithstanding, *it isn't organized that way in fact, and won't be even after reform of the judiciary.*[1198]

This, of course, is a matter for another work.

1192 Susan C. Wawrose, *Griswold v. Connecticut*, 79. Note 917.

1193 Duncan Kennedy, *A Critique of Adjudication (fin de siècle)* (Cambridge, Mass.: Harvard University Press, 1997), 97.

1194 *Ibid.*, 133.

1195 *Ibid.*, 318.

1196 Peter deMarneffe, "Popular Soverignty and the Griswold Problem", *Law and Philosophy*, 13 (1994): 110.

1197 Please see Justice Roberts' opinion in the decision, Parents Involved in Community Schools v. Seattle School District No. 1, 551 U.S. 701, 127 S.Ct. 2738, 75 U.S.L.W. 4577 (2007), metioned above.

1198 Kennedy, *Critique*, 206. Note 1384 (Emphasis mine.)

In Case Two/Norway, the legal institution was not involved as intimately in the abortion and gender equality laws in Norway as the American judiciary had been in that half of this Case. That, in itself, is a significant cultural difference between how law was used to incorporate social change in these two countries. The co-productionist idiom is clearer in the Norwegian portion since we have the political personalities and their maneuvers, as well as the vote in the Parliament to review. In the American half, assuming that the motivation for Justice Douglas' decision in Griswold was not only legal, as the Freidan speeches and texts in Douglas' Griswold files would seem to indicate, the only option that remains is to speculate as to motivation. One could argue that Douglas was only following his oath of office – and the maxim of *stare decisis* – in rendering his decision, but that is not very satisfying as an explanation. In the Norwegian half of this Case study, the debate was influenced by politics, social movements, religion, medicine – even exorcism – in a heady, "sticky" mixture of action and reaction. But, in the end, it was more public than how the law was co-produced in the United States. Only one major legal case, albeit an important case, was launched in reaction to the abortion law in Norway.

Case Two/Norway exemplifies the legislative route to law making. The framing and re-framing of arguments by various sectors of the Norwegian political spectrum spanned all the nuances of the 1978-abortion/gender equality laws that could be entertained. But issues attached to reproductive technologies do not exist in isolation. As we saw in Case One/Indiana, the right to vote for women existed side by side with the "fact" that educated women in particular were not having enough children, and commonly portrayed as preferring dogs to babies. This type of rhetoric was not seen in Case One/Norway but the birth control and abortion issues were debated, and indeed linked, to the sterilization law. In the American half of Case Two, birth control in Connecticut soon became linked with abortion and, in Norway, abortion was linked with gender equality. None of these issues could have existed in isolation because of the structures, schemas and resources that were implicated. Societal coherence – or disarticulation – rests on interdependencies and articulations of structures, schemas and resources. The model of Norwegian society had also changed over the intervening years in line with the Pescosolido model moving from a pre-modern to modern society.

In the case of Norway, a large social movement that had developed – again, over the decades – that was already in the first stages of internal disintegration in 1978. But for one moment in 1978, however, a moment imbued with Sewellian sense of historicity, the Women's Movement had enormous power. I have discussed this moment as the Sunday in June when the religious service in Ullern was disrupted – before God, King and the Mayor of Oslo. In short, before the apparent heads of the political and religious institutions of Norway, feminists and gay men disrupted the Church service, protesting against the use of the pastoral letter by DNK on abortion. What had happened between 1934 and 1978 that allowed this type of activity by these people? During World War II, DNK had, and maintained, a prophetic voice against the Quisling regime but by 1978, a social movement who force DNK to reassess its opinions.

What had happened in the 40+ years after the passage of the sterilization law, was that women had entered the labor market, in a country where a significant role had been played by the labor movement. But they were disillusioned, as Willy Martinussen has demonstrated. And, as Table 6.6 shows, above, it was not only women but also men that were disillusioned. In 1969, in the age group 20–30, upwards of 80% - 90% of vocationally trained workers were disillusioned. Professional workers were also disillusioned but not to the extent that vocational-trained workers were. In addition, the influence of the state Church in Norway had diminished since World War II, used primarily for marking life passages rather than for day-to-day inspiration or for guidance on political matters. DNK had gone from being a *de jure* as well as a *de facto* national Church to being only a *de facto* national Church for many citizens.

Debate over abortion and gender equality legislation was played out in the public sphere. But the emotional hysteria of the times was also played out in the hexical possession of a young girl. This brought religious and medical institutions into conflict, psychiatry and exorcism into the public consciousness. Debate became less and less "reasoned", even among Church leaders on the national television station, NRK. At the lead in acrimonious assaults – in the name of the "just" cause – was FASA, the People's Action Against Self-Determined Abortions. This religiously motivated membership would use almost any means necessary to win their battle for "unborn life." One Pastor Knudsen embodied the tension between DNK as a national Church and the political debates that were occurring by proposing a strike by Church priests. Only one other priest joined this strike, but his case did eventually end in the Supreme Court of Norway.

We can see at this time another important societal schematic disarticulation not only in the body but also in the identity of a woman. Was a woman who was a member of the Arbeiderparti in Norway, a woman first or a worker first? This question was played out in the vote by the Women's Secretariat of the Ap whether or not to support the 1978 abortion legislation. Aud Svindland cast the determining vote that had that body supporting the legislation. Rather than align themselves with workers who had various disagreements with the legislation, two of the four members voted to identify themselves as women first and workers second. This was an unique moment in Norwegian labor history.

7.2 Conclusions Based on the Jasanoff Fields and Idiom of Co-production

With regard to Case One, we see that various types of bodies became the focus of the law at this epistemically uncertain time. I conclude that whether it be parliamentary-created law in Norway or legislatively-created law in the United States, at a time of "moral panic" or Pescosolido shifts, law incorporates societal norms as legal norms so that real, human bodies are affected, usually bodies belonging to intersubjective categories, i.e. the "weak we." With regard to Case Two, where judge-made law became the vehicle for social norm inclusion in the United States as opposed to parliamentary-created law in Norway, the reverse process can be seen. Social norm changes take place through shifts in the co-production of knowledge by social institutions, identities, discourses and representations. This is after the process described by Sheila Jasanoff and her "co-productionist idiom" as she describes it pertaining to the co-production of knowledge in the field of science. Despite the two countries having a number of geographic, demographic and economic dissimilarities, the intersubjective categories formed along the same lines in both, i.e. along lines of gender, race/ethnicity, etc. And, despite the dissimilarities in legal theory, similar laws were passed. With regard to both cases, we can see that epistemic uncertainty did not exist only within society at large but also within jurisprudential arenas, i.e. within the framework of what was take to be sound or unsound legal theory.

In Both Case One and Case Two, the representations that I considered were those that Science made in the public space. The intersections of Science with Religion and/or Law were also considered. I also considered social institutions in both Cases. They were in the process of change due to shifting societal structures, schemas and resources. These shifting societal structures were examined. In Case One /Indiana, social kinship ties were under stress as children left farms to work in automobile plants in Detroit. The intersection of races and ethnic groups became inevitable. Patriarchy was under stress in that women had had access to education for some time and were demanding the vote.

Discourses as a source of co-production were also considered. In Case One/ Indiana, the discourse of "race suicide" was often a commentary on educated and upper-class women limiting family size as well as being a criticism of large immigrant families. The discourse of "degeneration" was also tied to gender in this fashion as well as being tied to the sterilization of "confirmed criminals." Discourses often do not work alone and the eugenics-race suicide discourses complemented each other very nicely. But each had its unique corollary discourses. Representations of what was "natural" in the social world created boundaries that individuals crossed only at their peril. Masturbation was "unnatural" and displayed a lack of self-control. Help to control this impurity, a focus for Comstock and his allies, was found in the most advanced technology the medical profession had to offer – a vasectomy. The main researcher in this area, Dr. Sharp, and his circle of male medical professionals, politicians and social activists saw a way to help society "progress." Social schemas surrounding ideas of "purity" and "obscenity" combined with the polysemious resources these men possessed insured the passage of the Indiana sterilization law.

Later, in Norway, the same processes came into play. The names of those with resources were different, but the same sort of schemas, institutions and discourses were similar in form and content. When Margaret Sanger visited Norway in 1934, she saw similar doctors with similar ideologies in Norway as in the United States. What she found was that Norwegian women were already fully engaged in the same process with the same birth control/abortion ideology. But there were "parasites" on the Norwegian body politic and these needed to be exterminated just as weeds in a farm acreage. Progress needed to be efficient and productive. In Norway, the object of this "parasite"/"degenerate" discourse had changed from "confirmed criminals" to the mentally ill and developmentally delayed. The boundaries of this law were no more secure than were the boundaries of American law vis-a-vis criminals.

In Case Two/Connecticut I had the opportunity to examine how the religious institution of the Roman Catholic Church entered into the reductionist discourses of what the proper role for a woman was. This is not unique to this denomination but it was the one Church that was most obviously at work in Connecticut at this time and place. The ideology of the "family" was set into play by this religious institution with regard to birth control legislation. Jon Bernardes writes that:

> 'Family ideology' is...a multi-layered system of ideas and practices which hold "the family" to exist, to be 'natural' and universal. 'Family ideology' interlocks with gender ideology and wage labour ideology to form the major part of contemporary dominant ideology.[1199]

Given these interlocking layers of ideas of practices, which I investigated, it is not difficult to see why the battle was waged with such intensity. Given this Church as an institution and the legislature as an institution plus the discourses and representations from both as to what a "real", a "natural" woman was and did, it is also not difficult to see why, even in the early 1960s, the Connecticut state legislature was not anywhere near repealing its "little Comstock" law even if the majority of medical doctors insisted it should be repealed.

I also examined, as part of the Jasanoff idiom, the role of co-production of identities. These two societies were firmly in the grip of the forces of modernization. Women were joining the work force in numbers not seen since World War II and the "pill" was making this easier to do. Women were perceived as deserting the "private sphere" for the "public sphere", a forum that was "unnatural" for them. And, by the turn of the 20–21st century, the female body would be "not-wholesome" again. The discourses would have changed 180 degrees from one in which medical professionals wanted to prevent the birth of "defectives" and "degenerates" to one in which medical professionals would be technological "fathers/mothers" to better, even "perfect" children that some insisted upon.

As Alexis de Tocqueville had earlier noted with reference to America, "Scarcely any political question arises in the United States that is not resolved, sooner or later, into a judicial question."[1200] This is exactly what happened in Case Two/Connecticut

1199 Jon Bernardes, "'Family ideology': identification and exploration", *Sociological Review*, 33 (1985): 291, 288.
1200 Alexis de Tocqueville, *Democracy in America* (1835), Vol. 1, Chapter 6.

as legal practitioners joined forces with the women's birth control movement, shaping and refining a set of facts in a series of cases until one eventually made its way to the Supreme Court. Not only did this half of Case Two provide an opportunity to dissect judge-made law but it is also a powerful contrast to the Norwegian half of Case Two in which the political question was resolved in the political venue. Justice Douglas' opinion in Griswold, while ostensibly pertaining only to married couples that sought to buy and use birth control technology, essentially opened a fifteen-year era of legal refinement of the "right to privacy", from considerations of abortion (Roe[1201]) to sodomy (Bowers[1202]). The original "body" boundary had been loosened, in a manner similar to Case One, but this time from that of a married woman to unmarried citizens, heterosexual and homosexual.

In Case Two/Norway, a bloody political battle that wearied the majority of the population took place. Again, the main institution, apart from political parties that engaged in the legislative process was a religious institution. Again, the 1978 Norwegian law on abortion and gender equality took place later than in did in the United States. But in the time period between Case One and Case Two in Norway, forms of religiosity had decreased and the "national" Church of Norway, DNK, had become a nationalistic icon used for socio-cultural significant events. This is not to say that the People's Action Against Self-Decided Abortion, FASA, which was rooted in DNK identities and discourses was not a vocal and a strong movement. But, in the end, it was this intensity that was its undoing.

In a country with a strong labor movement, large segments of the working population were "disillusioned" and felt as if they were being discriminated against. The women's movement in Norway had also reached its zenith and with the saliency of FASA and DNK reduced, the 1978 law on abortion was passed. But the further passage of an ERA in Norway is especially significant when contrasted with how the ERA is dormant in the United States. While a discussion of the reasons for its passage in one country and not the other is well beyond the scope of this work, some of the factors involved surely included the labor movement history in Norway and the law on the right to work as well as the change in societal schemas that made living together as "samboer" ("co-inhabitants") and having children easier, eventually culminating in various laws on the rights of unmarried mothers and fathers and their children. Roughly half of all births in Norway as of this writing are outside of the institution of marriage. In addition, more emphasis was placed

---

1201 Please see Emily Bazelon, "The Place of a Woman on the Court" in *New York Times Magazine*, 7 May 2009, accessed on Novemeber 5, 2009 at http://www.nytimes.com/2009/07/12/magazine/12ginsburg-t.html?pagewanted=1&_r=1. Justice Ginsburg is quoted as saying that she thought there was a concern "about population growth and populations we don't want to have too many of."

1202 The case Bowers v. Hardwick, 478 U.S. 186 (1986) overturned a sodomy law that criminalized sodomy between consenting adults.

on the rights of children in Norway than in the United States. Norwegian children are secure in their right to the material needs of life rather than, for example, in the America where the focus is on abstractions such as "life, liberty and the pursuit of happiness."[1203]

As Jasanoff points out, "social theory and research have taught us that the boundaries separating regions of power are seldom innocent and that between the law and policy is no exception."[1204] These boundaries are "laboriously achieved" by

> effort and resources – material, economic, discursive to produce them and to hold them in place. Not all actors have equal means to participate in, let alone effectively criticize, the boundary work performed by major social institutions.[1205]

The actors involved in Case One/Indiana such as the criminal, the immigrant, the African-American, and the institutionalized poor/sick could not effectively criticize the major social institutions of the day. Therefore, their bodies were, sooner or later, the focus of "body-law", which just happened to use the technology of surgical sterilization. Their bodies became visible. This situation was completely reversed in Case Two, were these groups had significantly more power than at any other time in history. The same could be said for Norway with the insertion of Sàmi and taterne for African American or immigrant. Because of how the law was co-produced, we can expect the boundaries of the law to move, which is what happened.

So we are left with no real assurances that a given law that is passed by a legislature or a Parliament, or adjudicated in the United States or Norway, will be closer to any one end or the other of the Case One-Case Two spectrum. Over and over again, we saw that good intentions are simply that and no predictor of a "just law." My conclusion is that the one of the major predictors of "good law" is what the status of intersubjective markers is at that time and place/in the world. And these factors will hardly ever be scrutinized unless law is de-mystified.

1203 Please see, to begin with, 8 April. nr. 7 1981 *Lov om barn og foreldre (barnelov)*. Norway is also a signatory to the United Nations Convention on the Rights of the Child as of 1999.
1204 Sheila Jasanoff, "The Life Sciences and the Rule of Law", *The Journal of Molecular Biology*, 319 (2002), 894.
1205 *Ibid.*

7.3 Intersubjective Bodies as Barometers of Moral Panic, Structural Change and Epistemic Uncertainty

> It is perhaps conceivable that an epistemology without an ethos may exist, but we have yet to encounter it. As long as knowledge posits a knower, and the knower is seen as a potential help or hindrance to the acquisition of knowledge, the self of the knower will be at epistemological issue.
>
> Lorraine Daston and Peter Gallison[1206]

> The bodies we meet [...] are a singularly sorry lot: bodies [...] afflicted with disease, bent by paralysis... These are certainly not the bodies spotlighted by Greek philosophy or existential phenomenology, which are hale and healthy organisms, upright, agile, agential bodies that move with ease and alacrity through the *Lebenswelt*; Philosophy's bodies are active and well, every one a *corpus sanum* cut to fit a *mens sana*, a fit organ of the soul or a suitable seat from which to launch intentional acts.
>
> John D. Caputo[1207]

French sociologist Pierre Bourdieu thought that besides politics, something else was at work in society, something he termed a "double naturalization." This took place **in bodies and things** through a "silent and invisible agreement between social structures and mental structures."[1208] What Bourdieu called the "law of the social body" was converted into the "law of the physical body" and this was no more apparent than in the "dominated habitus" of gender, culture and language.[1209] The social world was one of domination, of unequal distribution of "symbolic capitol" and the "inescapable dialectic of distinction and pretension it activates."[1210] And, as Bourdieu knew, there can be a "disconnect" or a "maladjustment" in society which can, with difficulty, be utilized to shatter the status quo.

A mere change in consciousness is not enough. But, should the field of politics enter, he thought that then alternative political futures were a possibility. One good example of Bourdieu's "disconnect" and of how bodies become both the subject and object of the medicine took place prior to the American Civil War (1861–1865). In 1860, Dr. Samuel Cartwright discovered a new illness that he called "draptomania." The symptomology for this new illness was that black slaves ran away from their masters and that they did this repeatedly.[1211] Cartwright's analytical mental process

1206 Lorraine Daston and Peter Gallison, *Objectivity* (New York: Zone Books, 2007), 40.
1207 John D. Caputo, *The Weakness of God* (Bloomington and Indianapolis: Indiana University Press, 2006), 132.
1208 *Ibid.*
1209 *Ibid.*
1210 *Ibid.*, 21.
1211 Troy Duster, "Lessons from History: Why Race and Ethnicity Have Played a Major Role in Biomedical Research" in *Journal of Law, Medicine and Ethics*, 34 (2006), 495.

might have been to ask why would a black slave want to run away from a kind master, assuming of course that a strict or even brutal master was better than no master – for the slave. Obviously, the slave must be medically ill. And, the scientific method proves this. Cartwright's hypothesis was that slaves who run away from owners have a disease. His method might have been to see if one puts a slave with an owner, will that slave run away? Cartwright's data was that this happened to numerous slave owners. The experiment was even repeatable. Cartwright combined ideology with science to "medicalize" the effort of slaves to seek freedom.[1212] The same type of process happens in the hybrid medico-legal field that I investigate in this work, i.e. "body law."[1213]

There is a great deal of comparative historical evidence showing a "relationship of medical knowledge to both transformations in basic science knowledge and to social and political reformulations about what bodies and populations mean to society."[1214] I assume that the practice of science informs society and vice-versa within both the medical and the socio-political and cultural arenas – which the law mediates. Discussions of one's national population, its vigor, lack of vigor or the less-than- "normal" traits of its darker-skinned inhabitants often rest for their political salience on science of a sort, in addition to politics, social constructions – or even religion.[1215] I assume that the reformulation of what a body means, for example, of an immigrant, a mentally ill person, an alcoholic, a non-white person, a poor person, and a woman is also continuously in play in any society.

What I refer to, as "body of Law", is fairly straightforward. In a given society, after some sort of legislative process, positive law – by definition – is written down and published. As such it is then available to literate citizens – subjects of the law – who may, or may not, also happen to be the objects of the law. However, included within that short description are several assumptions. I assume that society can be inscribed on and in the body; it is the site for "incorporated history."[1216] Sociology and sociologists have described and theorized various ways in which the body has been inserted "into a signifying order."[1217] This is because, as Berthelet continues, it is "the particu-

---

1212 This is only my conjecture. Cartwright could have been in the same position as American scientists who worked for cigarette manufacturers in the 1950s.

1213 It is worth noting that the year before the Civil War began included many elements of a "social/ moral panic" which I discuss below.

1214 Lock, *Cultivating the Body*, 145.

1215 This is not a feature buried in some ancient history; I need only mention 1962 Nobel-laureate Dr. James Watson in this context and his rapid departure from the renowned Cold Spring Harbor Laboratory in October, 2007 after making remarks that questioned the intelligence of Africans. See "Controversial Nobel Winner resigns at: http://cnn.site.printthis.clickability.com/pt/ccpt?/acctioin=cpt&title=Controversial+Nobel, last accessed 7 November 2007.

1216 Pierre Bourdieu, *Language and Symbolic Power* (Polity Press, 1919), 13.

1217 J.M. Berthelet, "Sociological Discourse and the Body" in Mike Featherstone, Mike Hepworth and Bryan S. Turner (eds.), *The Body: Social Process and Cultural Theory* (London, Newbury Park, New Delhi: Sage Publications, 1991), 398.

lar site of an interface between a number of domains: the biological and the social, the collective and the individual, that of structure and agents, cause and meaning, constraint and free will."[1218] In short, the body has a "particular status in sociology: *not that of an object but rather that of an epistemic index.*"[1219]

I believe this epistemic index includes the normative values of the time and place. And this describes the investigation that I undertake here, i. e. how the body vis-à-vis the judicial system becomes an "epistemic index" of society itself. And, how the law is "helpless" for lack of a better word, to do anything but reflect on a sometimes-wicked society that creates a wicked law in an occasional book or article. This is precisely because of the supposed safeguards that positivistic law has developed, i.e. they only begin after the process of legislation is complete. This occurs despite all the claims the body of Law makes to objectivity, legislative beneficence and interpretive brilliance; it can also happen because of its rejection of input from social science sources, as in the case of the United States, and because it refuses to acknowledge that some sorts of moral norms are always at play in the legislative process.[1220]

In the late twentieth century, sociologists have given consideration to how the body incorporates society and societal norms, e.g. in considerations of anorexia and other illnesses. But, within the last five years or so, a new term has been coined to deal with how society and the body interact, i.e. "somatechnics." In 2005, Professor Susan Stryker used the word "somatechnics" to signify the "inextricable" connection between the "soma and techne of the body (as a culturally intelligible construct), and the techniques in and through which bodies formed are transformed."[1221] Some researchers have confined their research into the techne portion of the above definition to include "dispositifs and 'hard technologies'."[1222] Michel Foucault used

---

1218 *Ibid.*

1219 *Ibid.* (Emphasis mine.) When I use the word "object" to refer to a body's status in a law, I will mean "epistemic index."

1220 This is most clearly seen in the USSC's refusal to use social science data as to the race of victim and perpetrator from the Baldus Study in death penalty cases. Please see McCleskey v. Kemp, 481 U.S. 279 (1987). What the USSC decides to do in any given case depends on the composition of the Court. Citing statistical contamination in previous studies, McGuire and Stimson claim that the Justices are affected by public opinion "to a degree far greater than previously documented" and that they are "highly motivated by their personal preferences." Kevin T. McGuire and James A. Stimson, "The Least Dangerous Branch Revisited: New Evidence on Supreme Court Responsiveness to Public Preferences" in *The Journal of Politics*, 66 (2004), 1033.

1221 Goldie Osuri, "Media Necropower: Australian Media Reception and the Somatechnics of Mamdouh Habib" in *Borderlands e-journal*, 5, (2006), paragraph 3 at http://www.borderlands.net.au/vol5no1_2006osuri_necropower.htm, last accessed 18 July 2008. While "techne" is used primarily with reference to cultural changes, such as tattoos, I see no reason why it cannot be applied in the context of laws written upon the body.

1222 Please see, The Fifth International International Somatechnics Conference: The Technologisation of Bodies and Selves at http://www.conferencealerts.com/seeconf.mv?q=ca1xa08H, last accessed

the word "dispositifs" (apparatus) in 1977 at a round table discussion by historians. There, he used the word to mean

> A thoroughly heterogeneous ensemble consisting of discourses, institutions, architectural forms, regulatory decisions, **laws**, administrative measures, scientific statements, philosophical, moral and philanthropic propositions – in short, the said as well as the unsaid. Such are the elements of the apparatus.[1223]

Other researchers have focused on the use of "hard technologies" that can be used in "body projects" to conform the body to societal expectations, e.g. liposuction, face lifts, etc. Most of the work done within Sociology within this field at this point has been done in the very recent past.[1224]

Drew Leder has discussed the body and its "dys-appearance."[1225] This is an idea that I also incorporate into my definition of "body law" since it accurately describes how the body becomes in the world after the passage of body-law. While Leder writes primarily about the individual body in society, he does extend his ideas and focus on when the bodies "dys-appears" due to the objectifying gaze of the "other."[1226] In one chapter, Leder begins with a discussion of pain and ends with the observation that the dys-appearance of the body in times of pain exists because "this structure plays a part in the broadest patterns of social behavior and power distribution."[1227] As he notes, political power can be seen in the pain of individual torture. A person with the pain of a psychiatric disease may feel both it and the power of the hospital where she is being cared for, as an institution, and even the doctor as a more immediate extension of an oppressive medical institution. Furthermore, social dys-appearance "may lead to biological dysfunction" such as anorexia nervosa.[1228] And finally:

18 July 2008. Often, somatechnics seems to take on the appearance of anthropology, concentrating on cultural decoration such as tattoos, piercings, etc.

1223 Michel Foucault, "The Confession of the Flesh Interview" in Colin Gordon (ed.), *Power/Knowledge, Selected Interviews and Other Writings* (New York: Pantheon Books, 1980), 194–228. Also see at, http://foucaultblog.wordpress.com/2007/04/01/what-is-the-dispositif/, last accessed 18 July 2008 (Emphasis mine.)

1224 See, for example, Mike Featherstone, Mike Hepworth and Bryan S. Turner, *The Body,* Chris Shilling, *The Body and Social Theory* (2nd ed.) (London, Thousand Oaks, New Delhi: SAGE Publications, 2003), Bryan S. Turner, The Body and Society: Explorations in Social Theory (2nd Ed.) (London, Thousand Oaks, New Delhi: SAGE Publications, 1996).

1225 Drew Leder, *The Absent Body* (Chicago and London: The University of Chicago Press, 1990).

1226 *Ibid.*, 92–99. (Emphasis mine.)

1227 *Ibid.*, 99.

1228 *Ibid.*

> Biological dysfunction may inaugurate social dys-appearance, such as is frequently experienced by the handicapped and disabled. The body is at once a biological organism, a ground of personal identity, and a social construct.[1229]

As part of my thesis, I think one can convincingly argue that in times of societal "pain", otherwise known as "social/moral panics", that the bodies of some begin to "dys-appear" when "the primary stance of the Other is highly distanced, antagonistic, or objectifying." The bodies that do not dys-appear are John Caputo's "hale and healthy organisms, upright, agile, agential bodies that move with ease and alacrity through the *Lebenswelt*."[1230] I use the term "body-law" to mean laws that are either judicially or legislatively created during times of social upheaval or "moral panic" alone or in tandem with major structural changes in societal structure, which, in turn, depend on a number of factors, but most significantly on who is the "strong we" and the "weak we" during these times.[1231] Body-Law makes the physical body both an object (index) and a subject of the law and can affect its societal and legal dys-appearance.

Here I saw that specific bodies that are more likely to be selected as objects of normative law formation during these unstable times are taken from inter-subjective categories based on gender, race, class, ability, citizen status and variations thereupon. These bodies may not be the original sites for normative law attachment, but if legal norms attach to non-intersubjective[1232] bodies, i.e. white male bodies, the original laws can be eventually invalidated. However, at least in the case of sterilization, they do not disappear and are quietly moved to apply to intersubjective bodies. The same effect, originally meant for one group, may well continue in either a legal or an extra-judicial fashion on intersubjective bodies. As Charles Lemert notes, this is but one example of the "sneaky epiphanies of power" – that some people and their bodies deserve less prestige than others.[1233]

An example of one of these sneaky ephiphanies is that the involuntary sterilization of "habitual" criminals originally applied only to imprisoned males. Oklahoma's

---

1229 *Ibid.*

1230 John D. Caputo, *The Weakness of God* (Bloomington and Indianapolis: Indiana University Press, 2006), 132.

1231 The idea of a "strong we" and a "weak we" is taken from Charles Lemert, *Dark Thoughts* (New York and London: Routledge, 2002).

1232 The term "intersubjective" is taken from feminist theory. Although it is a word associated with psychoanalytics, it can also be used in sociology to mean a shared understanding that shapes our relationships and epistemic realitites. It is also known as intersectionality. Intersectionality can be defined as the idea that identities are socially constructed and that societal oppression is a multi-level process that brings together many types of interlocking oppressions. Please see Patricia Hill Collins and Margaret Andersen (ed.), *Race, Class, and Gender: An Anthology* 6th Ed. (Belmont California: Wadsworth Publishing, 2007).

1233 Charles Lemert, "Mysterious Power of Social Structures" in Barbara A. Arrighi (ed.), *Understanding Inequality: The Intersection of Race/Ethnicity, Class and Gender*, (Lanham, Md.: Rowman & Littlefield Publishers, Inc., 2001), 8.

equivalent of the 1907 Indiana law was overturned on due-process grounds barely 25 years after Indiana passed its law.[1234] Thus, male chicken thieves, such as one Oklahoma felon, Mr. Skinner, were saved from sterilization. The timing of Mr. Skinner's appeal roughly corresponded to the height and beginning denouement of the eugenics movement in the United States. After World War II and confirmation of Holocaust horrors, the eugenics movement was said to go into remission. But, as Allison Carey points out, non-white and non-wealthy women continued to be sterilized well into the 1970s, many forcibly; this also continued in Scandinavia. In the main, intersubjective groups compose the pool from which bodies are usually – or, eventually – normatively selected. This pool of bodies is, in the main, the "weak we", an idea developed by sociologist Charles Lemert.[1235]

As for the concept of "Law", I find that the inherent Hobbesian promise of "law and order" was essentially disregarded by both nation states. In the Norwegian case, this is so since those particular bodies were the object of the sterilization law had not, in fact, broken any law. And the same can be said for Indiana since the belief was that the law was as good as broken at some time in the future by these criminals, i.e. prescriptive law with proscriptive consequences. The precarious nature of having one body, as opposed to having another, different type of body, prefigures a later legal philosopher's notion of the "veil of ignorance."[1236] Societies generally expect control through law but this equation breaks down at various times in various places and depends, in the main, according to what body one has. Rather than wait for the passage of time to reflect on our potential legal "mistakes", I ask is there a way to be pro-active when it comes to the passage of "body-Law"?

As I demonstrated above in both cases, there was a claim that each law was "objectively" made and applied and this served as legitimation for the new laws. One could argue that objectivity itself can help to create unjust laws but I opt here for a much easier argument, namely that the ideology of "objectivism" helped to legitimate the injustice of sterilization laws. The intersections of schemas, societal structures and resources also engaged in the entire process. But, having said that, it was also true that objectivism was a well-stocked ideological commodity because, as we have seen, so many "degenerate" bodies were marginalized in the "objective" reasoning process.

1234 Please see, Skinner v. Oklahoma ex rel. Williamson, 316 U.S. 535 (1942).

1235 Please see Charles Lemert, *Dark Thoughts: Race and the Eclipse of Society* (New York and London: Routledge, 2002).

1236 Please see John Rawls, *A Theory of Justice* (Oxford and New York, Oxford University Press, 1972).

7.4 Legal Objectivity as Scientific Objectivity?

If society can be inscribed on various bodies and various times, then a problem exists when one is trying to be legally objective, whether in law or science. And that problem leads us back to the well-known observation that body and mind had been earlier dichotomized where Reason is a type of Baconian Protestantism and it was carved into law by one Christopher Columbus Langdell.[1237]

Howard Schweber has written quite convincingly of the historical connection between law and the natural sciences.[1238] He writes that, at the beginning of the 20th century, American legal sciences looked to the natural sciences for its "metaphors, its methods, and its legitimating claims."[1239] It was in America that antebellum[1240] natural legal scientists manipulated the public discourse of "science" for use in law schools. Schweber calls this public discourse "Protestant Baconianism" and teases out four primary characteristics of this type of discourse:

> 1. a commitment to natural theology,...
> 2. a commitment to a limited form of inductivism that defined science as fundamentally an exercise in taxonomy...
> 3. a belief in a grand synthesis that bound all forms of knowledge together in a system of analogies,...and
> 4. a claim that science was a public undertaking that would produce moral and political uplift.[1241]

This approach was taken by Professor Christopher Columbus Langdell (1826–1906) who was appointed the Dane Professor of Law at Harvard Law School in 1870; he also became Dean there in 1875.

Along with his successor, J.B. Ames, Langdell revised the law school curriculum in the United States to include inductive studies of the law based on actual cases, commonly called the "case-law method" or the "casebook method" which survives to the present as a major component of law school education.[1242] The most famous quotation attributed to him is from this speech where he notes that,

> We have also constantly inculcated the idea that the library is the proper workshop of professors and students alike; that it is to us all what the laboratories of the university are to the chemists

---

1237 And, this is kept in place by the work of sociologists such as Arthur Stinchcombe. For a current antidote to Stinchcombe's reliance on formalism, please see, Lucas A. Powe, Jr., *The Supreme Court and the American Elite, 1739–2008* (Cambridge, Mass.: Harvard University Press, 2009).

1238 Howard Schweber, "The "Science" of Legal Science: The Model of the Natural Sciences in Nineteenth-Century American Legal Education" in *Law and History Review*, 17 (1999).

1239 *Ibid.*, 422.

1240 The War Between the States, the American Civil War, was fought 1861–1865.

1241 *Ibid.*

1242 *Ibid.*, 457.

> and physicists, what the museum of natural history is to the zoologist, what the botanical garden is to the botanists.[1243]

If this natural science approach was injected into the law in the mid-1860s, it was also injected, in various forms, into the study of societies, i.e. the social sciences. At this point in time, a large body of literature would argue that this scientific model thesis is, at the very least, under stress.

Legal theorist Eric Engle elaborates on this idea by writing that the law is not "nomothetic."[1244] It is less exact than Physics is, for example. If water is heated "it expands...[and] if water is sufficiently heated at 1 atmosphere of pressure it will eventually boil and evaporate."[1245] Water has no volition and so this happens at all times, in all places. It is a "nomothetic" process, i.e. its physical laws cannot be derogated from; "it poses principles which themselves are laws *strictu sensu*."[1246] This is not the case with the social, human sciences. Therefore, as Engle concludes, human sciences "cannot discover 'laws' but only general trends and tendencies – which nonetheless is knowledge."[1247] Regularities can be seen in social science research. It can also happen that this research can change how people behave while stating or not-stating a natural law will not change anything.

With the benefit of hindsight, I can hypothesize that, had there been more people such as Edward Miller in Indiana, had there been a social movement organization organized and used for self scrutiny and had the progressive movement not been wedded to the eugenics movement at that time and place, perhaps the particular policy rationales at work in the Indiana Legislature might not have produced such a law. However, there can be little doubt that the ideology of "objectivism" in addition to the co-production idiom outlined above played their particular roles in the passage of this law.

The "objectivity" of the law depended on a number of theories still in place today, or at least attempting to stay in place such as for example, adherence to a proper, earlier enacted, legislative procedure. As Daston and Gallison point out, albeit with regard to science, "it is fear that drives epistemology, including the definition of what counts as epistemic vice or virtue."[1248] One of the fears at work was a fear emanating from the early Enlightenment, that is, that some religious or moral entity might seek to impose their epistemic values and/or vices on a civil society. And, in order to offset

1243 *Ibid.*, 459.
1244 Erik Engle in "Law: Lex vs. Ius" in *The Journal of Jurisprudence*, 1 (2008), 33.
1245 *Ibid.*
1246 *Ibid.* Engle appears not to be the originator of this term. He cites to Christianne and Ota Weinberger, *Logik Semantik Hermeneutik* (München: Beck'sche Elementarbücher, 1979), p. 38 and also to Stanley I. Paulson, "Kelsen on Legal Interpretation" in *Legal Studies*, 10 (1990), 136–52.
1247 *Ibid.*
1248 Daston and Gallison, *Objectivity*, 49. Note 1398.

this possibility, the Autonomy Thesis in the United States, and some form of the same in Norway, pervaded legislative conduct.

The jurisprudential idea that supports the claim of legal objectivity is the Separability Thesis, also known as the Autonomy Thesis (ATL). It has to do with legal reasoning and, while held by prominent positivists, natural law scholars also adhere to this thesis. As I noted above, it is clear why the ATL came to be. Not only does it generally have a good "fit" with ordinary legal practice but also there are good reasons why it exists. But, when things go terribly wrong, it can be reduced to a thin philosophical veil covering both benevolent motivations as well as those not even remotely close to benevolent. Although the sociological methodology I have used in the main body of this work indicates the ATL was breached, an evaluation of the ATL from a philosophical angle is another matter altogether. The ATL is a complicated theory and Gerald Postema reduces it to three core ideas; these are the Limited Domain Thesis (LDT), the Pre-emption Thesis (PT) and the Sources Thesis (ST).

The LDT means that law "defines a limited domain of practical reasons or norms for use by officials and citizens alike."[1249] The LDT is not based on the content of the law or on how sound that content is but is based on "substantively neutral social facts about how the norms were created or came into existence."[1250] In the case of sterilization laws, this means that the subject of the law is not considered and only the method of its enactment is considered. In addition, the PT looks at the LDT and looks at "reasons that preclude acting for certain other reasons...falling outside the domain."[1251] What this means, in effect, is that the PT helps to add "new reasons and norms to the stock of practical considerations" and to separate them from the more brutish practical reasoning process.[1252] The ST says that when legal reasoning is "proper", the "*content* of the legal norms can be determined without appeal to moral or evaluative argument."[1253]

Looking at these three core ideas in relation to the sterilization and "bodily privacy" laws passed in both Norway and the United States, we can see several problems. For example, with regard to the ST, when a court looks at a law and tries to decide what reason(s) existed for the decision, i.e. the "why" of the case, there is an evaluation being carried out. And when O.W. Holmes wrote that "Three generations of idiots is enough", he was not only "appearing" to evaluate, he was evaluating.[1254]

1249 Gerald Postema, "Law's Autonomy and Public Practical Reason", in Robert P. George ed., *The Autonomy of Law: Essays in Legal Postivism* (Oxford: Clarendon Press, 1996), 82.
1250 *Ibid.*, 83.
1251 *Ibid.*
1252 *Ibid.*
1253 *Ibid.*, 95.
1254 This is against the position of Joseph Raz, who thinks that the activity only "appears" even by interpreters who are not like-minded. *Ibid.*, 96–97.

Or, when W.O. Douglas "found" the right of privacy in the "penumbra" of the Constitution, one could hardly deny his appeal to a moral, or ethical, argument.

Legitimacy of the ATL is one matter, but using it as an "isolation strategy" is yet another, as Postema points out. As he argues, the more isolation is needed to induce social cooperation, "the more difficult it will be to meet this legitimacy condition."[1255] If a matter is so socially divisive, having a law might be worse than having no law. A facet of the isolation claim is the "neutrality claim" which says that, while the law itself may not be neutral in content or enforced neutrally, it still means that the "lawmakers occupy some position which is neutral relative to the moral and political views which are in conflict."[1256] And this, Postema says is "entirely gratuitous."[1257] An ancillary idea, that law-makers might be "experts" is also doomed since as "Leslie Green observed, 'There are experts on whales, but not on whether we should save the whales'."[1258]

And, in this work, we saw not only how gratuitous the neutrality of lawmakers and eugenicists and scientists and medical doctors and judges was, but also that no expertise, in the sense that Green allows, was at work. Not only was this the case, but also the angst of the times was at work. While perhaps difficult to quantify, this does not mean that this angst did not exist and did not become a factor that affected the processes. Not only was there social anxiety but there was also epistemic anxiety. Daston and Gallison examine in their book *Objectivity*, how this anxiety affected medical atlases. Of this, they note that

> Anxiety about virtue, epistemic or otherwise, is neither omnipresent nor perpetual. But when epistemic anxiety does break out, scientific atlases by their very nature register it early and emphatically.[1259]

This observation fits very nicely with my own thesis, that societal anxiety, when it does break out, is registered in the body, in a fixation on the material composition and qualities of the physical body.

So, despite the myriad claims to objectivity or neutrality posited in jurisprudential theory, one cannot count on positivism, as a general practice, either to not be affected by or to affect societal norms, sometimes to their detriment. For those who embrace practical reason[1260], and only practical reason, this is a fairly banal conclu-

---

1255 *Ibid.*, 104.
1256 *Ibid.*, 107.
1257 *Ibid.*
1258 *Ibid.*
1259 Daston and Gallison, *Objectivity*, 49.
1260 Many philosophers including Aristotle, Aquinas, and Kant have addressed "practical reason." It is a "rational capacity by which (rational) agents guide their conduct." (See http://www.britannica.com/EBchecked/topic/473575/practical-reason, accessed August 17, 2009. "Pratical reason" is not the

sion. But one important point to be made, from a sociological and historically comparative perspective is that this phenomenon is trans-national, i.e. trans-cultural. This would tend to lend credence to the conclusion that there does exist a fundamental component with regard to positivism, and that it has, as some attachment, a capacity to engage with society in an valued manner, or a moral manner, especially with angst is an inducement.

Given the current state of all types of positivisms, are we to assume a future that holds, crudely conceived, yet another Inquisition of sorts? Must we assume another Thirty Years War? The short answer is probably "no" as modifications are bound to be made.

One of the more practical ideas that I have read comes from Jeremy Waldron. As he writes, some positivists are interested in one facet of law or another, i.e.

> some are interested in the separation of the law and morality at the retail level; some are interested in the textual and/or rule-like qualities of law, for reasons that go beyond or stand apart from the separability thesis [ATL]; some are interested in law as a distinctive institution and its institutional characteristics; and some are interested in the ethical autonomy of various legal-professional rules, such as judging.[1261]

Waldron calls this "Menu A."

Some positivists might be also be interested in the functions of law such as peace, predictability, control of power, democracy or conditions of social coordination. This is Waldron's "Menu B." For Waldron the problem in approaching positivism comes when general positivists fear normativists might have "foisted" something on them from Menu B. According to Waldron, theorists – such as Postema – are not trying to "foist" normativism on anyone. What they are doing is saying that to focus on one or another item from Menu A "is not intelligible on its own and cannot credibly be presented as a matter of pure 'analysis.' To be intelligible, it must be motivated."[1262] To have a fully comprehensible idea of positivist law, we must "map a choice from Menu A onto a choice from Menu B."[1263] This, we call the analytical outlook.

same as intuitionism. It is a "framework of moral principles..." (*Ibid.*) For Kant, "practical reason" is "concerned with freedom rather than the natural good or the human end. Kant's practical reason attains the kind of rigor based on pure *a priori* principles, which would by impossible in the ethics of Aristotle, Albert and Thomas who are content with a science of practical reason whosedomain is contingent and changeable acts. The secure foundatioin which Kant sought for every moral choice would be considered beyond the scope of practical reason formulated by themedieval commentators...." Please see http://plato.stanford.edu/entries/pratical-reason-med/, accessed August 17, 2009.

1261 Jeremy Waldron, "Normative (or Ethical) Positivism" in Jules Coleman ed., *Hart's Postscript: Essays on the Postscript to the Concept of Law* (Oxford: Oxford University Press, 2001), 432–433.

1262 *Ibid.*, 433. This remark is remarkable since it seems that motivation allows room for consideration of epistemic values as Daston and Gallison have argued above.

1263 *Ibid.*

Another outlook, which I have labeled as intersectional, comes from Rainer Forst, a political theorist. Forst has analyzed the debate between "'context-forgetful' liberal-deontological theories and 'context-obsessed' communitarian theories" by looking at how people, with bodies, are situated in four normative contexts, the ethical, legal, political and moral.[1264] If we go directly to Forst's discussion of the moral context, wherein a human being is seen as an end in herself and not as an instrument, the question, as is sometimes spelled out in legislative debate, should not be "what is the right thing for us to do?" Instead, the question must be asked in terms of the "context of being human."

The "context of being human" means that the community of human beings is the "justification community" and that "moral norms must not...be understood in an abstract manner."[1265] It also means that communities "must not fall below" some "minimal" standard of recognition and also that "persons as human beings have a basic right of justification."[1266] Moral norms, in this environment, are "not 'context-transcending' norms in the sense that they are valid only for 'ideal,' bodiless beings; rather they are valid for all, and that means for every moral person vis-à-vis every other."[1267] When bodies that were invisible suddenly become visible as "abnormal", then they fall beneath that minimal level of recognition and justification.

While I may have drawn more extensively on American legal thought than on its Norwegian counterpart, the above thoughts about positive law are also not without commentary in Norway. Knut Bergo writes in the final pages of his book *Text and Reality in the Sources of Law* that his book was not meant as a history of how to open Norwegian law to modern scientific philosophy "after having lived through Ross' love of natural science or Eckhoff's sense of half-abstract sociology."[1268] Bergo's book was meant to be an irritant,[1269] like a rock caught in a fixed position where the rock is constantly moving just a little. Bergo complains of the "hegemonic" use of "psychological realism in Norwegian legal sources and the scientific analysis of the legal process that leads to a partially norm driven, law giver-friendly [yet] misleading process."[1270] He dismisses deconstruction as not really coming from a neutral standpoint and points out that "to present a normative criticism with such a lack of foundation is like shoot-

1264 Rainer Forst, *Contexts of Justice: Political Philosophy beyond Liberalilsm and Communitarianism* (Berekely, Los Angeles and London: University of Californai Press, 2002), 5.
1265 *Ibid.*, p. 171.
1266 *Ibid.*
1267 *Ibid.*
1268 Knut Bergo, *Text and Reality in the Sources of Law*, (Oslo: Cappelen Akademisk Forlag, 2002), 1042.
1269 Einar Haugen, *Norwegian English Dictionary* (Oslo, Madison: Universitetsforlag University of Wisconsin Press), p. 334. Definition of verb "å rokke."
1270 Bergo, *Text and Reality*, 1044.

ing oneself in the foot while kicking...with the other."[1271] To immerse oneself in the "anti-normative" project reflects a "certain naivete" and results in no lack of material on the subject. What is needed, he writes, is for those "famous actors" who write/propose new laws to be more "responsible."[1272]

I close with this mention of Bergo since he complains about how the juridical method used in Norway can have concrete – and political – results, something I have also complained about, but coming at this issue from 180 degrees in the opposite direction. Bergo warns that to have a method that is "pragmatic, lacks criticism, shifting, concrete, context-orientated and flexible" is not always appropriate.[1273] As Bergo so eloquently puts it, what happens, given this scenario of adjudication, is that subjects of the law "can't see where the axe is coming from, because it can come from all sides."[1274] Nevertheless, the fact is that both Norway and the United States, with differing systems of legal thought and adjudication, passed similar body-laws as I have pointed out here. What mattered in my view, and produced these laws were not the sources of law, or the jurisprudential gaze or the philosophical abstractions employed. Both juridical systems failed and then turned to employing "body-law" as an antidote to communal human rights. What mattered was not the "how" but the "why", the motivation and the co-productive forces in society.

7.5 The King's Two Bodies and the Body Politic

> Our unspoken assumptions have the force of revelation. How else could we know that whoever is the first of us to seek assent and votes in a rich democracy will be the last of us and have killed our language? Meanwhile, if we miss the sight of a fish we heard jumping and then see its ripples, that means one more of us is dying somewhere.
>
> Seamus Heaney[1275]

I have argued here that the specific bodies selected as objects of normative law formation during these unstable times were taken from inter-subjective categories based on gender, race, class, ability, citizen status and variations thereupon. These bodies may not be the original sites for normative law attachment, but if legal norms attach to non-intersubjective[1276] bodies, i.e. white male bodies, the original laws can be eventu-

1271 *Ibid.*
1272 *Ibid.* 1045.
1273 *Ibid.* 1046.
1274 *Ibid.*
1275 Seamus Heaney, *The Haw Lantern* (New York: The Noonday Press, Farrar Straus Giroux, 1987), 19.
1276 The term "intersubjective" is taken from feminist theory. Although it is a word associated with psychoanalytics, it can also be used in sociology to mean a shared understanding that shapes our relationships and epistemic realitites. It is also known as intersectionality. Intersectionality can be

ally invalidated. However, at least in the case of sterilization, they do not disappear and are quietly moved to apply to intersubjective bodies. The same effect, originally meant for one group, may well continue in either a legal or an extra-judicial fashion on intersubjective bodies. As Charles Lemert notes, this is but one example of the "sneaky epiphanies of power" – that some people and their bodies deserve less prestige than others.[1277]

In order to invalidate these laws or reverse both the shadowy and more open extra-judicial processes based on these laws, individuals and SMOs often participate together at the same opportunistic period to reverse cultural and social paradigms. At a macro-level, the production of epistemic knowledge also changes. In order to examine this process, I use a critical discourse analysis of print media and also secondary sources from the two countries and the two time periodsThe "wicked" laws that I mentioned above in Chapter 1, as well as the sometimes-wicked legal systems currently in place, should give one hesitation when considering new "body-law."[1278] In some ways, all law is "body-law." But many laws directly impact the body more than others, i.e. however incorporeal laws seem, they actually touch human bodies through the direct or indirect actions of others, whether voluntarily or involuntarily. David Dyzenhaus, after his studies on both South African apartheid law and Nazi Germany, concludes rather mutedly "positivism discourages sound legal practice."[1279] Gustav Radbruch, more boldly said that it "paved the way" for Nazi Germany.[1280] But the problem with such statements is that they hide paradoxes, that, like Russian matryoska dolls, could be – and often are – only other paradoxes within the first, or second – or more layers. The paradox within the Dyzenhaus-Radbruch observation is that, as Jean Clam notes,

> The positivism of law also builds a paradoxical moment into the centre of modern law production. The paradox of positive law is that of the conservation of strong and full legal validity in spite of the relativity and constant transformation of law through legal re-vision and reform. Positive law has its validity by means of its alterability. The paradox here is that of the grounding of validity on provisionality. Positive law is law that can be changed at any moment without

---

defined as the idea that identities are socially constructed and that societal oppression is a multi-level process that brings together many types of interlocking oppressions. Please see Patricia Hill Collins and Margaret Andersen (ed.), *Race, Class, and Gender: An Anthology* 6th Ed. (Belmont California: Wadsworth Publishing, 2007).

1277 Charles Lemert, "Mysterious Power of Social Structures" in Barbara A. Arrighi (ed.), *Understanding Inequality: The Intersection of Race/Ethnicity, Class and Gender*, (Lanham, Md.: Rowman & Littlefield Publishers, Inc., 2001), 8.

1278 David Dyzenhaus, *Legality and Legitimacy: Carl Schmitt, Hans Kelsen and Hermann Heller in Weimar* (Oxford: Clarendon Press, 1997), 1. The extension of my argument to include law and biotechnology is as natural.

1279 *Ibid.*

1280 *Ibid.*

> being [made insecure] in its validity by that prospect. Politics is the instance that promotes legal change and from whose system the directives for change are imported. It thus plays the role of a parasite of law.[1281]

Clam may be right but I believe that this work shows that politics and Law have developed, at different times and places, either a parasitic relationship or a rather different relationship – a symbiotic (mutually beneficial) one. Clam's view is still upheld by perhaps the majority of jurisprudential thinkers, although that number is now becoming fewer.[1282] Frederick Schauer maintains that the idea of "the over willingness of legal officials to suspend moral judgment and thus to apply and enforce bad laws (or to apply and enforce laws badly) just because they are the law" is, specifically, an American legal academic phenomenon.[1283] Schauer writes that anyone who might hold this "distorted version of legal positivism" is one with a "scant historical or philosophical provenance."[1284] He, on the other hand, notes that positivism "as traditionally understood" is not the "cause of the problem...but...a potential solution to it."[1285]

Nonetheless, in the face of a current propensity for genetic essentialism and a mixture of recessionary economics and reactionary politics, I believe that to say solving the problem is impossible and resorting to a convenient paradox or a set of nested paradoxes is simply not an option today. Michael Stollies, another scholar of "wicked" laws and governments, notes that some historians continue to divide subject and object and "deny that it is possible to derive "ought" from past "is." From this assumption,

> follows a rejection of the notion that the writing of history should be duty-bound by the present, even if the desire springs from the best intentions of political [or sociological] pedagogy. Historians, who take this position[,] have... in a sense, lowered their expectations to the outside world...[1286]

I agree with Stollies that to take this position only lowers expectations and presents sociologists of history and law no current duty to the times in which they live.

1281 Jean Clam, "The Reference of Paradox: Missing Paradoxity as Real Perplexity in Both Systems Theory and Deconstruction" in Oren Perez and Gunther Teubner (eds.), *Paradoxes and Inconsistencies in the Law* (Oxford and Portland Oregon: Hart Publishing, 2006), 87. (Emphasis mine.)

1282 While this is an exaggeration, we need only think of the "conversion" of jurisprudential thinker, Neil MacCormick. This is also seen in the number of books in which numerous authors have sought to qualify positivism and their own position in relation to it, as, e.g. storng or weak, inclusive or exclusive, and ethical or normative.

1283 Frederick Schauer, "Positivism as Pariah" in Robert P. George ed., *The Autonomy of Law: Essays on Legal Positivism* (Oxford: Clarendon Press, 1996), 32.

1284 *Ibid.*

1285 *Ibid.*

1286 Michael Stolleis, (trans. Moshe Zimmermann), *The Law under the Swastika: Studies in Legal History in Nazi Germany* (Chicago and London: The University of Chicago Press, 1998), 38.

This is not to say that there are not significant problems with questioning the role of positive law to any degree. One of the most serious problems is that "justice" for one person may be a type of "fascist law" for another.[1287] One could argue that concepts of economic social "justice" require the nationalization of energy companies in the United States; but those same companies would be quick to cry "injustice" under yet some other principle. As Fatima Kastner points out:

> The insight that the idea of justice beyond legal legitimation introduces masked or unmasked authoritarian anti-democratic consequences is as common as it is easy to have after the totalitarian consequences of the twentieth century.[1288]

But it may also be that the owl of Minerva has already flown and as Olsen and Toddington have argued, there is "no sensible point in prolonging the traditional debate concerning the 'necessary' or 'contingent' relationship between law and morality, i.e. legitimacy."[1289] As they write:

> The crucial interdependence of law and morality, both conceptually and practically, is not seriously open to question. The issue is whether or not, and in what form, morality can survive the transformation from its natural state, through the process of institutionalization and autonomy, to the situated and shifting contexts of its indirect application. Whatever this form might take, it is always characterized by an interplay between legal form and moral interpretation. This relationship must be made explicit in the legal decision, and the very notions of authority and legitimacy demand that we are able to retrace and reveal the normative background for the decision... Such transparency is a condition of the validity of the system...[1290]

Therefore, I argue here, that to depend on "body-law" – whether it be either enacted or interpreted – as objectively legitimate, at those times of national cultural instability, legal epistemic uncertainty and "moral panic" would be a mistake, unless the relative positions of the "strong we" and the "weak we" are also taken into account. I believe it is those relative positions that provide the transparency that Olsen and Toddington espouse. If we resort to allowing morality to be combined with law we are only prolonging another age-old debate, which is "Whose morality?" The intersubjective categories can be used to create a clearer line separating good from bad law.

If we conclude that severe societal structural and schematic disarticulations occur at the same time as laws that affect the body are passed, can we also conclude the reverse, i.e. when major shifts occur in the value schemas of a body politic, that

---

1287 We need only consider reactions to new laws on smoking in public places,, in Greece among other places.

1288 Perez and Teubner, *Paradoxes and Inconsistencies*, 168.

1289 Henrik Palmer Olsen and Stuart Toddington, *Law In Its Own Right* (Oxford and Portland, Oregon: Hart Publishing Company, 1999), 158.

1290 *Ibid.*

we will encounter legislation and legal decisions that pertain to the human body, specifically to reproductive roles and schemas? Perhaps so, since society at large will begin to look for a "weak we" to instrumentalize the shift, thus entering into a vicious circle of cause and effect that only another disarticulation can curtail.

In his book, *The King's Two Bodies*, Ernst Kantorowicz made the argument that, when we look at the grave of any dead King/Ruler we are essentially looking at only one of his bodies. That dead body had once ruled a nation, made decisions, fashioned laws, fought wars and left a legacy – good, bad or mixed – to his or her nation. The other body – the State – was not subject to physical decay, however. Here, instead of focusing on a King or Ruler, I focused on the manner in which the Sovereign rules and disciplines, controlling the population within his or her territory – by controlling the body.[1291] But which bodies? As an indication, or measure, of the historicity of these social shifts, we can expect to find bodies associated with the feminist theory of intersubjectivity to be the ones affected. The "weak we" bodies become the sites of articulation and disarticulation of structures in historical events and legislation of laws. It is bodies that mediate the articulation and dis-articulation of societal schemas at various times in history.

But until the world of positive law in the United States and the rationalization aesthetic can be changed, Stephen Toulmin has, what I consider to be the best advice.

> The future belongs not so much to the pure thinkers who are content – at best – with optimistic or pessimistic slogans; it is a province, rather, for reflective practitioners who are ready to act on their ideals. Warm hearts allied with cool heads seek a middle way between the extremes of abstract theory and personal impulse.[1292]

A lot depends on whether or not the challenges to positive law can be answered in the near future. David Dyzenhaus has captured this tension in an article that addresses the contemporary lessons that the collapse of the Weimar Republic has for us.[1293] He cites German legal philosopher Hermann Heller who believes that "politics is not a normative vacuum" and that political institutions are the best place for the contestation and revisitation/revision of fundamental values. As Dyzenhaus summarizes:

> The rule of law is then the institutional mechanism of democracy. Its justification is the same as the justification for democracy itself. And that justification requires both a fully argued commitment to the rightness of democracy and a recognition that democratic politics must be **much** more than liberals today commonly express.[1294]

1291 This is not a new thought, given the works of Michel Foucault.

1292 Stephen Toulmin, *Return to Reason* (Cambridge, Mass.: Harvard University Press, 2001), 214.

1293 David Dyzenhaus, "Legal Theory in the collapse of Weimar: Contemporary Lessons?" in *American Political Science Review*, 91 (1997): 121–133.

1294 *Ibid.*, 133 (Emphasis mine.)

7.6 How to Guess the Color of a Chameleon

I mentioned the theory created by Brian Tamanaha in Chapter 2 and want to return to it here. Would it be useful to imagine law that could be explained from the "the bottom up"? With the idea that legislated law is a generative process, perhaps it would be better to conceive of it as a combination of processes "from the bottom up" as well as "from the top down"? Perhaps it would be better to conceive of law as operationalized through the medium of language but still embedded in the social as Tamanaha says and which then interacts with societal structures, schemas and resources? Ultimately no easy – or short – solution exists as to the questions these processes pose.

The above questions have not gone unnoticed by others, specifically, by Luc Wintgens. He coined the term "legisprudence" to mean jurisprudence from the perspective of the legislator rather than the judge. As Wintgens writes, by

> shifting the attention to the legislator, the same questions [of norm validity, norm meaning and legal structure] arise, such as in what sense the legislator has to take the systematicity of the legal order into account and what counts as a valid norm...[1295]

With this vantage point, we can finally step across the Berlin Wall that separates the legislator from the adjudicator.

Kaarlo Tuori adds another distinction, which may seem like an obvious one to sociologists but not to legal theorists, i.e. that there is a difference between legal norms and legal practice. We can perhaps all acknowledge that legislation involves politics but Tuori posits that this legislative "cluster of political practices does not necessarily mean legal practices, except with regard to norm formulation."[1296] Legislation is later transformed from "not yet law" into "law" through legal practice and it is in legal practice that there can be found the regularity that is so prized. Legislation is merely the "surface level" of the legal order that is later systemitized through the use of legal principles. As Tuori notes, the "legal order is connected on this deeper level with morals, without being identical to it." Law and politics have the same relationship. They are "connected on the surface but remain autonomous at the deeper level."[1297]

While there have been a number of critics of the way that Law is "done" in the United States, especially from the Critical Legal Studies (CLS) movement, beginning in the mid-1980s but now – apparently – in remission, I am not familiar with a major

---

1295 Luc J. Wintgens, "Rationality in Legislation – Legal Theory: Legisprudence: An Introduction" in Luc J. Wintgens (ed.) *Legisprudence: A New Theoretical Approach to Legislatio: Proceedings of the Fourth Benelux-Scandinavian Symposium on Legal Theory* (Oxford and Portland: Hart Publishing Co., 2002), 2.
1296 *Ibid.*, 2.
1297 *Ibid.*

theoretical tome regarding the failure of the law to be objective in its creation or adjudication. The United States' legal system has continued to espouse the ideology of objectivity and to continue with a certain Janus-faced schizophrenia as evidenced in both its education and practice of law.[1298] Meanwhile, in Europe, other scholars such as Tuori and Wintgens continue to address the problem.

Tuori's theory of "critical positivism" uses a multi-layered law formation process. Tuori argues that there are three levels of law that can be investigated. The surface level (SL) is one in which we find statutes, ordinances, court decisions and various works on the way in which law should be interpreted. At a middle level is the level at which experts of the law create a culture of their own, similar to what Gary Edmond terms the "law set."[1299] This level also includes the "general legal culture of the ordinary citizens" although the expert "core set" is "deemed more important in the framing of legal phenomenon."[1300] This middle level also includes the canons of interpretation such as *lex superior, lex posterior, lex specialis* and patterns of argumentation in legal adjudication.[1301] At the third lowest level we find the deep structure of law, which corresponds to "Michel Foucault's notion of the episteme."[1302]

Under the surface level, the Tuori model includes an intermediate "Level 2" which is divided into two parts. This lower level, just above the lowest level, is the discourse-theoretical deep structure level or DSLL-DTF. This frame is "the axiomatic ground of legal validity and legal rationality, plus the two conceptual claims and the felicity conditions of adjudication effected" and it contains, among other notions, the "criteria for justice."[1303] The DSLL-PI level, above the PSLL-DTF, includes an identification and interpretation of the *ratio* of a case "in light of the set of ideological fragments involved" which is further affected by the "specific rule of law criteria for a well-functioning system of precedents."[1304] In other words, the DSLL-PI level is further "up" these different levels of rationality and reasoning. The lowest level is the infrastructure level of law (ISLL) and here we find the area of norm formation in legal philosophy. It is here that we find the "prelogical and preconceptual" foundations of legal

1298 Please see for example, K.C. Worden, "Overshooting the Target: A Feminist Deconstruction of Legal Education" in *American University Law Review*, 34 (1984–1985), 1141.

1299 Gary Edmond, "The Law-Set: The Legal Scientific Production of Medical Propriety" in *Science, Technology and Human Values*, 26, (2001), 191. Also see further, H.M. Collins, "The Place of the 'Core-set' in Modern Science: Social Contingency with Methodological Propriety in Science" in *History of Science*, 18 (2001), 6–19.

1300 Raimo Siltala, *A Theory of Precedent From Analytical Positivism to a Post-Analytical Philosophy of Law* (Helsinki: University Printing House, 1998), 158.

1301 In general, *lex superior* means that a law with a higher rank has precedence, *lex posterior* means that a law that is more recent has precedence over an older law and *lex specialis* means that a more specialized law takes precedence over a less specialized law.

1302 Raimo Siltala, *A Theory of Precedent*, 158.

1303 *Ibid.*, 155–63.

1304 *Ibid.*, 155.

norm composition and thus, also, of "precedent-based judicial signification."[1305] It is also the most controversial of the four levels.

Tuori's theory was derived from another theory of law, one developed by Sakari Hänninen; his is generally described as "Marxist." Tuori's version however, has allowed Hänninen's Marxist frame to "recede", making room for ideas drawn from, among other, François Ewald and Jürgen Habermas.[1306] In order to distance himself from the Marxist version, Tuori uses the term "critical positivism" for this model.

The surface level of Tuori's model exists at the level of legal dogmatics or what we find in legal documents. This surface-structure level (SSL) of law is about the *ratio* (reasoning) of a particular case and it is found in what is written and published. The legal norm production is in the *ratio* and *dicta* (language) within the case. In that sense, it distinguishes the case from other cases. The judicial significance is that a meaning is formed for the *ratio* and others may read the case and find that meaning.

The second level is called the deep-structure level of law (DSLL) or what we usually find in legal theory. It addresses how we know the premises of the precedent norm in the SSL. There are two ways we can use to do this; first, through a look at the precedent ideology and second, through the discourse-theoretical frame. The precedent-ideology (PI) includes identification and interpretation of the *ratio* "in light of the set of ideological fragments involved" and as affected further by the "specific rule of law criteria for a well-functioning system of precedents."[1307] The discourse-theoretical frame (DTF) is "the axiomatic ground of legal validity and legal rationality, plus the two conceptual claims and the felicity conditions of adjudication effected."[1308] In terms of legal signification, the ideological premises at this level contain references to "argumentative closure, systematicity, binding force, (source)/effect, criteria of justice, and method of argument under the judge's precedent-ideology."[1309]

The third level is perhaps the most contentious of the three. It is called the infrastructure level of law (ISLL) and here we find the area of legal philosophy. It is here that we find the "prelogical and preconceptual" foundations of legal norm composition and thus, also, of "precedent-based judicial signification."[1310] Siltala has simplified the Tuori Model as follows.

1305 *Ibid.*
1306 *Ibid.*, 159.
1307 *Ibid.*, 155.
1308 *Ibid.*
1309 *Ibid.*, 157.
1310 *Ibid.* The levels may, in fact, include a fourth level that Siltala describes as depending "on whether a judge's ideological commitments and the discourse-theoretical frame of law are collected under the common heading of the 'deep-structure level of law', or whether they are treated on an individual basis. The ISLL level is also "slightly contestable" since it does operate in the DSLL as well. Siltala at 155–56.

Level 1	**Operative Surface-Structure Level (SSL)** ***Ratio* (reasoning) and *dicta* (language) of a Case** (Requalification, ↓↑ Morality of Aspiration Restructuring)
Level 2	**Ideological Deep Structure (DSLL-PI)** **Legal theory in the case** **1. Precedent-ideology (PI) of the case** (Requalification, ↓↑ Condition of Possibility Restructuring) **2. Discourse-Theoretical Deep Structure Level (DSLL-DTF)** (Requalification, ↓↑ Condition of Possibility Restructuring (and Impossibility)
Level 3	**Prelogical and Preconceptual** **Infra-Structure Level (ISLL)** **Legal Philosophy**

Figure 7.1: Siltala simplification of the Tuori vertical relations between the levels of law[1311] (edited)

1311 Siltala, *A Theory of Precedent*, 163.

Tuori's theory posits that these three levels exist in relation to each other. They act upon or are acted upon in a number of ways. Tuori calls these six vertical relations, 1. sedimentation (SD), 2. constitution (CT), 3. concretization (CZ), 4. limitation (LM), 5. criticism (CM) and 6. justification (JS). Sedimentation (SD) occurs when the statutes, etc. at the surface level impact the other two levels so that "each individual enactment or judicial ruling at the same time produces, reproduces and modifies the level of legal culture and the deep structure of law."[1312]

If we compare both the Tamanaha and Tuori[1313] Models, it is possible to imagine a visible "tip of the iceberg" surface level, i.e. macro-objective/SSL. Beneath that level lies the bulk of metaphorical iceberg however, i.e. the macro-subjective and micro-objective/DSLL-PI and DTF and the lowest level, the micro-subjective/ISLL, respectively. I think that these two models are compatible and might be capable of being used simultaneously and/or interchangeably to trace the work of norms in the two sets of laws that I begin to examine in Chapter 3. In other words, how to guess the color of a chameleon at a given time, place, society and history.

The idea that law is historically and socially situated may seem overly obvious to many, especially in Norway. This idea can serve to introduce the larger question of what the idea of being "situated" means for the philosophy of jurisprudence? In asking this question we can immediately feel the wind rushing from below as we fall feet first into a kind of jurisprudential pit. This trap was most recently carved out of some fundamental bedrock by the positive law of the Third Reich and laws legislated by an apartheid South Africa. Were these laws merely some form of immoral law? Were they merely some sort of positivistic hiccup, albeit one that cost the lives of millions of individuals, and inflicted suffering on millions more? Should they be considered to have been laws at all?

For my purposes here, I want to go back to the mid-nineteenth century for a minute, to a Scottish legal philosopher named Dugald Stewart. As Mary Poovey tells us, Stewart – with the best of intentions – wanted to open up new vistas with his work, to produce "not certainty but hope."[1314] In order to do this, he created a philosophical process that involved two separate steps, both leading to the phenomenon of abstraction.

1312 *Ibid.*, 161.

1313 More information on the Tuori model can be found in the following: Kaarlo Tuori, "Legislation Between Politics and Law" in Luc J. Wintgens, (ed.) *Legisprudence: A New Theoretical Approach to Legislatio: Proceedings of the Fourth Benelux-Scandinavian Symposium on Legal Theory* (Oxford and Portland: Hart Publishing Co., 2002), pp. 99–107, Kaarlo Tuori, Zenon Bankowski and Jyrki Uusitalo (eds.), Law and Power: Critical and Socio-Legal Essays (Liverpool: Deborah Charles Publishing, 1997).

1314 Mary Poovey, *A History of the Modern Fact: Problems of Knowledge in the Sciences of Wealth and Society* (Chicago: University of Chicago Press, 1998), 270. Citing to Dugald Stewart, *Philosophy of the Human Mind*, 99. (Emphasis mine.)

> The first move consists of elevating the signs used to designate phenomena over the phenomenal objects that these signs signify. The second involved demoting the distinguishing features of particular objects in favor of features they can be said to share, so that the philosopher can emphasize – and name – the class to which a series of phenomena belong instead of being distracted by particulars. Stewart subsumes these philosophical operations into the method he calls "abstraction."[1315]

Abstraction, in Stewart's account, was related both to Cartesian analysis and to the theory of nominalism[1316] more generally. According to Stewart, abstraction breaks objects down into their component features so that philosopher can "attend...to some...qualities or attributes, **without attending to the rest**."[1317]

When law does not have to "attend to the rest" then this is what a fact looks like. This situation, when combined with the abstraction of the law, can mutate into an ideological objectivism leading to an imbalance between the "strong we" and "weak we." One machine simply sets another machine in motion, without "attending to the [the human person inside the human body]." Abstract philosophy – as well as jurisprudence and legal theory – deals with the dichotomous "*corpus sanum* cut to fit a *mens sana*", as noted in the quotation by John Caputo, above. This "corpus sanum" is usually not a diseased body or a black body or a female body or a poor body or a body of different abilities. Abstraction also often relieves the law of the obligation to relate to the "other" and to other bodies and, at times, only assists in their dys-appearance. The problem for this type of law is that history can be used to prove these abstractions as sometimes fundamentally deceitful.

1315 *Ibid.*

1316 Nominalism is a concept from the philosophy of language whose proponents included John Locke and George Berkeley. The American Heritage Dictionary defines it as "the doctrine holding that abstract concepts, general terms or *universals* have no independent existence but exist only as names." Basically, the term means that things or ideas have not existence outside of the mind, or imagination. Objects have nothing in common besides their name, therefore the name "nominalism." The philosophy denies the existence of universals. Nominalism exists on a continuum from extreme nominalism to near-realism. http://newadvent.org/cathen/11090c.htm, accessed April 9, 2009.

1317 Poovey, Fact, 270. Note 302.

8 Appendices

8.1 Appendix A – NYSSV Membership

New York Society for the Suppression of Vice (NYSSV), Short biographies of some of the original founders.

Thatcher M. Adams Lived at 63 E. 79th Street in New York after buying 123 acres of land from Emile Grigsby, mistress of Charles Yerkes, Chicago street car magnate.

Cornelius R. Agnew (1830–1875) Physician who was appointed the Surgeon General of New York in 1858. Founded the Brooklyn ear and eye hospital in 1868 and was elected President of the York Medical Society in 1872.

J.M. Cornell Along with J.B. Cornell, he owned a wrought and cast iron company that supplied materials for the Washington Monument.

William Earl Dodge, Jr. (1805–1883) Businessman and abolitionist. Builder of the Macon and Brunswick Railroad, after the Civil War. Influential in the post-war Native American reform movement.

Morris Ketcham Jessup (1830–1908) First President of the YMCA. Banker and philanthropist. One of the founders of Syrian Protestant College, later called the American University in Beirut. Organizer of the American Museum of Natural History. One of the original trustees of the Slater Fund, along with Rutherford B. Hayes and William E. Dodge.

Elbert B. Monroe Trustee of the Hampton Institute, a black, mulatto and Indian university founded after the Civil War in Hampton, Virginia. His wife was the niece of Frederick Marquant (1799–1882) a jeweler and merchant who retired at age 40 to devote his life to philanthropy.

John Pierpoint Morgan (1813–1890), Banker, who in the late 1800s founded the most powerful banking house in the world. The company, J.P. Morgan & Co., financed the formation of the U.S. Steel Corporation and arranged the merger of Edison General Electric and Thomson-Houston Electric companies to form General Electric. The company also bought and reorganized 4 of the 5 major American railways between 1869 and 1899.[1318]

8.2 Appendix B – Indiana's Sterilization Statute

Indiana's Sterilization Statute (Full Text)
Passed 1907
House Vote: 59–22
Senate Vote: 28–16

1318 Ibid.

Table 8.1: CMHVS members and number of committee appointments

CMHVS Members and Number of Committee Appointments	**Coble (2)**	**Cox (6)**	**Keller (4)**	**Porter (5)**	**Read (5)**	**Scholl (7)**	**Simison (5)**	**Vizard (4)**	**Wade (4)**	**Total Number of CMHVS on Committee**
Affairs of Reformatory						X				1
Affairs of State Prison		X								1
Banks		X								1
Benevolent and Scientific Institutions				X	X					2
Building Loan		X				X				2
Education					X		X			2
Engrossed Bills								X		1
Federal Relations							X			1
Fees and Salaries						X				1
Legislative Apportionment	X									1
Manufacture and Commerce							X			1
Mileage and Account				X						1
Public Libraries									X	1
Reformatory Institutions									X	1
Rights and Privileges			X	X				X		3
Rivers and Waters					X					1
Roads								X		1
Phraseology of Bills							X			1
Printing				X						1
Sinking Fund		X							X	2
Soldiers Monuments						X				1
State Library						X				1
State Medicine, Health and Vital Statistics	X	X	X	X	X	X	X	X	X	9
Statistics and Immigration		X	X							2
Telegraph and Telephone						X				1
Trusts and Funds					X					1
Ways and Means			X							1

AN ACT to prevent the procreation of confirmed criminals, idiots, imbeciles and rapists: Providing that superintendents or boards of managers of institutions where such persons are confined shall have the authority and are empowered to appoint a committee of experts. Consisting of two physicians, to examine into the mental condition of such inmates. WHEREAS, heredity plays a most important part in the transmission of crime, idiocy, and imbecility:

THEREFORE, BE IT ENACTED BY THE GENERAL ASSEMBLY OF THE STATE OF INDIANA, that on and after the passage of this act it shall be compulsory for each and every institution in the state, entrusted with the care of confirmed criminals, idiots, rapists and imbeciles. To appoint skilled surgeons of recognized ability, whose duty it shall be, in conjunction with the chief physician and board of experts and the board of managers. If in the judgment of this committee of experts procreation is inadvisable, and there is no probability of improvement of the mental and physical condition of the inmate, it shall be lawful for the surgeons to perform such operation for the prevention of procreation as shall be decided safest and most effective. But this operation shall not be performed except in cases that have been pronounced unimproveable. Provided that in no case the consultation fee be more than three dollars to each expert, to be paid out of the funds appropriated for the maintenance of such institution.[1319]

8.3 Appendix C – Composition of CHMVS and Committee Appointments

Committees, 1907 Indiana General Assembly
Committee on Health, Medicine and Vital Statistics (CHMVS), as reported in *Indianapolis News*, 14 January 1907, p. 3.

CHMVS: Porter, Coble, Cox, Keller, Read, Scholl, Simison, Vizard, Wade
Chairman: Dr. A.W. **Porter** (R), Martin and Orange Counties. Member of 5 committees, Chair of CHMVS.
Members:

- Rep. **Coble** (D) of Dubois and Pike Counties, resided in Stendal. Member of 3 committees.
- Senator Lincoln A. **Cox***, (), Marion County: on 6 committees.
- **Keller** (R) of Marion County: Member of 4 committees.
- Dr. Horace D. or G. **Read**, (R), Tipton and Hamilton Counties: Member of 5 committees.
- Rep. Dr. **Scholl** (R), Carroll, Howard and Miami Counties: Member of 6 committees.

1319 Document URL: http://www.kobescent.com/eugenics/statute.html, accessed May 1, 2014.

- Rep. Dr. J. Frank **Simison** (R), Montgomery and Tippecanoe Counties: Member of 4 committees.
- Dr. John Wellington **Vizard** (D), Adams County, Pleasant Mills: Member of 4 committees.
- Frank J. **Wade** (D), Posey County: Member of 3 committees

* There were two legislators named Cox, and one was Lincoln A Cox on the CHMVS.

Other Doctors in the Legislature:

In the Senate:

- Dr. Richard R. McCain of Kentland, Chair of Senate Committee
- Dr. O.M. Keyes of Dana
- Dr. Charles R. Lane of Ft. Wayne
- Dr. McDowell of Sullivan and Knox Counties

8.4 Appendix D – Composition of the 1934–1936 Norwegian Storting by Party Affiliation, Region and Occupation

Composition of 150-Member 1934–1936 Norwegian Storting by Party (Source: http://www.norgeslexi.com/politikk/storting/representatnt/34-36.html last accessed 9 December 2007)

Party Affiliation

Labour Party (Arbeiderparti) – 68

T. Haaverstad – Aust-Agder, A. Udland – Vest-Agder, O.J. Olsen – Vest-Agder and Rogaland, I.J.S. Førre – Vest-Agder and Rogaland, K.M. Nordanger – Akershus, H. Halvorsen – Akershus, B. Korslund – Akershus, **Fru Helga A.A. Ramstad – Akershus**, J. Samuelsen – Bergen, G.O.O. Bakke – Bergen, C. Hornsrud – Buskerud, N.A. Steen – Buskerud, H.J. Jensen – Buskerud, A.R. Moss – Buskerud, A. Nygaard – Buskerud, K.H. Berg – Finnmark, A.K. Mikkola – Finnmark, O.V. Nilssen – Hedmark, O. Sæter – Hedmark, K.T. Sjøli – Hedmark, P.E. Vorum – Hedmark, K. Fonstad – Hedmark, C.F. Monsen – Hedmark and Oppland, N. Ødegaard – Hedmark and Oppland, K.O. Bergsvik – Hordaland, G.B. Forstøm – Hordaland, O.B. Oksvk – Møre and Romsdal, A.L. Alvestad – Møre and Romsdal, J.U. Olsen – Møre and Romsdal, A.J.H.H. Moan – Nordland, C.L. Enge – Nordland, C.E.C. Bonnevie – Nordland, J.O. Steffensen – Nordland, J.A. Andrå – Nordland, Troms and Finnmark, J.B. Olsen – Nordland, Troms and Finnmark, J. Bøe – Oppland, L.M. Moen – Oppland, M. Smedby – Oppland, A.M. Madsen – Oslo, M. Nilssen – Oslo, O.J. Johensen – Oslo, **Fru Helga A. Karlsen – Oslo**, I.K. Hognestad – Rogaland, A.M.A. Lothe – Sogn and Fjordane, O.M.K. Stennes – Telemark, O.A. Versto – Telemark, O.T. Vegheim – Telemark, O. Solberg – Telenmark and Aust-Agder, A. Nilssen – Telenmark and Aust-Agder,

M.N. Foshaug – Troms, W.A. Ingebrigtsen – Troms, A.J. Johansen – Troms, A.J. Moen – Nord-Trøndelag, J. Wiik – Nord-Trøndelag, J. Nygaardsvold – Sør-Trøndelag, S.K.E. Skarholt – Sør-Trøndelag, M.A. Salbubæk – Sør-Trøndelag, S.K.E. Støstad – Sør and Nord-Trøndelag, I. Aarseth – Sør and Nord-Trøndelag, J. Mathassien – Vestfold, A.M. Jenssen – Vestfold, K.A. Christiansen – Vestfold, J.O. Bergersen – Østfold, P.O. Thorvik – Østfold, A.T. Svendsen – Østfold, J.E. Pettersen – Østfold and Akershus, J.L. Johannesen – Østfold and Akershus, A. Akre – Østfold and Akershus.

The Liberal Party (Venstre) – 25

C. Stray – Aust-Agder, G.J. Eiesland – Vest-Agder, B. Olsen-Hagen – Vest-Agder and Rogaland, L.K.N. Rygh – Vest-Agder and Rogaland, R.E. Peersen – Vest-Agder and Rogaland, J.L. Mowinckel – Bergen, O.M. Mjelde – Hordland, O.J. Myklebust – Hordaland, M.A.A. Kårbø – Hordaland, O.R.K. Flem – Møre and Romsdal, J.M.J. Strand – Møre and Romsdal, P. Ø Syltebø – Møre and Romsdal, R. Anderssen-Ryst – Møre and Romsdal, J.J. Caroliussen – Nordland, J.I. de Kobro – Nordland, Troms and Finnmark, K.K. Kleppe – Rogaland, K. Edland – Rogaland, J.M.A. Lothe – Sogn and Fjordane, H.K. Seip – Sogn and Fjordane, N. Valen –Telemark, A. Alexander – Telenmark and Aust-Agder, A.K.H. Jakobsen – Troms, H.M. Five – Noard-Trøndelag, S.O. Leinum – Sør-Trøndelag, N.M. Tvedten – Vestfold.

Conservative Party (Høyre) – 30

J.M. Ørbeæk – Aust-Agder, B.A.B. Skeibrok – Vest-Agder, S. Nielsen – Vest-Agder and Rogaland, K. Jacobsen – Vest-Agder and Rogaland, O.L. Bæroe – Akershus, H. Gram – Akershus, T.B. Mowinckel – Bergen, J.R. Aas – Buskerud, S.A. Svensen – Buskerud, C.R. Olsen – Finnmark, J.A. Svendsen – Hedmark and Oppland, I.J. Bleiklie – Hordaland, E.H.P. P. Præsteng – Nordland, O. Fjalstad – Nordland, Troms and Finnmark, C.J. Hambro – Oslo, E. Getz – Oslo, A.H.E. Nordlie – Oslo, T. Vinje – Rogaland, S.C. Brinch – Telenmark and Aust-Agder, E.A. Johansen – Telenmark and Aust-Agder, M.S.P. Laberg – Troms, J.O.O. Asmundvaag – Sør-Trøndelag, I. Lykke – Sør and Nord-Trøndelag, **Frk. Signe Swennsson – Sør and Nord-Trøndelag**, N.J. Shjerven – Vestfold, S.F. Brunn – Vestfold, T. Sverdrup –Vestfold, H.J. Sollie – Vestfold, I. Undrum – Østfold, H.S. Bakke – Østfold and Akershus.

The Farmers' Party (Bondepartiet) – 23

N. Nerstan – Aust-Agder, G.E. Moseid – Vest-Agder, J. Sundby – Akershus, K.H. Tandberg – Buskerud, O. Øst-Deglum – Hedmark, L.O. Aukrust – Hedmark, J.N. Vik – Hordaland, R.O. Langeland – Møre and Romsdal, M. Trædal – Møre and Romsdal, L.S. Rommundstad – Møre and Romsdal, N.K.N. Mjaavatn – Nordland, H.N. Hanssen – Nordland, K. Ørud – Oppland, E. Bjørnson – Oppland, N.M. Kverneland – Rogaland, G.A. Hegernes – Sogn and Fjordane, P.T. Hovland – Sogn and Fjordane, J.F. Hundseid – Telemark, I.L. Kirkeby-Garstad – Nord-Trøndelag, E. Müller – Nord-Trøndelag,

M.H. Handberg – Sør-Trøndelag, A. Maastad – Østfold, B. Braadland – Østfold and Akershus.

Society Party (Samfundsparti) – 1 B.D. Brochmann – Bergen
Kr and F – 1 N. Larvik – Hordaland
R and F – 1 A. Mjøen – Oppland
F and F – 1 R.R. Ræder – Sør and Nord-Trøndelag

Occupations
Arbeidsformann (Work Foreman) – 1
Assistant – 1

Bakermester (Master Baker) – 1
Bankdirektør and gårdbruker (Bank Director and Farmer) – 1
Banksjef (Bank Manager) – 1
Bibelskolebestyrer and gårdbruker (Bible School Prinicipal and Farmer) – 1
Bokhandler (Bookshop) – 1
Bryggearabeider (Construction Worker) – 1

Direktør and ingenør (Director and Engineer) – 1
Direktør and major (Director and Major) – 1

Fabrikkarbeider (Manufacturing Worker) – 3
Fisker (Fisherman) – 3
Fisker and småbruker (Fisherman and Small Farmer) – 1
Fiskeriinspektør (Fishery Inspector) – 1
Fullmektig (Law Clerk) – 1
Fylkeskasserer (District Treasurer) – 1
Fylkesmann (Chief Administrative Officer of a District) – 1

Gårdbruker (Farmer) – 29
Gårdbruker and bankasserer (Farmer and Bank Cashier) – 1
Gårdbruker and fanejunker (Farmer and Highest Non-Commissoned Officer) – 1
Gårdbruker and fisker (Farmer and Fisherman) – 2
Gårdbruker and landbrukslærer (Farmer and Agriculture Teacher) – 1
Gårdbruker and poståpner (Farmer and Post Opener) – 1
Gårdbruker and statsrevisor (Farmer and State's Accountant) – 1
Generalsekretære (General Secretary) – 1 Gullsmed (Jeweler)– 1

Havne- og transportarbeder (Ocean and Transportation Worker) – 1
Herredskasserer (Township Treasurer) – 1 Hovedkasserer (Head Cashier) – 1
Høyesterettsadvokat (Attorney entitled to practice before the Supreme Court) – 2

Jordbrukkonsulent (Agricultural Consultant) – 1

Kaiarbeider (Wharf Worker) – 1
Kontorsjef (Office Manager) – 2
Kjøpmann (Merchant) – 4
Kommunearbeider (Municipal Worker) – 1
Kommunerevisør (Municipal Accountant) – 1
Konsul (Consul) – 1
Kontrollør (Inspector) – 1

Lagerarbeider (Warehouse Worker) – 1
Landsbrukssekretær (Agriculturer Secretary) – 1
Landbrukslærer (Agricultural Teacher) – 1
Landbruksskolebestyrer (Agricultural School Principal) – 3
Lektor (Secondary School or University Teacher)– 1
Lege (Doctor) – 1
Lensmann (Administrative Official) – 3
Lærer and Gårdbruker (Teacher and Farmer) – 1
Lærer (Teacher) – 7

Major and Skogeier (Major and Forest Owner) – 1
Marinekaptein (Sea Captain) – 1
Maskinist (Machinist) – 1
Murmester (Masonry Master) – 1

Oberstløytnant and gårdbruker (Lieutenent General and Farmer) – 1
Overingeniør (Head Engineer) – 1

Papirarbeider (Paper Worker) – 1
Prost (Cathedral Dean) – 1

Redaktør (Editor) – 8
Rektor (President of University/Principal of Secondary School) – 1

Sagarbeider (Sawmill Worker) – 1
Skipsreder (Ship Owner) – 1
Skolebestyrer (School Princpal) – 3
Skoleinspektør (School Inspector) – 3
Skreddermester (Master Tailor) – 1
Småbruker (Small Farmer) – 8
Småbruker and fisker (Small Farmer and Fisherman) – 2
Snekker (Cabinet Maker) – 1

Sorenskriver (Chief Judge of a Rural District) – 2
Sosiologisk Forfatter (Sociology Author)– 1
Statsråd (Cabinet Minister) – 3
Statsadvokat (Prosecuting Attorney) – 1
Statsminister (Prime Minister) – 1
Statsrevisor (State Accountant/Treasurer) – 1
Steinarbeder (Stone Worker) – 1

Telekontrollør (Telegraph Inspector) – 1
Telegrafissst (Telegrapher) – 1

Underfoged (Assistant Tax Collector) – 1

Vaktmester (Caretaker) – 2 Verkmester (Plant/Mill Manager) – 2

Party Distribution in 150-Member Storting
Labour Party (Arbeiderparti) – 68 Members (45.3%)
Conservative Party (Høyre) – 30 Members (20%)
Venstre – 25 Members (16.6%)
B Party – 23 Members (15.3%)
Society Party (Samfundsparti) – 1 Member (0.6%)
Kr and F Party – 1 Member (0.6%)
R and F Party – 1 Member (o.6%)
F and F Party – 1 Member (0.6%)

Approximate Occupation Percentages of 150-member Storting
Bank/Merchant/Manager – 16 (10.6%)
Blue collar – 18 (12%)
Farming – 46 (30.6%)
Fishing – 4 (2.6%)
Professional (Attorney/Doctor/Engineer/Lector/Rector) – 6 (4%)
State Administrative/Professional – 20 (13.3%)
Teacher – 10 (6.6%)
White Collar – 30 (20%)

8.5 Appendix E – Translation of Storting Debate, 1934[1320]

Translation of the transcript from the 9 May 1934 Storing Committee meeting, called to order at 12:15 P.M. The President was Eiesland. The meeting lasted 2 hours and 10 minutes and handled 8 items. The seventh item was the "Instilling fra justiskomiteen til lov om adgang til sterilisering m. v. (Innst. O. nr. 46). The debate was taken from Volume 8 of the 1934 multi-volume Stortingsforhandling, published by the Central-trykkeviet in Oslo, 1934. The debate began on page 157 of Volume 8 and ended on page 161, followed by a copy of the law.

Committee Members

- Storting Representative E. Bjørson (Bonde Party) from Oppland District
- Storting Representative Bonde (Alternate for B.D. Brochmann) (Samfundsparti) from Bergen District
- Storting Representative C.E.C. Bonnevie (Labour Party) from Nordland District
- Storting Representative O. Fjalstad (Conservative Party) from Nordland, Troms and Finnmark District
- Cabinet Minister Sunde

Sak Nr. 7	Item Number 7
Instilling fra justiskomiteen til lov om adgang til sterilisering m.v. (Innst. O. nr. 46)	The Report from the Justice Committee regarding the Law on Access to Sterilization submitted as Odelstinget Proposition Number 46.
Saka i det heile vart sett under debatt.	The entire Report was open for debate.
Bjørnson (Komiteens ordfører): Det er naturlig at valget til å fremlegge denne proposisjon er falt på en bonde. For der er ingen som gård brukerne der daglig kan iaktta den uhyre fordel som en gjennomført rasehygiene har for gårdsdriften og dermed for det hele land Dette gjelder ikke bare buskapen, men også alle nyttevekster som landbruket er avhengig av. På den ene side går våre bestrebelser ut på å sikre en kraftig, avlsdyktig og ydende stamme, på den annen side å befri den for snyltedyr og ukrutt. Bare ugresset koster landet mange millioner kroner om året.	**Bjørnson** (The Chair of the Committee): It is natural that the choice of someone to talk about this bill has fallen to a farmer. For there is no one like a farmer who can, on a daily basis, observe the enormous advantage that comes from race hygiene in the management of the farm and therefore for the entire country. This concerns not only animal husbandry but also all the new crops that farming is dependent upon. On the one hand are our efforts to produce powerful, genetically sound and productive stock and, on the other hand, is our ability to free this stock from the parasites and weeds cost the country millions of kroner annually.

1320 My sincere thanks to Professor Sissel Jensen Nefzaou and to Professor Sætnan for their assistance in this translation; all mistakes in translation or meaning are ultimately mine.

Stortinget har ved lovkraft og bevilgninger i mange år støttet arbeidet for å fremme folkehelsen og deler med videnskapen æren for at folkets gjennomsnittsalder i betydelig grad er gått frem. Mens den for vel 50-år siden lå under folkets kraftigste alder, ligger den nu adskillig år over. Som et samlet folk er vi idag nesten tyve år eldre enn den generasjon var som våre forfedre tilhørte. Man kan si at der aldri før har levd i Norge en så gammel folkegenerasjon. Det bør man merke sig, og det ser ut som grensen ennu ikke er nådd, for så virksomt arbeider videnskap og folkeviljen hånd i hånd om å trygge de enkeltes liv. En naturlig utvikling av de forandrede forhold har vært at det arbeidsdyktige samfund er blitt belastet med økede utgifter til alderstrygd og sykebehandling samt andre byrder i forbindelse hermed. Mens det for 40 à 50 år siden var en skam å komme på forsorgen er det i de nye tiders forholds medfør blitt en selvfølgelighet at samfundet trygger en sorgfri alderdom og hjelper de ikke arbeidsdyktige til utkomme. Skattene og avgiftene stiger og umiliggjør selv for den flinkeste og sparsomste å legge såpass til side at han kan sørge for sig og sine. Det er ikke tvil om at det moderne samfund allerede i så henseende viser tegn på at det er overbelastet. Det gjelder derfor mer enn nogen sinne at den arbeidsdyktige stamme ved rasehygiene blir så kraftig som mulig, så den kan overkomme kravene uten å miste sitt livsmot.	Over many years the Storting, through its laws and appropriations, has supported the work to advance the health of citizens and shares with science the honor to have increased the average age of our citizens to a meaningful degree. Fifty years ago the average age was less than the age when people are at their strongest but now this age has been increased by several years. As a nation, we are today nearly 20 years older than the generation to which our parents belonged. One can say that there has never before lived in Norway a generation that has lived to such an advanced age. One should pay attention to this and it looks like the limit hasn't been reached yet because science and the will of the people, working hand in hand, works in such an effective way to secure the life of the individual. A natural development from the changed situation, has been that the those who are the able-bodied workers* of society have become saddled with rising taxes for the old age pensions and hospital care together with other burdens in connection with this. While, forty or fifty years ago, it was a disgrace to receive welfare, we now have a new situation in which it is obviously a matter of common knowledge that society secures a worry-free old age and helps those who are not able-bodied workers to have enough at their disposal. Taxes and fees are rising making it impossible for even the most capable and parsimonious to put something aside so that he can provide for himself and his own family. There is no doubt that modern society, in this respect, already shows signs that it is overburdened. It is important therefore, more than ever, that the able-bodied working stock of people, through race hygiene, become as powerful as possible, so that they can overcome all these demands without losing their own will to live.
Det er med dette syn på fremtiden at Tyskland er gått til tvangssterilisering for å befri de kommende generasjoner for å trekkes med an overbelastning av degenererte mennesker. Det skjer således til fordel for dem som har gjort sin plikt like overfor samfundet og nu som gamle kun kan følge begivenhetene, så vel som til fordel for den yngre generasjons sundhet og utdannelse. Av frykt for at der ikke skal bli nok unge krefter	It is with this view of the future that Germany has enacted forced sterilization in order to free the coming generations from being burdened with degenerate humans. This benefits those who have done their duty to society and now as aged can only watch and follow whatever happens. There will also be an advantage for the health and education of the younger generation. Out of fear that there will not be enough young people to bear the

til å bære byrdene, utbetales der nu i Tyskland flere hundre millioner kroner til fremme av nye ekteskaper. Så alvorlig tar de saken der.

burdens, there is now in Germany the disbursement of many hundred millions of kroner to help new marriages. So seriously do the Germans take these matters.

Det er allerede klart for enhver som setter sig inn i disse spørsmål, og som vil se at forholdene utvikler sig i den retning at det blir imperativt nødvendig for et folk i den henseende å drive folkebruk, som man nu driver gårdsbruk, dersom man vil trygge folket en lykkelig og trygg fremtid. Med denne tvingende nødvendighet som bakgrunn er det forebyggende lovforslag et spakfer (page 158) dig tiltak. Våre efterkommer vil kanskje komme til å bebreide oss at vi ikke straks går til mer drastiske forholdsregler, da nødvendigheten herav sikkerligen er til stede, og arvelighetslovene tilsier en å handle både hurtig or grundig. Dette lovforslag gir også anledning til allerede nu å gå et skritt videre, og åpne adgang til tvungen seksualinngrep, og blir der optatt forslag herom, akter iallfall, jeg å stemme for dette. Når vi i komiteen ikke har fremsatt forslag herom, var det av frykt for at det da kunne gå med denne lov som med den jeg sist forsvarte har i Odelstinget, som vi desverre ikke fikk det mer konservative, og kanskje mer bigotte Lagting til å gå med på. Jeg mener loven om å gi kvinnene samme rett til å bli prester som menn. Dertil kommer at selve loven som vi foreslår den, er i og for sig en utmerket lov, som med et slag setter vårt land in rang med de mest fremskredne land på dette område.

It is already clear to anyone who is trying to understand these questions and who is willing to see that conditions are developing in such a direction that will make it imperative to breed people and one now breeds animals if one will be able to secure for the population a happy and secure future. With this type of force of necessity as background before us, this bill is a mild attempt. Our descendants will perhaps criticize us that we did not immediately take more drastic measures when the necessity for them was assuredly in place, and the law of genetics demand that we deal with this quickly and thoroughly. This bill also gives us the possibility to even now go a step further and open access to forced sterilization. And, should this proposal come about I, for one, intend to vote for it. When we here in the committee have not advanced the bill to that point, it was out of fear that the result would be the same with this law as happened to the last bill I defended here in the Odelsting, which we unfortunately couldn't make the more conservative and perhaps more biased Lagting to go along with. I refer to the law that would have given women the same right as men to become priests. In addition, this law itself, in the way we propose it, is a remarkable law which, with one sudden blow, sets our country in the same position as the most progressive countries in this area.

Jeg synes ikke jeg kan avslutte dette mitt innlegg uten å få takke statråd Sunde for at han har tatt denne sake op og fremlagt det utmerkede lovforslag, som vi nesten uten endring har fulgt. Men jeg vil også fra denne plass få sende vår anerkjennende takk til de menn og kvinner som har modnet denne sak i vårt folk, så den nu idag vil gå sin sikre vandring til lov. Særlig vil jeg nevne Den norske rådgivende komité for rasehygiene med dens utrettelige leder dr. Alfred Mjøen, som ved denne loves vedtagelse vil få den anerkjennelse også i vårt land, som han for lengst har erhvervet ute i verden.

I don't feel that I can close my introductory remarks without thanking minister Sunde since he has picked up this cause and proposed this splendid bill, which we have followed almost with any change. But, at this time, I also want toextend dan appreciative thanks to those men and women who have matured this cause with our citizens, so that now, today, it will certainly follow its certain path into law. I want especially to thank The Norwegian Advisory Committee for Race-Hygiene and its indefatigable leader Dr. A. Mjøen, who, with this law's passage, will also get the recognition in our country which he has had for such along time out in the world.

Til slutt må jeg gjøre opmerksom på at annen linje i §7 skal det stå << befatning med steriliseringssaker >> istedenfor ordene << behandling med steriliseringssaker >>.	In closing, I want to point out that the second line in §7 should read "connection with sterilization cases" instead of the words "treatment of sterilization cases."
Bonde: Jeg har ikke det samme syn på det lovforslag som her er fremlagt, som komiteens ordfører nettop gav uttrykk for. Jeg finner at dette lovforslag, som idag er lagt frem for Odelstinget er et av de farligste lovforslag som overhode har sett dagens lys i landet.	**Bonde:** I do not feel the same about this bill, which has been proposed by the committee Chairman who just spoke for it. I find that this proposal that is placed before the Odelsting today is one of the most dangerous proposals ever to see the light of day in this country.
Det er jo klart det må være et visst forhold mellom samfund og individ, men der er i dette tilfelle rettet et angrep på individet, hvorved man i høi grad retter baker for smed. Vi må jo husker på at forbryderne blir ikke forbrytere i kraft av sig selv, men de blir forbrytere ikke minst i kraft av det miljø, de omgivelser de lever i. Det er de samfundsforhold vi lever under som skaper forbryterne, - de forbryter vi har det er prisen vi må betale for de dårlige samfundsforhold. Når vi legger sedelighetsforbryteren hans forbrytelse til last og dømmer ham, så er vi på feil vei. Det er underlig at vi i et land, hvor vi snakker om 900 års kristendom, fullstendig har glemt vår barnelærdom. Det var en mann for 1900 år siden som sa i en lignende situasjon: Den som er uten skyld, han kaste den først sten. Men vi i Norges Stortinget, anno 1934, vi kaster sten alle sammen. Vi innbys her i Odelstinget til å dømme individet for det som vi selv gjennom vår samfundsorden har ansvaret for. Løsningen av dette spørsmål er ikke den at vi skal gå til voldelige inngrep på individet, men løsningen, den eneste varige løsning – og også den eneste mulige rasehygiene i lengden - er den ting at vi får endret på de samfundsforhold vi lever under og dermed redusert forbrytelsenes antall. Jeg mener der er barbarisk og middelaldersk å la individet lide for det som samfundet har skylden for.	It is clear that there has to be a certain relationship between society and the individual, but, in this case, the law directs an attack on the individual, which, to large degree,makes the innocent suffer for the guilty. We have to remember that criminals do not become criminals by virtue of themselves but they become criminals, not the least through the environment and the surroundings in which they live. It is these societal influences that we live in that create the criminals, – these criminals that we have, that's the price we must pay for the bad social conditions. When we accuse and convict the sexual criminal for his crime, we are on a mistaken course. It is strange that in a country, where we talk about 900 years of Christianity, that we have completely forgotten our catechism lessons. There was one man 1900 years ago who, placed in a similar situation who said, "Let he who are without guilt caste the first stone." But we here in the Norwegian Parliament, in the year 1934, we are all casting stones. We are invited here in the Odelsting to judge the individual that we, through our own social order, have responsibility for. The solution to this question, to this violent attack on the individual, theonly lasting solution – and also the only possible race hygiene in the long run – is that we must change societal conditions under which we live and through this secure a reduction in the number of criminals. I believe that it is barbaric and medieval to let the individual suffer for something that society has the blame for.
Min oppfatning er at det er en slett forberedelse det fremlagte lovforslag har vært gjenstand for. Det er jo klart at den nye videnskap som går sin seiersgang over hele verden, den nye psykologi og psykoanalyse har et helt annet syn på	My opinion is that the proposed law that is before us has been badly prepared. It is clear that the new science which goes in a triumphant procession around the entire world, the new psychology and psychoanalysis has a totally different attitude

forbryterer og forbrytelser enn den gamle hedensk-romerske opfatning som ligger til grunn for vårt juridiske system. Det er jo på det rene at en sedelighetsforbryter utfører sin forbrytelse i en sjelelig nød, det er de sjelelige forhold ved individet som skaper forbryteren og man forbedrer ikke en forbryter ved å sperre ham inne i et fengsel. Vil man være sikker på at man ikke skal få uskadeliggjort en sedelighetsforbryter så skal man sette ham i et fengsel en 2-3 år og så slippe ham ut igjen, for da er det noget som er helt klart at han er ti ganger verre enn da han blev satt inn. Men den nye videnskap er fullt klar over at en sedelighets (page 159) forbryter kan sjelelig helbredes gjennom psykologisk påvirkning. Psychoanalysen har nettop som opgave å gjøre også forbrytere til nyttige samfundsmennesker igjen. Det er en utredning av de forhold, vi savner i forberedelsen til denne lov.

towards criminals and crimes than does the old pagan-roman experience that lies at the foundation of out legal system. It is clear that a sexual criminal commits his crime in a state of mental despair and it is this mental state that creates the crime and one cannot cure the criminal by locking him up in a prison. If one intends not to cure the criminal, then one should put the sexual criminal in jail for 2—3 years and let him out again because there is nothing clearer than that he is ten times worse than when he was put in prison. But the new science is clear on that point that a sexual criminal can be mentally cured through the influence of psychology. Psychoanalysis has as its goal to remake criminals into useful social persons again. It is an account of these conditions that we miss in the preparation of this law.

Jeg vil på det bestemteste advare mot at man treffer nogen beslutning om dette lovforslag idag. Jeg vil foreslå at saken utsettes, inntil den også er utredet på det område den nye videnskap her er kommet til, og som hele verden over nu vekker den største opmerksomhet.

I would warn very strongly against a decision on this bill today. I would suggest that the issue be set aside, until looked at in light of the new science that is receiving great attention now throught the world.

Bonnevie: Jeg tror at denne sak har fått en meget omhyggelig forberedelse. Det som kunde sies å mangle i lovens forberedelse og forarbeid er vel dette ene at de synsmåter som samfundspartiet representerer, ikke har fått gjøre sig gjeldende, men ellers mener jeg at den i alle deler er vel forberedt. Jeg mener også at de uttalelser representanten Bonde kom med i virkeligheten helt skyter over mål. Så lenge lovforslaget ikke har møtt motsigelse fra noget annet hold enn samfundspartiet, og da vi her står foran en enstemmig instilling, akter jeg ikke å komme nærmere inn på denne lov og det alvorlige materiale den gjelder. Jeg vil bare som sagt presiser at hr. Bonde skyte over mål.

Bonnevie: I believe that this issue has been given a great deal of painstaking preparation. The one thing one could say is missing in this preparation of the law and prepatory work of the law is the view represented by the Samfundsparti, which has not been considered, but otherwise I think that in all respects the bill is adequately prepared. I also think that the comments by Representative Bonde have actually missed the mark. As long as the bill has not encountered discrepancies other than those held by the Samfundsparti and as we have before us a unanimous proposal, I do not intend to pay any closer attention to this law and the serious content it contains. I only want, as I have said, to point out that Mr. Bonde has overshot his mark.

Dette lovarbeid gjelder jo dels sterilisering og lignende forholdsregler overfor dem som frivillig samtykker i det; dernest gjelder det seksualinngrep overfor sinnssvake og åndssvake personer, nærmere angitt i loven. Dette siste inngrep er i realiteten et slags tvunget inngrep fordi disse sinnssvake eller åndelig mindre

This prepatory law work concerns partly sterilization and similar measures concerning those who voluntarily partake in it; thereafter, it concerns the sterilization** of the mentally ill and the mentally weak***, more thoroughly explained in the law itself. This last intervention is in reality a type of forced intervention because these mentally ill

utrustede, de samtykker ikke selv – det er ikke nødvendig, det er en verge eller kurator som samtykker. Men det som hr. Bonde nevnte og kom inn på, er den tredje gruppe. Det er tvangsinngrep overfor sedelighetsforbrytere, som altså hverken har gitt samtykke og som heller ikke er sinnssvake eller åndelig mindre utrustet. Og hvad denne tredje gruppe, altså disse sedelighetsforbrytere, angår så har ikke proposisjonen noget forslag, og den enstemmige komitéinnstilling har heller ikke på dette tidspunkt kommet med noget forslag. Det er bare slik at flere av komiteens medlemmer, som hr. Bjørnson sa, har forbeholdt sig der å stå fritt, og det kan man vel komme tilbake til ved behandlingen av den spesielle paragraph. Jeg skal bare på dette tidspunkt få tilføie at efter min opfatning må selvsagt individets rett veies overfor samfundets rett. Men det som har bidratt til at dette lovforslag som dette kommer frem, er naturligvis et dypere syn både på samfundets interesser og en dypere følelse av ansvar overfor efterslekten og de resultater i det hele tatt som arvelighetsforskningen har medført. Jeg vil sluttelig bare si at lovforslaget som det er tilblitt hos oss, er ikke et resultat bare eller fortrinvis av hvad man i Tyskland under Hitler har foreslått. Leser man proposisjonen eller leser man straffelovkomisjonens instilling eller andre forarbeider, ser man jo at det er arbeidet med denne sak også i andre land in Norden som utenfor Norden. Og en enkelt mann bør vel nevnes her, det er overlæge Johann Scharffenberg, som i høi grad med sine bidrag i pressen og for øvrig har bidratt til å reise denne sak.

or mentally less endowed, they cannot consent on their own behalf – it is not necessary – there is a guardian or a social worker who consents. But that which Mr. Bonde has mentioned and brought forward is this third group. It is the forced sterilization of the sexual criminals that have neither given consent nor are mentally ill or mentally less endowed. And what concerns this third group, these sexual criminals, has not been referred to in the proposal nor has the unanimous committee report come up with a proposal at this time. It is only so that many of the members of the committee, which Mr. Bjørnson has said, have not taken a decision on it and it may be that one can come back to it by treatment in another special paragraph. At this point in time I shall only add that, in my opinion, the right of the individual must obviously be weighed against the right of society. But what has contributed to the fact that this bill has been advanced is naturally “a deeper view” of both society’s interest and a deeper feeling of responsibility to our descendents and to the results that genetic research has brought forth. Finally, I want only to say that the bill, which has come before us here, is not the result only or primarily a result of what has been proposed in Germany under Hitler. If one reads the bill or if one reads the criminal commission’s report or other prepatory work, one would see that there is work of this type in other countries both inside Scandinavia and outside it. And one individual man should clearly be mentioned here, and that is Medical Director Johan Scharffenberg, who has to a great extent contributed in the press and in other fields in bringing this bill to this point.

(The proposal is physically taken to the President’s table and put on it.)

Presidenten: Representanten Bonde har teke op dette framlegget: << Ot. prp. 17 for 1934 tas ikke under behandling av inneværende års Odelsting. >>

President: Representative Bonde has brought up this proposal: << Ot. prp. nr. 17 for 1934 should not be taken into consideration during the present year by the Odelsting. >>

Fjalstad: Den ærende representant hr. Bondes angrep på proposisjonen og innstillingen må hvile på en total misforståelse av hvad lovutkastet går ut på. Forholdet er nemlig det at ifølge proposisjonen og den enstemmige innstilling vil der ikke være anledning til seksualinngrep

Fjalstad: The honorable representative Bonde’s attack on the bill and its recommendation must rest on a total misunderstanding of what the draft law sets out to do. The case is that according to the bill and the unanaimous recommendation there will not be permission to sterilize a normal

like overfor normale personer, selv om de er sedlighetsforbryterer, med mindre de selv samtykker i det. Og hvad sinnssyke personer og personer med sterkt nedsatt tilregnelighet angår kreves det samtykke av vergen. Forslaget bygger på frivillighetsprincippet. Jeg skal ikke si mer om saken i sin almindelighet. Jeg forbeholder mig å komme tilbake til det spørsmål som det har vært en del diskusjon om i komiteen, når vi kommer til den spesielle paragraf. Jeg vil bare her ha fremholdt at det må være misforståelse av hvad loven går ut på, som ligger til grunn for representanten Bondes angrep på proposisjonen. (page 160)

person even if they are sexual criminals, unless they consent to it. And as far as concerns mentally ill people and people with gravely diminished responsibilities, consent of a guardian would be required. The bill builds on the principle of voluntary action. I won't say anything more about the case in general. I reserve the right to come back to the question that has been discussed in the committee when we come to that specific paragraph. I want only here to call attention to the fact that there must be a misunderstanding on what the law sets out to do which is the basis for Represenetative Bonde's attack on the bill. (page 160)

Statsråd Sunde: Efter det som er uttalt av de to siste ærnde talere, kan jeg fatte mig i den største korthet. Hr. Bonde talte om slett lovforbedredelse. Det forekommer mig at man før man bruker den slags uttrykk, burde bemøie sig med å lese iallfall selve lovforslaget og helst også preposisjonen.

Minister Sunde: After what has been expressed by the last two honerable speakers I will be very brief. Mr. Bonde spoke about a poor preparation of the law. It strikes me that before one uses this type of language, one should take the trouble, in any case, to read the bill that has been suggested and preferably also the report itself.

Bonde: Det var typisk å høre hr. Bonnevies uttalelser, hvor han gjorde sig til talsmann for at de meninger som jeg forfekter, kunde det ikke tas hensyn til fordi de kom fra en enkelt man, mens det stod en enstemmelig komitéinnstilling mot mig. Det er jo så her i Stortinget at den individuelle mening teller ikke, det er bare partimeningen. Og når jeg da representerer et helt parti, vil jeg sette stor pris på om det blev tatt hensyn til den mening som jeg forfekter. Det er så at ingen kan benekte den ting at der i utredningen vedrørende dette lovforslag ikke er tatt hensyn til de nye resultater som man gjennem den nye psykologi og psykoanalysen er kommet til ut over verden, det kan statsråden ikke benekte, det kan ingen benekte. Og da har jeg rett til å karakterisere tingen sådan som jeg har gjort, fordi jeg mener det er et vesentlig punkt i tingen. Og jeg mener det er i høi grad påkrevd av Odelstinget å vise den største forsiktighet like overfor de voldelige inngrep som her er antydet like overfor individet. Og man kan heller ikke komme forbi den ting at man retter baker for smed, når man tar fatt på individet utelukkende for de ting som også samfundet har den største skyld for. Jeg vil så innstendig jeg kan, henstille til Odelstinget at det ikke vedtar denne

Bonde: It was typical to hear Mr. Bonnevie's words where he made himself the spokesman and claimed the opinions that I defend and which could not be taken into consideration becaue it comes from an individual man while an unanimous committee recommendation stood against me. It is like this here in the Storting, that an individual opinion means nothing and that there is only the party opinion. As I represent a whole party I would greatly appreciate it if you consider the opinion that I am putting forward. It is true that nobody can deny that, in the way that this bill has been prepared, the new results that one has seen from the new psychology and psychological analysis from all over the world has not been paid attention to; the Cabinet Minister cannot deny this, noone can deny it. And then consequently, I have the right to characterize the thing just as I have done, because I believe it is an essential point in that thing. And I believe it is to a high degree necessary for the Odelsting to show the greatest care in relation to such a violent intervention presumed to directly affect the individual. Nor should we forget whereby one makesthe innocent suffer for the guilty, when one concentrates exclusively on the individual for the things which society also has the greatest guilt for. I want to

skjebnesvangre lov nu iår, men nærmere overveier spørsmålet til neste år.	propose to the Odelsting as urgently as I can that it should not pass this fateful law now this year but more thoroughly review the question next year.
Bjørnson: Vi i komiteen blev fra hr. Bonde bebreidet at vi hadde ikke fremlagt denne sak i dens hele dybde, kan jeg vel si. Jeg vil sannelig til hr. Bonde selv komme med adskillige bebreidelser. Han kommer i et langt, oratorisk innlegg og skal angripe oss, uten at han vitterlig har lest loven. Det fremgår da tydelig hvad han sa. Han uttalte at samfundet vil gå frem med vold. Ikke på nogen måte, hr. Bonde! Det står til individet selv å bestemme hvor vidt han vil la sig seksualoperere, og er individet slik at han ikke har sin fulle åndsfullkommenhet, så har han en kurator eller en verge som skal bestemme for ham. Det står i vår lov. Så bebreidet han oss at vi ikke har tatt hensyn til den moderne linje, som hr. Bonde taler om. Det viser mig atter hvor lite hr. Bonde har lest denne lov. Hvis han ser efter i §4, så står det at medisinaldirektøren eller i tilfelle det sakkyndige råd bestemmer seksualinngrepets art. Det er med andre ord efter denne lov intet i veien for at man kan gå inn på den linje som hr. Bonde mener man skal redde samfundet efter.	**Bjørnson:** I suppose I can say that Mr. Bonde has criticized us in the committee for not having discussed this law in all its depth. I will truthfully criticize Mr. Bonde himself with devisive criticism. He comes here with a long, oratorical speech and attacks us, obviously without having read the law. This is evident from what he has said. He said that society would use violence. By no means, Mr. Bonde! It is for the individual himself to decide whether he wants to allow these sexual operations or not and if it is an individual who does not have full mental comprehension then he has a social worker or a guardian who can decide for him. That is included in our law. Then hecriticized us that we have not paid attention to the modern line – as Mr. Bonde speaks about. It shows me again how little Mr. Bonde has read this law. If he looks carefully at §4 it says that either the Medical Director or, if that's the case, an expert committee, decides the nature of the operation. There is, in other words, nothing in this law that prohibits the line that Mr. Bonde believes would save society.
Denne sak er av en overordentlig stor betydning. Hvis man har lest all den litteratur som er fremkommet om denne sak, vil man komme til det. Det viser sig i allfall in Danmark, hvor man har statistikk både over lovens virkninger, likesom man også har statistikk over fødselsprocenten innen de forskjellige leire, at mens fødeselsprocenten går ned hos de levedyktige individer, de ansvarlige familier, så har den steget i en voldsom grad nettop hos de defekte familier, og for å kunne være med og råde bot på dette og få en sterk slekt er det heller ikke minst at man har gått til denne lov, en lov som har gått sin seiersgang over hele verden og som jeg ikke tviler på at Odelstinget vil se berettigelsen av. La så samfundpartiet få lov til å stå der! Det er ikke første gang jeg kjemper mot den reaksjonære linje i dette partis program under navn av en frihet som vi andre ikke forstår.	This case has extraordinarily far-reaching implications. If one has read all of the literature that has come outon the issue, one would realize that this can be shown in Denmark at any rate where one has both statistics about the inplementation of the law, and about the birth rate in different categorie; that while the birth rate decreases in the homes of healthy individuals, the responsible families, the birth rate has increased to a horrible extent exactly in the defective families and, in order to get a strong stock, it is not least in order to repair this and to achieve what we have proposed this law, that has gone in a triumphant march around the world and which I have no doubt the Odelsting will see the justification for. Let the Samfundsparti just stand there! This is not the first time that I have fought against the reactionary line in that party's program that goes under the name of a freedom that the rest of us can't understand.

Bonnevie: Hr. Bonde har ennu ikke kunnet overbevise mig om at han overhodet har lest proposisjonen og innstillingen. Det er denne og lignende grunner som gjør at jeg ikke kan tillegge hans ord særlig vekt, ikke fordi de kommer fra ham eller samfundspartiet. Hadde hr. Bonde lest proposisjonen og innstillingen og ennu mer de utrykte dokumenter, vilde han kunnet se at det er vårt lands første psykologer, bl.a. menn som professor Ragner Vogt og overlæge Scharffenberg, som har arbei- (page 161) det med i denne sak. Den er utredet av folk som kjenner sakens både psykologiske og fysiske side.	**Bonnevie:** Mr. Bonde has still not convinced me that he has read the bill and the report at all. It is because of this and the similar reasons that I can't give his words any special weight not because they come from him or from the Samfundsparti. Had Mr. Bonde read the bill and the recommendations in the report and, additionally, the documents that were not printed, then he would have been able to see that they are from our country's foremost psychologist, among others, Professor Ragner Vogt and Medical Director Scharffenberg, who have work- (page 161) ed on this bill. It has been worked on by people who know both the psychological and the physical dimensions of the proposal.
Presidenten: Hr. Bonde har havt ordet tvo gonger og har order til ein stutt merknad.	**President:** Mr. Bonde has spoken two times and has the floor for one closing remark.
Bonde: Jeg vil bare gjøre opmerksom på at jeg selvfølgelig har lest proposisjonen og dens forarbeider meget inngående, og jeg behandler tingen ganske enkelt ut den ånd og den mening som ligger i loven, og som fører til kastrering av sedelighetsforbryteren som mål. Jeg vil bare sette fingeren på at det videnskapelig sett er erkjent nu at det er andre måter å løse det hovedspørsmål på som loven tar sikte på å løse, der er andre måter enn ved voldelig inngrep på individet, og ut fra den forutsetning mener jeg at man skal være forsiktig med å vedta en så brutal lov som denne. Når hr. Bonnevie nevnte at det har vært forelagt psykologer som doktor Vogt og doktor Scharffenberg, så vil jeg bare gjøre opmerksom på at den psykologi som de representerer ikke har noget med den psykologiske gren å gjøre som jeg tenker på, nemlig psykoanalysen, og jeg fastholder at lovforslaget ikke er forberedt under hensyntagen til det som faktisk idag foreligger på psykolgiens videnskaplige område.	**Bonde:** I only want to point out that of course I have obviously read the bill and the prepatory works and have studied it very carefully and I treat this thing quite simply from the spirit and the meaning that is in the law and which leads to the castration of the sexual criminal as its goal. I wantonly to point out that, scientifically speaking, it is now acknowledged that there are other methods to solve this main question that this law intends to solve, there are other means than such a violent intrusion on the individual, and from this assumption I believe that one should be careful about approving such a brutal law as this. When Mr. Bonnevie mentioned that the bill was submitted to psychologists such as Dr. Vogt and Dr. Sharffenberg, I will only point out that the psychology that they represent has nothing to do with the branch of psychology that lam thinking about, namely psychoanalysis, and I maintain that the proposed bill was not prepared with attention to what actually is being discussed in the scientific areas of psychology.
Presidenten: Hr. Bonde har sett fram eit utsetjingsframlegg som ein må avgjera fyrr ein går på tilrådinga. Framlegget lyder slik: << Ot. prp. Nr. 17 for 1934 tas ikke under behandlingen av inneværende års Odelsting. >>	**President:** Mr. Bonde has put forward a suggestion for postponment that must be decided before the proposal. The proposal is as follows: << Ot.prop. nr. 17 for 1934 is not taken under consideration by this year's Odelsting. >>
Røysting: Framlegget frå Bonde vart mot 1 røyst ikkje vedteke.	**Voting:** The suggestion from Bonde was rejected receiving only one vote.

Nemnda hadd tilrådt Odelstinget å fatte følgende	The Committee had proposed that the Odelsting should take up the following
Beslutning til lov om adgang til sterilisering m.v.	Resolution regarding the law allowing access to sterilization.
§1	§1
En operasjon eller annen behandling som til sikter å opheve en persons forplantningsevne eller kjønnsdrift (seksualinngrep) kan foretas såfremt tillatelse innhentes efter reglene i denne lov.	An operation or other treatment which is intended to annul the reproductive ability or the sex drive of a person can be performed so long as permission is provide according to the rules set out in this law.
Tillatelse kreves dog ikke når inngrep av medisinke eller andre grunner er rettmessig efter rettsregler utenfor denne lov.	Permission of this type is not required when the procedure, due to medical or other reasons, is lawful according to the rules set out in other laws.
§2	§2
Tillatelse efter §1 gis av medisinaldirectøren.	Permission according to §1 may be given by the Medical Director.
Gjelder inngrepet en person som er mindreårig eller sinnssyk eller som har mangelfult utviklede sjelsevner, gis tillatelsen av et sakkyndig råd, som skal bestå av medisinaldirektøren som formann og 4 andre medlemmer, opnevnet av Kongen. Blandt mendlemmene skal det være minst en kvinne, en dommer og 2 læger.	If the procedure concerns a person who is a minor or who is mentally ill or lacks mental development, permission must be given by an expert panel, consisting of the Medical Director as Chairman and four other members, appointed by the King. Among the other members there shall be at least one woman, one judge and two doctors.
§3	§3
På en person som selv begjærer det, kan et seksualinngrep tillates foretatt når begjæringen har en aktverdi grunn. Er han under 21 år eller sinnssyk eller er hans åndsevner mangelfullt utviklet kreves også samtykke fra vergen eller den i §6 nevnte kurator.	If a person himself makes an application, the sexual intervention can be permitted, carried out when the reason is acceptable. If he is nder 21 years of age or mentally ill or has a lack of mental development, approval is needed from the guardian or the social worker as mentioned in §6.
§4	§4
På sinnssyke og personer med særlig mangelfullt utviklede sjelsevner kan sesksualinngrep tillates foretatt efter begjæring fra verge eller den i §6 nevnte kurator, når det ikke er håp om helbredelse eller vesentlig bedring og det er grunn til å anta at vedkommende ikke vil bli i stand til ved eget arbeide å sørge for sig og avkom, eller at en sykelig sjelstilstand eller en betydelig legemlig mangel vilde bli overført på avkom, eller at han på grunn av en abnorm kjønnsdrift vil begå sedelighetsforbrytelser.	Sexual intervention on the mentally ill and persons with a lack of mental development can be permitted, carried out at the request of the guardian or the social worker mentioned in §6 when there is no hope of recovery or essential improvement and there is reason to presume that the person will not be able to work in order to care for himself or his offspring, or that the mental condition or the serious physical defect will be conveyed to the next generation, or, that due to his abnormal sex urge, he will commit sexual crimes.

Begjæring om seksualinngrep kan i slike tilfelle også fremsettes av politimesteren i det distrikt hvor vedkommende bor; har vedkommende ikke fast bopel, kan den fremsettes av politimesterin i distrikt hvor han opholder sig. Er vedkommende anbragt i fengsel eller tvangsarbeidershus eller i pleie – eller opdragelsesanstalt, som står under offentlig tilsyn, kan begjæring tillike frem (page 162) settes av anstaltens bestyrer. I begge de her nevnte tillfelle kreves dessuten samtykke fra verge eller kurator.	A request for sexual intervention can, in such a case, also be proposed by the Police Chief of the district where the person lives; if the person has no stable residence, then the Chief of Police from the district where the person is currently living can propose it. If the person is located in a prison or in a work house or in care – or in a closed educational institution which is under administrative supervision, the request can also be made by the supervisor of the institution. In bothcases mentioned here, a guardian or a social worker must also approve the request.
§5	§5
Medisinaldirektøren eller i tilfelle det sakkyndige råd bestemmer seksualinngrepets art, foreskriver hvor inngrepet kan finne sted, og av hvem det skal utføres. Det skal som regel foretas i et offentlig eller kommunalt sykehus eller i et privat sykehus som i dette øiemed er godkjent av rådet.	The Medical Director or, when elevant, the expert panel, can decide the nature of the sexual intervention, where the intrusion shall take place and who shall perform it. Normally, this can be undertaken in a public or a county hospital, or in a private hospital which has been approved by the panel for this purpose.
§6	§6
Hvis en som er sinnssyk eller har mangelfullt utviklede sjelsevner, ikke er umyndig, skal herreds – eller byretten efter begjæring av medisinaldirektøren opnevne en kurator når det opstår spørsmål om seksualinngrep efter §§3 og 4. Det sakkyndige råd kan beslutte at det for en som umyndig, av herreds – eller byretten skal opnevnes en kurator, såfremt vergen ikke antas skikket til å avgi erklæring om seksualinngrep.	If a request has been received or behalf of a person who is mentally ill or lacks mental development but who is not a minor, then the district court shall, at the request of the Medical Director, appoint a social worker. If a request has been received under §§3 and 4, the expert panel can decide that there should be named a social worker for one who is a minor, if the minor's guardian is not seen as competent to represent the minor for a sexual intervention.
Denne beslutning av de sakkyndige råd kan under en frist av14 dager av vergen innankes for vedkommende department.	This decision of the expert panel can, within a deadline of 14 days, be appealed to the appropriate Ministry.
§7	§7
Enhver som i medhold av denne lov får befatning med steriliseringssaker, plikter å bevare taushet overfor uvedkommende med hensyn til hvad han i stillings medfør har fått kjennskap til. Over tredelser av taushetsplikten straffes med bøter, hvor ikke strengere straff følger av andre lovbestemmelser.	Pursuant to this law, everyone who has dealings with sterilization cases has a duty of silence regarding the persons involved in relation to the knowledge that he received in the undertaking of his job. Breaches of this duty of silence will be punished with fines if there is no stronger punishment under other laws.

§8	§8
Før det blir gitt samtykke til seksualinngrep på en gift person, skal ektefellen så vidt mulig få adgang til å uttale sig om begjæringen.	Before consent may be given for sexual intervention on a married person, the marriage partner shall, as far as possible, be given access to be heard on the request.
§9	§9
Kongen gir de nærmere regler som ansees nødvendige til gjennomførelsen av denne lov.	The King will further spedify the rules which are presumed to be necessary for the xecution of the law.
Røysting: Tilrådinga frå nemnda vart vedtaken mot 1 røyst.	Voting: The advice from the Committee was taken against one vote.
Etter framlagg frå presidenten vart samrøystes vedteke: Lovvedtaket vert sendt Lagtinget.	After a suggestion from the President an unanimous vote was taken: The law was sent to the Lagting.

* Page 573, "arbeidsdyktige" has been translated as "able-bodied workers" although it has the connotation of "productive" as well as "capable."
** Page 578, "seksualinngrep" has been translated as "sexual intervention", i.e. castration.
*** The Norwegian phrases "åndelig mindre utrustede" (page 578) and "åndsevner mangelfullt utviklet" (page 585) have been translated as "mentally less endowed" and "lack of mental development." In the social science language of the earlier 20th century, this might have been translated as "mentally retarded" and in the language of the late 20th and early 21st century this is a reference to those that are "developmentally delayed."

8.7 Appendix F – Comstock Act

An Act for the Suppression of Trade in, and Circulation of, Obscene Literature and Articles of Immoral Use

Be it enacted by the State and House of Representatives of the United States of America in Congress ssembled, That whoever, within that whoever, within the District of Columbia, or either of the Territories, or other place within the exclusive jurisdiction of the United States, shall sell, or offer to sell, or shall give away, or offer to give away, or shall have in his or her possession with intent to sell or give away, any obscene or indecent book, pamphlet, paper, advertisement, drawing, lithograph, engraving, wood-cut, daguerreotype, photograph, stereoscopic picture, model, cast, instrument, or other article for indecent or immoral nature, or any article or medicine for the prevention of conception, or for causing abortion except on a prescription of a physician in good standing given in good faith, or shall advertise the same for sale, or shall write or print, or cause to be written or printed, any card, circular, book, pamphlet, advertisement, or notice of any kind, stating when, where, how, or of whom, or by what means, any of the said obscene or indecent articles, or those hereinbefore mentioned, can be purchased or obtained, or shall manufacture, draw, or expose to have sold or exposed, or shall print any such article, shall, on conviction thereof, be imprisoned at hard labor for not less than six months nor more than five years for each offense, or fined not less than $100. nor more than $2,000. with costs of court.

Sec. 2. That section one hundred and forty-eight of the act to revise, consolidate, and amend the statutes relating to the Post Office Department, approved June 8, 1872, be amended to read as follows:

Sec. 148. That no obscene, lewd, or lascivious book, pamphlet, picture, paper, print, or other publication of an indecent character, or any article or thing designed or intended for the prevention of conception or procuring of abortion, nor any article or thing intended or adapted for any indecent or immoral use or nature, nor any written or printed card, circular, book pamphlet, advertisement, or notice of any kind giving information, directly or indirectly, where, or how, or of whom, or by what means either of the things before mentioned may be obtained or made, nor any letter upon the envelope of which, or postal cared upon which indecent or scurrilous epithets may be written or printed, shall be carried in the mail; and any person who shall knowingly deposit, or case to be deposited, for mailing or delivery any of the hereinbefore mentioned articles or things, or any notice or paper containing any advertisement relating to the aforesaid articles or things, and any person who, in pursuance of any plan or scheme for disposing of any of the hereinbefore mentioned articles or things, shall take or cause to be taken from the mail any such letter or package, shall be deemed guilty of a misdemeanor, and, on conviction thereof, shall, for every offense, be fined not less that $100 nor more that $5,000, or imprisoned at hard labor not less than one year nor more than ten years, or both, in the discretion of the judge."

Sec. 3. That all persons are prohibited from importing into the United States, from any foreign county, any of the hereinbefore mentioned articles or things, except the drugs here-inbefore mentioned when imported in bulk, and not put up for any of the purposes before mentioned, under a penalty of $1,000 for each importation, to be imposed upon due conviction of such offense; and all such prohibited articles in the course of importation shall be seized by the officer of customs and condemned and destroyed.

Sec. 4. That whoever, being an officer, agent, or employee of the Government of the United States, shall knowingly aid or abet any person engaged in any violation of this act, shall be deemed guilty of a misdemeanor, and, on conviction thereof, shall, for every offense, be punished as provided in section two of this act.

Sec. 5. That any judge of any district or circuit court of the United States before whom complaint of any violation of this act shall be made, supported by oath or affirmation founded on knowledge or belief, may issue, conformably to the Constitution, a warrant directed to the marshal, or any deputy marshal, in the proper district, directing him to search for, seize, and take possession of any such obscene or indecent books, papers, articles, or things, and to make due and immediate return thereof, to the end that the same may be condemned and destroyed by proceedings, which shall be conducted in the same manner as other proceedings in case of municipal seizure.

Comstock Law Excerpted from U.S. v. One Package, 86 F.2d 737, 739 (1936).

8.8 Appendix G – Ethnic and Religious data for New Haven, 1939

Ethnicity and Religion in New Haven, 1939

By its own count, the Roman Catholic Diocese of Hartford Connecticut had 603,467 members in 1929; this population had essentially doubled since the end of Bishop Michael Tierney's term in 1908 when the population had been 325,000.[1321] The economic growth of the Hartford Diocese can be tracked in the following chart since, in the main; it was voluntary contributions that built the institutions.

Table 8.2: Percent change, Catholic personnel and institutions, 1844–1929 Diocese of Hartford, Connecticut (Numbers positive unless noted.)

Bishops	Population	Churches	Missions	Priests	Schools	Religious	School Children	Academies	Orphanags
William Tyler (1844–1849)	15,000	13	0	8	0	0	0	0	0
Bernard O'Reilly (1850–1856)	35,000	22	16	22	10	41	2,500	2	2
Per Cent Increase (1849–1856)	133.3	69.2		175					
Francis P- MacFarland (1858–1874)	140,000	76	69	77	18	100	8,000	2	2
Per Cent Increase (1856–1874)	300	245.5	331.3	250	80	143.9	220	0	0

1321 Right Reverend Thomas S. Duggan, *Catholic Church in Connecticut*, Centennial Edition (New York City: The States History Company: 1930), 608.

continued **Table 8.2** Percent change, Catholic personnel and institutions, 1844–1929 Diocese of Hartford, Connecticut (Numbers positive unless noted.)

Bishops	Population	Churches	Missions	Priests	Schools	Religious	School Children	Academies	Orphanags
Thos. Galberry (1876–1878)	150,000	83	74	83	23	160	10,100	3	3
Per Cent Increase (1874–1878)	7.1	9.2	7.2	7.8	27.8	60	26.3	50	50
Lawrence McMahon (1879–1893)	250,000	96	54	180	40	485	16,000	3	3
Per Cent Increase (1878–1893)	66.7	15.7	-27	116.9	73.9	203.1	58.4	0	0
Michael Tierney (1893–1908)	325,000	156	51	280	69	1,115	30,275	3	3
Per Cent Increase (1893–1908)	30	62.5	-5.6	55.6	72.5	129.9	89.2	0	0
John J. Nilan (1910 -)	603,467	235	51	546	101	2,197	48,293	8	3
Per Cent Increase (1908–1929)	86.3	50.6	0	95	46.6	96.9	59.5	166.7	0

8.9 Appendix H – Waterbury, Connecticut Roman Catholic Church Proclamation, 11 June 1939

Proclamation read at all Roman Catholic Churches in Waterbury, Connecticut on 11 June 1939.

> Whereas, it is the teaching of the Catholic church that birth control is contrary to the natural law and therefore immoral, and
>
> Whereas, it is forbidden by statue law to disseminate birth control information for any reason whatsoever or in any circumstance, and
>
> Whereas, it has been brought to our attention that a so-called birth control clinic, sometimes called a maternal health center, is existing in Waterbury as admitted by the superintendent of Chase Dispensary, according to the papers, therefore be it

> Resolved, that this association go on record as being unalterably opposed to the existence of such a clinic in our city and we hereby urge our Catholic people to avoid contact with it and we hereby publicly call the attention for the public prosecutors to its existence and demand that they investigate and if necessary prosecute to the full extent of the law.[1322]

8.10 Appendix I – Demurrer to Criminal Information

The following is a detailed account of the legal maneuvering in the Chase Case.

A number of counts of violation of the 1879 Connecticut anti-contraception statute were filed against the three who all pled "not guilty." J. Warren Upson and Lawrence L. Lewis represented the three defendants on Friday, June 23. The two doctors were described as "young doctors"; Nelson was 30 and Goodrich was 29 years old. McTernan was 40 years old. After Lewis argued for parole into his custody of the three, Judge Wynne commented that the information about the case was "sketchy" but he believed all three to be connected in some professional capacity with the clinic. Wynne also commented that he thought the case was about "religious, moral or ethical" differences of opinion and since the three probably thought they had a right to do what they did, he could see no reason for the posting of a $500.00 bond. Nelson was charged with three counts of giving birth control assistance, on 17 January 1939, to a 27-year-old married woman, on 18 October 1939 to a 21 year old married woman and on 27 February 1939 to a 27 year old woman. Goodrich and McTernan were each charged with three counts also, of providing birth control information on 31 January 1939 to a 22 year old married woman, on 8 November 1938 to a 23 year old married woman and on 22 November 1938 to a 22 year old married woman. The penalty for violation of the statues was at least 60 days in jail with the possibility of up to one year in jail and a $50.00 fine or both. The trial would be held in September although Lewis retained, on the record, the right to withdraw the "not guilty" pleas.

Roman Catholic lay organizations soon became involved in the affair. The Notre Dame Alumni Association passed a resolution in support of "the stand taken by priests of the city" in which the clinic was condemned.[1323] The Knights of Columbus ("KOC") would also get involved.[1324] Once organized, they did the bidding of the clergy on

---

1322 John W. Johnson, *Griswold v. Connecticut: the Constitutional Right of Privacy* (Lawrence: University Press of Kansas, 2005), p. 22.

1323 *Waterbury Democrat*, 14 June 1939, p. 1. Again and again the *Democrat* implicitly asks the Bishop to take action saying that he "may" issue a statement. Also, the *Democrat* – again and again – wrote about the possibility of a need for a statewide investigation, as if it were advocating this.

1324 http://www.archdiceseofhartford.org/archdiocesehistory.htm, accessed on January 7, 2008. Father Michael J. McGivney had originally founded that group on 29 March 1882 in the basement of St. Mary's Church in New Haven, the town next door to Waterbury. McGivney, now a candidate for sainthood, originally organized the group so that it would "prevent our people form entering Secret

many fronts over the years.[1325] But the KOC was also a response to "strong anti-foreigner" sentiment among New Englanders. New Haven had attracted a large number of immigrants because of the jobs in railroads and industry there and competition with "nativist" New Englanders was a problem.[1326] Earlier, in the 1850s, the "Know-Nothing" political party had been organized; the majority of its members joined what became the modern day Republican Party in the 1860s. This nativist party actively – and enthusiastically – worked against the interests of immigrants, into the twentieth century. The Knights of Columbus, while providing solicarity for Catholic men and a buffer for xenophobia also carried out the wishes, the political wishes, of the hierarchy in whichever diocese they existed.

On Thursday, 29 June 1939, the lead story for the *Waterbury Democrat* was the Chase Dispensary Case. Splayed across the front of the paper was the headline, "Demurrer Filed in Alleged Birth Control Case" along with "Attorneys For Accused Physicians, Nurse Say Law Unconstitutional" below.[1327] J. Warren Upson had filed a demurrer on behalf of the three defendants and made a brief statement to that effect before Judge Kenneth Wynne.[1328] State's attorney William B. Fitzgerald had filed an amended complaint, adding the fact that Goodrich and Nelson were "duly licensed physicians" and the McTerhan was a "duly qualified nurse" thereby, according to the *Democrat*, making the case "a real test." Upson and Fitzgerald agreed to the defense brief by 25 July and the state's answer on 15 August. The trial would not be held until the September criminal term.[1329]

Upson's statement to the Court settled the issue of whether or not the Chase Dispensary was a birth control clinic. He said

> Both doctors are engaged in private practice, and voluntarily gave their services to the birth control clinic at the Chase dispensary, which is the outpatient department of the Waterbury Hospital.[1330]

Societies by offering the same if not better advantages to our members" and to unite the men of our faith throughout the diocese of Hartford, that we may gain strength to aid each other in time of sickness; to provide for decent burial, and to render pecuniary assistance to the families of deceased members.

1325 The Knights of Columbus continue to be used by clergy for support of various political issues that implicate the Church. As mentioned above in footnote 1726, in Washington, D.C. in summer, 2006, the KOC tried to organize Catholics to write in support of the "Defense of the Family Act" that defined marriage as an institution composed of one female and one male. Their material was inserted into Our Lady of Lourdes (Bethesda, Maryland) weekly parish bulletin. Please see: http://religousmovements.lib.birginia.edu/Knights.html. Also, please see: Christopher J. Kauffman, *Faith and Fraternalism* (New York: Harper & Row Publishers, 1982).

1326 *Ibid.*

1327 *Waterbury Democrat*, June 29, 1939, 1. Flush left.

1328 A "demurrer" was essentially an answer to a complaint which says that the defendants acknowledge everything the complaint alleges, makes legal arguments and then asks, in essence, "so where is the crime/harm?" This document is reprinted in Appendix IX at page 580.

1329 *Ibid.*

1330 *Ibid.*

In the defense demurrer §6246 of the Connecticut General Statutes was alleged to be unconstitutional because it interfered with the individual liberties of state citizens as well as being a violation of the due process clause of the federal Constitution. It "sets no reasonably precise standards of guilt and in that it sets forth no maximum fine." The demurrer also alleged that the law did not make exceptions for doctors engaged in trying to save the life of their clients or in protecting their health. The state's warrant was "fatally defective" in that the accused may have given birth control information "for reasons of health", as opposed to only for contraception.[1331] In a rare move, the *Democrat* printed the entire text of the demurrer for the public to read.[1332]

On Monday, 3 July 1939, Warren Upson was back in Superior Court before Judge Frank P. McEvoy (1878–1945) arguing a motion for dismissal of the entire case.[1333] McEvoy had been born in Waterbury. Both of his parents died in his early childhood and so he was sent to live with an uncle, Reverend Patrick P. Lawlor, then the pastor of St. Mary's (Catholic) Church on Hillhouse Avenue.[1334] He graduated from Yale School of Law in 1907 where he was editor of the Yale Law Review. He had worked for years in a partnership with Francis P. Guilfoile.[1335] In 1930 he was appointed by Republican governor, John H. Trumull (1925–1931), to fill the vacancy created by the death of Superior Court Judge L.P. Waldo Marvin, although McEvoy was a member of the Democratic Party.[1336] At the time of this hearing, he was a member of Blessed Sacrament Church in Waterbury, the sponsor of a Boy Scout troop as well as a member of the Holy Name Society at that church. As his obituary read,

> Partly as a result of his early life with his uncle in New Haven, but principally of his innate religious convictions, he was a devout communicant of the Roman Catholic church....It is hardly possible to conceive of a layman more thoroughly imbued with this religion than Judge McEvoy, or more devoted to is principles. And yet he was no bigot.[1337]

If this were true, it might be worthwhile asking why he did not recuse himself from the case.[1338] That Upson did not ask McEvoy to recuse himself is clear enough; this was to be a test case.

1331 *Ibid.*

1332 *Waterbury Democrat*, June 29, 1939, 4.

1333 *Waterbury Democrat*, July 3, 1939, 1. Flush left.

1334 Please see Obituary Sketch of Frank P. McEvoy at http://www.cslib.org/memorials/mcevoyf.htm, last accessed on January 7, 2008.

1335 Although I have been undable to confirm this, Guilfoile may have been a brother to McEvoy's wife, Gertrude.

1336 *Ibid.* Guilfoile would later become counsel to the city of Waterbury and its Mayor for four terms.

1337 *Ibid.*, 3.

1338 "Recusal" is a procedure whereby a Judge or attorney can remove him or herself fro a proceeding due to a conflict of interest.

Upson argued a theory of "*mens rea*", that the state had produced no evidence that the items confiscated were "kept for the purpose of violating the criminal law." McEvoy chose not to make a ruling on the motion and ordered that the issue be briefed; the defense brief was due on July 25 and the state's brief on August 15, the same days as ordered in Judge Wynne's Court. William B. Fitzgerald argued that he was prepared to prove "beyond a reasonable doubt" the intent to commit a crime citing to the North Shore Mothers Health Office of Salem, Massachusetts case the Margaret Sanger case of New York.

On a desk in the courtroom that July day were "several bagsful" of items as well as booklets that had been seized by the police in their raid of the Chase Dispensary.[1339] In his rebuttal, Fitzgerald produced a stipulation signed by both himself and Upson that the articles in the bags belonged to the Connecticut Birth Control League and the Waterbury Maternal Health Center. Exactly how the issue came before the Court is unclear but at some point, the destruction of the articles came into issue. It may be that the issue is intentionally unclear as Mr. Fitzgerald had to change is position in mid-hearing. Upson is reported as arguing against the state since it asked for a condemnation order under Section 6441, saying the state had not met its burden of proof. This fact is buried on page 4 after Fitzgerald is reported, on page 1, as saying the items would be needed for the trial. It might have been that Fitzgerald anticipated pleas of guilty and submitted the order for destruction prematurely. Or, Fitzgerald was not familiar with criminal trials and the need for the items to be admitted into evidence subject to defense challenges to the "chain of evidence."

Upson went on to give his argument in full, eventually pointing out that there was a split of opinion in the United States between various jurisdictions on the legal issue; the prosecution relied on a Massachusetts case while the defense relied on several U.S. Court of Appeals cases. The state's attorney argued that Upson's constitutional claims were "not proper claims" in that they had been tried before and rejected. Fitzgerald brought up the case of Carolyn Gardner and other who operated the North Shore Mothers' Health Office at Salem, Massachusetts, all of whom who had been convicted on May 26, 1938. Their case had gone to the Massachusetts Supreme Court, where the Massacchusetts equivalent of the Comstock Act was upheld. Fitzgerald noted that Connecticut courts paid "respectful attention" to Massachusetts's courts. He also referred to Margaret Sanger saying the statute had been effect since 1879 and had to be "enforced, unless it is repealed."[1340]

The following is the text of the demurrer, which is identical in text except in the names of the accused:

1339 The items were consolidated and identified as one item.

1340 *Waterbury Democrat*, July 3, 1939, 1, 4. See Kenneth C. Sears, "Legal Control..." in *Michigan Law Review*, 44 (1946): 69 for reference to the North Shore case.

STATE OF CONNECTICUT V. ROGER B. NELSON, Superior Court for New Haven County at Waterbury June 28, 1939.

DEMURRER TO INFORMATION
The defendant, having reserved his rights to plead to the information as on file, demurs to all counts of the information, and for reasons therefor, assigns the following:

I.

The information, and all three counts thereof, is based upon Section 6246 of the General Statutes of the State of Connecticut, and said Section is unconstitutional for the following reasons:

a. it constitutes an unconstitutional interference with the individual liberty of the citizens of the State of Connecticut;

b. it constitutes an unconstitutional interference with the individual liberty of the citizens of the sate of Connecticut under the provisions of the Constitution of the Untied States and the Constitution of the State of Connecticut;

c. it constitutes a deprivation of life, liberty and property without due process of law, under the provisions of Article 14 of the Amendments to the Constitution of the Untied States and under the provisions of Section 9 of Article First of the Constitution of Connecticut;

d. it fails to contain a reasonably precise standard of guilt;

e. it fails to fix minimum fine which may be imposed by the Court, and by virtue of the express provisions of the Statue, the Court might impose an unlimited fine, although the sole power to fix the limits of the fine or penalty reposes in the legislative branch of the government;

f. if the information correctly sets forth the crime under Section 6246 of the General statute, said Section is unconstitutional because it applies.

(1) where a married woman makes use of drugs, medical articles or instruments for the purposed of preventing conception upon the recommendation and advice of a physician;

(2) where a married woman makes uses drugs, medicinal articles or instruments for the purpose of preventing conception upon the advice of a physician under circumstances in which all physicians would agree that a pregnancy would jeopardize her life.

(3) where a married woman makes use of drugs, medicinal articles or instruments for the purpose of preventing conception upon the advice of a physician where for health reasons the use thereof is necessary for such purpose;

(4) where a married women makes use of drugs, medicinal articles or instruments for the purpose of preventing conception upon the advice of a physician where such contraceptive measures are necessary to protect and procure the best possible state of health and well being;

g. inasmuch as the information does not except the right of the medical profession to prescribe the use of drugs, medicinal articles or instruments for the purpose of preventing conception where the life or health of a patient is at stake, the information, and each count thereof, is unconstitutional and said Section 6246, if it is so construed, without a clause protecting the right of any physician to prescribe drugs, medicinal articles or instruments for the purpose of preventing conception, is unconstitutional.

II.

If said Section 6246 is so construed as to protect the right of any physician to prescribe drugs, medicinal articles or instruments for the purpose of preventing conception, the information, and all three counts thereof, is fatally defective for the following reasons:

a. the information, and each count thereof, contains no allegation that the "married woman" has been charged with the violation of Section 6246 of the General statues or convicted thereof;

b. under the law of this State, an accessory to a crime cannot be charged and convicted as an accessory in the absence of the allegation and proof of the commission of the offense by the principal;

c. under the law of this State, an accessory to a crime cannot be charged and convicted as an accessory in the absence of the allegation and proof the conviction of the offence by the principal with which he is charged;

d. the information fails to charge a crime under the Statutes of the state of Connecticut;

e. because on its face the information fails to negative the fact that the physician caring for a married woman might have been advising the use of the contraceptive devices by reason of the physical condition of the patient or by reason of the fact that all physicians would agree that the life of the patient would be jeopardized if contraceptive devices were no furnished ore where, for the reasons of health and well being of the patient, contraceptive practices were necessary, the information, and each for the three counts thereof, is fatally defective;

f. the information, and all three counts thereof, contains an inadequate description of the crime, in that the date upon which the crime is supposed to have been committed is not set forth therein; and in that the place where the crime is supposed to have been committed is not set forth therein.

DEFENDANT
By J. WARREN UPSON L.L. LEWIS His Attorneys[1341]

1341 *Waterbury Democrat*, 29 June 1939, p. 4.

Selected Bibliography

Government Records, Judicial Records, and Other Primary Source Materials

Baker v. Carr, *369 U.S. 186 (1962), 82 SCt 691, 7 Led2d 663,* case decided in the U.S. Supreme Court

Bakke v. Regents of the University of California, 438 U.S. 265 (1978), case decided in the U.S. Supreme Court

Bowers v. Hardwick, 478 U.S. 186 (1986)

Brown v. Board of Education, *347 U.S. 483 (1954),* case decided in the U.S. Supreme Court

Buck v. Bell, *274 U.S. 200 (1927),* case decided in the U.S. Supreme Court

Comstock, Anthony. "The Extirpation of the Crime-Breeders of the Day a Public Necessity", in *Bedford's Magazine* (June 1880), APS Online

____________. "The Suppression of Vice", in *The North American Review,* Vol. CXXXV, no. CCCXII (November 1882), APS Online

Files of Justice William O. Douglas at the Manuscript Room at the Library of Congress in Washington, D.C.

Griswold v. Connecticut, *381 U.S. 479 (1965),* case decided in the U.S. Supreme Court

Hoffman, Frederic L. "Race Traits of the American Negro", in *Publications of the American Economic Association,* Vol. XI, nos. 1, 2, 3 (New York: Macmillan & Co., 1896)

Journal of the House of Representatives of the State of Indiana, Sixty-Fifth Session of the General Assembly, Commencing January 11, 1907, Regular Session, Vol. I (Indianapolis: Wm. B. Burford, Contractor for State Printing and Binding, 1907)

Linda Lewis, City of New York, New York Health and Hospitals Corporation Cesar Perales v. Tommy G Thompson *("Linda Lewis v. Grinker") 252 F. 3d 567 (2nd Cir.* 2001), case decided in the U.S. Court of Appeals for the Second Circuit

Lov om likestilling mellom kjønnene (9 June 1972)

McCullough, Oscar. *Tribe of Ishmael: A study of social degradation* (Indianapolis, 1881)

Norges Lover 1687—2003, compiled by Hans Flock, Birger Stuevold Lassen, Henrik Bull, and Anne-Marie Tronslin (Oslo: Det juridiske fakultet, Universitet i Oslo & Gyldendal Akademisk Forlag, 2004)

1 June 1934 Lov om adgang til sterilisasjon (1 June 1934 Law on Access to Sterilization)

Papers of Margaret Sanger, 1926—1928, at the Library of Congress, Washington D.C.

Parents Involved in Community Schools v. Seattle School District No. 1, *551 U.S. 701 (2007), 127 S. Ct. 2738, 75 USLW 4577,* case decided in the U.S. Supreme Court

Planned Parenthood of Southeastern Pennsylvania v. Casey, *505 U.S. 833 (1992),* case decided in the U.S. Supreme Court

Planned Parenthood of Minnesota, North Dakota, South Dakota; and Carol E. Hall, M. D., Plaintiffs and Appellees, v. Mike Rounds, Governor, and Larry Long, Attorney General of the State of South Dakota, in their official capacities, Defendants and Appellants, case no. 05-3093 (2007), case decided in the 8th Circuit Court of Appeals, South Dakota

Schroeder, Theodore Albert. *"Obscene" Literature and Constitutional Law: A forensic defense of freedom of the press* (New York: Privately printed, 1911)

Statistisk sentralbyrå (Oslo), website at http://www.ssb.no/

Storting drafts, memoranda and debates, 1934, 1978

U.S. v. One Package of Japanese Pessaries, *86 F. 2d 737 (2nd Cir. 1936),* case decided in the U.S. Court of Appeals for the Second Circuit

Vital Statistics of the United States, 2000 (Hyattsville, Md.: U.S. Department of Health and Human Services, Centers for Disease Control and Prevention National Center for Health Statistics, 2002)

Williams et al. v. Smith, *190 Ind. 526 at 526, 131 N.E. 2 (1921)*, case decided in the Supreme Court of the State of Indiana

Books

Aasen, Henriette Sinding. *Rasehygiene og menneskeverd* (Oslo: Institutt for offentlig rettskriftserie, nr. 4, Kvinnerettslige studier, no. 28A, 1989).

Arrighi, Barbara A. (ed.). *Understanding Inequality: The intersection of race/ethnicity, class, and gender* (Lanham, Md.: Rowman & Littlefield, 2001).

Bates, Anne Louise. *Weeder in the Garden of the Lord: Anthony Comstock's Life and Career* (Lanham, Md.: University Press of American, 1995).

Beisel, Nicola. *Imperiled Innocents: Anthony Comstock and Family Reproduction in Victorian America* (Princeton, N.J.: Princeton University Press, 1997).

Bergo, Knut. *Text and Reality in the Sources of Law* (Oslo: Cappelen Akademisk Forlag, 2002).

Blom, Ida. *Barnebegrensing – synd eller sunn fornuft* (Bergen: Universitetsforlaget, 1980).

___________ *Totalitetsøkonomi: En oversikt over Samfundspartiets ideologi og retningslinear,* 3rd ed. (Bergen, 1966).

Bourdieu, Pierre. *Language and Symbolic Power,* ed. by John B. Thompson; trans. from French by Gino Raymond and Matthew Adamson (Cambridge, Mass.: Harvard University Press, 1991).

Carpenter, Daniel. P *The Forging of Bureaucratic Autonomy: Reputations, networks, and policy innovation in executive agencies, 1862—1928* (Princeton, N.J.: Princeton University Press, 2001).

Christensen, Chr. A.R. *Norge Under Okkupasjonen*, 2nd ed. (Oslo: Fabritius & Sønners Forlan, 1965).

Cohen, Stanley. *Folk Devils and Moral Panics: The creation of the mods and the rockers* (London: MacGibbon & Kee, 1972).

Dahl, Hans Fredrik. *Norge mellom krigene/Det Norske samfunnet krise og konflikt 1918—1940* (Oslo: Pax Forlag A/S, 1971).

Douglas, Mary. *Natural Symbols: Explorations in cosmology* (London: The Cresset Press, 1970).

Duggan, Rt. Rev. Thomas S. *The Catholic Church in Connecticut* (New York: The State History Company, 1930).

Dyzenhaus, David. *Legality and Legitimacy: Carl Schmitt, Hans Kelsen and Hermann Heller in Weimar* (Oxford: Clarendon Press, 1997).

Ezrahi, Yaron. *The Descent of Icarus: Science and the Transformation of Contemporary Democracy* (Cambridge, Mass.: Harvard University Press, 1990).

Foss, Øyvind (ed.). *En seksualfiendtlig kirke?* (Oslo: Gyldendal forlag, 1978).

Garrow, David J. *Liberty and Sexuality: The Right to Privacy and the Making of Roe v. Wade* (New York: Macmillan Publishing Co., 1994).

Haave, Per. *Sterilisering av tatere, 1934—1977: En historisk undersøkelse av lov og praksis* (Oslo: Norges forskningsråd, 2000).

Hagen, Ingar. *Den Norske kirke i storm* (A.S. Lunde & Co's Forlag, 1967).

Hardcastle, Rohan J. *Law and the Human Body: Property rights, ownership and control* (Oxford and Portland: Hart Publishing Co., 2007).

Hasian, Marouf Arif, Jr. *The Rhetoric of Eugenics in Anglo-American Thought* (Athens, Ga.: University of Georgia Press, 1996).

Hawkins, Mike. *Social Darwinism in European and American Thought, 1860—1945: Nature as model and nature as threat* (Cambridge: Cambridge University Press, 1997).

Hull, N.E.H. and Peter Charles Hoffer. *Roe v. Wade: The abortion rights controversy in American history* (Lawrence, Kansas: The University Press of Kansas, 2001).
Hvinden, Bjørn (ed.). *Romanifolket og det norske samfunnet: Følgene av hundre års politikk for en nasjonal minoritet* (Bergen: Fagbokforlaget, A.S., 2000).
Jasanoff, Sheila (ed.). *States of Knowledge: The co-production of science and social order* (London: Routledge, 2004).
Jensen, Magnus. *Fra 1905 til våre dager* (Oslo: Universitetsforlaget, 1968).
Johansen, Per Ole (ed.). *På Siden av Rettsoppgjøret* (Oslo: Unipub Forlag, 2006).
Johnson, John W. *Grisvold v. Connecticut: Birth control and the constitutional right of privacy* (Lawrence, Kansas: The University Press of Kansas, 2005).
Kennedy, Duncan. *A Critique of Adjudication (fin de siècle)* (Cambridge, Mass.: Harvard University Press, 1997).
Kevles, Daniel J. *In the Name of Eugenics: Genetics and the uses of human heredity* (New York: Alfred A. Knopf, 1985).
Lemert, Charles. *Dark Thoughts: Race and the eclipse of society* (New York and London: Routledge, 2002).
Lønnå, Elizabeth. *Stolhet og Kvinnekamp: Norsk Kvinnesaksforenings historie fra 1913* (Oslo: Gydendal Norsk Forlag, 1996).
Lundby, Knut and Ingun Montgomery (eds.). *Statskirke i etterkrigs samfun: Kirkehistorie og sosiologiske syndspunkter på Den norske kirke etter 1945* (Oslo: Universitetsforlaget, 1981).
MacKinnon, Catherine A. *Towards a Feminist Theory of the State* (Cambridge, Mass.: Harvard University Press, 1989).
Marks, Lara V. *Sexual Chemistry: A history of the contraceptive* (New Haven, Conn.: Yale University Press, 2001).
Martinussen, Willy. *The Distant Democracy: Social inequality, political resources and political influence in Norway* (New York and London: John Wiley & Sons, 1977).
McAdam, Doug, John D. McCarthy, and Mayer N. Zald (eds.). *Comparative Perspectives on Social Movements: Political opportunities, mobilizing structures, and cultural framings* (Cambridge: Cambridge University Press, 1996).
Mohr, Tove. *Katti Anker Møller – en banebryter* (Oslo: Tiden Norsk Forlag, 1968).
Moses, Jonathon. *Norwegian Catch-up: Development and globalization before World War II* (Aldershot and Burlington: Ashgate, 2005).
Oberschall, Anthony. *Social Conflict and Social Movements* (Englewood Cliffs, N.J.: Prentice-Hall, Inc., 1973).
Oftestad, Bernt T., Tarald Rasmussen, and Jan Schumacher. *Norsk kirkehistorie,* 2nd ed. (Oslo: Universitetsforlaget, 1993).
Phillips, Clifton J. *Indiana in Transition: The emergence of an industrial commonwealth, 1820—1920,* vol. IV (Indianapolis: Indiana Historical Bureau and Indiana Historical Society, 1968).
Powe, Jr., Lucas A., *The Supreme Court and the American Elite, 1739–2008* (Cambridge, Mass.: Harvard University Press, 2009).
Ritzer, George. *Sociological Theory,* 7th ed. (Boston: McGraw-Hill, 2008).
Rock, John. T*he Time Has Come: A Catholic doctor's proposals to end the battle over birth control* (New York: Alfred A. Knopf, 1963).
___________ and David Loth. *Voluntary Parenthood* (New York: Random House, 1949).
Rommetveit, Ragnar. *Social Norms and Roles: Explorations in the psychology of social pressures with empirical contributions from inquiries into religious attitudes and sex roles of adolescents from some districts in western Norway* (Oslo: Akademisk forlag, 1955).
Rothman, David J. *The Discovery of the Asylum: Social order and disorder in the New Republic* (Boston: Little, Brown & Co., 1971).

Sætnan, Ann Rudinow, Nelly Oudshoorn, and Marta Kirejczyk (eds.). *Bodies of Technology: Women's involvement with reproductive medicine* (Columbus: Ohio State University Press, 2000).
Self, Helen, J. *Prostitution, Women and the Misuse of the Law: The Fallen Daughter of Eve* (New York and London: Routledge, 2003).
Sewell, William H., Jr. *The Logics of History: Social theory and social transformation* (Chicago: University of Chicago Press, 2005).
Shilling, Chris. *The Body and Social Theory* (London, Thousand Oaks, New Delhi: Sage Publications, 2005).
Siltala, Raimo. *A Theory of Precedent: From analytical positivism to a post-analytical philosophy law* (Helsinki: University Printing House, 1998).
Smith, Dwight E. *Goodly Heritage: One Hundred Years of Craft Freemasonry in Indiana* (Franklin, Ind.: 1968).
Stinchcombe, Arthur L. *When Formality Works: Authority and abstraction in law and organizations* (Chicago: University of Chicago Press, 2001).
Støren, Thordis and Tone Schou Wetlesen (eds.). *Kvinnekunnskap* (Oslo: Gyldendal Norsk Forlag, 1976).
Sundby, Nils Kristian. *Om normer* (Oslo: Universitetsforlaget, 1974).
Turner, Bryan S. *Regulating Bodies: Essays in medical sociology* (London: Routledge, 1992).
Walsh, Justin E. *The Centennial History of the Indiana General Assembly (1816–1978)* (Indianapolis: The Select Committee on the Centennial History of the Indiana General Assembly and The Indiana Historical Bureau, 1987).
Wawrose, Susan C. *Griswold v. Connecticut: Contraception and the Right of Privacy* (New York: Grolier Publishing, 1996).
Weber, Max. *Economy and Society: An outline of interpretive sociology,* ed. by Guenther Roth and Claus Wittich; trans. from German by Ephraim Fischoff et al. (Berkeley and Los Angeles: University of California Press, 1978).
Hvem, Hva, Hvor 1979: Aftenpostens Aktuelle Oppslagsbok (Oslo: Chr. Schibsteds Forlag, 1979).

Articles and Book Chapters

Andersen, Kristen. "Abortus provactus med særlig henblikk på dens mulige sociale og humanitære indikasjoner", in *Tidsskrift for Den norske Lægeforening,* Vol. 49 (1929): 1191–1215.
Benford, Robert D. "An Insider's Critique of the Social Movement Framing Perspective", in *Sociological Inquiry,* Vol. 67, no. 4 (Fall 1997): 409–430.
___________ and David A. Snow. "Framing Processes and Social Movements: An overview and assessment", in *Annual Review of Sociology,* Vol. 26 (2000): 611–639.
Berthelet, J. M. "Sociological Discourse and the Body", in Mike Featherstone, Mike Hepworth, and Bryan S. Turner (eds.), *The Body: Social process and cultural theory* (London, Newbury Park, New Delhi: Sage Publications, 1991).
Carey, Allison. "Gender and Compulsory Sterilization Programs in America, 1907–1950", in *Journal of Historical Sociology,* Vol. 11, no. 1 (March 1998): 74–105.
Clam, Jean. "The Reference of Paradox: Missing paradoxity as real perplexity in both systems theory and deconstruction", in Oren Perez and Gunther Teubner (eds.), *Paradoxes and Inconsistencies in the Law* (Oxford and Portland, Oregon: Hart Publishing, 2006).
Crocker, Ruth Hutchinson. "Making Charities Modern: Business and the reform of charities in Indianapolis, 1879–1930", in *Business and Economic History,* 2nd series, Vol. 12 (1983).
Diduck, Allison. "Legislating Ideologies of Motherhood", in *Social and Legal Studies,* Vol. 2, no. 4 (1993): 461–485.

Duster, Troy. "Lessons from History: Why race and ethnicity have played a major role in biomedical research", in *Journal of Law, Medicine & Ethics,* Vol. 34, no. 3 (Fall 2006): 2–11.

Edmond, Gary. "The Law-Set: The legal scientific production of medical propriety", in *Science, Technology, & Human Values,* Vol. 26, no. 2 (Spring 2001): 191–226.

Glæver, Øyvind. "Abortion and Eugenics: The role of eugenic arguments in Norwegian abortion debates and legislation, 1920–1978", in *Scandinavian Journal of History,* Vol. 30, no. 1 (March 2005): 21–44.

Goode, Erich and Nachman Ben-Yehuda. "Moral Panics: Culture, Politics, and Social Construction", in *Annual Review of Sociology,* Vol. 20 (1994): 149–171.

___________. "No Need to Panic: A bumper crop of books on moral panic", in *Sociological Forum,* Vol. 15, no. 3 (September 2000): 543–552.

Gugliotta, Angela. "Dr. Sharp and His Little Knife: Therapeutic and punitive origins of eugenic vasectomy – Indiana, 1892–1921", in *Journal of the History of Medicine and Allied Sciences,* Vol. 53, no. 4 (October 1998): 371–406.

Haines, Michael. "The Urban Mortality Transition in the United States, 1800–1940", *Annales de démographe historiques,* No. 1 (2001): 33–64.

Knodel, John and Etienne van de Walle. "Lessons from the Past: Policy mplications of historical fertility studies", in *Population and Development Review,* Vol. 5, no. 2 (June 1979): 217–245.

Krippendorff, Klaus. "The Expression of Value in Political Documents", in *Journalism Quarterly,* Vol. 47 (Summer 1970): 510–518.

Larsen, Øyvind. "Doctors, Migration, and Professional Career", in Øyvind Larsen and Bent Olav Olsen (eds.), *The Shaping of a Profession: Physicians in Norway, past and present* (Canton, Mass.: Science History Publications, 1996).

Lock, Margaret. "Cultivating the Body: Anthropology and epistemologies of body practice and knowledge", in *Annual Review of Anthropology,* Vol. 22 (1993): 133–155.

McCall, Leslie. "The Complexity of Intersubjectivity", in *Signs: Journal of Women in Culture and Society,* Vol. 30, Issue 3 (March 2005): 1771–1800.

___________. "Explaining Levels of Within-Group Inequality in U.S. Labor Markets", in *Demography,* Vol. 37, no. 4 (2000): 415–430.

McGee, Michael Calvin. "The 'Ideograph': A link between rhetoric and ideology", in *The Quarterly Journal of Speech,* Vol. 66, no. 1 (February 1930): 1–16.

___________. "The Ideograph as a Unit of Analysis in Political Argument", in Jack Rhodes and Sara Sewell (eds.), *Proceedings of the Summer Conference on Argumentation* (Annandale, Va.: Speech Communications Association, 1998).

Mitchell, David and Sharon Snyder. "The Eugenic Atlantic: Race, disability and the making of an international Eugenic Science, 1800–1945", in *Disability and Society,* Vol. 18, no. 7 (December 2003): 843–864.

Olsen, Bent Olav. "Recreation or Professional Necessity? – The Study Tours of Nineteenth Century Norwegian Doctors", in Øyvind Larsen and Bent Olav Olsen (eds.), *The Shaping of a Profession: Physicians in Norway, past and present* (Canton, Mass.: Science History Publications, 1996).

Pescosolido-Rubin, Bernice A. and Beth A. Rubin. "The Web of Group Affiliations Revisited: Social life, postmodernism, and sociology", in *American Sociological Review,* Vol. 65, no. 1 (February 2000): 52–76.

Stern, Alexandra Minna. "We Cannot Make a Silk Purse out of a Sow's Ear: Eugenics in the Hoosier heartland, 1900–1960", in *Indiana Magazine of History,* Vol. 103, no. 1 (March 2007): 3–38.

van Leeuwen, Theo and Ruth Woodak. "Legitimizing Immigration Control: A discourse-historical analysis", in *Discourse Studies,* Vol. 1, no. 1 (1999): 83–118.

Victor, Jeffrey S. "Moral Panics and the Social Construction of Deviant Behavior: A theory and application to the case of ritual child abuse", in *Sociological Perspectives,* Vol. 41, no. 3 (1998): 541–565.

Wooley, Owen. "Locating Masterframes in History: An analysis of the religious masterframe of the abolition movement and its influence on movement trajectory", in *Journal of Historical Sociology,* Vol. 17, no. 4 (December 2004): 490–516.

Additional Literature

Government Records, Judicial Records, and Other Primary Source Materials

Boye, Th. And Olaf Lundamo (compilers). *Norsk Medicinallovgivning. En kronologisk samling av lover og bestemmelser vedkommende Norges medicinalvæsen for aarene 1921–1925* (Oslo: i kommission hos H. Aschehoug & Co., 1928).

Books

Bijker, Wiebe E., Thomas P. Hughes, and Trevor Pinch (eds.). *The Social Construction of Technological Systems: New directions in the sociology and history of technology* (Cambridge, Mass.: MIT Press, 1989).

Bonde, Gjert Edvard. *Nyorientering* (Oslo: Frie Samfunds forlag, 1936).

Broberg, Gunnar and Nils Roll-Hansen (eds.). *Eugenics and the Welfare State: Sterilization policy in Denmark, Sweden, Norway, and Finland,* Rev. paperback ed. (East Lansing: Michigan State University Press, 2005)

Chamberlin, J. Edward and Sander L. Gilman (eds.). *Degeneration: The dark side of progress* (New York: Columbia University Press, 1985).

Dowbiggin, Ian. *The Sterilization Movement and Global Fertility in the Twentieth Centurey* (Oxford: Oxford University Press, 2008).

Emberland, Terje. *Religion og Rase: Nyhedenskap og nazisme i Norge 1933–1945* (Oslo: Humanist Forlag, 2003).

Hagemann, Gro. *Kjønn og industrialisering* (Oslo: Universitetsforlag, 1994).

Hantrais, Linda. *International Comparative Research: Theory, Methods and Practices* (Houndmills, Basingstoke: Palgrave Macmillan, 2009).

Hart, H.L. A. *The Concept of Law* (Oxford: Clarendon Press, 1961).

Kuhn, Thomas. *The Structure of Scientific Revolutions,* 3rd ed. (Chicago: University of Chicago Press, 1996).

Latour, Bruno and S. Woolgar. *Laboratory Life: The social construction of scientific facts* (Beverly Hills: Sage Publications, 1979).

McLaren, John, Robert Menzies, and Dorothy E. Chunn (eds.). *Regulating Lives: Historical essays on the state, society, the individual, and the law* (Vancouver: University of British Columbia Press, 2002).

Merton, Robert K. *Social Theory and Social Structure,* Rev. & enlarged ed. (New York: Free Press, 1968).

Nussbaum, Martha C. *Sex and Social Justice* (Oxford: Oxford University Press, 1999).

Prado, C. G. *Searle and Foucault on Truth* (Cambridge: Cambridge University Press, 2006).

Richardson, Angelique. *Love and Eugenics in the Late Nineteenth Century: Rational reproduction & the New Woman* (Oxford: Oxford University Press, 2003).

Rosen, Christine. *Preaching Eugenics: Religious leaders and the American Eugenics Movement* (Oxford: Oxford University Press, 2004).

Journal Articles

Bowdery, George J. “Conventions and Norms”, in *Philosophy of Science,* Vol. 8, no. 4 (October 1941): 493–505.

Hunt, Arnold. "'Moral Panic' and Moral Language in the Media", in *British Journal of Sociology,* Vol. 48, no. 4 (December 1997): 629–648.

March, James G. “Group Norms and the Active Minority”, in *American Sociological Review,* Vol. 19, no. 6 (December 1954): 733–741.

Morris, Richard T. “A Typology of Norms”, in *American Sociological Review,* Vol. 21, no. 5 (October 1956): 610–613.

Reid, John R. “Definitions, Criteria, Standards, and Norms”, in *The Philosophical Review,* Vol. 53, no. 3 (May 1944): 246–259.

Stouffer, Samuel A. “An Analysis of Conflicting Social Norms”, in *American Sociological Review,* Vol. 14, no. 6 (December 1949): 707–717.

Newspapers

Aftenposten (Oslo), 1934, 1978
Arbeiderbladet (Oslo), 1934, 1978
Bergens tidene, 1934
Boston Daily Globe, 1907
Indianapolis Morning Star, 1907
Indianapolis News, 1907
Indianapolis Star, 1906–1907
New Haven Evening Register, 1960
New Haven Register, 1961
Washington Post, 1907–1908
Waterbury Democrat, 1939
Waterbury Republican, 1939, 1960–1961
Waterbury Republican-American, 1961
Miscellanous other newspapers for the years 1900–1982, as cited in the text

Unpublished Materials

Leon, Sharon Mara. *Beyond Birth Control: Catholic response to the eugenics movement in the United States, 1900–1950,* Unpublished Ph.D. dissertation, University of Minnesota, 2004

List of Figures

List of Tables

Index

Bei Fragen zur Produktsicherheit wenden Sie sich bitte an:
If you have any questions regarding product safety,
please contact:

Walter de Gruyter GmbH
Genthiner Straße 13
10785 Berlin
productsafety@degruyterbrill.com